The Royal Household and the King's Affinity

The
Royal Household
and the King's Affinity

Service, Politics and Finance in England 1360-1413

Chris Given-Wilson

1986
Yale University Press
New Haven and London

For my mother

BEATRICE

Designed by Mary Carruthers
Typeset by Boldface Typesetters, London and printed in Great Britain by Bell & Bain Ltd, Glasgow.

Library of Congress Catalog Card Number 85–52145
ISBN 0 300 03570 5

Contents

Preface

SOME explanation is needed for the choice of the dates 1360 to 1413 for this book. Originally, I had intended to write a book on Richard II's household and affinity. This was to be a development from my own Ph.D. thesis on 'The Court and Household of Edward III 1360–1377' (1976), on which I proposed to draw only really for comparative purposes. Also, I had read Dr Alan Rogers' extremely comprehensive and illuminating Ph.D. thesis on 'The Royal Household of Henry IV' (1966), and knew that this too would be very useful for comparative purposes. When I submitted this idea to John Nicoll of Yale University Press, however, he suggested that I should broaden the work and make it into a full study of the royal household, drawing much more extensively on both my own earlier research and that of Dr Rogers. By this time, Alan Rogers had informed me that he had abandoned his original idea of converting his thesis into a book, and the idea of comparing the royal household under three successive kings was obviously attractive. Another reason for choosing these dates was that they afforded an opportunity to study the late medieval royal household at a time when it was not too heavily involved in the war, for it was really the household in peace-time, its role in domestic politics, that I wanted to examine. Finally, it soon became obvious to me that the more I said about the reigns of Edward III and Henry IV, the more sharply that of Richard II came into focus.

Alan Rogers' thesis has been absolutely invaluable. I thank him not only for allowing me to read it, but also for the very pleasant and helpful manner in which he did so. I wish also to thank two other scholars who, with equal courtesy, allowed me to read their doctoral theses, Robin Jeffs, for his thesis on 'The Later Medieval Sheriff and the Royal Household' (1960), and Kate Mertes for her thesis on 'Secular Noble Households in England 1350–1550' (1981). In addition, I have obtained through Inter-Library Loan a number of other unpublished theses, and my debt to these and to the published work of other historians is reflected in both my footnotes and my bibliography. My special thanks also go to two friends: firstly, to Nancy Wood who, with astonishing efficiency and cheerfulness, guided the successive drafts of this book through the St Andrews University computer, producing a succession of immaculate typescripts which I promptly rendered unintelligible again; and secondly, to Dr Michael Prestwich, who supervised my thesis on Edward III's household and who, even after he moved from St Andrews to Durham, proved a constant source of information and inspiration. This book owes a great deal to him. To Alice, who throughout the years that I have been working on this book has kept me sane by never allowing Edward III, Richard II or Henry IV into the house, I owe much more than thanks. And the same is true of my mother, Beatrice, a constant source of help and encouragement from a time long before I had ever heard of Richard II. To her, this book is dedicated.

Chris Given-Wilson
St Andrews

Introduction

The twelfth-century household

'THE history of the royal household,' said L.M. Larson, 'begins with the history of kingship.'[1] In theory, his statement was quite unexceptionable: once a king had a servant to make his bed, a treasurer to mind his treasure-chest, or a warrior to guard his body, he had a household. Yet in practice it is not until the early twelfth century, during the reign of Henry I, that anything like an over-all picture of the English royal household can be obtained. On the other hand, it is not difficult to comprehend the sorts of functions performed by the members of a king's household even in the earliest and darkest days of Anglo-Saxon history. If we ask the question, what functions did a king's household servants perform?, these can be divided into four principal categories. Firstly, they catered to his domestic needs: food and drink, clothing and shelter, leisure. Ceremonial duties should also be included under a king's domestic needs, for the magnificence of his domestic establishment was one of the yardsticks by which his political authority was judged. Secondly, the household served as a centre of government: within the household was the king's personal secretariat; from it emanated the orders, written or oral, which maintained the links between central and local authority, while to it came those who wished to make their ways in the king's service, or to obtain favours from him. Thus it was both centrifugal and centripetal, the first and most immediate extension of the king's will, and the political hub of the realm. Thirdly, and closely connected with its administrative role, the household included the personal financial department of the king. If he kept his treasure-chest under his bed, sooner or later he would need someone to receive it, count it, disburse it. And in time this 'someone' developed into a financial department which was to remain the controlling force behind royal finances for much of the medieval period. Fourthly, the king's household servants were there to guard his body and to fight for him. This often comprised no more than a personal bodyguard for the king, but he was always assured of rapid reinforcement if necessary. When a medieval king went to war, his household troops formed the nucleus of his army, around whom gathered the fyrd, the feudal knights, the mercenaries, the magnate retinues, and anyone else who had come to fight for him.

The problem of the 'expanded' as compared with the 'permanent' household is one which has sometimes confused discussion of the royal household in medieval England. The distinction is, at least in essence, a fairly clear one, however, and is encapsulated in the use of the words *domus* and *familia*. The permanent household, which coped with the king's bodily needs, provided his secretariat, and formed his bodyguard, was the *domus*. Beyond this, however, the household might be expanded for any one of a number of reasons into what is loosely known as the *familia regis*. The *familia* had no fixed membership: those who joined the king's *familia* when he led an army, those who attended the court in order to offer counsel or receive orders, those who made up the numbers on ceremonial occasions, might or might not receive rewards in money, land or offices from the king, might or might not think of themselves as primarily royal servants, but they were frequently styled *familiares regis*. There were, then, several different royal households, but only the first is capable of reasonably precise definition. It was a distinction understood by Walter Map in the twelfth century, when he wrote that Henry I 'scriptas habebat domus et familie sue consuetudines.'[2] Ordinances regulating the king's household deal almost exclusively with this small and permanent domestic establishment. That drawn up for King Stephen in 1136 was entitled *Constitutio Domus Regis*.[3]

The *Constitutio*, which consists of a list of the principal servants of the *domus* and a record of the wages and allowances due to each of them, was almost certainly drawn up in the early months of 1136, possibly by Henry I's last treasurer, Nigel of Ely, and was intended as a guideline for King Stephen.[4] Thus it describes Henry I's household at the end of that king's reign. It has recently been analysed in considerable detail by Professor Barlow.[5] What it reveals is an institution with a clear departmental organisation, a recognised hierarchy of officers and servants, a considerable degree of functional specialisation, and an established accounting procedure. The *Constitutio* divides the *domus* into five main departments, headed by the chancellor, stewards (*dapiferi*), master-butler, master-chamberlain, and constables (diagram 1, p. 3). The real domestic organisation of the household fell to the stewards and the master-butler; the master-chamberlain had overall supervision of the king's domestic chamber (that is, his private living quarters, the inner personal sanctum of the household), but he also had financial responsibilities which made him a national as well as a domestic officer; the constables likewise had important domestic functions. They had general responsibility for the king's horses, his personal bodyguard, and his hunting staff, but they too were figures of national importance, in military affairs. The chancellor's principal responsibility was as head of the king's secretariat, the chancery, but he also had charge of the king's chapel. The chancellor received 5s. a day, in court or out of court, which made him the highest-paid officer of the household. Although this may have given him a certain status by comparison with his fellow-officers, he was certainly not the

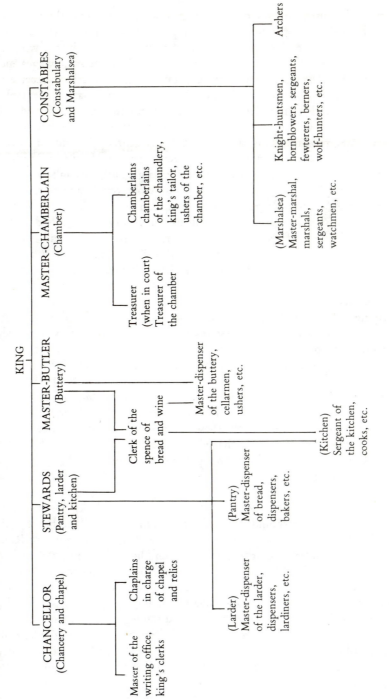

Diagram I: Organisation of the domus 1135–6, according to the Constitutio

KING

CHANCELLOR
(Chancery and chapel)

Master of the
writing office,
king's clerks

Chaplains
in charge
of chapel
and relics

STEWARDS
(Pantry, larder
and kitchen)

(Larder)
Master-dispenser
of the larder,
dispensers,
lardiners, etc.

(Pantry)
Master-dispenser
of bread,
dispensers,
bakers, etc.

(Kitchen)
Sergeant of
the kitchen,
cooks, etc.

MASTER-BUTLER
(Buttery)

Clerk of the
spence of
bread and wine

Master-dispenser
of the buttery,
cellarmen,
ushers, etc.

MASTER-CHAMBERLAIN
(Chamber)

Treasurer
(when in court)
Treasurer of
the chamber

Chamberlains
chamberlains
of the chaundlery,
king's tailor,
ushers of the
chamber, etc.

CONSTABLES
(Constabulary
and Marshalsea)

(Marshalsea)
Master-marshal,
marshals,
sergeants,
watchmen, etc.

Knight-huntsmen,
hornblowers, sergeants,
fewterers, berners,
wolf-hunters, etc.

Archers

man who supervised the domestic organisation of the household. This task fell to the stewards, of whom there were probably about four, serving in rotation at court, who received 5s. a day out of court, but only 3s. 6d. when at court. The master-butler and master-chamberlain received the same wages and liveries as the stewards but although the constables were also said to receive the same wages and liveries as the stewards, two of the three named constables apparently received no more than 1s. 2d. when in court and 2s. out of court.

The *Constitutio* suggests a *domus*, a permanent domestic establishment, of at least 100 persons. This was almost permanently itinerant, a factor which brought considerable additional pressures to bear on its system of provisioning and general organisation. Backed by the king's authority (although not necessarily with his blessing), it provided numerous opportunities for members of the household to indulge in petty corruption over such matters as the requisitioning of supplies. Walter Map tells us that Henry I reorganised his household and established a fixed rate of allowances for his servants, and it may well be that the reason he did so was in order to curb the indiscipline and extravagance of Rufus's court.[6] Both Eadmer and Henry of Huntingdon strongly censored Rufus for the violence and corruption (as well as the moral laxity) of the members of his household, and William of Malmesbury credits Henry with trying to reform the system: 'he made a regulation for the followers of his court, at whichever of his estates he might be resident, stating what they should accept from the locals without payment, and what they should purchase, and at what price; transgressors were punished by a money-fine or loss of life.' Walter Map adds that Henry, a man noted for his regular habits, issued proclamations saying where he was going and when, a month in advance, so that merchants could arrange to meet the household there and keep it supplied.[7] How effectively these reforms worked in practice is difficult to say, but it does seem likely that Henry tried to check at least the worst abuses associated with the problem of supplying the household. However, it was not merely around the household, but within it too, that corruption had to be checked, and here too there were strict regulations governing the preparation of food. Of the four bakers employed in the household, for instance, it was decreed that two should always be travelling ahead of the household to buy corn. They were to be given 3s. 4d. with which to purchase each Rouen *muid* (roughly a quarter) of corn, from which they were expected to bake forty superior simnels, 140 (or 150, according to one text) salt simnels, and 260 bakers' loaves. A superior simnel fed four men, a salt simnel two, and a loaf one man. The strict control of liveries envisaged in the *Constitutio*, the operation of a clear accounting procedure, and the regulations for supply, all suggest that Henry was well aware of the pitfalls involved in running a large domestic establishment; but one must always remember that ordinances and regulations present a picture of the household as its master hoped it would be, rather than as it necessarily was.

In administrative matters, the most important household official was the chancellor. He was also one of the three most important figures in the national administration (along with the justiciar and treasurer). Moreover, he remained within the *domus*, keeping the king's seal (except when sent out of court on business, in which case the seal was probably kept by his immediate subordinate in the *domus*, the master of the writing-office), and normally itinerating with the king.[8] The frequent absences from England of the first three Norman kings naturally meant that a 'secondary' administration had to be created to cope with matters in England, and, as is well known, this led to the establishment of the justiciars, who came to preside over the court of the exchequer. Yet the creation of a secondary administration in no way detracts from the importance of the chancellor and chancery within the *domus*, indeed the fact that they remained with the king emphasises the continuing importance of the chancery as the immediate extension of the king's will through the written word. The *Constitutio* does not specify the number of clerks working under the chancellor in the *domus*, but William I apparently had up to eight clerks working under his chancellor simultaneously, and it is difficult to imagine that Henry would have made do with less.[9]

The early history of royal finance is obscure, but it seems clear that before the Conquest the financial administration of the crown was centred firmly within the *domus*. Between 1066 and 1135, the organisation of the royal finances became more definitely departmentalised than any other section of the administration, and the crucial effect of this was to hive off certain sections of the financial apparatus from the *domus*. By 1135, there were three principal financial departments of the crown: chamber, treasury and exchequer. The latter two were separate from the *domus*, while the chamber remained an integral part of the *domus*. The treasury at Winchester was by now the principal depository for royal revenues in England: it was to Winchester that Stephen raced in December 1135, as had Henry I in August 1100. The exchequer, under the control of the justiciar, had a different function of auditing the accounts of the sheriffs and other royal ministers who brought in the king's revenues, and to assay such money. It first came into being in the last few years of the eleventh century or the first few years of the twelfth. The establishment, and increasing importance, of a separate treasury and exchequer at this time was largely due to the fact that the Anglo-Norman kings spent much of their time on the other side of the channel.

Yet in no real sense had the chamber within the *domus*, the *camera curie* as it was now called, declined in importance. By this time, and probably for some time before this, the word *camera* had acquired two distinct (though related) meanings: in one sense it was the king's bedchamber, the inner, private sanctum of the *domus* where he dressed, bathed, slept, and often dined or worked away from the hubbub of the household, closeted in privacy with a small inner circle of friends and counsellors. It is probable that the master-chamberlain was increasingly concerned with this domestic aspect of the chamber's work.[10] In its other sense, it meant the financial department which accompanied the king and *domus* wherever they went: the *camera curie*, his privy purse. Yet throughout the twelfth century it was much more than a privy purse. It was the principal spending department of the crown, financing not only the domestic expenses of the king but also military expeditions, the building and mainten-ance of royal castles, and so forth. It was the chamberlains of the *camera curie*, together with the treasurer of the chamber,[11] whose task it was to ensure that the king was always well supplied with money by organising its collection and transportation from the local treasuries in England and Normandy to the *domus*, wherever that happened to be. After the recovery of Normandy in 1106, when the king had a greater diversity of resources upon which to draw, the importance of the chamber as the central, controlling financial department was paramount.[12] In keeping track of the payments they made, the chamber-lains and treasurer of the chamber were assisted by the master-marshal, who was responsible for keeping the counterfoils of all tallies issued, so that he could act 'against all the king's officers a a universal witness'.[13] In Henry I's time, therefore, the controlling and dynamic force behind the royal finances remained very much within the *domus*, itinerating with, and subject to the immediate authority of, the king.

The military capability of the royal household was, throughout its history, a factor of prime importance in the establishment and maintenance of kingship. 'Everywhere in the Germanic world,' said F.M. Stenton, 'the ruler, whether king or chief, was attended by a bodyguard of well-born companions.'[14] From the warrior-companions of the *comitatus* described by Tacitus in first-century Germany, through the *gesiths* and thegns of Anglo-Saxon England, to the *housecarles* of Cnut's and Edward the Confessor's reigns, there is the same emphasis on the personal nature of the bond between ruler and warrior, the inviolability of the oath of loyalty, the disgrace of betrayal. What we often do not know is how many of them there were, how they were recruited, and under what conditions they served. The obvious recruiting-ground would be the youthful sons of the nobility, and Larson states that *gesiths* in the seventh century often joined the court while still young.[15] In the disturbed conditions prevailing in England during the first half of the eleventh century, the royal corps of *housecarles* probably came as close to forming a permanent military household as any other group of warriors in medieval English history. Larson estimates that there may have been 3,000 of them, and that they were probably recruited by Cnut between 1014 and 1018, specifically for the subjection of his new kingdom.[16] In addition to their monthly wages, they were granted estates of up to fifteen hides each. Naturally all of them were not with the king all the time, but many of them probably were for long periods at a time. From the early stages of their formation, it had been usual for some of the *housecarles* (in rotation, presumably) to return to their estates during the winter, and then to come together again during the summer to guard the realm (which might include garrison duty). They might also be used for administrative purposes, collecting revenues for instance, although every one of them was undoubtedly first and foremost a soldier. The elaborate regulations governing their conduct throw some interesting sidelights on ceremonial aspects of the medieval royal court (although it has recently been suggested that these may not be strictly contemporary). The *housecarles* had a strict order of seating precedence at the king's table, based on eminence in warfare, nobility of birth, and length of service; those found guilty of petty crimes, however, would be demoted; anyone found guilty of three or more crimes would be sent to sit at the lowest place at table, where none of the other *housecarles* would talk to him and all could hurl their gnawed bones at him. Treason was punishable by either execution or exile. The *housecarlegemot* was set up as a special court to decide disputes between them. It is far from impossible that other, non-military members of the Old English royal household were governed by similar kinds of regulations.

As Stenton pointed out, the *housecarles* must have acted as a constant reminder to Englishmen that Danish kingship in England had been achieved through conquest. Moreover, it was upon ordinary Englishmen that the burden of supporting the *housecarles* fell, for from the reign of Cnut through to 1051 a new tax, the *heregeld* (army tax), was regularly levied, out of which they were paid their wages. In 1051, however, the Confessor ceased to levy it. By this time the number of *housecarles* had declined, and many of them had ceased to accompany the king on a permanent basis and were now living on their estates. Nevertheless, like the household knights of later times, they remained ready to respond to the king's summons when needed, and formed an important professional element around which the last armies of the Anglo-Saxon kings gathered. This was their role at Hastings, after which they disappear from English history, although in Scandinavia, the guild of *housecarles* can still be found two or three hundred years later.[17]

In the years immediately following the Conquest, it may well be that the king kept a substantial body—hundreds, perhaps—of knights with him (the term 'knight' comes from Anglo-Saxon *cniht*, meaning 'household retainer', although it rapidly acquired a broader meaning). But, like the *housecarles* before them, it is probable that the knights of post-Conquest England began to be released from permanent duty at court and to settle on their estates once Norman rule had been firmly established. Recent research on the military household of Henry I has raised many questions about both the role and the value of enfeoffed knights in the armies of the Anglo-Saxon kings.[18] It has been argued, and convincingly, that the armies employed by Henry to mount his numerous campaigns in Normandy, and occasionally in England, owed much less than has been realised previously to the idea of enfeoffed knights performing their annual and statutory feudal service, and far more both to contracted retinues of mercenaries, and to a professional and intensely loyal core of knights retained to be of the *familia regis*. In fact, it has been suggested, the recruitment of royal armies under Henry I differed little from the recruitment of royal armies under Edward I.

The military *familia* consisted of a professional corps of young knights—'several hundred', suggests Dr Chibnall, while J.O. Prestwich, following Orderic Vitalis, estimated that one detachment alone might number 200–300. Each of these knights was in effect retained by Henry I at a minimum annual fee of £5, in addition to which each received wages of up to 1s. a day, reckoned from the day on which he left home, when summoned to the king's service. These household knights, drawn from diverse social and geographical back-grounds, but always including a good proportion of young nobles, formed the shock-troops of Henry's armies, around whom the bands of mercenaries and those fighting in order to fulfil their feudal obligations gathered. The tradition of family service among knights of the *familia* was strong, as was their loyalty to the king. Their organisation, when they came together on campaign, was centred in the *domus*. They were paid by the constable, who received his money from the chamberlains (hence the constable's place at the exchequer table; as well as supervising the muster, the constable also probably arranged for the supply of castles).[19] The constable's right-hand-man was the master-marshal who, with his four assistant marshals, was responsible for the billeting of the *familia* and for taking care of the horses.[20] Yet they did not always fight in the company of the king: they might also be employed for prolonged garrison service in the string of castles through which Henry maintained his hold in Normandy, and sometimes a detachment of the *familia* might be fighting in France while the king was in England. There are also examples of the king contracting retinues in a manner strikingly reminiscent of the fourteenth and fifteenth centuries.[21] Yet it would surely be premature to argue that feudal service was a relatively insignificant factor in the armies of the Anglo-Norman kings: whether or not quotas were imposed, military service was an important element in early English feudalism. Nevertheless, the distinction between feudal service and service for wages is evidently a blurred one. Moreover, the knights of Henry I's expanded household were clearly a vital factor in the war-fare of his reign. They provide important evidence of a military tradition, that is, a broad, outer circle of warriors of the king's *familia*, closely bound to the king and easily assimilated to the *domus*, which can be seen to stretch right through medieval English history, from the *gesiths*, thegns and *housecarles* of the Anglo-Saxon kings, to the household knights of Edward III.

In the early twelfth century, then, there is no doubt that the royal adminis-tration operates from within the *domus*, under the immediate supervision of the king. The chancellor, master-chamberlain, and constable are still the chief per-sonal servants of the king in their respective spheres of secretarial, financial, and military administration. They were important men, not perhaps as impor-tant as in France, where the steward, constable and chancellor were men of immense importance, but most of those who became constables, chamberlains or stewards to the Conqueror and his sons were extensive landholders (although only one became an earl: the Conqueror's steward William FitzOsbern, who was earl of Hereford *c.* 1067–71). The principal reason why these lay officers of the household failed to acquire the sort of personal power and influence which is usually attributed to their French counterparts is largely because each office was divided between a number of individuals. Yet there were other reasons too. Firstly, household offices were beginning to become honorary, and as a result hereditary. Already in the reign of Henry I the office of master-butler had been granted hereditarily to William d'Aubigny, and that of master-chamberlain to Aubrey de Vere, and by the early thirteenth century the offices of steward, marshal and constable had become hereditarily attached to the earldom of Leicester and the Bigod and Bohun families respectively.[22] This might not lessen the *personal* influence of the holder of one of these offices, but it inevitably removed the necessity for him to attend the king on a regular basis, for his domestic duties came to be performed by deputies. Secondly, as royal government became increasingly specialised, departmentalised, and generally busier, more government departments tended to be hived off, to move 'out of court', and thus the *domus* gradually ceased to be the administrative hub of the kingdom and became increasingly concerned with the domestic needs of the king. Although this did not necessarily reduce the political influence of members of the *domus*, it could have important political consequences. It necessitated, for instance, the increasing formalisation of the body which was to act as co-ordinator of the various government departments: the king's council. The composition of the king's council was a matter of regular, and often acrimonious, public debate in late medieval England. It also raised the question of the relationship between the king and the other government departments, most notably over the question of appointments, which was another matter for (occasionally bitter) dispute. Finally, it led to some questioning of the role of the *domus* itself: no-one denied the king's right to have a household, and the great majority of the king's subjects would undoubtedly have recognised that he had a duty to maintain high standards of entertainment there; but equally, as the administrative functions performed within the *domus* gradually decreased in number, as it became, more and more, the *domestic* establishment of the king, there was a growing chorus of voices demanding that its extravagance be modified, its servants pruned, and its capacity to devour funds measured in proportion to its usefulness.

Administration and finance before 1360

By the end of the thirteenth century there were again five chief officers of the *domus*: the steward, the keeper of the wardrobe (or treasurer of the household), the chamberlain, the controller, and the cofferer. Their titles, and their duties, reflect sharply the narrowed range of the household's activities for they were all primarily domestic officers of the king. In 1279 there had still been two stewards of the household, but fifteen years later there was only one.[23] The (single) steward remained the chief lay officer of the household for the rest of the Middle Ages, responsible for order, discipline, and over-all efficiency within the *domus*, and, jointly with the keeper of the wardrobe, for general supervision of the domestic expenses of the king. Under Edward I, he was always an important man of at least knightly rank, a member of the council, and almost invariably summoned to parliament.[24] The keeper of the wardrobe was the chief financial officer of the household, as he had been since the end of Henry III's minority and he was ultimately responsible for accounting to the exchequer for all money which passed through the household. The first really powerful keeper of the wardrobe was Peter de Rivaux (1232–4), and although few subsequent keepers achieved such an eminent political position as this all-powerful clerk briefly did, many thirteenth- and fourteenth-century keepers of the wardrobe were appointed to bishoprics. The importance of both the steward and the keeper is demonstrated by the fact that they were both included on the list of leading royal ministers who should, claimed the Ordainers in 1311, be appointed only with the consent of the baronage in parliament. Also included on that list was the controller. The office of controller of the household, also a clerical post, had developed in the 1230s as the right-hand-man of the keeper. He kept a counter-roll—hence his name—of the household's receipts and expenses, and was responsible for custody of the household's records and any other archives kept there. He was also, until the second decade of the fourteenth century, the keeper of the king's privy seal.[25] This made him the head of the king's personal secretariat once the chancery had moved 'out of court'. By 1318 the custody of the privy seal had been transferred to a specific 'keeper of the privy seal', but the controller was still a domestic officer of great importance, checking the quantity and quality of victuals brought into the household, and sitting with the steward and keeper at the (theoretically nightly) account of the household.[26] It was only natural that many controllers of the household went on to become keepers of the wardrobe.

If the controller was the keeper's right-hand man, the cofferer was his left-hand-man. This post really emerged during the reign of Edward I as the personal clerk of the keeper, although he was not always known as the cofferer until late in Edward II's reign.[27] In 1318 he was described as the 'treasurer's deputy', and was in charge of the counting-table (later 'counting-house'), where the cash, tallies and bills received and issued by the wardrobe were reckoned one against the other, where wardrobe creditors were paid and debtors called to account. He kept the keys to the coffers in which the cash and credit instruments were stored. The office of chamberlain, technically the deputy of the master-chamberlain (or chamberlain of England), but in reality appointed by the king, underwent a temporary eclipse in the thirteenth century. For most of Edward I's reign, for example, there were about ten chamberlains, who ranked as esquires, and whose duties seem to have been very largely domestic.[28] Towards the end of Edward I's reign, however, with the appointment of Peter de Champvent as chamberlain, the office began to acquire importance again.[29] In 1318, the steward, keeper and chamberlain were regarded as the three senior officers of the *domus*, and in the later years of Edward II's reign the post was held by none other than the younger Despenser. During Edward III's reign the post continued to be held by men who were of high (often lordly) status, and often close friends of the king. The list of leading ministers of the crown who, according to the Statute of 1341, were in future to be accountable for their actions in parliament, included all these five officers except the cofferer. The chief officers of the *domus* were undoubtedly figures of national importance, even if not for the same reasons as the chief officers of Henry I's household had been.

For the domestic organisation of the household as it had evolved by the reign of Edward II, our chief authority is the household ordinance promulgated by the king at York on 6 December 1318. The preamble to the ordinance states that it was drawn up, at the king's request, by the steward, chamberlain, keeper and controller. It is a long, and drearily repetitive, list of all (or almost all) the king's domestic servants, detailing the duties and accounting responsibilities of each of those servants, together with a statement of the wages and allowances due to each of them from the steward, keeper and chamberlain at the top, down to the garçons (grooms) who formed the broad base of menial service at the bottom. The number of these grooms is not always specified, so it is impossible to be precise about the total staff establishment of the *domus* at this time, but it appears to point to a figure of 450–500 domestic servants of the king.

Daily liveries naturally varied according to status. As a general rule, the 1318 Ordinance stated that the king, queen and lords should be served with four meat courses a day, everyone else with three, except for the grooms who received but two.[30] Liveries of candles and beverages were also regulated carefully, at least in theory. In addition, the great majority of household servants received wages and allowances for robes and/or shoes. In Henry I's time, according to the *Constitutio*, they had received only wages in addition to their daily liveries of food and drink, but by the reign of King John it was usual for at least some members of the household to receive money for robes and shoes.[31] Only the most senior lay officers of the household received annual fees (ten or twenty marks) from the king; the senior clerical officers received daily wages only until the king found suitable livings with which to present them. By the mid-fourteenth century, and probably for some time before this, certain groups of ecclesiastical benefices to which the king had the right of presentation were customarily reserved for his household clerks. Both lay and clerical officers of the household received annual robes allowances, usually set at eight marks but sometimes rising to sixteen for the steward, chamberlain and keeper. The next level of household servants, the clerks, sergeants of the offices, sergeants-at-arms, and esquires, received wages varying between 4½d. and 7½d. per day, and annual robes allowances of three or three and a half marks (occasionally up to six marks). The menial servants of the household, valets, carters, palfreymen, sumptermen and grooms, got between 1½d. and 3d. in daily wages, and annual robes allowances of between 6s. 8d. and £1. They also received a standard annual allowance of 4s. 8d. for shoes.

The departmental organisation of the household as revealed by the Ordinance of 1318 is shown in diagram 2 (p. 13). Comparison between the Ordinance of 1318 and the Black Book of Edward IV's reign, as well as abundant evidence from the period with which this book is principally concerned, reveals that the general lines along which the domestic establishment of the king functioned changed very little in the fourteenth and fifteenth centuries.[32] Service was divided between the hall, where the great majority of servants and visitors ate, and the king's chamber, where he and his personal friends, guests and advisors ate. The distinction was between the 'political' and 'domestic' households, in some ways resembling the later division between 'upstairs' and 'downstairs'. Beneath the keeper, controller and cofferer, the domestic offices of the household fell into three groups, each with a clerk responsible for presenting its accounts. Firstly, the pantry and buttery, secondly the kitchen (including the poultery, larder, scullery and saucery), and thirdly the marshalsea, which coped with the several hundred horses attached to the household.[33] Within each of these sub-offices there was at least one sergeant, supported by his staff of purveyors, valets, carters, and grooms. The clerical officers divided into those concerned with the internal finances of the household (clerks of the offices, accountable in the first instance to the cofferer), the king's personal secretariat (the office of the privy seal), and the king's chapel, headed by the king's confessor and the chief chaplain (known by 1347 as dean of the chapel). The king's physician and surgeon were also normally members of the *domus*, and other miscellaneous members of the household included the clerk of the market (a post often held by a layman in fact), who held the assizes of bread and ale in towns through which the household passed, the king's minstrels, archers, huntsmen, falconers, and even a hat-maker employed to make hats for the esquires of the household.

The Ordinance of 1318 was, explicitly, a reforming ordinance[34] for it is abundantly clear that the king's household, even in its purely domestic aspects, did not always run as smoothly and as efficiently as might have been desired. Reading it, it is difficult to understand how the steward and keeper and their fellow chief officers of the household could be regarded as *ex officio* politically important figures, but evidently they were, in 1311, 1341, and on many other occasions. Moreover, the theory propounded by some historians in the early twentieth century (with particular reference to the reign of Edward II),[35] namely that the household's political unpopularity was a result mainly of its being used by the king as an 'administrative haven', wherein he could escape the administrative controls imposed by an ever-vigilant baronage, has now largely been discredited.[36] In fact, the political unpopularity of the household sprang very largely from its domestic sphere of activity. The depradations of William Rufus's servants were often remarked upon. Peter of Blois, once Henry II's secretary, said that the royal household used to decimate areas through this it passed.[37] These aspects of the household are dealt with in some detail in the next chapter, but it needs to be emphasised that they were by no means peculiar to the fourteenth century. The abuse of its powers is one of the constant themes of the history of the royal household.

Problems of corruption and indiscipline were bound to arise with a royal establishment of around 500 or more people regularly moving around the country. But these were not the only complaints made about the king's

Diagram 2: Organisation of the domus according to the Ordinance of 1318

STEWARD*
KEEPER*

(Clerical)
- King's confessor
- chief chaplain
- (with 5 chaplains and 6 clerks of the chapel)
- almoner
- Clerk of the privy seal (with 4 clerks writing under the privy seal)

(Domestic)
CONTROLLER* OF THE HOUSEHOLD
- Clerk of the spicery
- sub-clerk of the spicery
- confectioner of spices
- sub-usher of the wardrobe
- esquire fruiterer
- sergeant chaundler
- naperer

(Great wardrobe)
Chief clerk-purveyor of the great wardrobe
- King's tailor
- king's armourer
- king's pavilioner

(Queen's household)
- Queen's steward
- queen's treasurer

(Miscellaneous)
- Physician
- surgeon
- clerk of the market
- sergeant-marshal of horses
- huntsmen
- trumpeters and minstrels
- messengers (12)
- foot-archers (24)
- hat-maker

(Service)

(Chamber)
CHAMBERLAIN*
- Ushers of the chamber
- valets of the chamber
- sergeants-at-arms (30)
- surveyor of the king's meats
- porter of the chamber

(Hall)
- knight chief usher of the hall
- marshals of the hall
- surveyor of the dresser of the hall
- sewers of the hall
- esquires (24)

(Accounting)
COFFERER* (with 2 clerks of the counting-table)

Clerk of the pantry and buttery
- Pantler
- waferer
- baker

Chief butler
- sergeant butler
- sergeant butler for the king

Chief clerk of the kitchen
- Buyers and cooks for poultery, larder, scullery and saucery

Chief clerk of the marshalsea
- Buyer of the averary harbingers of horses
- blacksmiths
- carters
- sumptermen
- valets of the stables

* Denotes five chief officers of the household

domestic establishment as criticisms of royal extravagance were frequently made, and there is no doubt that this question too contributed considerably to the household's unpopularity. We have no way of knowing how much money the Angevin kings spent on their households. King John's *Misae* roll for the twelve months from Ascension 1210 to Ascension 1211 records a total expenditure of something over £7,760, but the figure is incomplete and in any case does not include figures for daily food and drink.[38] From early in Henry III's reign, however, it becomes possible to compute with some accuracy the expenses of the *domus*. Henry III spent a steady averge of £9,000–£10,000 *per annum* throughout his reign.[39] Edward I's average was a little higher, with annual totals varying between £9,000 and £12,000, although in 1305, when it was proposed to adopt a *certum* (a fixed annual allowance) for the domestic expenses of the household, the sum of £250 a week, or £13,000 *per annum*, was evidently considered appropriate.[40] Edward II's domestic expenses continued at a level similar to that of his father's, although in the last few years of his reign (1323–6) they dropped markedly, staying below £10,000 *per annum*.[41] In the early years of Edward III's reign household expenses remained at a relatively low level, between £10,000 and £12,000 *per annum*, but by the middle of the 1340s they had begun to rise. The purely domestic expenditure recorded in keeper Walter Wetwang's account for the period April 1344 to November 1347 totals just over £77,500, making an annual average of £21,530.[42] For the twelve months from February 1353 to 1354 the equivalent total is £19,070.[43] In 1359–60, during a period of eleven and a half months, domestic expenses totalled about £20,500.[44]

Complaints about the king's extravagance were made during this period, but they appear to bear little relation to the level of expenditure. The proposal in 1305 to adopt a *certum* which the wardrobe could not exceed (an idea which was repeated in 1316–17)[45] clearly was, in theory, an attempt to restrict household expenditure below a maximum figure. But what really seems to have mattered to those who complained about the king's extravagance was whether or not the household was able to meet its bills. Neither in 1305 nor in 1316–17 could the *domus* be accused of unusual extravagance, yet on each occasion there was a general air of financial crisis, the crown was short of cash, and consequently the household which as a recurrent charge on the crown's revenues which could be modified only with great determination, had been failing to pay its debts.[46] In 1258 the situation was very similar for in that year too there was a financial crisis, and the discontented barons demanded that royal grants should be checked, and the 'ordinary' revenues of the crown should be reserved for the payment of royal debts and the expenses of the household. Between 1259 and 1261 attempts were made to implement this policy, but once he reained power Henry III did his best to ignore such demands.[47] In 1310 the household's inability to pay its way again created dissent, and the demand for the resumption of royal grants reached a new level: throughout the next decade it was a major constituent of the policy advocated by Thomas of Lancaster and his supporters. The point of clauses 4 and 8 of the Ordinances of 1310–11 was not to deprive the household of cash, but explicitly to ensure that it was supplied with sufficient cash to enable it to meet its debts. In the 1330s and early 1340s, when household expenditure remained generally modest but when once again the exigencies of war had left the crown short of cash, there were further complaints about the extravagance of the king and the non-payment of household debts, and further demands for the moderation of royal grants. Yet during the next two decades, when the king's expenditure on his *domus* reached a markedly higher level, there was a notable absence of complaints about his extravagance.[48] It seems that (within limits, obviously) no-one much minded how much the king spent on his *domus*, as long as its creditors were not left unpaid, and as long as there was no general financial crisis (the latter, naturally, was always likely to result in the former). In times of political and financial crisis, however, domestic expenditure was always an easy target. 'Be it noted to reform the household of the king and queen', minuted the barons of 1258.[49] Richard II was to find himself confronted by the same attitude in the 1380s, and it is important to remember that a correlation between the persistence of demands for moderation of the household's expenditure, and the actual level of that expenditure, does not always exist. Thus it was that, from the standpoint of those who made it their business to reform the royal government, there were good reasons from a purely domestic point of view why the chief officers of the king's household should be accountable not solely to the king, but also to their critics in parliament.

The range of routine administrative functions performed within the *domus* declined steadily through the thirteenth and fourteenth centuries. Following King John's loss of Normandy in 1204, the need for a 'dual administrative system' to cope with royal absences abroad was greatly reduced. The chancery now remained almost permanently in England, and its separation from the *domus* became increasingly marked during the thirteenth century. Already in John's reign the seal which the chancellor kept was coming to be known as the 'great seal', in contradistinction to the 'small seal' (the later 'privy seal') which was continually with the king. Eventually, after the death of Edward I's great chancellor Robert Burnell in 1292, the chancery finally moved 'out of court'.[50] The fourteenth-century chancellor was, in the words of Professor Wilkinson, 'no longer so much the secretary as the representative of the crown.'[51] It needs to be emphasised, however, that the chancery remained, except in very extraordinary political circumstances (1314–16, for example), firmly under the control of the king: the eventual political importance of the late medieval chancellors stemmed not from the fact that they headed an independent administrative machine, which they did not, but from their position of pre-eminence on the royal council.

The gradual establishment of the chancery at Westminster necessitated the development of a new personal royal secretariat within the *domus*, in order to authenticate mandates or warrants from the king when the chancery (great) seal was out of court. King John's small seal, which served this purpose, was kept by one of the officials of his chamber, who naturally remained with the king.[52] By 1318 at the latest, a specific 'keeper of the privy seal', with four clerks working under him, was appointed.[53] Yet gradually, such was the inexorable tendency towards bureaucratic departmentalisation, the privy seal office too moved out of court. Already in Edward II's reign it was sometimes used to authenticate the acts of council, and this tendency accelerated during the reign of Edward III. By the middle of Edward III's reign, the keeper of the privy seal was no longer in constant attendance on the king.[54] In its place had arisen the 'secret seal' or 'signet', which was, by the mid-fourteenth century, the principal immediate instrument under which the king's personal wishes were conveyed, and so it was to remain until the end of the Middle Ages.[55]

It has sometimes been argued that these 'personal' seals of the king—initially the privy seal, subsequently the signet—were of considerable political importance to successive kings.[56] The older 'state' departments, so it is argued, such as the chancery and exchequer, gradually acquired both a bureaucratic routine and a measure of political independence of their own, thus making them less responsive to the king's wishes and more susceptible to baronial or 'opposition' influences. It has been suggested that this development produced a reaction whereby the king attempted to restore his administrative initiative through an inner 'household' enclave by creating new and more personal administrative machinery which operated from within the household and which would therefore be subject to the immediate supervision of the king. This might then be used to circumvent 'opposition' influences within the 'state' departments. Thus, for instance, the privy seal or signet might be used to by-pass the great seal, or the wardrobe to by-pass the exchequer. The argument really stands or falls on the question of whether or not the chancery and exchequer were under the control of the king; if they were, there would be no point in developing more 'personal' administrative machinery for purposes other than practical convenience. And it has recently been argued that in the political circumstances which obtained normally in late medieval England, there is no serious reason to doubt that royal control over the whole administration was, as far as matters of political importance were concerned, more or less complete.[57] There was no real conception of 'state' departments as opposed to 'household' departments; no-one in the Middle Ages used the phrase 'household government'. The administration was regarded as a unity by king and barons alike, and in the fourteenth and fifteenth centuries the way in which the king's opponents might increase their political influence was by gaining representation on the royal council which, with the king, co-ordinated the whole administrative machine. Alternatively, they might try to ensure 'parliamentary' or 'baronial' consent to top ministerial appointments, but never just household appointments. Such demands show that these ministers could indeed play a significant political role, especially if they were *not* chosen by the king, but these requests were almost invariably ignored by the king, and the envisaged scenario of 'opposition' control of the whole administration hardly ever materialised.

There is, therefore, very little evidence that, at any time before 1360, either the privy seal or the signet were used by the king, or indeed regarded by his opponents, as the instruments of an alternative 'household' administration. This does not mean that the household lacked political or administrative importance, but it was a personal rather than an institutional importance. In other words, many of those employed in the household were of great political and administrative importance, but the household as an institution was only as important as the sum of those individuals within it who wielded influence. It was precisely because such men were able, or loyal, that they were given jobs in the household. Under Henry II, the king's chamber was the nursery of most of the principal royal administrators; under Edward I, 'nearly all the most important administrators' began their careers as wardrobe clerks. Those administrative changes which did occur (such as, for instance, the supplanting of the chamber by the wardrobe as the administrative heart of the household—'the brain and hand of the court'—in the early thirteenth century) were the product not of opposition pressures but of practical decisions taken by the king and his advisors.[58] In the Middle Ages, as long as England had an adult king, the exercise of political power at a national level remained essentially with those who were closest to the king. Only by taking the most drastic action, as in 1258, 1264, 1310–11, or 1386–88, could this situation be altered.

As for the matter of financial administration, the roles of the financial departments which remained within the *domus* (chamber and wardrobe, essentially) changed considerably during the thirteenth and fourteenth centuries.[59] Under Henry II, and even more emphatically under Richard I, the chamber was the great spending department of the crown. It remained permanently with the king, staffed by the chamberlains and the newly-emerged clerks of the chamber (clearly distinct from the clerks of the chapel even in the early years of Henry II's reign) and drew in cash from the series of castle treasuries dotted around the king's dominions, from loans, and from the 'great and occasional profits' of the crown, such as gifts, aids, escheats, wardships, temporalities *sede vacante*, and so forth.[60] It financed both the personal, domestic and occasional expenses of the king, and his wars and other military expenditure. Meanwhile, by the end of Henry II's reign, the exchequer with its functions of audit and assay, and the treasury, acting as the principal storehouse of the royal treasure, had merged and come to be known as the upper and lower exchequer. By the end of the twelfth century both upper and lower exchequer were normally established at Westminster, although they might still itinerate with the king if he wished them to. Thus they were clearly outside the *domus*, while the chamber, the 'controlling organ of the financial system', was definitely an integral part of it.[61]

After King John's death in 1216 the chamber rapidly declined in importance, and throughout the thirteenth century its role in the national financial system was minimal. In its place arose the wardrobe. The financial role of the wardrobe had first become important in John's reign, when it had been used as a storehouse for the chamber. In no sense was it a rival to the chamber. The distinction between the two departments was evidently extremely blurred, and domestic servants of the king were referred to quite indiscriminately as either 'of the chamber' or 'of the wardrobe'.[62] But as Henry III approached his majority, and as the influence of Peter de Rivaux grew from 1223 onwards, the wardrobe emerged as the principal financial department of the household. Like the twelfth-century chamber, it paid for the personal and domestic expenses of the king, and for his military campaigns. From the 1230s onwards, the post of treasurer of the household and keeper of the wardrobe were one and the same and when Henry III led campaigns abroad in 1229–30, 1242–3, and 1253–4, the cash to pay his armies was channelled through the wardrobe. There was, however, an important distinction between the Angevin chamber and the wardrobe under Henry III. The reforms of 1232–42 had stressed the importance of the exchequer as the department with overall responsibility for the collection and initial apportionment of royal revenues. Even in Henry II's time it had been customary for routine, recurrent revenues (such as the farms of the shire) to be paid into the exchequer/treasury, and from the 1230s onwards more and more types of crown revenue were paid into the exchequer. Thus the accountability to the exchequer of the king's spending departments including principally his household departments, was emphasised. It may be that this led to a theoretical distinction between the 'public' and 'private' revenues of the king, although the wardrobe might still draw directly on any source of royal revenue if and when need arose.[63] Nevertheless, it remains true that throughout Henry III's reign the wardrobe drew the vast majority of its cash from the exchequer, and thus quite naturally accounted for it at the exchequer. This did make it rather different from the chamber under the Angevins.

From the early years of Edward I's reign, the wardrobe came to occupy a much more important role in the crown's financial administration than it had done under Henry III. Although the principle of wardrobe accountability to the exchequer was, at least theoretically, maintained throughout the reign, it was no longer the case that the wardrobe received the majority of its cash from the exchequer. Even for the early Welsh wars of the 1270s and 1280s, it drew regularly on the customs, aids, taxation, and any other source of crown revenue. This made it difficult for the exchequer to balance its books, and a further series of reforms by royal ministers in the early 1290s tried to reimpose the principle that nearly all royal revenue should initially be brought to the exchequer, to be distributed thence to the spending departments. For a few years these reforms were quite effective, but from 1294 onwards, under the stress of constant war, political opposition, and a severe shortage of cash, the system rapidly disintegrated. Edward I used his wardrobe, just as Henry III had used his, and the Angevins had used the chamber, as the paymaster to the royal armies, the channel through which military expenses were distributed. It was thus the wardrobe, with the king constantly at the centre of operations, that needed the ready cash, and the exchequer was unable to provide that cash in sufficient quantity with sufficient speed. The wardrobe began to live on credit: not only did it pre-empt more and more crown revenues before they could be brought into the exchequer, it also began to issue written bills and debentures on its own behalf in return for cash or goods, to both royal ministers such as customs collectors and to private creditors. These bills were supposed to be redeemable at the exchequer. But often the exchequer was unable to redeem these credit instruments because the wardrobe was pre-empting so much of the cash which should have come to the exchequer, and the amount of cash available at the exchequer with which to redeem them was insufficient. The exchequer was thus unable to impose any sort of effective supervision over the crown's principal spending department during this last decade of the reign, while the vast sums needed by the wardrobe meant that the crown's debts mounted enormously. By 1307, Dr M. Prestwich has estimated that they stood at 'at least £200,000'.[64]

There was no 'constitutional policy' involved in all this. The king was not trying to escape exchequer control for it was royal policy just as much as it was 'opposition' policy (if such a term is applicable) to emphasise the exchequer's role as the department which supervised receipt and disbursement of crown revenue. It was pure practical necessity, occasioned by the intense demands of war and the time-honoured role of the household as paymaster to the royal armies. Nevertheless, the almost indiscriminate issuing of wardrobe bills and debentures probably did mean that the wardrobe came to be regarded with suspicion: a wardrobe bill, it came to be realised, might not be worth the parchment it was written on. Hence the demand of the ordainers in 1311 that all the crown revenues should be brought in to the exchequer in the first instance, a demand entirely in accord, whenever practically possible, with royal policy. Hence also the development during Edward II's reign of the exchequer's own system of credit, through tallies of assignment, which allowed to exchequer officials a greater say in determining who was to be paid first, as well as allowing them to keep a closer check on the level of credit pledged by the crown.

The role occupied by the wardrobe in the administration of crown finances during the first half of the fourteenth century was broadly similar to that which it had occupied under Henry III and Edward I. That is to say, in peacetime, it paid for the domestic expenses of the king, while in war-time it acted as a mobile war-treasury and paymaster to the army. Some changes are, however, worth noting. In 1324, it was decreed by Edward II and his advisors in the Westminster Ordinance that in future all crown revenues should be paid to the exchequer rather than to the wardrobe, with the exception only of receipts intimately connected with the household, such as personal gifts to the king and the profits of the court of the verge. At the same time it was decreed that the keepers of the king's stud, great wardrobe, and hanaper, the purveyors for his castles, and the king's butler, should in future account to the exchequer rather than to the wardrobe. The object of this was to speed up the wardrobe's accounting process, which had fallen in arrears, by removing extraneous accounts and restricting the wardrobe's peace-time responsibilities to the immediate domestic entourage of the king. Both decrees were purely administrative measures. They were by no means adhered to by Edward III in the period up to 1360, and again it was practical necessity, caused by the pressure of war, which forced the king to ignore them. In particular, Edward III's use of his wardrobe to manage his manipulation of the English wool-traders between 1338 and 1340 reflected as badly on the wardrobe as had the indiscriminate issuing of credit instruments in the later years of Edward I's reign, although it was for practical reasons that the king used the wardrobe rather than the exchequer for this purpose. The real objection was to the fact that the king was seizing wool, not the fact that the wardrobe rather than the exchequer was receiving the profits. Nevertheless, this episode served once more to bring the wardrobe's operations into disrepute, and in 1340 there were renewed demands in parliament that all crown revenues should be brought into the exchequer. After 1340, although the wardrobe continued frequently to receive the proceeds of taxation directly from source (and to issue bills and debentures in order to secure credit), the theory that these revenues were received via the exchequer was maintained by entering them under exchequer rather than 'foreign' receipt, and wardrobe accountability to the exchequer was thus again emphasised.

Finally, it is worth noting the revival of the chamber in the fourteenth century. The part played by the chamber in national finance was not great, but at times it acquired considerable wealth and could make some of that wealth available to either the exchequer or the wardrobe in emergencies. The fourteenth-century chamber was essentially the king's privy purse: while the wardrobe paid for his domestic expenses, the chamber paid for his private expenses. The chamber's sources of income were diverse but considerable. Not only were prerogative revenues still regularly received there, but from the early years of his reign, Edward II set aside a number of estates of which the profits were to be submitted to the chamber. After the rout of the Contrariants in 1322, much of their forfeited personal wealth was hoarded by the king in his chamber.[65] Although the system of chamber lands was discontinued in 1326, Edward III revived it from 1333 until 1356, when it was once again discontinued. All sorts of incidental, private profits of the king, such as ransoms and fines, were received in the chamber, and its wealth is demonstrated by the transfers which the king sometimes ordered to be made to other departments. In 1346–7, for instance, Robert de Burton, receiver of the chamber, passed £30,679 to Walter Wetwang, keeper of the wardrobe, to help pay for both domestic and military expenses during the Crécy-Calais campaign.[66] A record of the normal expenses of the chamber between 1345 and 1356 reveals considerable, although thoroughly erratic, expenditure on military and naval affairs, together with such items as a tent for the king to sleep in, or a painting costing £10.[67] The chamber had no defined role in the financial administration of the crown. It was the most personal of the king's spending departments, yet there is much evidence to suggest that the king's personal wealth was often considerable, and it was a useful fall-back in times of need.

It was logical that the wardrobe should act as paymaster to the English army, for throughout the thirteenth and the first half of the fourteenth centuries the royal household continued to form the nucleus of the English army.

When the king went to war, the *domus* went with him. It was augmented to form the army in two stages. Firstly, the bannerets, knights and esquires of the household, soldiers who were sometimes permanently, sometimes only temporarily, retained by the king, but who did not in normal circumstances reside at court, were summoned to join the king, to form his *familia*. Secondly, the whole English army—magnate retinues, mercenaries, county levies, and those performing feudal service—gathered around the *familia*. The first group was lodged 'within the verge', in other words, they were, for the duration of the campaign, of the household; the second group, the bulk of the army, was kept outwith the verge.[68] The organisation of the second stage, the 'outer circle' has more to do with the history of English armies than the history of the household, and need not be discussed here. The first stage, the 'inner circle' of soldiers personally bound to the king, often on long-term contracts, is well documented in the reign of Henry I, at which time the knights of the king's *familia* probably numbered several hundred. Whether Stephen, Henry II, Richard I and John maintained such large personal retinues of knights is difficult to prove, but it is quite probable for it is clear that throughout these reigns the household knight continued to be a vital figure in the king's military operations.[69] In the thirteenth and fourteenth centuries the number of knights retained by the English kings seems to have been considerably smaller than the number retained by Henry I, partly no doubt because of the long-term decline in the number of English knights and the rise in status of the esquires. From the 1220s, when Henry III first built up his own retinue of household knights, until the 1350s, the number of household knights and knights-banneret attached to the king at any one time varied between about thirty, in peace-time, and well over a hundred in war-time.[70] They were essentially fighting men, and this is why the king retained them. When summoned to join the king for a campaign they brought with them their *commiltones* (brothers-in-arms), and their retainers; the household contingent, which consisted of these knights with their retinues, as well as the esquires of the household, who numbered between fifty and a hundred and twenty and who also brought their own retainers, and the remaining servants of the household, all under arms, often contributed something like a quarter to a third of the entire army.[71]

Information relating to the king's personal bodyguard in peace-time is more abundant in the late thirteenth and fourteenth centuries than in the twelfth century. From at least the time of Edward I, there were three main elements of the bodyguard. Firstly and most importantly, the sergeants-at-arms, who received wages of 12*d.* a day and £2.6*s.*8*d. per annum* for robes, and were permanently based at court. In 1279 it was ordained that there should be twenty sergeants-at-arms, each keeping two or three horses.[72] In fact the number of sergeants-at-arms varied between fifteen and over thirty in Edward I's reign, and in 1318 their number was fixed at thirty.[73] They were all to be armed, and to keep three horses each at court. Each night four of them were to sleep outside the king's chamber, while the other twenty-six were to sleep in the hall, always ready to come if the king called. Each day the king travelled, all thirty were to ride before his person.[74] Under Edward III, however, this number does not seem to have been maintained and it seems that this king normally had between sixteen and twenty-two sergeants-at-arms.[75] Secondly, there were the king's foot-archers, who received 3d. a day plus 10s. *per annum* for robes, were also based permanently at court, and were also to go before the king when he travelled. The 1318 Ordinance implied that there should normally be twenty-four foot-archers, but numbers might vary between sixteen and forty-four.[76] Thirdly, there were the esquires of the household. They did not stay permanently at court, although the Ordinance of 1318 implied that twenty-four of them were expected to be at court at any one time, and it is probable that they served in rotation. They each received wages of 7½d. per day while at court, plus annual robes allowances of £2.[77] Thus the number of armed men who were supposed to be based at court at any one time in order to guard the king's body was about eighty, although in practice the number was often probably less than this, partly because full complements were not maintained, and partly because any esquire, foot-archer, or sergeant-at-arms was always liable to be sent out of court on some mission for the king.

Politics and the household 1360–1413

This outline of the history of the royal household in England before 1360, which is by no means intended to be comprehensive, but primarily to highlight the more important developments which occurred between the twelfth century and the fourteenth, makes it possible to analyse and perhaps to explain some of those developments. The need to service the king's domestic requirements, in a milieu appropriate to his station, was the principal *raison d'être* of the *domus*. Yet the scale on which those requirements were serviced was obviously variable. The growth in the size of the *domus* from around 100–150 persons in the early twelfth century to the 500 or more of the early fourteenth century is immediately apparent. Essentially this can be explained by an enhanced desire for ease, comfort, and splendour. It was a trend also clearly noticeable in noble households during the same period. It is associated too with developments in, for instance, castle-design where a greater emphasis on comfort, less on defensive qualities emerged.[78] The more sedentary nature of the fourteenth-century royal household as compared with that of the twelfth century may also help to explain this growth in size of the *domus*: the larger the household, the more difficult it would have been to maintain the sort of pace at which the Angevins moved around the country. This growth in size was certainly not accompanied by a growth in the administrative functions performed by members of the *domus*, in fact quite the opposite. From the late eleventh century onwards, the trend was steadily towards the shedding of routine administrative work, as first the treasury and (initially embryonic) exchequer, and later the chancery, as well as some of the less important royal departments, gradually moved 'out of court' and set up house elsewhere. Yet the word 'routine' is crucial in this context for the household remained the political heart of the kingdom, and as long as England had a king who ruled as well as reigned, not even the growing authority of the council could alter this fact. The steady movement of departments out of court is explained essentially by the steady growth of government business (particularly routine business), the formalisation of procedures, and hence the growth of bureaucracy. By the mid-fourteenth century, Westminster had clearly become the administrative heart of the kingdom.

It may be that these apparently contradictory trends—the simultaneous increase in size and decrease in administrative usefulness of the household—go some way towards explaining the harsh and frequent criticisms directed against the household during the years 1360–1413. The last years of Edward III's reign, and the reigns of Richard II and Henry IV, witnessed frequent political crises and whenever a crisis threatened, it seemed that the royal household was not far from the centre of the stage. The first major attack on the court in this period came in the deservedly famous 'Good Parliament' of 1376. At the instigation of the commons, led by their speaker Sir Peter de la Mare, a dozen or so courtiers and royal ministers were impeached and disgraced, and a continual council was set up to steer the king through the twilight of his reign. The political background to the Good Parliament has been analysed in detail by Dr Holmes.[79] What does need to be emphasised is the sharp contrast between the political atmosphere of the 1360s and that of the 1370s. The middle years of Edward III's reign, from *c.* 1345 onwards, were characterised by a striking series of English military victories against both France and Scotland, and a domestic political scene which was as trouble-free as any other period of similar length in the Middle Ages. Edward consolidated his military successes with the Treaty of Brétigny in 1360, and for the next decade or so England enjoyed a period of external peace, internal harmony, and relatively low taxation. All this was shattered by the renewal of the war with France in 1369. Within a year, the war had brought on the first of a series of financial crises which were to dog the government for the next two decades; taxation levels soared, and hostility to the government was compounded by military failures abroad, especially in 1372–3, when most of what had been gained in 1360 was once again lost. Edward himself was by now senile, and increasingly dominated by a small group of unpopular courtiers who gathered about the king in his dotage, most notorious of whom were the king's mistress Alice Perrers, and the chamberlain of the household, William Lord Latimer. It was these courtiers who were the butt of the commons' anger in 1376.

Edward III's death in June 1377 meant the replacement of a senile king by a juvenile one—Richard II was ten when he came to the throne—and though the influence of Perrers and Latimer and their friends was finally destroyed, little else changed. Expensive military failure gave way to just as expensive military stalemate. Taxation remained high. Among both the enfranchised and the unenfranchised members of the population, there was widespread discontent with the government, which was, nominally at least, in the hands of a series of continual councils between 1377 and 1380. In a succession of restless parliaments, the commons were increasingly critical of what they regarded as wasteful and ineffective government policies, and in 1381 the poor people of both town and countryside made their own feelings clear. That massive explosion of popular unrest, the Peasants' Revolt, ws provoked as much by political failure on the part of the government as by the new social and economic inequalities of post-Black Death England. Probably as a result of the Revolt— it was of course the third poll-tax which had provided the spark for rebellion— the level of taxation dropped quite considerably after 1381 but among the political classes, the early 1380s witnessed a steady build-up of tension. Within about a year of the revolt, Richard II had personally assumed charge of the government. Temperamentally, he seems to have been unsuited to kingship: he was capricious, quick to take offence, and easily led. His personal relations with several of the great magnates, notably his uncles John of Gaunt, duke of Lancaster, and Thomas of Woodstock, duke of Gloucester, as well as the irascible Richard Fitzalan, earl of Arundel, were distinctly uneasy. For their part, these and several other magnates regarded with distaste the king's courtier friends such as Robert de Vere, earl of Oxford, Michael de la Pole, earl of Suffolk, and Simon Burley, chamberlain of the household. In addition to these personal enmities, the government's financial position continued to deteriorate and, with the war in France continuing to go badly, there were serious disagreements over foreign policy.

Parliamentary criticism came to a head in the 'Wonderful Parliament' of 1386, when lords and commons united to refuse a demand for a massive subsidy of four tenths and fifteenths (tenths and fifteenths were direct subsidies payable as fractions of the population's movable goods; this was the standard way to collect royal taxation in fourteenth-century England). The king's chief ministers were dismissed, the chancellor (Michael de la Pole) was impeached, and the king was trammelled by the establishment, for one year, of a Commission of Government consisting of fourteen lords of the realm. As with the ordainers in 1310–11, the idea behind the commission was that power should be taken out of the hands of the king and his friends and given to those who would implement reforms. The infuriated king soon removed his household from the London area (where it might have been subjected to the scrutiny of the commissioners) and spent much of 1387 roaming the midlands and the north-west, trying to recruit supporters for his cause. In August he put his famous series of 'Questions to the Judges'; according to the replies given by the judges, all those who had been instrumental in securing the impeachment of de la Pole or the establishment of the commission were deemed to be worthy of a traitor's death. Richard's opponents, fearful for their lives, now came out in open opposition to the king and his friends, and demanded that an 'Appeal of Treason' be heard against five of Richard's most prominent supporters (de Vere; de la Pole; Alexander Nevill, archbishop of York; Chief Justice Robert Tresilian; and Nicholas Brembre, mayor of London). Because of this, the five main lords who opposed the king have come to be known as the Lords Appellant (Gloucester; Arundel; Thomas Beauchamp, earl of Warwick; Thomas

Mowbray, earl of Nottingham; and Henry, earl of Derby). With civil war looming, Robert de Vere was dispatched to Cheshire to raise an army for the king but just before Christmas 1387, his force was defeated at Radcot Bridge, near Oxford, by the Appellants and their retinues. The victorious lords then marched to London, confined the king, purged his household, imprisoned several of his courtiers, and forced him to summon parliament to hear the appeals against his friends. This parliament met on 3 February 1388. Robert de Vere, Michael de la Pole, and Alexander Nevill had all fled the country, but others were less lucky: before the conclusion of business in May, eight of the king's friends had been convicted of treason and executed, and another forty or so had been dismissed from court. Among those executed were the steward and chamberlain of the royal household, and the remaining victims of the parliament included numerous knights of the chamber and other members of the royal household. Not without reason is this assembly known as the 'Merciless Parliament'.

The aim of the king's opponents in 1388, just as it had been in 1376, was to destroy the circle that had gathered round the king. For more than a year after the Merciless Parliament the Lords Appellant remained in control of government, but in May 1389 Richard declared at a meeting of the council that he was now of age to rule (he was twenty-two), and that he intended henceforth to assume personal control of government. This he did, and with considerably more circumspection than he had shown before 1388, so that the next eight years were, politically, the most peaceful of the reign. The truce of Leulingham in May 1389 marked the effective end of the war with France until the end of the reign, and royal finances now improved markedly, which meant that there was much less parliamentary criticism of the government. Personal rivalries were patched up, or at least glossed over; John of Gaunt, who had been pursuing his dynastic ambitions in Spain during the crisis of 1386–9, was now back in England and had emerged as one of his nephew's foremost supporters. Beneath the apparent calm, though, the tensions remained, and from *c.* 1394 they began to resurface. Foreign policy was still a contentious issue. At court, too, a new inner circle of royal intimates was emerging, most notable of whom were the king's cousin Edward, earl of Rutland, Richard's half brother John Holand, earl of Huntingdon, and the new chamberlain of the household, William le Scrope. In the summer of 1397, the king decided that opposition had to be eliminated and he arrested the three chief Appellants of 1387–8, Gloucester, Arundel and Warwick. Gloucester was taken to Calais and murdered; Arundel, having been subjected to a mock trial in a parliament which was completely dominated by the king, was executed; Warwick was exiled to the Isle of Man. For the next two years Richard ruled as he pleased; his domestic extravagance soared, his vastly swollen retinue of camp-followers terrorised the countryside, his friends grew fat on the fruits of his generosity, and his arbitrary and vindictive actions, which have so often been described, made the king himself intensely unpopular and have earned for this period of his reign the appellation of 'Richard's Tyranny'. He went too far, however, and made too many mistakes. His decision to exile Henry of Derby (John of Gaunt's eldest son, and a former Appellant), in September 1398, was followed in March 1399 by his sequestration of Derby's Lancastrian inheritance once Gaunt died. This was contrary to the promise which he had made to Derby at the time of his exile. When the king left for Ireland in late May 1399, Derby returned, and soon found supporters flocking to his standard. Returning from Ireland, Richard was captured in North Wales and taken to London. On 30 September he was deposed; within a further five months he was dead, probably murdered, in Pontefract castle.

Derby, who now became Henry IV, was personally much more suited to kingship than Richard. He has suffered from the lack of a good biographer. A soldier of international renown, he was more level-headed, more conciliatory, less reckless than his predecessor. In different circumstances, he could have made a very good king; as it is, he did well just to hang on to his crown until his death in 1413. By strict primogenitary rule it was the earl of March, who was aged only eight in 1399, to whom the crown should have passed following Richard's deposition, but March's claim was ignored. The unavoidable fact of Henry's usurpation was to plague him throughout his reign, providing a ready excuse for four armed rebellions as well as a number of lesser conspiracies, all of which aimed to topple the usurper from his throne. The first major rebellion, in January 1400, was led by the earl of Huntingdon and other magnates who had been close to Richard, but there was little support for them and the danger was quickly over. Behind the other three rebellions, in 1403, 1405, and 1408, stood the domineering figure of Henry Percy, earl of Northumberland, who had been Henry's most powerful ally in 1399 but who had since become disenchanted with the king he had helped to make. On each occasion the king was able to muster sufficient armed strength to defeat the rebels, but, especially in 1403, it was a close call.

One of Henry's major problems was that he so often found himself fighting on two or three fronts at the same time. In addition to the domestic revolts, he was confronted with a major rebellion in Wales, led by Owen Glendower, which erupted in 1400 and plunged much of Wales into virtual anarchy for a decade and more; during the early years of his reign the situation on the Scottish border also demanded constant infusions of men and money, although the danger from this quarter was largely neutralised by the fortuitous capture of the heir to the Scottish throne, James, off Flamborough Head in March 1406. (Within a few days of his capture, James's father died, so he became nominal king of Scotland; nevertheless, he spent the next eighteen years in an English prison.) Ireland, however, proved a drain on the king's resources throughout the reign, and during the last few years of Henry's life he found it increasingly difficult to avoid intervening in France. These military commitments combined to strain Henry's finances to the limit. In addition, his expenditure on his household was far from meagre, and his precarious hold on the throne obliged him to buy support on a large scale. Thus despite the fact that he had added his own vast Lancastrian inheritance to the crown patrimony, he was constantly short of money, and constantly defaulting on his debts. This led to a succession of bitter attacks on the government—and in particular on the household, which was regarded by many as the chief culprit—in the early parliaments of the reign. These culminated in the long and acrimonious parliament of 1406, the result of which was a substantial shift of power away from the king and his close supporters, and in favour of the king's eldest son, Prince Henry. After this, the tension subsided for a few years. The king's military commitments were now less pressing, the household was forced to moderate its expenditure, and some semblance of order was restored to government finance. With the king increasingly incapacitated by the mysterious illness which afflicted him from *c.* 1407, Prince Henry became increasingly dominant, until by 1410–11 he was the virtual ruler of England. In late 1411 the king decided that the time had come for a trial of strength with his son: he resumed control of ministerial appointments, and replaced the prince's supporters on the council with his own. Although this nearly provoked an armed conflict between father and son in the summer of 1412, they managed to patch up their differences, and the ailing king lived out the last nine months of his reign in peace, and in charge. Henry IV's major achievement was that when, on 20 March 1413, his enfeebled body eventually gave out on him, his son became Henry V.

These are, briefly, the main events in the political history of England between 1360 and 1413. The remainder of this book is concerned with the part played by the king's household and affinity in that history.

CHAPTER I

The King's Servants

Royal residences

THE royal household was the sum of the persons employed in it by the king, and its sole function was to service the needs of the king. These needs were many, and required a large permanent staff—varying in the period 1360–1413 between about 400 and 700.[1] In addition, the household included many hundreds of horses, and a massive store of baggage: crockery and cutlery, hangings, furnishings, clothes and weaponry, wax, wine and storage vessels, parchment and quills, weights, measures, and so on.[2] These were very much a part of the household, rather than of the houses in which the household stayed. For the household had no permanent residence. There were certainly some places where it stayed more frequently than others, but it was unusual for the household to spend more than about two months consecutively in any one place; for much of the time, therefore, the royal residences—castles, palaces, or just 'houses'—were lifeless, almost empty, beautiful but statuesque, until suddenly transformed into a veritable maelstrom of activity by the arrival of the king and his followers.

Travel, or 'removing', as it was called, and which gives a much clearer idea of the operation involved, was a normal part of life for all medieval household servants; to a degree, indeed, that most of us nowadays would probably consider intolerable, even allowing for the much greater speed and comfort of twentieth-century travel. It was also a crucial factor in pushing up both the cost and the unpopularity of the household, for it meant not only that numerous extra servants (carters, purveyors, harbingers, and all those who cared for the pack-horses) had to be employed on a permanent basis, but also that *ad hoc* sleeping and eating arrangements often had to be made, hence the twin evils of purveyance and the requisitioning of lodgings.

Yet the rate at which the royal household moved about the country at this time had declined markedly by comparison with, for example, the almost frenetic peregrinations of the Angevin kings. Moreover, the radius of activity had narrowed, so that for the most part London was little more than a day's ride away. Typically, the royal household in the late fourteenth and early fifteenth centuries would stay for periods of between two weeks and two months at one of the small group of favoured royal residences in the vicinity of London, then pack up, move on (often by quite slow stages), and re-install itself for another few weeks or months in another favoured residence; only occasionally, and then usually for some specific purpose, did the king and his household move more than about thirty miles away from London. Three residences were especially favoured: Windsor castle, and the royal manors of Eltham and Sheen. Looking at the buildings in which the king's household resided most frequently can tell us a certain amount about the people who made up that household.

Every residence of every great lord in the Middle Ages had two focal points, the lord's chamber, and the hall. Chamber and hall symbolise the 'upstairs' and 'downstairs' elements of the household—and often quite literally, for the hall, where the lesser servants congregated, was usually on the ground or first floor, with the chamber at first or second floor level. The relationship between chamber and hall shifted significantly from the thirteenth century onward. This was in part (as has often been pointed out) as a result of a greater desire for privacy on the part of the lord: increasingly, the lord would eschew the hall, preferring to eat and take his pleasure in the more intimate surroundings of his chamber. But the desire for privacy can be over-stressed, for one of the consequences of the lord's preference for his chamber was that the chamber became a less intimate place. Chambers got bigger: more and more, in the fourteenth century, we hear of 'great chambers'. Edward III built a 'great chamber' at both Windsor and Eltham in the 1360s, as well as several subsidiary chambers.[3] More things were now done in the lord's (or king's) chambers, more eating, more discussion, more leisure activities. This is vividly demonstrated, with regard to the king's household, by the change in terminology of the knights attached to the royal household: knights 'of the household' (*de familia regis*) no longer feature in royal accounts after about 1370, but are replaced by knights 'of the chamber' (*camerae regis*).[4] The hall (*aula*) was increasingly the preserve of the lesser servants, although, being generally bigger than the chamber, it was still the natural place to hold banquets and other ceremonial activities, and on these occasions the king and his followers would still descend and meals were taken communally. It seems likely, then, that it was not solely the desire for greater privacy which drove lords and kings 'upstairs': it was also, in part, a consequence of the increasing size of both noble and royal households, and, perhaps, of a sharper social dividing line being drawn between greater persons and lesser persons (a trend in the social history of late medieval England which has frequently been commented upon in different contexts).[5] It is also worth pointing out that the seclusion of the king with a smaller and more intimate group of friends and advisors in his chamber may not be unconnected with the increasing number of accusations of 'chamber politics' in the fourteenth and fifteenth centuries. In both 1376 and 1388, when violent attacks were launched on the court, members of the king's chamber staff were prominent among the condemned.

Yet the separation of 'upstairs' and 'downstairs' in the fourteenth-century royal household should not be exaggerated. It is above all at Windsor castle, rebuilt by Edward III at a cost of over £51,000 between 1350 and 1377, and which the king clearly intended to be 'the Versailles of the age',[6] that it is possible to reconstruct the physical setting of the king's household, and Edward's work at Windsor leaves two clear impressions. Firstly, the great hall was still very much an integral part of the court. The setting for Edward's court was created in the magnificent new range of royal apartments built along the north side of the upper bailey at Windsor, on which over £40,000 was spent between 1357 and 1365.[7] The south range of this block was largely taken up by the two principal communal buildings of the household, the great hall and the chapel. To the west and north of these came the royal apartments, and the second clear impression left by the buildings at Windsor is of the extent and magnificence of these private apartments. Apart from his great chamber, the king himself had a further six chambers, as well as a closet (small retiring room, perhaps his most private sanctuary) and private chapel. The queen had four chambers, one of which had a private chapel attached. All these private apartments have since been destroyed, but there can be no doubt that they were built, finished and furnished to the highest standards of the time. The service buildings (kitchen and so forth) have also been destroyed, but they almost certainly lay along the north side of the block, thus connecting with both the hall and the chamber.

The multiplicity of chambers for both the king and the queen serves to emphasise the growing importance and size of the 'chamber' as distinct from the 'hall', while the integration of both private and public apartments into one block, with communal service facilities, continued to maintain the unity of the household. It was not just for himself and Queen Philippa, however, that Edward constructed new private apartments. Once the main block was completed, rows of private lodgings were built along the eastern and southern walls of the upper bailey, probably about twenty in all, undoubtedly intended for senior members of the household or high-ranking guests and friends of the king.

Although we are less well-informed as to the physical layout of the buildings at Sheen and Eltham at this time, documentary evidence makes it quite clear that the intention behind the rebuilding undertaken by Edward III, Richard II and Henry IV at both manors was the creation of a setting similar to that at Windsor (though, obviously, not on such a grand scale). The buildings at Sheen were divided into two courts, and here it was in the lower court, nearer to the Thames, and with its own great gate and bridge, that the residential accommodation was situated. Even before Edward III began his major rebuilding work at Sheen in 1358, there were already a number of private lodgings; between 1358 and 1370 the king added at least nine more, most if not all with fireplaces, and each with its private latrine. The old hall and chapel were apparently retained, but at least two new chambers were built for the king, floored with tiles and glazed with stained-glass, in each of which there were two fireplaces (indicating that they must have been chambers of a reasonable size).

Another new chamber, situated by the garden, contained eight fireplaces; this was probably the equivalent of the king's 'great chamber' at Windsor and Eltham. The dean of the king's chapel, the controller of the household, and Walter Whithorse, a trusted esquire of Edward's chamber, each had their own lodgings at Sheen, an interesting development reflecting as much as anything the frequency with which the household stayed there. Richard II was, until 1394, just as fond of Sheen as his grandfather had been, and took this move towards privacy one step further when he ordered the construction of a new, subsidiary lodging 'within a certain island called la Nayght at Sheen.' A paling was set up around the island, new steps and a wharf were constructed to allow the king to pass over in his new barge, and within the lodging itself the king and queen each had their own chambers, and Richard had a closet, a private chapel, and a bath-house decorated with 2,000 painted tiles. Sadly, Queen Anne died at Sheen in June 1394, and in the following year the unhappy king ordered the destruction of (apparently) the whole manor. As far as can be gathered he never went there again, and not until Henry V's time was this undoubtedly delightful royal manor rebuilt.

Edward, Richard and Henry all contributed considerably to the works at Eltham. Here there were at least two halls (since replaced by the one built by Edward IV, which still stands), a 'great chapel', and a host of private chambers. The king and the queen both had chambers with chapels attached, and there was a bath-house and dancing chamber, as well as a wardrobe for the king with a fireplace in it. An account of repairs undertaken at Eltham in the years 1384–8 reveals that the 'personalisation' of private apartments had occurred here as well as at Sheen: John of Gaunt, Robert de Vere, Thomas Mowbray, the chamber knights Baldwin Bereford and Nicholas Sharnesfeld, controller of the household Baldwin Raddington, and one of the queen's ladies in waiting, Lady Luttrell, all had their own chambers, to which evidently they would always be assigned when the household was at Eltham. There were also chambers for the steward of the household, the keeper of the wardrobe, and the chaplains of the king's chapel. Not content, however, with the standard of his personal accommodation, Henry IV overhauled the royal chambers entirely (as well as other parts of the manor) between 1399 and 1407, 'at a cost of not less than £1,000'. Next to the private royal chapel, he built a new chamber and study, a parlour, and a private buttery, kitchen and larder. His new chamber had two fireplaces and three windows with stained-glass; his study had seven stained-glass windows, and two desks, in one of which Henry kept his books. Once his own apartments were completed (and once he had remarried, presumably), he proceeded to the construction of a similar private suite for Queen Joan, consisting of two drawing-chambers, another chamber, and a parlour. It is hardly surprising that Eltham remained a favourite royal residence throughout the fifteenth century, and both Henry VI and Edward IV made further substantial additions to the buildings there.

More money was spent at Windsor, Sheen and Eltham because more time was spent there, but similar improvements were carried out at nearly all the royal residences at which the household stayed with any regularity. At King's Langley, for example, a new range of private lodgings called 'Le Longrewe' was built, probably by Edward III but perhaps by Richard II. This contained the private chambers of the king and queen, a bath-house with hot water, and personal chamber for, in the 1360s, Edmund of Langley and Thomas of Woodstock, and, in the 1380s, Robert de Vere, Thomas Mowbray, the king's confessor Thomas Rushook, and the steward, controller and knight marshal of the household. At Henley-on-the-Heath there were eleven private chambers apart from those assigned to the chief butler and the keeper of the wardrobe, while at Kennington there were separate chambers for the steward, controller and keeper, as well as for the esquires of the household (though these were probably not individual).[8]

Even if in the Middle Ages people clearly put much less store by privacy than we do nowadays, these splendid late fourteenth-century royal residences must still have made life for the senior members of the royal household very comfortable indeed. Yet it is worth emphasising even at the risk of repetition, that the community of the household was not sacrificed to the demands for greater privacy. The hustle and bustle of the hall was never more than a minute or two from the seclusion of the chamber. At Langley, for example, it seems that the new 'Longrewe' erected in the second half of the fourteenth century contained not only the private chambers noted above, but also a new great hall for the lesser servants. The over-all layout was thus not dissimilar to that at Windsor.

The process of 'removing' naturally involved everybody in the household to some degree. There were certain groups of people within the household, however, who had more specific duties connected with removing. One group of servants would always have travelled ahead of the king to make things ready. This group included the harbingers, who were meant to requisition lodgings for everyone, some of the purveyors (those described on occasion as the *precursores*), and the clerk of the market with his assistants, whose job it was to ride ahead of the household and proclaim the assizes of bread and ale within the verge (twelve miles radius from the place where the king spent the night). Each department had its own harbinger (over forty were listed in the 1318 Ordinance), and it is probable that this advance party of the household numbered little short of a hundred persons. Then came the king himself, preceded by his thirty sergeants-at-arms and twenty-four foot-archers marching in solemn procession, surrounded by his knights, esquires and clerks as well as any other friends or guests who happened to be staying at court, and followed by all the remaining servants of the household, driving and pulling the horses and carts which carried the massive baggage-store. (The 1318 Ordinance said that there should be twenty carts for the offices with five horses per cart, and thirty-four sumpter-horses with one sumpterman per horse; the number of sumptermen was often sixty or seventy in the later fourteenth century, so presumably the number of sumpter-horses was greater, too.)[9]

Removing was undoubtedly an affair of considerable magnitude. Yet in practice it must often have been a very staggered process, with the king himself quite often going on ahead with only his bodyguard and a few intimate servants (his *privata familia*, as it was called), or remaining behind so that all would be ready by the time he arrived. Sometimes the king even left his household for days or weeks on end and travelled around with only his *privata familia*. The normal travelling distance for the household was about fifteen miles a day, though this could be extended to twenty-five or so if necessary. As far as was possible, the king tried to plan his movements several weeks or even months ahead, so that residences could be prepared and sufficient stores laid in, but this was not always practicable, and in such circumstances everyone probably had to accept a rather lower standard of living and organisation.

Edward III in his later years spent a great deal of time apart from his household, presumably out of a personal desire for greater privacy in his old age. At the same time, his household spent more and more time at Windsor Castle, which for many of the household servants at this time must have acquired something close to the aspect of a permanent home. Royal itineraries can only be plotted in detail and with reliability when wardrobe account books survive. The surviving wardrobe account books during the years 1366–77 cover a total of 1,438 days (in 1366–7, 1369, 1371–3, and 1376–7), of which the household spent 990 days at Windsor Castle.[10] Yet incidental entries recording, for example, alms and gifts dispensed by the king or medicines purchased for him, continually show Edward himself to have been elsewhere, with his *privata* or *secreta familia*. Earlier in the reign, it had been much more usual for the king to take his household with him wherever he travelled. The wardrobe account book for 1353–4, for example, shows the household continually moving about southern England with the king, stopping with him for periods of up to ten weeks at places such as Thurrock, Salisbury, Gloucester, Northampton and Bury St Edmunds.[11] After 1360 the radius of the king's activity still spread further than the environs of London: until the last five or six years of his life he continued to spend regular periods at favoured residences such as Woodstock, Marlborough, Queenborough, King's Langley, and Hadleigh. More and more, though, he left his household behind. One account for the *privata familia* survives, covering the period 7 January to 15 May 1361.[12] During this time the king was itinerating around the home counties, accompanied by only some fifty persons or less, spending short periods at Thame, Sheppey (at Queenborough castle, presumably), Sheen, Moor End, Hadleigh, and Westminster. Meanwhile, the household remained at Windsor, with the queen. Only twice during this period did the king spend any length of time at Windsor, from 15–31 March, and from 22–28 April (for the St George's Day festivities, which he never missed). He also visited Windsor briefly on 9 January, 12 and 19 February.

This frequent separation of king and household continued until the king's death, and became even more marked during the last few years of his life (after *c.* 1372). During the last seven months of his life, while his household remained constantly at Windsor, Edward divided his time between Sheen and Havering-atte-Bower; he spent less than a week at Windsor, the period of the St George's Day festivities in late April 1377. Moreover, the number of residences which saw the king with any frequency after 1372 was much smaller, and they were all closer to London: Sheen, Eltham and Havering were almost exclusively the favoured abodes of the last five years. From here he could still travel to Westminster to deal with matters of state when required, and in fact there is considerable evidence to suggest that Edward continued to visit Westminster quite frequently right up until the last year or two of his life.[13]

The pattern of itineration of king and household during the last seventeen years of Edward III's reign thus shows two clear trends, both of which accelerated markedly during the last five years of the reign. Firstly, the radius within which both king and household moved around was continually decreasing, and secondly, the king preferred more and more to leave his household at Windsor and to move around his other favoured manors near London with only his *privata familia*. This had two consequences. Firstly, it meant that the household itself ceased for long periods to be a centre of government, and lost much of its political importance. Indeed it must have seemed a somewhat redundant institution, a collection of royal servants living at Windsor and not really serving their king at all for much of the time. Secondly, it created a royal court which was very much a separate entity from the household. Contemporaries referred to the court at this time as the *privata* or *secreta familia*, but it would be just as correct to say that what in effect had happened was that the 'chamber' had been removed from the rest of the household, for it was largely the staff of the chamber who made up the *privata familia*. It was in these circumstances that a small clique (*covyne*) of courtiers came to exercise an undue amount of influence over the king, or at least over the direction of royal policy, and it was these men who got their come-uppance in the Good Parliament. The seclusion and exclusivity of the court clique in the 1370s had undoubtedly contributed significantly to this state of affairs.[14]

Richard II's wardrobe accounts give a very different picture of the movements of king and household. Richard clearly preferred to take his household with him wherever he went. His favourite residences were certainly Sheen (until he had it burnt down in 1395) and Eltham, but the number of residences at which he liked to spend time was larger than had been the case in the later years of his grandfather's reign, and their geographical distribution was wider. Apart from Eltham and Sheen, the household was regularly to be found at Havering, King's Langley, Windsor, Clarendon, Easthamstead, Woodstock, Henley-on-the-Heath, Kennington and Berkhamstead. The last two had been inherited by Richard from his father the Black Prince, but all the others had been royal houses under Edward III. Yet even if the radius of Richard's activities was greater than his grandfather's, it was still very largely confined to the south-eastern quarter of England. The most striking feature of the distribution of the king's residences during the fourteenth century is their increasing centralisation around London, and naturally this is reflected in the itineraries of the late fourteenth- and fifteenth-century kings and their households. Between

1200 and 1377 the number of royal houses kept in repair had been roughly halved, from approximately thirty-five to approximately seventeen.[15] By 1377, the only royal manor-house north of the Chilterns was Clipstone (Notts.), while the furthest to the west was Clarendon (near Salisbury, Wilts.). The increasing centralisation of government departments at Westminster no doubt helps to explain this, together with the desire for higher standards of comfort and perhaps a growing reluctance to spend too many days in the saddle. The result was (within limits) a change in style of government, with less emphasis placed on personal itineration.[16] This is a trend found in the habits of the nobility at this time too: their households were becoming more sedentary, while their principal residences were being built to a higher standard of luxury.[17]

The itinerary of king and household under Richard II was normally planned to take them from one royal residence to another, spending periods of a few weeks or months at each. Apart from the favoured manor-houses, there was also a small number of castles at which they stayed occasionally, such as Corfe, Wallingford, Southampton, Devizes, and Nottingham. Repairs or refurbishing often had to be put in hand rapidly in order to make them ready for the king's visits.[18] There were times, however, when the king found it either necessary or desirable to spend some days or even weeks at a place where there was no royal residence. The most popular alternative to a royal house was a religious house, particularly an episcopal palace. It was in the archbishop of York's palace that Richard stayed when he visited York between 24 March and 5 April 1396, while Christmas 1398 was spent in great style in the palace of Richard's friend Tideman of Winchcombe, bishop of Worcester. According to the *Vita* the king was accompanied by a great number of followers, tournaments were held every day, and about 26 oxen and 300 sheep were consumed each day, as well as 'volatile quasi sine numero'.[19] For the Gloucester parliament of 1378 the king lodged by turns at Gloucester and Tewkesbury abbeys; with their monastery over-run by the household, the monks of Gloucester had to dine in their dorter, from where they watched footballers and wrestlers sporting themselves on the lawn of the cloister.[20] On numerous occasions the itinerary of the king and his household took them—deliberately, it seems—through a series of religious houses. Journeying from Windsor to Woodstock in December 1389, for example, they stayed for two nights at Reading (Benedictine abbey), five nights at Notley (Augustinian abbey), and two nights at Oseney (Augustinian abbey again). After celebrating Christmas for two and a half weeks at Woodstock, they returned via the Benedictine abbey of Abingdon (for two nights), Wallingford castle, Henley-on-the-Heath manor-house, and so back to Windsor.[21]

Longer periods were sometimes spent at religious houses. Between 23 May and 2 June 1393 Richard made a pilgrimage to Canterbury, staying in the archbishop's palace; in the late summer of the same year he and the household spent twenty-five days at the Cistercian abbey of Beaulieu (Hants.), while between 5 November and 23 December 1395 they were at Abingdon abbey. On a leisurely progress from Corfe Castle back to Eltham in June/July 1384, six nights were spent at Wimborne (college of canons), six nights at Breamore (Augustinian monastery), six nights at Beaulieu, two nights at Southampton castle, two nights at Southwick (Augustinian abbey), and two nights at the episcopal palace in Chichester.[22] Such visits were not always popular. Thomas Walsingham said that in the summer of 1383 King Richard and Queen Anne with a multitude of followers (including numerous Bohemians) went on a tour of English monasteries expecting them to pay for his keep. He was 'vagabundus . . . per patriam et domus religiosorum', and he came not to give, but to take. According to Walsingham it cost the abbot of Bury 800 marks to entertain the royal household for ten days, after which the king and queen took their followers on to Thetford priory and Norwich cathedral to continue sponging.[23] It was indeed an expensive business to entertain the royal household. For instance, when Richard took his household to stay at Winchester in July 1393, Bishop Wykeham invited them to lunch on the 25th and Richard brought 180 followers with him for whom Wykeham laid on a magnificent spread including crab, salmon, eels and shrimps. Wykeham's household expenses, which normally averaged about £3 a day, rose to £23. Two months later the king was back, dining with the bishop on two consecutive days, 16 and 17 September, at Wolvesey palace. On 16 September there were swans, crab, lobster and grapes on the menu, and the cost was over £15. On 17 September 'rex et regina et tota familia' ate with Wykeham, the same sort of food was provided, and the cost was nearly £26.[24] If the whole royal household really did stay at Bury for ten days in 1383, Walsingham's estimate of 800 marks could well be right. It is worth remembering that Richard was desperately short of money for his household in 1383, and an itinerary which included several lengthy stays at wealthy religious houses might be seen as part of a cost-cutting exercise.[25] Casual visits for a night or two were unlikely to be resented: no doubt they aroused a certain amount of excitement and provided an opportunity for the host to win a little royal favour, and there must always have been an element of 'King Richard slept here'. But when casual visits turned into blatant sponging, the protests began.

Itineraries which could be planned around royal residences and religious houses were obviously preferable, but clearly this was not always possible. There are numerous examples of king and household spending a night or two at places where it is very difficult to know exactly where either the king himself or his hundreds of servants might have slept. In July 1390, for example, the household journeyed from Woodstock manor to Oakham castle (held by the king at this time, though only briefly) in four days. The wardrobe account book states that the four nights *en route* were spent at Brackley, Daventry, Lutterworth and Market Harborough.[26] There was a Cluniac priory at Daventry where the second night may have been spent, but there were neither royal residences nor religious houses of any size at Brackley, Lutterworth, or Market Harborough, nor were they very large towns. Presumably the best house in the town was found for the king, or he may have stayed in a neighbouring house or castle belonging to a friend (when Richard visited Leicester on 15 February

1387, for example, he stayed with John Lord Beaumont at Beaumanoir; but when he came back to Leicester eight months later, he stayed in the Augustinian abbey).[27] For the rest of the household, though, either tents must have been set up, or the scramble for lodgings must have been intense. That private lodgings were frequently requisitioned is undoubted, and the wardrobe account books for both Richard II's and Henry IV's reigns record several payments to householders whose premises had been damaged in some way while requisitioned for members of the household. Lodgings must have been limited, though, and no doubt it paid to have an efficient harbinger for one's department. The royal household must have swamped not just small towns, but the whole neighbourhood. This was why the verge of the household extended for a radius of twelve miles: the 1318 Ordinance said that all those who could not find lodgings within the house or the town in which the king was staying were to be lodged within twelve miles, with the offices themselves to be as near as possible to the king.[28] Even when the king was staying at a religious house or royal residence, there must have been considerable requisitioning of lodgings, for there were few places which could accommodate the whole of the household. Tents or marquees were also used frequently, and not just in the summer. When Richard went to Calais to meet Charles VI of France and marry his daughter in November 1396, he was, according to Walsingham, eating and sleeping in a tent.[29] The king's tent was doubtless very large and luxurious, but whether many of the lesser servants of the household had much more than a piece of canvas over their heads and a few blankets to wrap around them is doubtful.

The royal household under Richard II, therefore, was very much more active than it had been during the later years of Edward III's reign, and the reason for this was that Richard nearly always preferred to take his full household with him wherever he went. During the last four or five years of the reign, when the household grew substantially in size, and especially during the last two years of the reign when the king's personal bodyguard of over 300 Cheshire archers apparently accompanied the king wherever he went (in addition to his other household servants), the disruption and expense caused by these frequent itinerations must have been very considerable. Moreover, the king's fondness for Cheshire and its people meant that on several occasions now he moved out of the south-eastern quarter of the country (he also called the adjourned parliament to Shrewsbury in January 1398, spent Christmas 1398 at Worcester, and led armies across England and through Wales in both 1394–5 and 1399).[30] In general, a larger number of English people were made aware of the royal household in these years, and there was a larger royal household to be aware of.

Only two wardrobe account books survive from Henry IV's reign, covering the years 1402–3 and 1405–6. Like his cousin, Henry clearly liked to take his household with him wherever he went. Unlike his cousin, he was constantly troubled by rebellions both in England and Wales during the first half of his reign, which made his movements often rapid and (presumably) unpredictable, and this is reflected in the itineraries given in both these accounts.[31] The

1405–6 account, which actually covers the period 1 October 1405 to 7 December 1406, is also untypical in that it covers almost the whole period of the long 1406 parliament, which meant that Henry had to spend much of the year in London. Between 7 January and 7 December 1406 (a total of 334 days), the king and household spent no less than 248 days in London, staying usually either at Westminster palace or at the Tower. Between 1 October 1402 and 30 September 1403 they also spent fifty-three days at Westminster palace, and visited the Tower of London briefly on a further three occasions, so it does seem that, whether out of choice or out of necessity, Henry did tend to spend more time in the capital than either of his predecessors. For recreation, he retired principally to Eltham (which he also largely rebuilt). Although he did not visit Eltham once during the period of the 1405–6 account, he spent more time (seventy-eight days) there than at any other residence during the period of the 1402–3 account, and it was to Eltham that he took his new queen, Joan, straight after their wedding, and again (for eight weeks) after her coronation. Hertford castle, which had been one of John of Gaunt's favourite residences, was also clearly a favourite of Henry's. He visited Hertford on six occasions in 1405–6, spending two weeks there in December 1405. The only other Lancastrian castles where he spent more than a day or two were Leicester and Kenilworth; at the latter, which was the administrative headquarters of the Duchy of Lancaster, he spent nearly a month in October 1405. Otherwise, with the exception of Sheen which had been destroyed, his preferred residences were not dissimilar to Richard's, and included Windsor castle, Berkhamstead, Clarendon, Kennington, Henley-on-the-Heath, and Woodstock. He did occasionally stay at religious houses (he spent eleven days at Reading in January 1403, for example, presumably at the abbey), but not nearly as often as Richard had. This may have been through personal choice (Henry's relations with the church in general were not nearly as good as Richard's),[32] or it may have been because his rather hectic itinerary made it difficult to fit such visits in.

It is very likely that after 1406 Henry's movements became much more restricted. The worst period of rebellions was now over, and the king himself was increasingly an invalid. After 1406, too, the household almost certainly decreased quite considerably in size. During the first half of Henry's reign, however, an inflated household was regularly moving around through wide areas of the kingdom. Thus in 1405 the household went to Winchester in February, to Shrewsbury in July (to battle with the Percies), then north to York and back to Nottingham before once again moving west to Hereford and entering South Wales on 23 September. In October 1405 the household was again in the Hereford-Worcester area, while in July and August 1406 (while the parliament was adjourned) Henry took his household on a progress to northern Norfolk and Lincolnshire. The Welsh and Scottish campaigns, as well as the domestic rebellions in the north, involved a great deal of household itineration during these years. During the years *c.* 1394–1406, therefore, a combination of circumstances meant that the household was moving outside its south-eastern base rather more frequently than was normal—or at least than had been normal for the previous thirty or forty years. This coincides with a period of exceptionally high-spending in the household, and of inflated numbers. Although the increase in size and cost of the household at this time was certainly not caused by this increased activity, it did mean that the pressure of the household on the areas through which it passed must have increased, and doubtless this contributed to the household's unpopularity.[33]

The staff of the household

Over the years 1360 to 1413, there are clearly identifiable trends in the size of the royal household (see Appendix III). During the last seventeen years of his reign, Edward III's household declined steadily. The figure of 579 for 1359–60 is distorted by the fact that at this time the household was mobilised for war: thus it included about fifty household bannerets and knights, forty-five archers, eight smiths, and probably a number of other men who had been drafted into the household for the campaign. In fact the total household complement in peace-time around this time was probably little different from the 447 of 1366–7, and may well even have been less. The figure of 368 for 1353–4 indicates that Edward did not normally keep an excessively large household in the 1350s. The figure of 447 for 1366–7 is also swollen, this time by the fact that in May 1360 the king had decided to merge Queen Philippa's household with his own, and as a consequence up to eighty or ninety of the queen's servants were now included in the roll-call of the king's household.[34] Thus the 1366–7 figure does represent a reduction from 1360, and by 1369, with a total of 387 (still including the queen's household; she died in August and the account ends in June), this reduction is more marked. It continued until the end of the reign, when the figure was 338.

The reduction occurred very largely at the bottom end of the household. In fact the drop from 163 to 78 in the number of valets of the stables accounts for very nearly the whole of the reduction, while the number of valets of the chamber and of the offices actually increased. During the first seven or eight years of Richard II's reign the household remained at more or less the same size as at the end of Edward III's. The figures for Richard's household are more complete than those for his grandfather's, because Richard began to pay £1 annually to each of the garçons (grooms) in his household (technically a gift rather than a wage), which means they are listed. The grooms were the lowest servant listed in household accounts; as their name suggests, they were young boys. There were certainly grooms in Edward's household, probably about as many proportionately as in Richard's, so in order to compare the full size of Edward's household with Richard's we should probably add about fifty to each of the totals before 1377. Financial evidence suggests that the size of Richard's household may have increased between 1384 and 1386, but not by much.[35] Not until 1390 does a more significant increase occur.

However, the increase in 1390 occurred partly among the lesser servants (the valets of the stables, for instance), but also more importantly among the esquires of the household, and it can be fairly precisely dated. The 1389–90 account book lists sixty-three esquires given allowances for robes of £2 each, and sixty-five given only 15s. 3d. each. These allowances were calculated on a *pro rata* basis, the accounting period running from 1 October to 30 September.[36] Thus the allowance of 15s. 3d. represents 139 days of service in the household, which means that these men were given robes allowances as from 14 May 1390. The significance of this is that the celebrated ordinance on livery and maintenance of 1390 was finally issued by the king on 12 May, to take effect within ten days. The ordinance said that no lord was to give livery of company to any person who was not either formally retained by him for life, 'or unless he is a servant and family retainer dwelling in his household'.[37] Forty-four of these sixty-five had not been in the household before (although six of them had been described as king's esquires, but this is not the same), and it seems probable that, in accordance with the terms of the ordinance, the king was pulling into his household men who had until now been more loosely bound to him, and who would now be legally entitled to wear his livery. There is other evidence to suggest that Richard tried during the 1390s (at least up until 1397) to keep within the terms of the ordinance while developing his affinity.[38] The other twenty-one esquires who received allowances only from 14 May are more problematic, for they had all been described as esquires of the household in the 1383–4 account. It is possible—although this is only really speculation—that they had been dismissed from the household by the Appellants in 1388, and were now being reinstated to their old post. The chroniclers certainly state that a fairly drastic purge of the household occurred at the beginning of 1388 (although it is difficult to believe that it was on the scale described by them), and that as far as the lesser household men were concerned (as opposed to the dismissed chamber knights and clerks), it was for financial as much as political motives.[39]

The increase in the number of esquires of the household was the most significant factor in the increased over-all size of the household in the 1390s. The 1392–3 figure of 101 esquires in fact represents a reduction on the 1389–90 figure, while numbers of other servants in the household remained almost exactly the same, but by 1395–6 the number of esquires had reached a massive 168. This heavy recruitment of esquires should be seen in conjunction with Richard's other attempts to increase the number of gentry in his affinity during the mid-1390s, and again it points to the fact that Richard was still staying within the terms of the 1390 Ordinance. It is pertinent to ask, though difficult to answer, whether the ordinance led to a corresponding increase in the size of nobles' households. However, it was not just the number of esquires that increased between 1393 and 1395. Amongst almost every rank of servants in the household (excepting the top rank, the officers and chamber knights), there was a significant increase during this period, so that the total complement of household staff rose from 433 in 1392–3 to 598 in 1395–6 (and there was no queen's household in 1395–6 to account for a proportion of this total).

Whether the household continued to increase in size after 1396 is not possible to say with certainty because there are no wardrobe books for the last three years of the reign, but financial evidence suggests that it may have.[40] What is clear is that Richard's household from at least 1395 onwards was excessively large, and excessively costly. The Ordinance of 1390 helped to account for this, but it is difficult not to believe that royal extravagance and the king's desire to maintain a magnificent court were at the heart of it.

What is more surprising, considering the criticisms made of the royal household in 1397 and 1399, is that Henry IV made little effort to reduce it in size. In 1402–3 the total figure was 552. The reduction had been achieved entirely by halving the number of esquires, while among the lesser servants there were some significant increases. Three years later, Henry had actually surpassed Richard's figure, the total now being 644. Admittedly there was now a queen's household attached to the king's, but even so this represents an increase of around fifty percent on the household which Edward III and Queen Philippa maintained in the 1360s. Under Henry, the significant increase came in the lower ranks of the hierarchy, among the valets in particular, and the grooms, which may reflect more concern with standards of service than with any more 'political' considerations. After 1406, Henry evidently did reduce the size of his household, though only after prolonged and fierce criticism. In general, there can be little doubt that those who complained of the size and extravagance of the king's household in the period between 1395 and 1406 had good reason to do so.

Purveyance

The pressure which the household exerted on the neighbourhoods through which it passed, or in which it stayed, was felt above all by those who suffered the attentions of the royal purveyors. The task of provisioning the royal household was an immense one: several hundred persons, most of whom were well-versed in the art of conspicuous consumption and accustomed to a high standard of living, took more feeding than most medium-sized towns in medieval England. The level of consumption varied considerably during this period, and there are few commodities for which we have more than passing information, but, of those which can be quantified over a meaningful period, it seems that on average the household consumed about 2,250 quarters of wheat, 1,000 tuns of wine, 1,600 oxen, and perhaps 20,000 sheep each year between 1360 and 1413. At times the level was much higher than this, in the mid-1360s, for example, or between 1395 and 1406.[41] Naturally, too, the pressure varied according to the season of the year: the twelve days of Christmas were always celebrated in great style, with numerous guests and retainers attending the court and daily expenses doubling or even tripling; Easter, St George's Day, and certain other great feasts also saw swollen daily totals, and events such as weddings, funerals and coronations were usually followed by massive banquets lasting several days. A certain amount of food and drink could be carried around, but in general the household looked to the local population to provide it with what was required for today, tomorrow, or next week. To search out and collect the provisions it needed, each of the household offices had a number of purveyors attached to it. In all, there were probably between thirty and fifty purveyors operating in the royal household at this time, constantly engaged in the business of scouring the vicinity, requisitioning food and drink, and arranging for it to be transported to wherever the household happened to be. They were among the most detested royal officials in medieval England. William of Pagula said that purveyors were 'sent to do in this world what the devil does in hell'.[42] In 1362, the commons requested that 'the hateful name of purveyor ' be changed to 'buyer'.[43] On average, there was a complaint about purveyance in one out of every two parliaments held between 1360 and 1413, and purveyors' activities were constantly deplored in chronicles, political pamphlets, and popular literature.[44] What was it that purveyors did, to make them so hated?

Purveyance for the royal household was a separate issue from military purveyance. Military purveyance was a major political issue in the late thirteenth century, and during the first half of the fourteenth century (particularly, for example, in 1297, 1311, and 1339–41), but by 1360 royal policy concerning military purveyance had changed, with the result that it was hardly an issue at all in the period 1360–1413. Whereas previously it had been organised on a shire-by-shire basis, which could often lead to gross corruption and injustice, from the 1350s onwards the crown tended to abandon the purveyance system for its military needs and instead to make contracts with merchants for bulk-provisioning, which seems to have reduced considerably the unpleasantness involved.[45] Complaints against purveyance in the later fourteenth and early fifteenth centuries were concerned almost entirely with purveyance for the household (the 'great statute of purveyors' of 1362 deals solely with household purveyance), which was organised very differently from military purveyance

The great mass of routine purveyance for the household was conducted in two main ways: firstly, by bulk-buying at ports and markets throughout the country, sometimes through merchants, local officials, or others under contract, and sometimes by household purveyors themselves; secondly, by local, village-to-village or even house-to-house purveyance, in the area in which the household happened to be. Since the household was most often in the home counties, the heaviest burden naturally fell on those who lived within a radius of about thirty miles from London. On the other hand, the bulk-buying of non-perishable commodities meant that remoter areas were frequently subjected to demands for victuals for the household as well, and this was often a source of bitter complaint.

Fish, for example, was bought mostly at the East Anglian and Lincolnshire ports, usually it seems through the services of local merchants or officials of the crown such as bailiffs or collectors of customs. The activities of Geoffrey atte Hethe, a fishmonger from Cromer in north Norfolk who worked for the royal household early in the fifteenth century, may serve as an example.[46] From at

least 1402 until his death in 1407, Hethe was responsible for purveying fish for
the household from the fishing towns and villages along the north Norfolk
coast. He received over £615 from various crown sources, mostly from John
Elyngham, collector of customs at Lynn, and, working with two other men,
Henry Stokes of Yaxley and John Parker, he regularly toured the towns and
villages in his vicinity, taking saltfish, stockfish and herrings from local fishermen and fishmongers, hardly ever, it seems, paying on the spot. After his
death, those from whom he had purveyed were to complain *en masse* that they
had been consistently underpaid, and they were almost certainly telling the
truth. Hethe's accounts reveal that while the total value of the fish purveyed
by him was over £732, payments made by him totalled just over £615, almost
exactly the same amount as he had received from the crown. Thus the fact that
he had not always paid promptly or in full was by no means his fault: he could
hardly be expected to disburse on the crown's behalf more than the crown was
prepared to make available to him.

The town of Blakeney (also in north Norfolk) was under obligation at this
time to provide the royal household with a certain number of fish each year,
and on more than one occasion the townsmen were accused by the king of trying to evade their responsibilities. Purveyors of fish were also sent regularly to
Great Yarmouth, hub of the East Anglian fishing industry, as well as to the
Kent and Sussex fishing ports.[47] Once salted, fish could be kept for months,
and thus were in effect non-perishable. Meat, too, could be preserved with salt,
and was sometimes bought in bulk from faraway places: in 1356, for example,
a large quantity of animals was 'slaughtered in the parts of the north for the
expenses of the king's household' and shipped from Newcastle to London.[48]
Wine was purchased by the butler at the main English ports: according to the
Ordinance of 1318, the steward and keeper of the wardrobe were to inform the
butler at the beginning of each year how much wine was likely to be required
by the household during the year, and where it should be sent to await the
king's arrival.[49] There is also evidence that wheat (inferior grains were hardly
ever used in the household except to provide horse-fodder) was sometimes
bought in bulk and shipped to wherever the household happened to be, but it
not clear how often this was done.[50] In general, it is probably true to say that
the only victuals consistently bought in bulk from distant places were fish and
wine; others might be, but it was probably more usual to purvey them locally.
Most purveyance of meat for the household, for example, was probably on the
scale shown in a list of expenses at Westminster during the latter part of
Edward III's reign, when on one day six legs of pork, one ox, eight capons,
eighteen snipe and fifty larks were bought in London, carried to St Paul's
wharf, and then taken by boat to the household at Westminster.[51]

In this aspect of purveyance, the daily taking of relatively small quantities of
victuals from local villages, markets, and individuals, that the household
records say least about, although there is no doubt that it went on all the time,
and was almost certainly the major source of grievance against household purveyors. William of Pagula spoke in bitter terms of the royal purveyor who

would take from a poor old woman a hen from which she might get four or five eggs a week, at a price well below that at which she wished to sell it, or seize the only sheep belonging to a poor man who had brought it to market in order to get money to pay his rent.[52] Items such as vegetables, beer, fruit, eggs, milk, fodder and litter for the horses, wood and coal for heating and cooking, were either too bulky or too perishable to be stored or transported for long, so that each of the household offices had a number of men who were employed in the continuous process of acquiring whatever was needed for the moment. There were nine purveying offices in the household: the pantry, or bakehouse, for corn and bread; the buttery, for wine and beer; the kitchen, for all food not covered by other offices; the poultery, for poultry, game-birds, and eggs; the stables (or avenary, or marshalsea), for hay, oats and litter for the horses; the saucery, for salt and whatever was needed for sauces; the hall and chamber, for coal and wood for heating, and rushes; the scullery, for crockery, cutlery, storage vessels, and coal and wood for cooking; and the spicery, for spices, wax, soap, parchment, and quills. The three largest and highest-spending offices were the buttery, the kitchen and the marshalsea.

When the household was stationary for weeks or months, the purveyors from each of these offices probably found regular sources of supply; at those places where the household stayed frequently, such as Sheen or Eltham or Windsor, there must have been well-established arrangements for supply, which no doubt went some way towards mitigating the rigours of the system (although William of Pagula lived in Windsor Forest, and he spoke out fiercely against the effect of purveyance on the local population). When the household was on the move, the clerk of the market would ride ahead to see that victuals were made ready, and to proclaim the assize of bread, wine, ale and oats in each market which was going to be within the verge that night. He was accompanied by a clerk who requisitioned carriage to transport any victuals purveyed, and by representatives of each of the purveying offices, described as *precursores* by William of Pagula, who would tour the vicinity searching out victuals suitable for their offices.[53] Victual selected for purveyance were probably marked with an appropriate sign to await collection. William of Pagula claimed that whole villages would tremble at the approach of the royal purveyors, and that he himself waited in terror for them to knock at his door.[54] However, he was writing around 1330. By the second half of the fourteenth century, house-to-house purveyance was probably a thing of the past. Vociferous and repeated complaints against purveyance in parliament and elsewhere had led to the establishment of the principle that on entering a village the household purveyors were to liaise with the village constable who, assisted by sworn local men, was to be responsible for selecting and pricing the victuals taken, and to ensure that those whose goods were taken were paid for them.[55] Obviously this system was not entirely effective, but it is worth noting that it was often through their constables that villagers whose goods had been requisitioned in return for tallies or bills of debenture received subsequent payment, and if constables were regularly used as intermediaries this must have reduced the opportunities for the petty corruption by purveyors which had formed the subject of so many petitions presented to parliament before 1362. The situation described by William of Pagula, where one *precursor* would arrive demanding hay and oats, quickly followed by a second demanding hens and fowls, and then by a third demanding corn, was an unfortunate consequence of the fact that each of the household offices purveyed separately, but it does seem to be the case that after 1362 there was closer supervision of purveyance at local level, and consequently a lower incidence of petty abuse. Complaints in parliament which referred specifically to corruption by purveyors certainly decreased in number.

Once the rest of the household had caught up with the clerk of the market and the *precursores*, men would be sent out from each of the offices to collect the goods and arrange their transport to the household. One of the major grievances associated with purveyance was the fact that passers-by and local men with carts or beasts of carriage were requisitioned to transport the victuals from the village or market to the household, and they seem rarely to have been paid for their services. Complaints about the extra burden imposed by the obligation to carry purveyed goods certainly did not cease after 1362, and it may be that the shortage of labour following the plague, and the resultant rise in the cost of transport, contributed to the anger felt on this score.[56]

It was at the time of collection that payment was meant to be made: 'readie mony for daylie payment estemed', stated the Black Book, and the parliamentary commons thought likewise. The statute of 1362 said that all purveyors were to pay for goods at the time they were requisitioned, at the prices obtaining in the locality, and in cash.[57] It is abundantly clear that these regulations were consistently ignored. Evidence as to the prices paid by the household for its goods is limited, but the general impression to be gleaned from the accounts is that although the price paid for most goods was in accordance with prices obtaining generally, this disguised the fact that household purveyors consistently claimed and received an *incrementum* or *avantagium*, which amounted in practice to the requisitioning of extra quantities of victuals for which no payment was made. Corn, for example, was purveyed by the nine-gallon rather than the eight-gallon bushel; in addition, one measure of corn was taken, *gratis*, for every twenty purveyed. Taken together, these increments meant that the household was receiving approximately an additional twenty percent in *avantagium* on top of the corn it was paying for.[58] The chief butler also had the right to take certain quantities of wine at English ports at greatly reduced prices. This right, known as the *recta prisa*, enabled the butler to take 'one ton from ships laded with from 10 to 19 tons of wine, and 2 tons, one from before and one from behind the mast, from ships laded with 20 or more tons of wine.'[59] Incidental entries also mention the exaction of an *incrementum* or avantagium on ale and meat, but perhaps more revealing is the petition submitted to the treasurer by the fishermen of north Norfolk concerning the activities of Geoffrey atte Hethe and his associates between 1402 and 1407.[60] The fishermen claimed that they had been quite systematically underpaid over a number of years. In the fourth year of the reign, when a hundred saltfish were worth £6, they had been paid £4, in the eighth year, when a hundred saltfish were worth £9. 6*s*. 8*d*., they had been paid £7. 6*s*. 8*d*., and so on. It may be that the household purveyors were ordered to purchase goods at specified rates, and that they incurred personal loss if they exceeded those rates. At any rate, it is clear that the rights claimed by the household in this respect were lucrative, and resulted in profit to the king and loss to the vendors. The situation had not, however, deteriorated to the extent that it had by the late sixteenth century when the 'queen's price' was normally 'about one-quarter of the current market value'.[61] Under-payment was a problem in the fourteenth century, but a far greater problem was the possibility that a vendor might not be paid at all.

As far as can be gathered, purveyors hardly ever handed over cash at the time when goods were requisitioned. The household's accounting procedure was, quite explicitly, geared to the expectation that purveyors would initially pay with credit instruments ('private' tallies, usually), which would either be redeemed in the wardrobe during the next few days, if this was practicable, or replaced in the wardrobe with bills cashable at the exchequer.[62] There can be no doubt that this caused considerable inconvenience, and often lengthy delays in securing payment. At Cuxham in Oxfordshire, 'the accounts of the 1340s are full of the expenses of journeys "to get money" (*pro denariis petendis*) for the corn that the royal officials had taken'.[63] For those who lived in areas where the household visited less frequently, although the volume of purveyance was reduced, so were the opportunities to secure payment. Hence a petition presented by the commons of various midland and west midland counties in the parliament of 1406, when it was claimed that great quantities of victuals had been taken from them, 'and the said poor Commons have pursued, and still pursue daily, the Treasurer of the said Household, to have payment for their said victuals, and no payment do they have except sticks, and tallies, and bills.'[64]

Judging by the endless complaints made against the whole system of purveyance during this period, there must have been a very considerable amount of loss as well as inconvenience and delay caused to those who were unfortunate enough to have their goods purveyed for the household. Contemporaries commonly blamed the purveyors themselves, which is quite understandable; whether they were right to do so is a different matter. The root cause of non-payment really had nothing to do with the purveyors themselves. There were good reasons why they should pay initially with credit instruments: if it was known that they carried large sums of money around with them, for instance, they would soon become tempting targets for robbers. They were meant to bring the counterfoils from the credit instruments which they disbursed into the various offices for which they purveyed within a week of making the purchase, and once the goods had been checked in, the creditors could then present their credit instruments in the counting-house and there receive either cash or bills cashable elsewhere.[65] Once the purchase had been made, therefore, the question of whether, or how promptly, or how much, creditors were paid, was out of the hands of the purveyors themselves. What mattered was whether there was any cash in the coffers of the counting-house with which to pay them. Ultimately, therefore, what mattered was whether there was money in the exchequer, partly because the household throughout this period was almost entirely dependant on the exchequer for its cash flow, and partly because, if the household's coffers were empty, creditors would themselves then be given bills to take to the exchequer in the hope of securing payment there. Thus the level of payment or non-payment for purveyed goods was related directly to the overall financial health of the household. This problem is discussed elsewhere.[66] Before leaving the subject, however, one further point needs to be emphasised: it was very easy for the king's household servants to abuse their right of purveyance, for they had royal authority and, no doubt, a strong right arm on their side. This meant that purveyance could play a vital role in the household's financial system, operating as a safety-valve, so to speak, when funds were low. By continuing to build up credit, the household could go on feeding and supplying itself even when the exchequer was unable to pass any money on to it. There are certain times during this period when this is exactly what it seems to have been doing, and it was, in the eyes of ordinary people, the single most important reason for the household's unpopularity.

As to the purveyors themselves, it would be unfair to condemn them too harshly. The orders given to them, repeated again and again in more or less the same words throughout the Ordinance of 1318 and the Black Book, were 'faire lez achatez en due manere a greignour profit le roy, et a mendre greuance de people'.[67] The reconciliation of these two principles can hardly have been an easy task. There were certainly some corrupt purveyors, but the nature of the job they did was bound to make them unpopular from the start.[68] They were seldom given cash to pay with, although by statute they were required to pay; they were under orders to requisition carriage without payment, although this too was forbidden by statute; their purchases were reckoned on the assumption by their superiors that they had enforced the king's right to the usual *avantagium*, even though some of these rights too had been forbidden by statute. When they brought their purchases into the household, these were subjected to a rigorous series of checks and counter-checks for both quality and quantity. Victuals of inferior quality would be discarded, with the loss falling on the purveyor. Purchases made without due warrant might be disallowed, and the purveyor left to make good his personal loss as best he could. For those who submitted unsatisfactory accounts, a graded scale of punishment was enforced, while if one of the sergeants of the offices allowed his account to fall into arrears, he might be pardoned only by the king, after examination by the steward. If he died in office, there was a good chance that his lands, goods and chattels would be seized into the king's hands until his outstanding accounts had been cleared. Naturally, the system was not entirely inflexible: sometimes, men who lost goods accidentally were pardoned by the king. But on the whole the sheer quantity of goods passing through the household made it imperative that checks were enforced. The purveyor was the man in the middle caught between, on the one hand, the expectation that he would enforce the king's (often technically illegal) rights to the hilt, and on the other hand, hatred and resistance, often violent resistance, from those whose livelihoods he threatened. It is not surprising that he became almost a symbol of royal oppression in late medieval England, or that whole villages apparently trembled at his approach.[69]

Finally, though, it must be noted that there was another side to the coin. For the people of London, for example, there are indications that, unlike smaller and less privileged communities, they were able not only to resist, but even to benefit from, the demands of some of the servants of the royal household. In his *Speculum Regis*, addressed to the young Edward III, William of Pagula summed up his general attitude to the king's household with the comment that 'nulla patria desiderat adventum tuum' (no region welcomes your approach), but then qualified this, interestingly, with 'unless it be the citizens of London, where you do not buy any commodities for a lesser price than that for which the vendor wishes to give them.'[70] Equally interesting is the Westminster chronicler's account of an incident in December 1387, when Richard II was at loggerheads with the Lords Appellant:

> It was at this time that the king transferred himself from Windsor to the Tower of London: he proposed to commandeer lodgings for his followers whether inside or outside the city walls, in the way he had done elsewhere, as the fancy took him. At this, the mayor and aldermen told the king that the allotment of accommodation in this way was quite out of the question in London, where it was unheard of for any of his royal predecessors to turn any merchant out of his own premises because at any given time the king's presence brought large numbers of people to London: without their wares the merchants could not make their living there, and without their houses they would be unable to show them to purchasers, since they had no means of keeping them [elsewhere]: moreover, when in the past, on the occasion of a royal coronation or some other rarely seen spectacle, great crowds had flocked to London, everybody had hitherto been quite comfortably accommodated without any sort of billeting. After listening to these arguments the king relented and abandoned his intentions.[71]

The London merchants' obvious desire to be in the city at the same time as the royal household was there serves as a reminder that conspicuous consumption as practised by the king and his followers could be a source of great profit to some, as well as a source of loss to others. The powerful London merchants must have jumped at the chance to supply luxury items for the court, or even everyday wares in bulk.[72] The probability must be, however, that while the profits were enjoyed by the few, the losses were sustained by many. Such at least is the picture suggested by the great majority of comments made by contemporaries about the late medieval royal household.

The court of the verge

What made the activities of the purveyors and the harbingers doubly objectionable was the fact that in the enforcement of their duties they could look for support to the legal arm of the household, the court of the verge. The court of the verge (or court of the steward and marshal of the household, or Marshalsea court; the three terms were interchangeable) was the institution through which household officials not only maintained discipline within the household, but also attempted to bring to justice those who refused to co-operate with the king's servants, or who committed certain types of crimes within the verge of the household. It was a subject of regular complaint during this period, and indeed throughout the late Middle Ages. In particular, the parliaments held in 1376 and 1377 witnessed a host of complaints about the court's activities, and there was good reason for this. For the operations of the court were central to the dispute between John of Gaunt and the Londoners which erupted during the last few months of Edward III's reign. The Londoners were especially affected by the court, because the king and household were so often in and around the city. Yet the steady stream of complaints shows that the court was generally unpopular, and the evidence certainly suggests that those responsible for running it were frequently inclined to over-step their rights.

The powers and procedure of the court in the fourteenth century have been investigated in considerable detail by W.R. Jones, and it is not worth doing more than to summarise his findings briefly here.[73] The court had two primary functions. Firstly, it tried 'pleas of the hall', which included cases such as trespass within the verge, contempt of the royal purveyors, and pleas of debt between members of the household; these cases were presided over by the steward of the household, the earl marshal, and their lieutenants. The steward was the judge of the court, and the source of justice for all would-be suitors. He had a lieutenant who acted for him when he was not available.[74] The earl marshal was rarely present, and his duties as 'enforcer of (the court's) will and as its policeman and jailer' were normally performed through his deputies, the two knights marshal of the hall. Although these deputies were probably appointed by the earl marshal, they were essentially servants of the king. Secondly, the court was responsible for holding the assizes of victuals in towns or markets through which the household passed. These were held by the clerk of the market (or coroner of the household, as he was also known). This post was not in fact held by a clerk but by one of the esquires of the household. He was accountant and chief administrator of the court, he levied fines on those who used false measures or were guilty of defrauding or obstructing the household, and managed the court's finances and submitted its accounts. His office equipment was simple: an inventory of it drawn up in August 1377 records weights, measures, wax, seals, writing materials, and a stool.[75]

The court usually convened every other day, or sometimes every day when the household was travelling. It was attractive to suitors, whether or not they were members of the household, because it did not entail the same degree of expense or technicality as the common law; it was also easily accessible. Litigation was originated by bill or plaint before the steward and was considerably cheaper than a common law writ. The court was also very useful to the king personally. Through a member of his household, he often brought cases in the court against those outside the household who had violated his rights, and goods forfeited by those who were found guilty of committing crimes within the verge were frequently used by him as minor rewards for his servants. The court's profits were paid into the wardrobe, where they were received annually under two headings: 'profits of pleas of the hall' (that is, the steward's court), and 'profits of his (the clerk of the market's) office' (that is, profits from the assizes held by the clerk). They were entered under *recepta forinseca*. 'Pleas of the hall' normally accounted for about two-thirds of the total, which was not great. Between 1360 and 1375 the entire profits of the court amounted to about £150 *per annum*, while between 1383 and 1406 they amounted to about £105 *per annum*.[76] Between 1375 and 1383, however, the court's profits were rather higher, averaging a little over £255 *per annum*.[77] Whether this represents an extension of the court's activity during these years is impossible to say with certainty, but it is worth noting that it was at this time that the complaints about the court of the verge were at their height.

There were criticisms of both aspects of the court's jurisdiction. In the Good Parliament of 1376, two petitions were submitted which complained of the clerk of the market's habit of imposing communal fines on towns in which individual traders had been found guilty of using false measures. One was from the commons as a whole, and one from the citizens of Rochester.[78] That such communal fines had frequently been imposed is indisputable[79] and although the king promised that in future fines would be levied only on individuals, Richard II had to make the same promise in the parliament of January 1390, which suggests that the practice did not cease entirely. In 1390 the king also promised that the clerk would not travel with more than six horses, that he would not stay in any place longer than was necessary, and that he would in future desist from imposing fines outwith the verge, which clearly indicates another abuse of his powers. For the Londoners, the problem was a different one: in October 1399 they complained that their own assizes were being delayed because the clerk of the market claimed that they could not be held without his presence; in 1406 the commons of Southwark claimed that the clerk was hearing their assizes and thus usurping their jurisdiction.[80] The frequent presence of the household around London clearly caused problems, and this was true also of the other side of the court's work, that is, the pleas heard by the steward.

The complaints about the 'pleas of the hall' were essentially concerned with the extent of the steward's jurisdiction. This had originally been limited by the *Articuli super cartas* of 1301, which tried to ensure that the court of the verge did not impinge on the jurisdiction of the common law courts, that it acted only within the verge, and that cases were dealt with promptly. On occasions, the commons simply requested that the limitations agreed in 1301 should be enforced. Yet clearly it was difficult to keep the steward's jurisdiction within bounds. One of the charges brought in 1368 against the disgraced John de la Lee (steward from 1360 until 1368) was that he had summoned people from outside the verge as well as from within it to appear before him.[81] It was in the three parliaments held between April 1376 and December 1377 that controversy over the court really reached a head. A total of twelve petitions relating to its activities were presented in these parliaments. One problem was the now almost complete separation of king and household.[82] The commons requested that the extent of the verge be calculated from either the king's presence or from the location of the household, 'and not from the one and the other simultaneously if they are not together'. They also asked that it be reduced from twelve miles to three. They received little joy, however. The royal reply was that the twelve-mile radius should be maintained, and that it should be taken from either the king's presence or from the household (although Edward agreed that it should not be taken from both at the same time, he did not specify from which it should be taken, which was clearly unsatisfactory from the commons' point of view).[83] Further petitions claimed that the court was interfering with the processes of the common law, that it was imposing fines on whole towns where prisoners of the Marshalsea were found taking sanctuary, and that it was illegally enforcing rights of carriage claimed by purveyors but forbidden by statute. The latter petition concluded ominously, 'et remembrez, seigneurs, del Marechalsie nostre Seigneur le Roy, quar y lui ad trop grante pleinte d'icelle par tout le Roialme.'[84]

In January 1377 the Londoners submitted a petition that dishonest traders and other criminals were in the habit of crossing the Thames to Southwark, where they could not be brought before the city authorities because the court of the Marshalsea was so often there and claimed jurisdiction over the area; they requested that no officer of the Marshalsea be permitted to exercise his jurisdiction in the area, which the king refused to grant because he said he would be impinging on the powers of others.[85] The relationship between the people of London and the king's household servants must have been getting gradually more strained. The Londoners claimed that Southwark was under the city's jurisdiction, but when the king was at Sheen or Eltham, it was also within the verge, and that was now increasingly the case. So sedentary had the royal entourage become, that in 1373 Edward III wrote to the 'good men of the town of Southwark to build in the high street . . . a house, 40 ft long and 30 ft wide, in which to hold the pleas of the Marshalsea of the king's household, and to keep the prisoners of the Marshalsea in the said town, and to hold all other the king's courts.'[86] In the revolt of 1381, hatred of the Marshalsea was manifested in the destruction of this building and the murder of its keeper, the royal sergeant-at-arms, Richard Imworth.[87] At the time of their petition in the January 1377 parliament, however, the Londoners were probably unaware of what John of Gaunt had in mind for them.

It was on 19 February 1377, three days before the parliament ended, that plans were drawn up by Gaunt and Henry Lord Percy (newly-appointed marshal of England) to extend the marshal's jurisdiction in the city. None of the accounts of this incident make it clear as to just how this was to be done, but it has generally been assumed that it was to be through the machinery of the court of the verge, and the Londoners themselves apparently thought that the court's jurisdiction was to be used.[88] The Londoners were already incensed by

Gaunt's support for Wyclif and by his treatment of Bishops Courtenay (London) and Wykeham. Rumours now fuelled their hatred of the duke: it was said that the city was about to be taken into the king's hands, and the mayor replaced with a royally-appointed 'captain'. Lords Brian and Fitzwalter told an angry meeting of citizens that a prisoner was being illegally detained in Percy's house in London, whereupon the citizens rioted, sacked the marshal's house, released the prisoner, and went in search of Gaunt and Percy. These two were dining at the house of John d'Ypres, a Lancastrian official of high standing and steward of the royal household. Warned of the riot in the nick of time, just as they were about to sit down to eat, they swiftly fled to the river, found a barge, and rowed downstream to join Princess Joan at Kennington.

The Londoners' behaviour, however, failed signally to solve their problems. Their petition to parliament was rejected, the city was forced to apologise publicly to John of Gaunt, and in May five aldermen were removed from the city's Common Council for failing to support the extension of the marshal's jurisdiction.[89] In the same month the mayor and aldermen appeared before the king at Sheen to put their case against this curtailment of their liberties, but their reasons were not regarded as sufficient. It was not until the new reign had begun that peace was restored between Gaunt and the Londoners; the question of the extension of the marshal's jurisdiction over the city was then quietly dropped. Not surprisingly though, the affair could not be forgotten so quickly. In the first parliament of Richard's reign, that of October 1377, a further five petitions complained of the court's activities, of which two came from the Londoners. One of these repeated the claim that criminals were finding a refuge from the city's jurisdiction in Southwark, and asked the king to confirm that Southwark was a part of London and that only officials of the city could exercise jurisdiction there. This the king refused, on the grounds that it would be prejudicial not only to himself but also to the bishops of Canterbury and Winchester (both of whom held franchises there). The second petition from the Londoners was directly related to the events of February to May 1377: they claimed that they did not have to obey any mandates from the officers of the court of the verge, the court of admiralty, the constable's court, or the courts of other great lords, but only those of the king himself, and asked Richard to confirm this. The royal reply was, ambiguously, that these matters should be dealt with as they had been in times past.[90]

The Londoners, then, had failed to secure an undertaking from the king that the court of the verge would desist from impinging upon the jurisdictional competence of their own courts. They had, however, successfully resisted the formal curtailment of their own liberties, even if only at the cost of a public humiliation. The problem remained, however, for the court tended to remain in the London area, and after 1381 the Marshalsea prison was rebuilt and continued to be based in Southwark. This led to further complaints of a general nature, not simply from the Londoners, in the parliaments of 1390, 1399, 1401, January 1404, and 1406. On the whole these simply raised the old problems anew: that the jurisdiction of the court was being exercised outside the verge, that it was hearing cases which ought to be heard in the courts of common law, and that the court's officers were charging excessive fees.[91] As was the case with purveyance, it is difficult not to believe that these repeated complaints, harping over and over again on the same themes, reflected the continuing, almost institutionalised, abuse of their powers by the officers of the king's household. It would be churlish not to recognise that an institution of the size of the royal household needed some sort of accepted and legally-backed machinery to help it to overcome problems, not only of internal discipline, but also of supply, lodgings and transport.[92] Equally, it would be surprising if the operation of that machinery did not sometimes conflict with the interests of those who lived in the areas through which the household passed. Yet the frequency of the complaints against the court of the verge suggests more than occasional infringement of people's rights. Only in 1376–7, when attempts were made actually to extend the court's jurisdiction (and in London, moreover, whose citizens were never slow to resist threats to their liberties), did the court really emerge as a major political issue, but there can be little doubt that throughout the later Middle Ages it was regarded with widespread suspicion and hostility. As the author of the *Anonimalle Chronicle* makes clear, the people of Kent felt just as strongly about it as did the people of London,

> On this same Wednesday (12 June 1381) and before the hour of Vespers, the commons of Kent, to the number of sixty thousand, arrived in Southwark where the Marshalsea was. They broke up and cast to the ground all the houses of the Marshalsea and removed all the prisoners imprisoned there for debt or felony. They then beat to the ground a fine place belonging to John (*recte* Richard) de Imworth, then Marshal of the Marshalsea of the King's Bench and warden of the prisoners therein. All the houses of the jurors and professional informers belonging to the Marshalsea were also thrown to the ground during that night.[93]

Richard Imworth was a royal sergeant-at-arms; not only was his house destroyed that night, but two days later he was brutally dragged from sanctuary in Westminster Abbey and beheaded in Cheap. Nor was he the only royal sergeant-at-arms to lose his life at the hands of the rebels in 1381. John Legge, who had been a prominent member of the commission to reassess the poll-tax, and who was thoroughly unpopular, was also a sergeant-at-arms, and was one of those taken from the Tower and beheaded on 14 June. It is quite probable that both of them were rather unpleasant men (the *Anonimalle* chronicler described Imworth as 'a tormenter without pity'), but their murders in 1381 also highlight the general unpopularity which attached to the king's sergeants-at-arms.[94] Indeed they seem to have been disliked almost as much as the royal purveyors were; and like purveyors, although they were officially members of the household, their duties meant that they probably spent as much time out of the household as in it.

Sergeants-at-arms

The king's sergeants-at-arms were men of some standing. Their standard rate of remuneration was set at 12*d.* a day plus an annual robes allowance of £2. 6*s.* 8*d.* (as compared to the 7½*d.* and £2 of the esquires of the household). The Ordinance of 1318 had stated that their number should not exceed thirty, and that each night four of them should sleep outside the king's chamber, while the other twenty-six should sleep in the hall. During the first half of the fourteenth century, and through until the late 1360s, it seems to have been normal for about twenty sergeants-at-arms to reside in the household, but during the last thirty years of the fourteenth century there were never more than seven (and usually only three or four) sergeants-at-arms receiving allowances in the wardrobe.[95] On the other hand, about ninety men were described as sergeants-at-arms in Richard II's reign, of whom about sixty-five were working for the king at one time. Their activities aroused regular complaint. In the 1386 parliament the commons protested that 'there are such great numbers of sergeants-at-arms now, who make great oppressions and extortions by colour of their office on the people', and asked the king to restrict their number in accordance with 'the statute for his household', presumably the 1318 Ordinance. This request was repeated in 1390, when the commons requested a reduction to the 'accustomed' figure of twenty-four (Richard pointed out that actually it was thirty), again in 1394, and even in the generally submissive parliament of September 1397.[96]

The clue to this discrepancy in numbers is given—at least in part—by the 1390 petition, which stated that many of these sergeants-at-arms received no wages from the king, and implied that this was why they resorted to oppressions. What in fact seems to have happened is that the sergeants-at-arms had been divided into two groups: a small inner group of about four, officially appointed to be 'assigned to the royal standard when the king in person attends the army in war',[97] but also identical to those who received allowances in the wardrobe, and therefore almost certainly comprising those who slept outside the king's chamber at night (under Richard II, these men were John Farringdon, Roger Atte Gate, John Orwell, and Thomas Sayvill, all of whom acted from 1379–80 until the end of the reign), and a much larger group of sixty or so at any one time, some of whom received wages and some of whom did not; they were not attached to the household in a permanent capacity, but the king could call upon them at any time to undertake special commissions. Quite often their work was of a military nature, but it could be very varied. An idea of the sort of work which a royal sergeant-at-arms might be asked to do can be gleaned from an expenses claim submitted by Robert Markeley.[98] In May 1389 he was ordered to arrest all ships carrying more than forty tuns of wine or more along the coast of East Anglia; in July he was sent to investigate a rumour that a quantity of gold had been found in Essex, and in October he was sent to make 'certain enquiries' in Sussex and Hampshire; in June of the following year he was asked to tour several of the counties to the north of

London and collect arrears from farmers of royal lands there, and was then ordered to take various (unspecified) commissions for the king in Kent, Surrey, Sussex, Devon and Cornwall; in 1394 he spent over three months at Eltham manor supervising repairs to the king's buildings there. In each case he received 2s. expenses per day.

Some of these duties probably involved Markeley in friction with those whom he had to deal with, others may not have. Some of the other tasks entrusted to sergeants-at-arms certainly provoked hostility. Several of them (including John Legge) were appointed to the commissions for the reassessment of the poll-tax in March 1381. It was a royal sergeant-at-arms who was sent by the king into East Anglia in the autumn of 1387 in a last-minute attempt to recruit men against the Appellants (for which he was arrested near Cambridge and thrown in prison), and it was another sergeant-at-arms, Thomas Usk, who was executed at the behest of the Merciless Parliament, probably for trying to raise forces against the Appellants in London.[99] During the last two years of the reign, they acted as the king's agents for the enactment of many of the more distasteful aspects of his tyranny.[100] It was not surprising therefore that they became so unpopular, and if they were not paid by the king on a regular basis, then presumably they had all the more reason to indulge in sharp practice in order to make a living. There is certainly evidence to bear out the statement by the commons in 1390 that they were not properly paid. In 1389, Nicholas Adam was said to have served the Black Prince and Richard II as a sergeant-at-arms for thirty-three years without wages, and was only granted the customary wages in November of that year; John Atherstone had been a royal sergeant-at-arms in January 1383, specifically without wages, and did not receive a grant of wages until 1391. Perhaps the king began to pay wages to more of them after the parliamentary petition of 1390, but John Hereford, who was described as a sergeant-at-arms as early as 1382, was not granted wages until October 1393.[101] The king did pay lip-service to the terms of the petition: after 1390 Richard commonly appointed men to be 'one of the thirty sergeants-at-arms of the king lately prescribed in the Parliament at Westminster',[102] but the number in practice remained about double the number prescribed, and their popularity failed to increase. It is interesting also to note that their employment by the king as special agents could be double-edged: on 27 December 1387, the day on which the Appellants entered London, but the day before they confronted Richard in the Tower, two of the king's longest-serving sergeants-at-arms, Thomas Sayvill and John Elyngham, were ordered to arrest Michael de la Pole because he was 'intending to withdraw himself' from the kingdom. Although warranted by the king, it is difficult to believe that this order really came from him.[103] Under Henry IV the number of sergeants-at-arms seems to have been much the same as under Richard, with four receiving wages and robes in the wardrobe, and fifty or more others close at hand. However, there is no evidence of complaints about their behaviour, in parliament or elsewhere. It may be that their unpopularity under Richard, especially at the end of his reign, had impressed upon Henry the need to lower their profile a little.

Work, rest and pleasure

So far, this discussion of the king's household servants has concentrated largely on their 'outward' face, the effect which they had on those whose paths they crossed. It is time now to turn to more 'inward' matters, to try to build up a picture of the internal structure and organisation of the household. The size of the household has already been discussed. Concerning remuneration, conditions of service, and so forth, there is a mass of evidence, but it is best to restrict this discussion to a few generalisations. A job in the royal household was undoubtedly a good one, and surely much sought-after. Apart from the prestige and excitement of proximity to the royal court, the king seems to have paid better. In a noble household in fourteenth- and fifteenth-century England for instance, the average annual wage for a valet was *c*. £2, less than 1½*d*. a day;[104] the king's valets usually received 3*d*. a day, and some of them received annuities (usually 5 marks or £5) at the exchequer, too. In the 1390s William of Wykeham was paying between 4*s*. and one mark a year in wages to the grooms of his household, whereas the king's grooms got 1½*d*. or 2*d*. a day plus an annual gift of £1 from the king.[105] In addition to wages, there were annuities at the exchequer for most of the knights and esquires and some (less than half) of the valets, good and plentiful livings for the clerks, and always the chance, even for quite lowly servants of the household, to pick up a minor wardship or lesser office in the king's gift. As would be expected, therefore, the rate of continuity among servants in the household was high. For instance, sixty-five percent of those 454 persons employed in the household in 1389–90 were still there in 1396. From one reign to the next, however, the continuity was not so high: only forty-two percent of Edward III's 338 household servants in 1376–7 were retained by Richard in their jobs, and only 10·5 percent of Richard's servants in 1395–6 were still in the royal household in 1402–3. The latter figure, of course, crosses a revolution as well as two reigns, which no doubt helps to explain why it is so low. Also, Henry was already a full-grown man with a sizeable household of his own before he became king, and he had this as well as John of Gaunt's household to draw on in 1399. Richard, by contrast, had but a small household (*c*. twenty-five persons) before he became king, although he too drew considerably on the former servants of his father the Black Prince. Continuity was generally most marked among the clerks of the household, probably because they were doing a specialised job. For instance, ten of Henry's household clerks in 1402–3 had been in Richard's household in 1395–6, and this excludes the politically contentious ones.[106] Continuity from one reign to the next was lowest among the upper reaches of the hierarchy. None of Henry's thirteen chamber knights in 1402–3, only five of his eighty-eight esquires, and only one of his thirty-four valets of the chamber, had been in Richard's household. Originally, none of Richard's household officers were given posts in Henry's household, but four of them were employed by Henry in 1401–2 (three of them at least at the insistence of the commons in 1401).[107]

As with any institution of size, there were always opportunities for promotion, but it should be emphasised, firstly, that only a small minority of household servants were ever promoted, and secondly, that it was most unusual indeed for a man to move more than one rung up the ladder, however long he stayed in the household. For instance, twenty-four of the sixty-five valets of the offices in the household in 1359 were still in the household in 1377: twelve of them were still valets of the offices, while the other twelve had been promoted to either esquire or sergeant of an office (but none of them was ever promoted further). Again, eighteen of the forty-seven grooms in 1389 had become valets by 1395 (promotion from the bottom rung of the ladder was easier), but none of them progressed further. There were a few notable exceptions, but they were very few: Richard Stury had first entered the household as a valet in the 1340s, was an esquire of the chamber by 1359, and a knight of the chamber by 1365. He remained a close companion and trusted counsellor to two kings for the remaining thirty years of his life. Thomas Brounfleet began as a clerk of the buttery in the 1380s, defrocked himself and became sergeant of the buttery before 1392, and rose to be king's butler (under Richard II), controller, and eventually keeper of the wardrobe (only the second layman to hold that post) under Henry IV. He was knighted by Henry, and established a landed family of distinction in his native Yorkshire. His son Henry, who started life as a household esquire under Henry IV, was summoned to parliament as Lord Brounfleet and Vescy in 1449.[108] It was more common, however, for men to be brought into the household at all levels when vacancies had to be filled. Men from the more substantial gentry were recruited as knights and esquires of the household, while men of lesser gentry status (those who by *c.* 1400 were known as gentlemen rather than esquires) were recruited as valets. Grooms were probably (as their name 'garçons' implies) younger members of this lesser gentry, but they are usually too obscure to figure much in the records.

Thus the royal household certainly could act as an agent of social mobility, raising men from 'gentlemen' to esquires, from esquires to knights, even occasionally providing a man like Thomas Brounfleet or John Stanley with the opportunity to establish a landed family of real note.[109] Whether or not these men chose to invest their money in land, there can be little doubt that service in the royal household would have enriched them, but the number of men who experienced a real and lasting rise in status as a consequence of a career in the royal household must always have been limited. Nevertheless, if service of one sort or another was the principal road to advancement in later medieval England (and it surely was), then service in the royal household, being one of the most prestigious and lucrative forms of personal service, certainly played its part in that process.

Recruitment to the royal household is a subject on which there is little direct evidence, but it is possible to make certain generalisations. Occasionally there are clear territorial patterns of recruitment, such as Richard II's fondness for men from his father's earldom of Cheshire, or Henry IV's employment of

Lancastrians, which are easily explicable. Edward IV's Black Book of the Household stated that the esquires of the household should 'be of sondry sheres, by whome hit may be knowe the disposicion of the cuntries', and such ideas were also current at the beginning of Henry IV's reign. Yet even if there was, broadly speaking, a policy to try to recruit household servants from different parts of the kingdom, there can be little doubt that the principal method by which men were recruited to the household was by personal introduction. Personal introductions might arise from service in the household of another lord or a member of the royal family; they might arise from chance meetings or private recommendations; but above all they arose from that ever-potent social force, the family tradition of service. Whole clans of Walweyns, Clements, Mackeneys, Humberstanes, Archebalds, Lyngeyns, Felbridges, and a host of others too numerous to mention, cousins, nephews and brothers-in-law as well as fathers and sons, regularly succeeded each other in the household and other offices in the king's service, the effect of which was that the staff of the household was recruited as much by chance as by design. The same process operated with regard to the king's retinue and affinity, and it has long been recognised as a powerful factor in the recruitment of noble households and retinues.[11] it bridged both reigns and revolutions (just as traditions of service to a lord usually survived changes in territorial lordship), although naturally it operated more powerfully during the lifetime of one king. It was at the heart of medieval service.

Of the 400–700 members of staff of the household in this period, the majority were lesser servants (below the rank of esquire, sergeant, or clerk). Under Edward III and Richard II, about sixty percent of the staff fell into this category; under Henry IV, the figure rose to about seventy percent, largely accounted for by the fact that Henry reduced substantially the number of esquires in the royal household while maintaining or increasing the number of valets. Every one of the lesser servants was attached to an office: they were not just 'valets' or 'garçons' but 'valets of the buttery', or 'garçons of the sumpterhorses', and so forth. Each office, or department, was headed by a sergeant, and the four major accounting offices (kitchen, marshalsea, buttery, and spicery) each had a clerk; the smaller offices were grouped together under the supervision of the clerk of one of the four major offices, to whom the sergeant presented his accounts. The tasks performed by these lesser servants were on the whole routine and largely self-explanatory.[112] By far the largest department of the household was the marshalsea, or avenary (to be distinguished from the Marshalsea Court), which throughout this period employed at least 100 valets and grooms, and sometimes nearer 200.[113] Their task was to care for, purvey for, feed and groom both the horses attached to the household and those brought to court either by visitors or by members of the household.[114] The other three large departments in terms of staff numbers were the kitchen, buttery, and chamber, each of which normally employed between twenty-five and fifty valets and grooms. Those attached to the chamber attended personally to the king; those attached to the kitchen were responsible for purveying, preparing and cooking food, while those in the buttery purveyed and prepared wine and ale. Among the other departments mentioned at various times during this period were the pantry (often attached to the buttery), wafery, bakery, cellar, poultery, larder, saucery, scullery, chandlery, spicery, napery, ewery, confectionary, laundry, apothecary, counting-house, almonry, and hall (responsible for fuel and rushes in the great hall). Occasionally mentioned too are servants such as the valet of the garbage, of the gate, of the fisher, and of the ferreter.[115] Most of these offices were staffed by less than ten, and often only two or three, servants; the scullery, however, which was responsible for coal and wood for cooking, and for crockery, cutlery and storage vessels, might have up to twenty valets and grooms, and the spicery (especially when it was combined with the chandlery, confectionary and apothecary, which was often the case) a similar number. The clerk of the spicery received most of his provisions from the keeper of the great wardrobe; as well as spices and wax, he provided medicines for both the king and the other members of the household.

The working structure of the household is mirrored in the buildings in which its members worked. At Eltham, for example, there are references during this period to the construction of a kitchen, saucery, and larder in 1358–9; and of a chandlery, spicery, almonry, great and privy sauceries (new ones, presumably), storehouse, bakery, office of the waferer, chamber of the porters, and a roasting-house with a circumference of 132ft, all in the 1380s. When Henry IV built his new suite of royal apartments at the beginning of the fifteenth century, he included a private kitchen, buttery and larder. At Windsor a new spicery, with its own 'Spicery gate', was built, also a new great kitchen, larder, salting-house, pastry-house, and dresser (room for dressing meat).[116] Information concerning the physical layout of these buildings is very limited, but presumably the service rooms were grouped around either the kitchen or the hall, and since kitchen and hall were never far apart, quite often both. At Eltham, for example, there is reference to the 'saucery next to the hall', and as far as can be gathered, the service facilities at Windsor were placed to connect with both the great hall and the royal suite of chambers. In addition to the valets and grooms attached to these offices, there were a few other groups of servants whose tasks are self-explanatory: cleaners, of whom there were usually only two (one for the king's chamber, and one for the hall; they were usually women), messengers, and carters, of whom there were between thirteen and twenty-one listed in the account books.[117] The household was supposed to have twenty carts, so presumably each carter had charge of one cart.

The internal staff structure of the household was thus highly departmentalised, with each group of servants responsible for the daily performance of quite specific tasks, and each probably going about those tasks with little reference to those employed in other offices; what brought this network of functional units together was their ultimate accountability to the steward and keeper, their communal worship each morning in the great chapel, communal eating and sleeping in the hall, leisure activities, ceremonial duties, and in the last resort the knowledge that they existed in order to make life comfortable for those who lived 'upstairs'.

Meals were taken in the hall, in two shifts, for obvious reasons. It was forbidden to remove food from the hall. Liveries of food and drink (as well as of candles and napery) were issued in 'messes', strictly according to rank, just as they had been in Henry I's time and as they would still be in Edward IV's time.[118] In an institution of the size of the royal household, close control of liveries was vital if expenses were to be kept within reasonable bounds. It was in the hall, too, that many of the lesser servants slept. Sleeping arrangements in general seem to have been very informal (virtually nothing is said about them in the regulations), but those who did not sleep in the hall probably distributed themselves around the passageways and vestibules, huddled in winter around the great fireplaces, lying on their straw mats (pallets) which may have been single or double.[119] Many of the more senior members of the household must also have frequently been reduced to sleeping wherever they could find space. In the Ordinance of 1318, for example, it was said that of the thirty sergeants-at-arms, four were to sleep each night outside the king's chamber, while the other twenty-six were to sleep in the hall, and the sergeants-at-arms received higher allowances than the esquires. On the other hand it was allowed to the two clerks of the counting-table that they might sleep in the king's wardrobe, which was clearly a privilege.[120] Such informality could clearly create problems: the 1318 Ordinance also stated that each week the marshals were to search the household for hangers-on and eject them, that no member of the household staff was to keep a wife or other woman at court, and that any prostitute found at court for the third time was to be imprisoned for forty days. Edward I had had to issue similar injunctions in 1279.[121] Yet the problem of prostitutes following the court was evidently insurmountable: it was an age-old custom, but still spelt out in 1370, that the clerk of the market held his post 'provided always that he have and hold the serjeanty of being marshal of the prostitutes of the household, dismembering adjudged malefactors . . .'; in tracts dealing with the offices of marshal and constable of England it was sometimes said that one or other of them had the right to take 4*d.* each week from 'chescune femme de fole vie' who followed the court. Another treatise on the marshal stated that he should employ twelve 'damoiselles' to inform him as to whether there were whores frequenting the court. It is clear that these 'damoiselles' were themselves prostitutes, and were, in effect, protecting their own livelihood.[122] In an almost exclusively male society, where men were forbidden to keep their wives at court, and where they were not allowed either to marry or to leave court without (theoretically, at least) the king's permission,[123] it is hardly surprising to find that something in practice not far removed from an organised brothel seems to have been attached to the royal household. Whether this had always been the case is difficult to say but there are several earlier references, going back to the twelfth century at least, to the serjeanty of guarding the court prostitutes, but different kings probably had different attitudes to the question.[124]

Too much emphasis on the duties of household servants and the regulations which governed their lives (at least in theory) leads to the neglect of another vital aspect of the household, namely, that it served as a centre of social life. Many of those who populated the royal court, lesser as well as greater servants, must have enjoyed a considerable amount of leisure time. Edward IV's Black Book stated that,

> the esquiers of houshold of old be acustumed, wynter and somer, in after nonys and in euenynges, to drawe to lordez chambrez within courte, there to kepe honest company aftyr theyre cunyng, in talkying of cronycles of kinges and of other polycyez, or in pyping, harpyng, synging, other actez marciablez, to help occupy the court and acompany straungers, tyll the tym require of departing.'[125]

Whether or not Geoffrey Chaucher really did formally declaim his poems to gatherings of Richard II's followers, such scenes can hardly have been uncommon in the household. Meals as well as informal gatherings were frequently accompanied by music, with between five and fifteen minstrels normally attached to the royal household, and visiting musicians often invited to give performances.[126] There was also much gambling and playing of chess, as well as practising of the martial arts such as archery and sword-play.[127] More formal entertainments normally took the form of either tournaments (of which Edward III, as is well known, was a particular patron) or hunting parties. To celebrate the arrival of the king of Cyprus in 1363, for example, Edward III organised a great hunting-party to Clive, Nottingham and Sherwood forests, while the Westminster chronicler said that following his discomfiture in the Merciless Parliament Richard II 'from now until the end of the autumn . . . took his pleasure in the chase.'[128]

Walsingham said that Edward III went hunting and hawking whenever he could, and to judge by the amount of money which he spent on them, Edward certainly seems to have been more addicted to these traditionally noble pastimes than either Richard II or Henry IV.[129] The cost of maintaining the king's dogs and falcons, and the wages of the men who cared for them, were recorded in the wardrobe accounts (although this by no means represents the full cost, for sheriffs and other local officials were frequently ordered to pay for the upkeep of either the animals or their keepers staying in their counties). The wardrobe during Edward's later years was spending on average about £80 a year on the king's dogs and his huntsmen. This was the cost of feeding fifty to seventy dogs, and paying fifteen to twenty huntsmen (who got 1½d. or 2d. a day). Under Richard II and Henry IV, the total never passed £18 in any year. Falconry was considerably more expensive than hunting: Edward's wardrobe spent about £200 a year on maintaining the king's falcons, although the figure could go over £600, as it did in 1367–8. Richard II's wardrobe spent between £50 and £100 a year on falconry, while Henry IV's recorded expenditure was £196 in 1402–3, and £158 in 1408–9. Edward III seems to have kept between fifty and sixty falcons of all types, gerfalcons, goshawks, tiercels, and lannerets among others. Most of them cost 1d. a day to feed, but the superior birds (the gerfalcons) cost 1½d. a day. About forty falconers were also employed, receiving wages of 2*d.* a day for the most part. The king's chief falconer, however, was paid 1*s.* a day and ranked as an esquire of the household.

Both hunting and falconry were taken very seriously by the nobility and royalty of medieval England (and Europe); they had to be carefully organised, and were surrounded by elaborate rituals and conventions. Hunting was normally a summer pastime, falconry a winter one, although the seasons were flexible.[130] The king's hunting has often been described, but falconry has generally received less attention, and deserves more. The reason why falconry was a more expensive pastime than hunting was because it was more labour-intensive, and the training involved for the birds required a greater degree of skill than that required for the hunting-dogs. The birds were based at the royal mews at Charing, by Westminster, and the post of keeper of the mews was always held by an intimate of the king. Under Richard II, for example, it was held successively by Simon Burley, Peter Courtenay, and Baldwin Bereford, all knights of the chamber; under Henry IV, the king's son John was keeper of the mews. Training continued throughout the birds' lives, and for this they were constantly being sent away into the country, where their trainers were normally told to take wages and food for them from local officials of the crown. With the approach of the winter, they were expected to be available to be brought to the king whenever he should summon them.[131] Other preparations had to be made too: special robes were often issued to courtiers and friends of the king for the hawking season (just as they were for the hunting season, 'contra seisonam venationis');[132] in October 1373 the sheriff of Oxfordshire was ordered to repair all the bridges in his county at once 'for the king's sport with his hawks in the approaching winter season'.[133] It is interesting, too, to note that when Rotherhithe manor was being renovated in the 1350s, a special partition was set up in the king's chamber 'for the king's falcons to perch on'.[134] Really good birds were much prized, and individually named. In 1370 Edward III wrote to the duke of Milan thanking him for various falcons which the duke had sent as a gift, and in particular one called 'the Cyprian' with which Edward had been especially delighted, but which had since unfortunately died. Gifts between nobles and kings were often associated with both hunting and falconry. In January 1367, Charles V of France sent Edward thirty wild boars as a present; presumably they were intended in the right spirit.[135]

Entertainments of one sort or another, such as hunting and falconry, martial competitions, or listening to music, were an important adjunct to court life, but essentially the household acted as a centre of social life because it was here that the great men of the kingdom congregated, to talk to each other and to the king, to negotiate or bargain, and to discuss matters of policy in an atmosphere less formal than the council or parliament chamber. Some were even brought up at court. During the last years of Edward III's reign both Robert de Vere and John Lord Beaumond were minors in the king's wardship, and both were being brought up in the royal household.[136] Both were later to become very close friends of Richard II, and it may well be that their intimacy with Richard was founded on childhood friendships formed at the court of his grandfather, for the future king must often have been about the royal court at this time too. Young noblemen were commonly brought up in the households of other nobles, whether or not they were minors, and they came to learn not simply how to hunt or to joust, but, much more importantly, the noble way of life. Thus at the beginning of Henry IV's reign, Thomas Mowbray, son of the king's late adversary the duke of Norfolk, who had just died in exile, petitioned the king that he might be allowed 'to reside with the queen, where he has resided before this time, in order to learn honour and gentleness, and in order the better to serve your highness and to do your pleasure in time to come.'[137] Naturally, more formal instruction was not lacking: in 1366, for example, Edward Palmer received £4 from the king for Edward's youngest son, Thomas (of Woodstock), 'to be instructed in the science of grammar'.[138] But it was not for such formal education that young men were brought up in noble households as there were many other places where that could be had. It was for the opportunity to meet other young men of a similar status, and to acquire the art of living nobly.

The household in arms

'Living nobly' included going to war. There were some functions of the household as a whole which never changed. Serving as a centre of social life was one of them, and accompanying the king *en masse* when he went to war was another. Not only the natural 'fighting' men, such as the knights and esquires, but also the clerks, valets, grooms, carters and so forth, from the highest to the lowest servants, would be expected to arm themselves and ride or march with the king wherever the campaign took them, and the senior members at least would be expected to bring other fighting men with them. To cite but one example from thousands, as unlikely sounding a soldier as Ralph Repingdon, who was clerk of Richard II's kitchen, received war wages for the Irish expedition of 1394–5 of 2s. a day plus 1s. a day for an esquire who accompanied him.[139] The list of *vadia guerre* for the 1359–60 campaign includes the name of almost every person who received robes in the wardrobe that year; for the futile sortie from Sandwich in 1372, the entire household was said to be *in navibus* from 27 August to 15 October, when adverse weather finally forced the expedition to be cancelled.[140] On such occasions the household expanded to four or five times its normal size because of the extra men which individual members brought with them. For the Scottish campaign of 1400, for example, the household contingent was 244 men-at-arms and 1,227 archers; for the Scottish campaign of 1385, the 'Tynell du Roy' was 800 men-at-arms and 2,000 archers, out of a total force of 4,590 men-at-arms and 9,144 archers.[141] Dr Prestwich found that during Edward I's reign the king's household servants and their retinues often contributed about one-third of the paid cavalry in the royal army (although not so much in the later years of the reign).[142] By the late fourteenth century the household contribution to the army seems not to have been quite as great, perhaps a fifth or a sixth on average but it was still substantial, and it was naturally the element closest to the king. One of the main reasons why the household proportion had dropped was because of the abandonment of the system of household knights, a development discussed at greater length below.[143]

For the expedition to Scotland in 1385 weaponry from the privy wardrobe was issued to members of the king's *hospitium*, as well as to those of his *familia*, and to others of his *comitiva*.[144] This illustrates clearly the stages by which the household was expanded to create the army. The *hospitium* was the household, the inner core of permanent royal servants, now armed and accompanied by their own retainers; the *familia* meant, in this context, the king's retinue, which naturally included members of the household, but also included men such as king's knights and king's esquires,[145] and other knights and esquires who had contracted directly with the king rather than with one of the lords bringing separate retinues to the muster-point (naturally, these knights and esquires also brought retainers with them). Such contracts could well be for the duration of the campaign only. For the Irish expedition of 1394–5, for example, the king's retinue included seventy-nine knights and 182 esquires; of the knights, thirteen were chamber knights, and another thirty-three were king's knights; of the esquires, 112 were esquires of the household, and another nine were king's esquires. Thus nearly 100 of the senior members of the retinue were men who were not retained by the king, and there must have been many more (such as the esquire who served with Ralph Repingdon mentioned above) who were of the king's retinue but not of the household, and not mentioned by name in the list of war wages because not personally contracted.[146] The *comitiva*, in this context, seems to refer to the whole of the rest of the army, that is, the king's retinue together with the magnates' retinues.

Those who were attached to the king, by life retaining contracts, for example, or by the fact that they received annuities from him, were clearly expected to join his retinue when called upon to do so, whether or not they were of the household. Both Richard II and Henry IV frequently issued general summonses to annuitants and retainers to join them for campaigns. When the king's knights got too old for fighting, Henry sometimes issued them with specific exemptions from service with him in war.[147] They could also, of course, be used for military purposes within the kingdom. In August 1397, for example, Richard summoned all his annuitants and livery-holders to join him at Kingston-upon-Thames for the triumphal march to Westminster to celebrate (and enforce) his parliamentary annihilation of the Appellants.[148] But even if the primary military duty of members of the royal household was to accompany the king personally in war, this did not mean that they were prevented from campaigning without the king if they had a mind to; the list of war wages paid in 1370–1, when Edward III was not campaigning in person, included numerous members of the household, who presumably had joined the expedition led by Robert Knolles in France, while in the summer of 1386, during the French invasion scare, various contingents from the household, led by such senior figures as controller Baldwin Raddington and under-chamberlain Simon Burley, were detached from the king and sent to garrison key south coast castles like Dover, Rye, Sandwich and Portchester.[149] Containing as it did a good number of senior and experienced soldiers, the royal household was always a useful reserve force for any type of military duty.

Many of the senior members of the household were also heavily involved in the organisation of warfare, as they had been under both Henry III and Edward I; unlike a century earlier, however, these men were hardly ever entrusted with army commands now—by the late fourteenth century these went almost exclusively to men of the rank of earl or above.[150] It was really as quarter-masters rather than as commanders that the household officers played a major role. For the Irish campaign of 1394–5, for instance, controller Baldwin Raddington, chamber knight Robert Witteneye, the king's knight John Stanley, and some fifteen household esquires and sixty lesser servants were sent on ahead of the army to make provisioning and lodging arrangements there before the king's arrival.[151] For the 1399 campaign it was again Witteneye and Stanley (who was by now controller of the household) who performed the same task.[152] John Stanley, a soldier first and foremost, remained heavily involved in military affairs after becoming steward of Henry IV's household in 1405. During Archbishop Scrope's rebellion of that year he and controller Roger Leche were sent to York to secure and govern the city, and during the next year or two he was in charge of the muster of the king's retinue.[153]

During peace-time, the military duties of the senior officers of the household were largely concerned with the organisation of the king's bodyguard. The four sergeants-at-arms who slept outside the king's chamber every night constituted the king's immediate bodyguard, but if need be the whole household was supposed to be able to defend the king. On occasions, they failed signally to do this. At the time of Richard II's encounter with Wat Tyler at Smithfield in June 1381, the author of the *Anonimalle Chronicle* recorded that 'almost all of the knights and squires of the king's household, and many others, were so frightened of the affray that they left their liege lord and each went his own way.'[154] In 1387, too, the household had proved incapable of providing any serious military support for the king. Possibly this was one reason why Richard was eager to develop his personal bodyguard in the latter half of his reign. The order to the chamber knight John Golafre to supervise archery practice by the lesser members of the household in 1392 is evidence of this, but it was not until 1397 that Richard really began to build up the military capability of his household.[155] His recruitment of over 300 Cheshiremen, divided into seven *vigilia*, and accompanying the king day and night wherever he went, swelled the royal bodyguard to unheard of peace-time proportions, and proved massively unpopular.[156] Early in Henry IV's reign there were again real fears about the personal safety of the king: in February 1400 the council advised Henry that 'from each county of the kingdom certain reputable armed esquires and archers should be chosen to stay for a time at the king's wages, outside his household, but close to him, keeping watch each night about the king. And that the king's steward be charged to furnish and order all domestic servants (*meynalx*) of the king to be armed and arrayed according to their estate for the safe keeping of the king.'[157] This was immediately following the earls' rebellion and was undoubtedly a reaction to it; the disaffected earls, it will be remembered, had hoped to catch Henry by surprise while he was celebrating Christmas at Windsor. However, no more is heard of this additional royal bodyguard in Henry's reign, and it is probable that, with the immediate danger gone, the idea was never really put into operation. Yet even if Henry's bodyguard never even remotely approached the size of Richard's during the last two years of the latter's reign, there would always have been plenty of men about the household capable of defending him by force of arms, and it was essentially up to the household officers to see that this capability was maintained at all times.

The officers of the household

Much more will be said about many of the senior members of the household in subsequent chapters. There are, however, a few points which are worth making about them, to clarify their functions and to illuminate general trends. The 'upstairs' of the household included a dozen or so officers, together with the chamber knights, the clerks and esquires of the household, sergeants of the offices, and sergeants-at-arms. The chamber knights are discussed in detail elsewhere.[158] There were usually about twenty sergeants of the offices during this period, most of whom had charge of one of the household offices (saucery, scullery, and so forth). In the larger offices, however, there were usually two or more sergeants: for the hall, for example, there were two sergeant-ushers responsible for seeing that fuel and rushes were provided and messes handed out in accordance with the regulations, and two sergeant-marshals, one in charge of seating arrangements, and the other to act as harbinger for the hall. Both the kitchen and buttery had two sergeants, one for the hall and one for the chamber, while there were at least three sergeants of the marshalsea.[159] The number of esquires of the household varied between sixty-three (in 1366–7) and 168 (in 1395–6). This figure included about twenty esquires of the chamber, who attended personally on the king. The esquires of the household almost certainly came to court in rotation. The Black Book said that Edward IV should normally have between forty and sixty esquires, of whom twenty were to be at court at any one time; the rather low figure of twenty-four esquires given in the Ordinance of 1318 probably refers not to the full complement but to those expected to be at court at one time. Thus it was probably normal in the late fourteenth and early fifteenth centuries for about twenty to thirty esquires to be at court, although when the total number rose as high as it did in the 1390s, there may well have been more. According to the Black Book, they were to be:

attendaunt uppon the kinges person, in ryding and going at all tymes; and to help serue his table from the surueying bourde, and from other places as the assewer woll assigne . . . They ete in the hall, sitting togyder at ony of the bothe meles, as they serue, som the furst mele, some the latter, by assent; this hath be alwey the maner amonges them for honour, profite to the king.[160]

The household clerks, who numbered between twenty and thirty-five in this period, fall into three groups. There were usually about ten clerks of the offices, of whom two (one senior and one junior) were responsible for the accounts of each of the four major offices (kitchen, buttery, marshalsea and spicery). They liaised with the sergeants and purveyors of the various offices, and drew up accounts of what had been acquired and disbursed, which were then presented to the cofferer and his clerks in the counting-house (the clerks of the counting-house also ranked as clerks of the offices). Secondly, there were the chaplains and clerks of the chapel, numbering between five and ten. They came under the supervision of the dean of the chapel, and were primarily responsible for the spiritual welfare of both king and household. Religious observance was a routine but important part of life in any medieval household; each day began with a mass in the great chapel, while holy days were celebrated with high mass and a sermon, often from a visiting preacher. The chaplains and clerks of the chapel officiated at these masses, heard confessions from members of the household, and so forth. By this time it was probably more common for the king to hear mass privately in the chapel attached to his chamber, and what is abundantly clear (this is especially true during the reign of Richard II) is that several of the king's chaplains became close friends of the king. Not surprisingly, many of them were promoted to the episcopacy.[161] Many of them were also graduates of either Oxford or Cambridge, and their duties within the household were educational as well as religious. According to A.B. Cobban, the English Chapel Royal 'incorporated a sort of independent grammar school' where not only the clerks but also the young nobles brought up in or sent to the royal household and 'all other members of the household who had a mind to use these educational facilities' could receive instruction in grammar and music. The Chapel Royal also had close links with the King's Hall at Cambridge. It was during the reign of Henry IV (whose credentials as a scholar and patron of learning are surely much more compelling than those of Richard II), that the first mention is heard of a household master of grammar (John Bugby).[162]

The third group of clerks in the royal household consisted of the clerks of the privy seal and signet. They numbered about eight, and it was their job to write out warrants which were then despatched under one or other of the king's seals. They were supervised by the keeper of the privy seal and the king's secretary, who kept the signet. The position of the keeper of the privy seal at this time was a little ambivalent. He was without doubt a royal minister of national importance, generally reckoned as the third great officer of state of the king, after the chancellor and treasurer; moreover, as T.F. Tout pointed out, by 1390 the privy seal had more or less come to be recognised as the seal under which the mandates of the king's council were usually despatched, even if it would be wrong to regard it as in a special sense the council's seal.[163] The keeper of the privy seal was also *ex officio* a member of the council, and must thus have spent a great deal of time away from the household. Nevertheless, he continued throughout this period to receive his robes in the wardrobe just as if he were a permanent member of the household, and whenever a new keeper was appointed, the exchequer officials were ordered to pay him his wages 'until order shall be taken for his continual abode in the king's household', which seems to suggest that, although the keeper was not normally residing in the household, this was still regarded as a temporary state of affairs.[164] Under whom, then, did the five or six privy seal clerks attached to the household work (for there was only one privy seal, and it could not be in two places at the same time)? The answer may well be that in practice they were clerks writing under the signet rather than the privy seal, but were still described by their traditional name because they still sometimes wrote under it, and because it was thought that at some future time the keeper with his privy seal might again be fully reunited with the household. The signet was certainly with the household; sometimes it was kept by one of the clerks or chaplains of the king's chapel, but from about 1380 onwards the 'king's secretary' becomes a clearly identifiable figure ranked among the officers of the household and receiving his robes regularly in the wardrobe. 'Clerks writing under the signet' are mentioned occasionally, but not very often.[165] Since most mandates despatched from the household which required a seal must surely have been sealed with the signet, it is highly likely that these so-called clerks of the privy seal were really clerks of the signet.

There was no precise number of officers of the household, but in this period between nine and twelve officials were classified as officers at various times. This group always included the keeper, steward, controller, cofferer, almoner, keeper of the privy seal, dean of the king's chapel, and chamberlain of the household. Also included on occasions were the king's confessor, his surgeon, his physician, his secretary, and the master of the king's horses (Robert Waterton, a close friend and long-serving Lancastrian esquire, held this post under Henry IV and received his fees and robes in the wardrobe). Of the clerical officers, the secretary, keeper of the privy seal, and dean of the king's chapel have already been discussed. The duties of the king's physician and surgeon are self-explanatory. The king's confessor does not seem to have always been considered as a permanent member of the household, although the nature of his job obviously meant that he was regularly in attendance on the king. Traditionally, he received an allowance of £69. 10s. 6d. *per annum* for the maintenance of himself, his horses, and his servants, and although this was 'in consideration of his continuous stay about the person of the king', it was payable in the exchequer rather than the wardrobe.[166] The confessors were often close personal friends of the kings whose sins they absolved, and Richard II's (particularly Thomas Rushook, exiled to Ireland in 1388) were thought to have an undue degree of influence over him.[167]

The king's almoner was the clerk responsible for distributing alms on behalf of the king. For all men of property in the Middle Ages, almsgiving was regarded as a duty. It was, in the words of Hilda Johnstone, 'as much part of daily ceremonial as eating or sleeping', and the impression given by the wardrobe account books for this whole period is that it was a thoroughly routine business which exercised the heart and mind of the king to a minimal degree.[168] The king's alms can be divided into two main categories: those given to the poor or sick to relieve their condition, and those offered at shrines or to religious houses. Almsgiving for relief of the poor was at a standard rate now, as it had been since the reign of Edward I. There is no evidence to suggest the sort of haphazard and spontaneous feeding of hundreds or even thousands of paupers in which Henry III had often indulged, as for instance when he ordered his almoner to 'feed in the great hall at Westminster as many as it will hold', or to 'feed as many poor as can get into the hall in the upper bailey at Windsor'. It was said that in addition to these impromptu gatherings, Henry used to feed 500 poor people each day; by the time of Edward I, this had been cut to 666 meals per week (although this king too sometimes ordered hundreds or thousands of additional meals to be given to the poor, so that in some years his almoner would distribute 100,000 meals or more). Under Edward III, Richard II and Henry IV, the king's *elemosina statuta* amounted to 4s. a day, which, at the probable rate of 1d. per meal, amounted to 336 meals a week, or 17,472 a year.[169] Edward III also used to distribute £25 in alms on each of the four great feasts of the year (Christmas, Easter, Pentecost, and Michaelmas), but Richard II discontinued this practise and instead began to give small sums of money to vast numbers of paupers each Good Friday.[170] In 1384 he gave 4d. each to 1,598 paupers, and 1d. each to a further 3,120 (which cost him £89. 12s.). The number gradually increased, however, and by Easter 1396, when he was staying at the palace of the archbishop of York, he distributed, with his own hands according to the account book, 4d. each to no less than 12,040 paupers, at a cost of just over £200. Henry IV continued his cousin's practise, and distributed 4d. to each of 12,000 paupers every Good Friday. All three kings also habitually gave 6d. each to 100 paupers on Maundy Thursday (a practise which continues today in slightly different form), although in 1406 only 40 paupers received their 6d. from Henry. All three kings also maintained a number of paupers on a regular basis, giving them each 2d. a day: Edward III usually maintained about twenty, while under both Richard II and Henry IV it was twenty-four. They were called the poor *'oratores'* of the king—presumably they were meant to pray for his soul. Presumably, too, they must have followed the court continuously.

On special occasions massive amounts of money were distributed in alms. At Queen Anne's funeral in 1394, for example, £67 were given away, while the figure for Edward III's funeral was £500. On feast days throughout the year, such as the Purification, the feast of St John the Evangelist, Ascension Day, the Assumption, Palm Sunday, St George's Day, All Saints, and the birth of St John the Baptist, the king would offer one gold noble (worth 6s. 8d.) or sometimes more. On the feast of the Epiphany he offered a gold noble together with incense and myrrh, in emulation of the three kings. On Good Friday another special ceremony was performed: the king would prostrate himself before a relic called the 'Cross Neith', and then offer at the altar three gold nobles and five silver shillings (total value 25s.) in alms; then these coins were replaced with different coins to the same value, and the original coins were melted down to be made into 'medicinal rings' to be given to those who suffered from epilepsy (they were commonly known as 'cramp rings'). This ceremony was performed by all the kings from Edward II to Henry IV.[171] When the king visited the shrine of St Thomas Becket at Canterbury, as he was meant to do in May each year, he offered three florins in alms. The wardrobe account books also record various other offerings classified as alms, such as one or two tuns of wine every year to each of a dozen or so favoured religious houses (often royal foundations), and gifts of £1 or £2 to preachers invited to give sermons to the household on feast days. To judge from the surviving account books, Richard II's two favourite preachers were John Depyng and Thomas Palmer, and it is worth noting that Thomas Palmer is also found preaching to Henry's household in 1403. He and Depyng were both friars preachers. Finally, the king attended mass every morning, and each morning at mass he offered 'one great penny' (value 7d.) in alms.

These official alms of the king must have attracted considerable numbers of paupers, cripples, invalids and general hangers-on to the court, especially on the great feast days or at occasions such as a royal funeral. There was also a less official side to almsgiving. According to the Black Book, for instance, the 'broken meat' from both sittings of the household was to be collected daily and 'distributed to such poore people as shall attend at the gate for the kinges almes'. (Any yeomen or grooms who tried to 'imbeasell' the meat were to lose six day's wages.)[172] As Hilda Johnstone pointed out, one sometimes wonders whether there were enough recipients for the king's alms. Could the household be assured of finding 336 paupers to whom to give meals each week? The king's *oratores* must surely have followed the court on a fairly permanent basis, and the likelihood must be that they were not the only ones who did so. Like the prostitutes who had to be regularly ejected from the household, there must also have been a floating body of paupers, several dozen or so, perhaps up to a hundred or more, who eked out a living by hanging around the court and feeding off the crumbs of the great. And with the king's almoner responsible for the distribution of between about £350 and £700 even in unexceptional years, some of them may not have been that poor.

The two remaining clerical officers of the household were the cofferer and the keeper. Before 1368, the office of controller of the household had always been held by a clerk too, but in 1368 the Lancastrian knight John d'Ypres was made controller, and from this time onwards it was regarded as a layman's post. The keepership of the wardrobe, one of the three most important offices in the household, remained a clerical preserve until 1406, when (under pressure from the commons) it was given to the former knight of the chamber, John

Tiptoft. This gradual laicisation of the top appointments in the household no doubt reflects the growth of lay literacy in late medieval England, but the post of cofferer at least remained in the hands of the clerks. The cofferers ran the counting-house and disbursed the household's cash. They were generally long-serving, rather unremarkable men; three of them went on to be keepers of the wardrobe (Richard Beverley, John Carp, and Thomas More). The keepers, too, were on the whole not very distinguished, although there are some exceptions to this rule: Thomas Brantingham and Henry Wakefield were both elevated to the episcopacy when they ceased to act as keepers (in 1370 and 1375 respectively), and the two lay keepers at the end of Henry IV's reign, Tiptoft and Thomas Brounfleet, were obviously highly talented. In general, the clerical keepers were men who had served long in the royal administration, and for whom the keepership was the climax of a worthy but unexciting career. Before 1399, no great political importance seems to have been attached to the post. Under Henry IV, however, the keepership emerges as a more controversial appointment. In 1399, and again in 1405, Henry appointed as keepers clerks who, although long-serving Lancastrians, had little or no experience of the workings of household finance (Thomas Tutbury in 1399, Richard Kingston in 1405). In the parliaments of 1401 and 1406 respectively, their dismissal was demanded; they were probably considered to be incompetent keepers, and thus to have been, at least in part, responsible for the financial chaos of Henry's wardrobe. They may well have been incompetent. What is also worth noting, however, is that the controversy surrounding the appointment of the keeper in Henry's reign clearly reflects the financial nature of the criticisms voiced about Henry's household. Under Edward III and, to an even greater extent, Richard II, it was the stewards and chamberlains who were unpopular.

The posts of steward, chamberlain, and controller were the three most senior lay offices in the household. The controllers acted as deputies to both keeper and steward, checking the accounts of the clerks and sergeants of the offices, drawing up counter-rolls of the keeper's account books, and having general responsibility for supervising purveyance, harbinging, and eating arrangements in the hall. The post was one which undoubtedly demanded both literacy and organisational ability. After 1368 it was normally held by men who were knighted. Two of the controllers in this period went on to be stewards of the household (John d'Ypres in 1376, and John Stanley, who had been controller 1397–9, in 1405), while another, Thomas Brounfleet, went on to be keeper of the wardrobe. Demands for the parliamentary appointment of the controller show the importance of the post and, as with the keepers, political controversy played its part in the appointments made in Henry IV's reign. Henry's first controller, the Lancastrian esquire Robert Litton, was dismissed in the parliament of 1401, probably because of suspected incompetence, and in 1406 Henry was again advised (by the council) to change his controller, though this time he refused.[173]

The chamberlain of the household, or under-chamberlain to be correctly termed, for in theory he deputised for the chief chamberlain of England—was the closest personal servant of the king. The post was one which carried with it an immense amount of influence and responsibility, and it was almost invariably held by men who were close personal friends of the king. The chamberlains of this period included such men as (under Edward III) John Chandos, Alan Buxhull, and William Latimer; (under Richard II) Simon Burley, Thomas Percy, and William le Scrope; (under Henry IV) Thomas Erpingham and Richard Grey of Codnor. As this list demonstrates, it was always held by a man of at least knightly status, and usually by one of higher rank, a banneret or peer of parliament. Only in 1397–8 was it held by an earl, however, William le Scrope, elevated to the earldom of Wiltshire in 1397, and who relinquished the post to his brother Stephen when he became treasurer of England in 1398. The chief chamberlainship of England was held by earls, and it may have been considered demeaning for one earl to act as the deputy of another.

The influence of the chamberlains of the household had been great since the early fourteenth century (the younger Despenser was Edward II's chamberlain, at a time moreover, when there was no chief chamberlain of England), and it stemmed not only from their personal friendship with the king, but also from two specific duties which they performed. Firstly, the chamberlain had general responsibility for the treasure and jewels stored in the king's chamber. In practice the actual custody of and accounting for the king's treasure would usually be delegated to the receiver of the chamber, but as was made clear in 1376, the chamberlain had access to it: in the Good Parliament, William Latimer was accused not only of having made a usurious loan to the king, but of having 'borrowed' the money in the king's chamber to make the loan, and then of having pocketed the interest for himself before returning the principal to the chamber.[174] Secondly, and even more importantly, the chamberlain was responsible for controlling both written and personal access to the king. Petitions brought to the personal attention of the king would normally have been endorsed first by the chamberlain. But it was above all the physical presence of the chamberlain, as the man who actually attended personally on the king and either allowed men to pass through into the royal presence, or turned them away, which suitors to the king had to overcome. When John Hastings, earl of Pembroke, visited the king at Marlborough castle in the autumn of 1371 to complain about the behaviour of Reynold Lord Grey of Ruthin, he found Edward III sick and had instead to settle for an interview with William Latimer.[175] Even the king's mistress, Alice Perrers—and no-one had more influence with Edward III than she did during the king's final years—sometimes found her way to the king blocked by the chamberlain. In November 1376, Alice came to the king at Havering with a bill requesting a pardon for Richard Lyons, who had been condemned in the Good Parliament. Outside the king's chamber she met his chamberlain, Roger Beauchamp, whom she asked to give the bill to the king, but once he discovered what the bill contained, Beauchamp refused. Edward heard them arguing outside his chamber, came out, and dealt with the matter himself. In fact, he agreed to pardon Lyons (a move which Alice was later to regret), but the incident demonstrates vividly the role of the chamberlain in court politics, and the enormous responsibilities of the job.[176]

Not surprisingly, contemporaries often believed that the royal chamberlains abused their power. It may be that the increasing separation of hall and chamber during the later Middle Ages enhanced the influence of the chamberlain by isolating the king from suitors and restricting access to his person. At any rate, several chamberlains during this period were highly unpopular: William Latimer (chamberlain 1371–6) was impeached, dismissed from office and imprisoned in 1376; Simon Burley (chamberlain 1377–88) was executed in the Merciless Parliament; William le Scrope (chamberlain 1393–8) was executed at Bristol in 1399. In each case, their unpopularity stemmed essentially from the belief that they had used their position irresponsibly, to influence the king evilly, even criminally, and to feather their own nests and those of their friends. The same, of course, was also said of Robert de Vere, earl of Oxford, chief chamberlain of England from 1382 (when he came of age) until he was driven into exile in December 1387; while John Holand, earl of Huntingdon (chief chamberlain 1390–9), was clearly regarded as one of the inmost circle of the king's confidants, and lost his life trying to restore Richard to the throne in January 1400.

If the chamberlain had over-all charge of the king's chamber, the steward was the man who was ultimately responsible to the king for the efficient running, discipline, and general organisation of the rest of the household. The author of the *Traison et Mort* described Richard II's steward Thomas Percy as the 'grand master' of Richard's household, and it was Percy who formally broke his staff of office in order to disband Richard's household in August 1399.[177] Like the chamberlains, the stewards during this period were generally intimates of the king, and normally drawn from the lesser peerage. Some men held both posts: William Latimer was steward from 1368 until 1371, before becoming chamberlain, while Thomas Percy was chamberlain from 1390 to 1393, then steward from 1393 until 1399. This suggests that the two offices were regarded as of equal status. Among other stewards during these years were (under Edward III) Guy Brian, John Nevill, and John d'Ypres; (under Richard II) John Montague and John Beauchamp of Holt; and (under Henry IV) Thomas Rempston, William Heron, Thomas Erpingham (also Henry's chamberlain earlier in the reign), and John Stanley. As heads of the household, and as men close to the king with personal influence almost as great as that of the chamberlains, the stewards too incurred considerable unpopularity. John atte Lee (steward 1361–8) was disgraced and dismissed from office following his trial on charges of corruption and over-zealous prosecution of his duties in the parliament of 1368; John Nevill (steward 1371–6) was impeached and dismissed along with his friend and colleague Latimer in the Good Parliament; John Beauchamp of Holt (steward 1387–8) was, like Burley, executed in 1388; Thomas Rempston (steward 1399–1401) was dismissed from office in the parliament of 1401, while Thomas Percy, earl of Worcester, who acted as steward under both Richard II (1393–9) and Henry IV (1401–2), lost his life rebelling against the king in 1403. (Walsingham said that Henry wanted to spare Percy's life after the battle of Shrewsbury, but that the king's friends insisted on his execution.[178] Percy may have been unpopular with many of the king's more established supporters in the household, for he had been closely associated with Richard II's later rule, and was probably foisted on the household as steward in the parliament of 1401, in the hope that his experience in the royal household might help to lessen the financial chaos.)

Both the chamberlains and the stewards were primarily household officers, but they were also without doubt officers of national importance. Indeed, in the 1380s they were sometimes referred to as two of the 'five principal officers of state', along with the chancellor, treasurer, and keeper of the privy seal.[179] The chamberlain's duties kept him close to the king, but the steward had more public functions as well, both in parliament and as a sort of public prosecutor for the king in trials of important persons. It seems to have been normal for the steward to take the roll-call of the knights and burgesses at the opening of parliament, for example. He is also sometimes found making the opening address to parliament, or negotiating with the commons over matters such as the granting of subsidies or the establishment of an inter-communing committee.[180] It was the steward Richard le Scrope who presided at the trial of Alice Perrers in the parliament of October 1377, while his successor, John Devereux, formally passed judgement on the 'traitors' in the Merciless Parliament. John Montague as steward presided at the trial of John of Northampton and twelve of his associates, held in the Tower of London in September 1384, on charges which included treason; he passed sentences of death on them, though these were later commuted. And it was Thomas Rempston as steward who chaired the proceedings when the rebellious earls of January 1400 were brought before a special court at Oxford, and again sentences of death were passed.[181] The steward, of course, was quite used to chairing court proceedings, for he also presided in the court of the verge.

In conclusion, it must be emphasised that it is impossible to estimate with any real precision just how many people were in attendance at court at any one time. Many of those whom the wardrobe account books define as permanent members of the household, such as chamber knights, esquires, purveyors, and so forth, must in fact have spent a fair amount of time 'out of court'. At the same time, there were always guests, visiting foreign dignitaries (with their own servants), and hangers-on of various sorts. Moreover, all the senior members of the household (sergeants, esquires, knights, and clerks) were entitled to bring their own servants to court, and though the number of followers which each was allowed to bring was restricted, this did increase the number for whom board and lodging had to be provided.[182] Thus, while the wardrobe account books provide us with evidence of a household staff complement varying in size between 400 and 700, it is not difficult to imagine that frequently the 'court' in fact numbered well over a thousand persons.

Contemporary complaints about the royal court leave us in no doubt as to the impact it made on any neighbourhood. 'Nulla patria desiderat adventum tuum': the stark admonition of William of Pagula rings down the centuries as a reminder of how we should view the medieval royal household. The harbingers who commandeered houses for the king's followers 'as the fancy took him'; the purveyors who were so hated that the commons in 1362 could hardly bear to pronounce their name; the sergeants-at-arms and the officials of the court of the verge, who seem constantly to have ridden (very well shod, no doubt) over both local liberties and the common law; all contributed to the ever-present hostility with which ordinary people greeted the royal entourage. And when the household expanded and travelled more widely, as in the years 1395–1406, this meant primarily that the hostility became more wide-ranging. The king's servants cared little on whose toes they trod for after all, the king and his ministers had a vested interest in maintaining them. At the very beginning of Richard II's reign, the new king's mother, Princess Joan, brought a case against thirteen men who, while Edward III lived, had committed an assault on her servants at Dartford and forcibly seized her goods. All the thirteen named were carters or sumptermen in the late king's household.[183] Even the king's daughter-in-law was not immune from the depredations of his followers. Nor was it just those who had royal letters to authorise their actions whom the locals had to cope with as the army of hangers-on, from prostitutes to alms-seekers, seem to have been an inevitable accompaniment to the medieval royal court, and they too must have made their impact on any neighbourhood.

For those who had some political clout (such as a voice in parliament), there were further reasons to criticise the court. It was seen as a refuge for aliens, never popular in medieval society. Thomas Walsingham described the Bohemians in Queen Anne's entourage as shameless and unwanted guests, who lived off the fruits of England and had forgotten about their own country, and the Westminster Chronicler had few kind words to say about them either. In 1406, the commons demanded the dismissal of forty-four 'aliens' (Bretons, mostly) from Queen Joan's household.[184] The household of a medieval queen was always liable to criticism on this count, and it is worth pointing out that Philippa of Hainault had done well largely to avoid similar criticism. At a more individual level, it is remarkable how many of those who held senior posts in the household (the stewards and chamberlains especially, but also the keepers and controllers in Henry IV's reign) were criticised for incompetence, corruption, or malpractice during this period. That some of these individuals were incompetent or corrupt is surely difficult to deny, but the sheer volume of criticism directed at the household and those who belonged to it is indicative of something more: a general disbelief in the idea that the royal household provided much more than an institutionalised forum for uncontrolled politicking and royally-backed law-breaking.

CHAPTER II

Finance

EXPENDITURE AND INCOME

THE complexities of medieval English government finance are considerable, and have been the subject of some controversy. The problem does not lie (as it does in France, for instance) in the survival of adequate documentation. Indeed it must be said at the outset that the records for a study of household finance in this period are, in summary form, almost complete, in addition to which there are more or less complete wardrobe account books which allow more detailed investigation of household finance for some twelve out of the fifty-three years. So it is possible to establish with almost total accuracy the official level of both income and expenditure for the wardrobe, great wardrobe, and privy wardrobe (though not for the king's chamber, for which there are virtually no accounts).[1] The problem lies in the interpretation of the accounts, and relates particularly to household income rather than to expenditure. It is vital, therefore, at each stage of the investigation, to be clear as to the questions needed to be asked of the records, and the first of these is, what was the level of expenditure in the household departments during the years 1360–1413?

The wardrobe of the household

There were four principal spending departments of the royal household: wardrobe, great wardrobe, privy wardrobe, and chamber. The most important—and the most expensive—of these was the wardrobe. The wardrobe had two principal areas of financial responsibility: firstly, the daily living expenses of the king and *domus*, and secondly, the recurrent personal expenses of the king. The day-to-day expenses of the *domus* were entered mainly under the *Dieta*, a daily total recording how much was expended in each of the service offices of the household (buttery, kitchen, and so forth) on each day of the accounting period. These expenses consisted, naturally enough, of food and drink for all those resident in the household at the time, coal, wood and faggots for heating and cooking, crockery, cutlery and storage vessels, candles, rushes, table- and bed-linen, hay, oats and litter for the horses, and the wages of those in court.

Apart from the *Dieta*, there were the 'foreign expenses', inevitably incurred by an institution of this size and itemised under various headings, most notably the fees and robes of household servants, the wages of huntsmen and falconers, the cost of buying new horses, and a whole miscellany of incidental expenses such as medicines, compensation for persons whose lodgings had been requisitioned for the household and damaged during the period of occupation, expenses of messengers and foreign ambassadors lodged at hostelries at the king's expense, minor repairs to houses where the king was staying, and everyday purchases such as ink-horns, parchment, bowls and jars. Many of these were classified under *necessaria*. Among the more personal expenses of the king may be classified medicines 'pro corpore regis'; gifts for good service, for example to a huntsman who had organised a good day's hunting, a cook who had prepared a special meal, minstrels, or the men from Essex who wrestled in Richard II's presence; gifts—often in the form of wine, received annually—to the king's personal friends; purchases of silver plate for the king's own use; and the routine alms of the king.[2] All these expenses were usually itemised under such headings as alms, necessaries, purchase of horses, replacement of horses, fees and robes, gifts, messengers, hunting expenses and hawking expenses. In general all items tended to rise or fall with the numbers in the household, although 'fees and robes' did not fluctuate as much as the others because on the whole large increases in household numbers occurred mainly at the lower (and thus cheaper) end of the hierarchy.

The table of wardrobe accounts in Appendix I show that these living expenses fluctuated very considerably, from a low of just under £12,000 in 1386–7, to a peak of over £37,000 in 1397–8. Looking first at wardrobe expenditure during the last seventeen years of Edward III's reign, two fairly clear trends are apparent. Firstly, a steady rise during the early 1360s, from an annual average of a little over £16,000 in 1360–1, up to a peak of over £25,000 in 1364–6, and remaining at a high level until 1368. Secondly, a sharp drop in 1368–9 from over £22,000 in the previous year down to *c*. £15,000, with this lower level of expenditure being broadly maintained through until the end of the reign (although the account for 1371–3, which included about £1,500 of expenses connected with the war, and the 1376–7 account, which included a roughly similar amount spent on Edward III's funeral, saw somewhat higher expenditure).

The steady rise in wardrobe expenditure during the early 1360s is to be explained by increasing personal extravagance on Edward III's part following the cessation of the French war in 1360, and it is a trend which is discernible in other household departments and in the office of the King's Works. Edward, basking in the glory of his French triumphs, and now slipping into middle age, took the opportunity afforded by the Treaty of Brétigny to rebuild and refurnish several of the royal residences, and generally to improve his standard of living. However, this shift in the pattern of expenditure away from military commitments towards domestic extravagance soon began to give rise to worries among both the officials at the exchequer and the commons in parliament, and from 1365 at least pressure was clearly mounting for the king to moderate his domestic spending.[3] No doubt this was a factor 'which helps to explain the sudden drop in wardrobe expenditure' in 1368, which is again apparent in other departments of the household, but at first sight the steep and sudden nature of this decrease is not easy to explain. It was not caused by the death of Queen Philippa (whose household had been merged with the king's in 1360) for she did not die until August 1369, nearly two years after the economies had begun.[4] It may have been, at least in part, the consequence of a cost-cutting exercise on the part of the new keeper of the wardrobe, Thomas Brantingham. The last account presented by Brantingham's predecessor, William Gunthorpe, lasted for a rather strange one year and twelve days, which strongly suggests that he was replaced at short notice, perhaps in order to bring in a new keeper capable of enforcing real economies. Brantingham was clearly a very able minister: he was to become treasurer of England in June 1369, and bishop of Exeter in May 1370. Despite his dismissal from the treasurership during the financial crisis of 1371, he later received a vote of confidence from the council when he was restored to the office in 1377, and Richard II again made him treasurer in May 1389. It may be significant that Brantingham and his successor Henry Wakefield, the two keepers of the wardrobe under whom expenditure was at its lowest, were the only two keepers of the wardrobe during this period whose ability was recognised by elevation to the episcopate.

Yet ultimately the determination to cut wardrobe expenditure must have come from the king himself, and here two factors were probably uppermost in the king's mind. Firstly, the pressure from parliament, manifested again in 1368 when the wool subsidy was renewed at a lower rate than that granted in 1365, and only at the price of certain royal concessions. Secondly, it must have been apparent to Edward by early 1368 that the peace with France was becoming increasingly precarious. English and French interference in Castile, the negotiations over Margaret of Flanders' marriage, and the restlessness of the Gascon lords under the oppressive rule of the Black Prince all served to heighten tension, and it was in June 1368 that the first *formal* appeal (that of Armagnac) was laid before the French *parlement*. These factors must have persuaded the king that large sums would soon be needed for the prosecution of the war again, and that accordingly he must moderate his domestic expenses. The growing need for money for the war during the last nine years of the reign, the declining activity of Edward himself, and the death of Queen Philippa and consequent reduction in the size of the household, all helped to keep expenses around this lower level (between £14,000 and £18,000) until Edward's death.

For the first seven years of Richard II's reign wardrobe expenditure was maintained at an admirably low level, varying between £13,500 and £16,000 except in 1381–2, when there was the king's wedding and Queen Anne's coronation to pay for and expenses for the year topped £18,000 (royal weddings, coronations, and funerals usually added at least £1,500 to the wardrobe's annual bill). From 1384 to 1386 there was a slight rise in expenditure, although it was still only marginally higher than during the last years of Edward III's reign. Nevertheless, the Commission of Government took power in November 1386 with a mandate to effect economies wherever possible, and despite the relative moderation of Richard II's household expenses during the early years of the reign, the commissioners proceeded to slash substantially the amount of money passed on from exchequer to wardrobe between 1386 and 1389, with the result that wardrobe expenditure during these years averaged only £12,800 *per annum*, making this the cheapest three-year period for the wardrobe throughout the years 1360–1413. Following Richard's resumption of power in May 1389, however, wardrobe expenses began to rise. Between 1389 and 1395 they rose gradually, but steadily, from *c*. £16,000 to *c*. £19,000. After 1395, the upward trend exploded. In 1395–6 Richard's wardrobe expenses reached £26,161, even though he had no queen to support. During the last three years of his reign, when he did have a queen to support (though she was still only a child, and could hardly have proved too costly), his wardrobe expenses averaged over £36,650 *per annum*. The expenses incurred in 1396–7 are to be explained partly by the magnificence with which Richard celebrated the conclusion of the twenty-eight-year truce with France and his own marriage to Isabella of France at Calais in late 1396. Walsingham reckoned that Richard spent over 300,000 marks (£200,000) on the Calais jamboree, and several other chroniclers commented on the splendour of the occasion. Even if the true figure (which is unobtainable) were only a tenth of Walsingham's obviously wild exaggeration, it was evidently a remarkably lavish affair and cost the exchequer a great deal of money.[5] What is perhaps more remarkable is that such a high level of expenditure was maintained for the following two years. The increased size of the household (including no doubt the cost of maintaining the bodyguard of Cheshiremen who apparently went everywhere with Richard during the last two years of the reign, and who numbered over 300), together with the inordinate extravagance and love of finery of the king himself, must be considered as the principal factors contributing to such recklessly high expenditure.[6]

Despite the criticism voiced about Richard II's extravagance at the time of his deposition, his supplanter continued to maintain wardrobe expenses at a fairly high level for most of the first seven years of his reign. Apart from a period of some eighteen months between March 1401 and September 1402 (when wardrobe expenses were around the £22,000 mark), Henry IV's wardrobe was spending over £27,000 *per annum* on average between October 1399 and December 1406. During the first eighteen months of the new reign expenditure was particularly high, averaging nearly £32,000 on an annual basis, although it must be said in mitigation of Henry that this figure includes certain expenses which had not normally been covered by the wardrobe during the second half of the fourteenth century. Nevertheless, the principal cause of this continuing high level of expenditure was not that the keeper of the wardrobe had taken on new financial responsibilities, but that the king continued to maintain a large and apparently extravagant domestic establishment. This led to repeated, often bitter, attacks on the royal household, most notably in the parliaments of 1401, January 1404, and 1406, so that eventually Henry was forced to bow to public pressure and reduce the cost of his household's daily expenses. Reform came with the appointment of John Tiptoft as keeper in December 1406 (the first layman to hold that post), and was broadly maintained during the last six years of the reign. Between December 1406 and March 1413 (when Henry IV died), wardrobe expenses averaged *c*. £19,700 a year, which, although still considered excessive by some of the king's critics, was clearly a marked improvement on the situation between 1395 and 1406. Henry's illness, and the consequent decline of his personal participation in government for at least part of the latter half of his reign, probably helped to keep wardrobe expenditure at a lower level.

The great and privy wardrobes

The second principal spending department of the household was the great wardrobe. From 1361 onwards, it was permanently situated in a large house just behind Baynard's Castle, close to both St Paul's and the Thames, which Edward III had purchased from John Beauchamp, brother of the earl of Warwick, in 1360, and which was to remain the home of the great wardrobe until it was burned down in 1666.[7] When required, however, the departmental staff might still be obliged to decamp and join the king and household, as they did, for instance, for the campaigns of 1385, 1394–5, and 1399.

The principal commodity of the great wardrobe was cloth. The keeper of the great wardrobe was however the head of a federation of royal servants all of whom were accountable to him and for most of the period considered here the four main sub-departments of the great wardrobe were headed by the tailor, armourer, pavilioner and embroiderer. Apart from cloth, the keeper of the great wardrobe also provided valuable commodities such as spices and wax for the household. His main link-man with the *domus* was the clerk of the spicery (or usher of the wardrobe) with whom he drew up regular indentures—as he did with his other four subordinates—detailing transfers of materials or provisions.

The keeper of the great wardrobe spent most of his money on purchasing cloth, furs and linen, which were then distributed by him to anyone to whom the king ordered him to distribute it, members of the household, personal friends of the king, or the king's Cambridge scholars, for instance. Much cloth was also used to make hangings, coverings and so forth at the various houses where the king resided. Robes and garters were made for the knights of the garter each year and in 1375, for instance, the king's armourer made 1,808 blue garters for the St George's Day festivities, each one embroidered with the motto 'honi soit qui mal y pense'.[8] It was also the responsibility of the keeper to provide cloth and robes for tournaments, marriages, funerals, anniversaries, and for the king to give to religious houses, and to keep the chapel royal within the household fully supplied with vestments, crucifixes, altar-cloths, missals, and portable altars. Trappings for the royal horses were also his business. At each of the principal royal residences remained an officer called the keeper of the king's beds, with whom the keeper of the great wardrobe liaised regularly to ensure that stocks were sufficient for a royal visit.[9] Clothes made for the king himself were made by the king's tailor and despatched to the keeper of the 'privy wardrobe of the king's chamber', not to be confused with the privy wardrobe in the Tower. Great events could prove very costly: for Princess Joan's funeral in 1385, for example, the keeper had to provide special mourning robes for four earls, ten bannerets, fifty-four knights, forty-eight clerks, 161 esquires and sergeants, 157 valets, eighteen minstrels, and a further 320 lesser servants of the king.[10] The cost of the truce-wedding festivities at Calais in 1396 was clearly enormous.

Great wardrobe expenses are shown in Table I on p. 82. They are complete apart from the periods 1387–90 and 1412–13, for which no accounts survive, and again they show considerable fluctuations, from the £1,383 of 1372–3, to the very untypical £17,717 of 1399–1400. Although the pattern of expenditure in the great wardrobe follows broadly similar lines to that of the wardrobe, there are at the same time significant differences. High expenditure in late 1360 and early 1361 may well be accounted for by provision of materials for the king's ceremonial visit to Calais to ratify the Treaty of Brétigny, but in the next year expenses dropped sharply before beginning to rise again through to the same peak in 1365–6 as has been observed in the wardrobe's pattern. In late 1367 there was a sudden fall in expenses, coinciding almost perfectly with the similar fall in wardrobe expenses which is observable from February 1368. Expenses continued to decline gradually until late 1371, when they dropped more sharply, and during the following three years (November 1371 to November 1374) they averaged only £1,464 *per annum*, making this by quite a long way the cheapest three-year period in this study (although the years 1387–90 may well have been equally cheap). The increased expenditure during the last few years of the reign is accounted for largely by the cost of providing cloth for Edward III's funeral. It is reasonable to assume that those same factors which had persuaded the king to moderate his wardrobe expenses were also responsible for persuading him to moderate his great wardrobe expenses.

For the first ten years of Richard II's reign expenditure in the great wardrobe remained at a thoroughly moderate level, reaching a peak of £3,823 *per annum* between 1381 and 1383 (when there was the king's wedding and Anne's coronation to provide for). It is a great pity that accounts for the period 1387–90 do not survive, for it would be interesting to know whether the Appellants were successful in enforcing economies in the great wardrobe to the same extent as they were in the wardrobe; the probability is that they were. From November 1390 the accounts begin again, and continue uninterrupted until the deposition. They show the same steep rise as in the wardrobe, only beginning three years earlier. From 1392 until 1394 Richard's great wardrobe expenses averaged nearly £8,000 *per annum*, and from 1394 onwards, just over

Table 1: Expenses of the great wardrobe 1360–1413

Period	Keeper	Expenses (£)	Annual Average (£)
1 Nov 1360–29 June 1361	John Newbury	5,051	7,650
30 June 1361–29 June 1362	Henry Snaith	3,921	
30 June 1362–29 June 1363	Henry Snaith	5,361	
30 June 1363–29 June 1364	Henry Snaith	7,859	
30 June 1364–29 June 1365	Henry Snaith	8,586	
30 June 1365–29 June 1366	Henry Snaith	11,718	
30 June 1366–29 Sept 1367	Henry Snaith	11,992	9,599
30 Sept 1367–29 Sept 1368	Henry Snaith	5,793	
30 Sept 1368–29 Sept 1369	Henry Snaith	4,612	
30 Sept 1369–29 Sept 1370	Henry Snaith	4,401	
30 Sept 1370–7 Nov 1371	Henry Snaith	3,580	3,234
24 Nov 1371–23 Nov 1372	John Sleford	1,533	
24 Nov 1372–23 Nov 1373	John Sleford	1,383	
24 Nov 1373–23 Nov 1374	John Sleford	1,478	
24 Nov 1374–30 Sept 1377	John Sleford	8,179 (two accounts)	2,871
1 Oct 1377–30 Sept 1379	Alan Stokes	4,284	2,142
1 Oct 1379–30 Sept 1381	Alan Stokes	5,835	2,918
1 Oct 1381–30 Sept 1383	Alan Stokes	7,646	3,823
1 Oct 1383–30 Sept 1385	Alan Stokes	6,872	3,436
1 Oct 1385–30 Sept 1387	Alan Stokes	7,064	3,532
1 Oct 1387–29 Nov 1390	Alan Stokes	no accounts	
30 Nov 1390–30 Sept 1392	Richard Clifford	8,032	4,382
1 Oct 1392–30 Sept 1394	Richard Clifford	15,838	7,919
1 Oct 1394–10 Apr 1398	Richard Clifford	45,226	12,826
11 Apr 1398–30 Sept 1398	John Maclesfield	3,770	7,954
1 Oct 1398–30 Sept 1399	John Maclesfield	11,924	
1 Oct 1399–30 Sept 1400	William Loveney	17,717	
1 Oct 1400–30 Sept 1401	William Loveney	8,665	
1 Oct 1401–30 Sept 1402	William Loveney	7,772	
1 Oct 1402–30 Sept 1403	William Loveney	10,343	
1 Oct 1403–30 Sept 1404	William Loveney	2,698	
1 Oct 1404–30 Sept 1405	William Loveney	3,571	
1 Oct 1405–30 Sept 1406	William Loveney	2,183	
1 Oct 1406–30 Sept 1407	William Loveney	3,290	
1 Oct 1407–30 Apr 1408	William Loveney	1,556	2,679
1 May 1408–30 Sept 1409	Richard Clifford	4,461	3,143
1 Oct 1409–31 Mar 1412	Richard Clifford	5,634	2,255
1 Apr 1412–20 Mar 1413	Thomas Ringwood	no account	

£12,000 *per annum*. As far as the surviving evidence allows of estimates as to the way in which this money was spent, it would seem that the inflation of great wardrobe expenditure was occasioned neither by the king's Irish expeditions, nor by any supplies of a military nature for the Cheshiremen during the last two or three years, but simply by the rapidly escalating acquisition of things beautiful—clothes, furs, and finery. For instance, of the £15,838 spent in 1392–4, a total of £6,203 was spent on mercery, £2,219 on furs, and £4,431 on drapery, bought mostly from London merchants.[11] The 1394–8 account, although lacking the same degree of detail as its predecessor, also includes large sums paid to London mercers and furriers, as well as very considerable amounts of cloth provided for the truce-wedding festivities at Calais in 1396.[12] Thus the evidence of both wardrobe and great wardrobe accounts for the later years of Richard's reign suggests that the sharply increased consumption of the household was caused principally by the conspicuous consumption of luxury goods which Richard was accused of by both Thomas Haxey and the chroniclers.

During the first four years of his reign, Henry IV's great wardrobe expenses remained very high, averaging £11,124 *per annum* between October 1399 and September 1403. After this, however, they fell dramatically and in 1403–4 great wardrobe expenditure totalled only £2,698. During the next eight years this moderate level was consistently maintained, the annual average expenditure for the whole period from October 1403 to March 1412 being only £2,752. There is no surviving account for the final year of the reign, but there is nothing to suggest that this low level of expenditure was not maintained through until Henry's death. The abnormally high level of expenditure during the first year of Henry's reign (£17,717) has been explained as the cost of a new king refurbishing his court, while in 1402-3, the only other occasion during the reign when the annual total passed the £10,000 mark, Henry had to pay for his own marriage and the coronation of his new queen; nevertheless, such a high level of expenditure can only really be explained by the altogether excessive generosity of the new king to his supporters, and the extravagance which he evidently thought befitting of his new station. The military campaigns of these years made little impression on the level of expenditure, for the great wardrobe was rarely involved to any significant degree in paying expenses of war.[13] It is worth noting, however, that the real decline in great wardrobe expenditure preceded by some three years the decline in wardrobe expenditure, which dates from 1406–7. This was probably due to pressure from parliaments (in 1401 and, more particularly, in January 1404) to moderate household expenses, as well as the king's own realisation that if he did not do something to cut the cost of his household, royal finances might break down completely. What this means is that while the period of really high expenditure in the wardrobe was from 1395 to 1406, the equivalent period in the great wardrobe was from 1392 to 1403, and there is doubtless some significance in this three-year 'interlude'. Very probably, it indicates the fact that it was considerably easier both to increase and to cut expenditure in the great wardrobe. The great wardrobe spent its money on *objects*, often beautiful and very expensive ones;

the primary factor determining wardrobe expenditure, on the other hand, was the number of *people* in the household. Inevitably the process of recruiting new members of the household and of discharging them from it was more drawn-out and, in the latter case, more strongly resisted by the king, than the process of acquiring or ceasing to acquire the trappings of luxury. Thus, while the increase in great wardrobe expenditure may be taken as, so to speak, 'evidence of intent' on Richard's behalf to spend more on his court from *c.* 1392 onwards, equally, the decline in great wardrobe expenditure suggests that from 1403 onwards Henry was serious in his desire to curb his domestic expenditure.

The privy wardrobe was, by a long way, the cheapest of the four main household spending departments, and was less intimately associated with the royal household than the wardrobe, great wardrobe, and chamber. It was essentially a storehouse for armour and weaponry, situated in the Tower of London, receiving and collecting supplies of military hardware and disbursing them as and when needed to royal armies or other royal servants. The stock of weaponry kept was impressive: an indenture drawn up in February 1396 when John Lufwyk took up the post of keeper of the privy wardrobe listed 796 basinets, 442 long lances, 8,076 'small lances called dartes', 2,328 bows, 740 aventails, 5 springalds, 1,392 coats of mail, 125 cross-bows, 11,300 quarrels (square-headed arrows for cross-bows) with 25,500 spare quarrel-heads, 14,280 arrows of various sorts for long-bows, 187 war-hatchets, 107 pounds of saltpetre, 1,356 cannonballs, and 350 tampions for cannons.[14] It is interesting to note that Richard II (or his advisors) put a new man, John Hatfield, in charge of the privy wardrobe on the very day that Edward III died—even though Edward only died at about 7 p.m.[15] Just as it was important for the king to keep a substantial cash reserve in his chamber in case of emergency, so was it important for him to keep a substantial reserve of weaponry under his personal control. Members of the household ordered out of court on military business were regularly provided with equipment from the privy wardrobe, and it is of some interest to note that when the king moved into the Tower to await the arrival of the Appellant army at Christmas 1387, men were promptly put to work to repair the cannons and to move two springalds from the 'great hall' within the Tower into the actual tower in which the king was to lodge.[16] The Tower, provided with massive defences, and providing ready access to the royal weapon-store, was the obvious place for any king to take refuge, be it from the mob of 1381 or the disaffected earls of 1387.

What is perhaps surprising is how little it cost the king to amass such a sizeable store of equipment. This was partly because the sheriffs were supposed to provide much of the weaponry kept there and arrange for it to be transported to the Tower, for which they deducted appropriate sums from their farms when they came to account at the exchequer. Nevertheless the cost of the privy wardrobe emphasises the fact that one of the most significant differences between medieval and modern warfare is that whereas in those days it was the payment of men which cost large sums of money, now it is the cost of weaponry. Accounts of the privy wardrobe survive for the whole period 1360 to 1407, after which they cease. During the last seventeen years of Edward III's reign privy wardrobe expenditure averaged just over £408 a year; under Richard II it averaged £209 a year, and between 1399 and 1406, £477. There are few fluctuations of any significance.[17] After 1407 the keepers of the privy wardrobe ceased to present accounts, and the weapon-store in the Tower dwindled into insignificance for the rest of Henry IV's reign. But of course this did not mean that the king had ceased to maintain a personal store of weaponry, but simply that Henry now used the chamber as the repository for it—which meant that it was even closer at hand. The king's gunner, Gerard Sprong, who worked within the chamber, was the man now responsible for keeping it. This was not the final demise of the privy wardrobe, however, for Henry V revived it during the early stages of his French wars.[18]

The chamber

The last of the four main spending departments of the household was the king's chamber. The chamber is both the most intriguing and the most elusive of the four, intriguing because it was so personal to the king, elusive because there are no proper chamber accounts surviving from this period. Accounts were almost certainly kept, but the receivers of the chamber probably accounted personally to the king rather than to the officials of the exchequer, and thus they have not been preserved. A few scrappy documents concerned with the chamber's business have survived, but they are usually just short lists of jewels or plate transferred from one place to another, or acquired at a particular time, and they afford no impression whatsoever of the overall receipts or expenses of the chamber. It is thus impossible to give a full picture of chamber finances. However, it is possible to record fairly precisely the amount of money passed from exchequer to chamber, for these sums are recorded in the exchequer issue rolls, and to assert with confidence, even though the picture is built up from impressionistic rather than statistical evidence, that there were times during this period when the wealth of the chamber was immense. In times of crisis, whether personal or financial, the importance of this personal hoard could be very great.

The money which the king kept in his chamber was his pocket-money. It was for his own personal and private expenses (as distinct from the money passed to the wardrobe, for instance, which was for the maintenance of his household and his *routine* personal expenses; almsgiving and gift-giving were very largely routine occupations for a king). He could spent it on precisely whatever he wished to spend it on, without having to justify his expenditure to anybody. Broadly, he did one of two things with it: either he spent it on himself, to buy jewels and plate, for instance, falcons, books, paintings, special gifts for friends and visiting dignitaries, occasional annuities even (John Golafre, Richard II's chamber knight, was in receipt of a £20 annuity in the chamber in

1386); or he ploughed it back into the exchequer to meet expenses, usually military, which the exchequer was unable to cover. Officially, money transferred to the exchequer (or wardrobe, as sometimes happened) from the chamber was often classified as a loan, but just how much of it was repaid is not always clear.[19]

Although the king might do what he liked with his chamber money, that did not mean that he could have as much money in his chamber as he wanted to do what he liked with. There was an element of 'accountability' for chamber expenditure, but it was enforced through regulation of the amount of money passed from exchequer to chamber rather than through audit of expenditure incurred. After the abolition of the system of reserving certain lands to provide revenue for the chamber (which lasted from 1333 to 1356, and which coincides with the close of the last proper chamber account of the fourteenth century), the chamber was normally financed by a *certum* from the exchequer—a fixed annual sum, handed over from the officials of the exchequer in theoretically regular instalments to the receiver of the chamber. This gives us at least a starting-point for estimates of chamber income, but it is no more than a starting-point, for it is abundantly clear that all three kings regularly drew upon many other, thoroughly miscellaneous, sources in order to swell chamber receipts. Fines, ransoms, profits of alien priories, temporalities *sede vacante*, licences for chantries, town charter fees, and traitors' chattels were some of the more common sources. These could increase chamber income enormously. When they were impeached in the Good Parliament, Latimer and Lyons were accused of selling licences to merchants allowing them to export wool to places other than Calais, at a charge of 11*s.* per sack; their defence was that they had done so with the knowledge of the king, and had dutifully passed all the money received from such licences into the chamber. If this were true, this could have made the chamber richer by about £6,000 or £7,000 *per annum*, about as much again as the official *certum*.[20] But we have no way of verifying this. It is just one of the many imponderables of chamber finance.

Table 2 below shows the actual amount of money passed from exchequer to chamber between 1360 and 1413, worked out over eight periods each of which has a certain unity.[21] Theoretically, a *certum* was in force from 1360 to 1377, 1380 to 1403, and 1408 to 1411, but in practice it is often difficult to disentangle payments made on account of the *certum* from additional sums requested by the king from the exchequer, and the exchequer officials themselves seem sometimes to have been unsure as to whether the money they were passing to the receiver was on account of the *certum* or not. There were three periods during which the amount of money passed from exchequer to chamber was substantial: from 1356 to 1377, from 1392 to 1399, and from 1406 to 1413. These periods only partially coincide with periods of high spending in the wardrobe and great wardrobe, which suggests that the chamber was not susceptible to the same degree of pressure (from parliament, or council) to moderate expenditure as were the wardrobes. Indeed there was virtually no overt criticism of any aspect of chamber finance throughout this period, probably because

Table 2: *Chamber receipts from exchequer (annual averages)*

Period	(*Certum*)	Total
1360–June 1377	(£6,667)	£6,667
June 1377–Sept 1380	—	£ 940
Sept 1380–Sept 1382	(£1,500)	£2,100
Sept 1382–Sept 1386	(£2,000)	£2,000
Sept 1386–Sept 1392	(? £2,000)	£3,400
Sept 1392–Sept 1399	(£4,000)	£7,000
Sept 1399–Dec 1406	(? £4,000)	£4,300
Dec 1406–Mar 1413	(? £5,333)	£8,000

it would have been considered as too personal a criticism of the king. The chamber, therefore, might be useful to the king as an alternative channel for funds: if he was forced to reduce receipt in the wardrobe or great wardrobe, he might increase chamber receipts to compensate—as it seems Henry IV did after 1406, and perhaps Richard II did too after 1386. What he then did with these funds was nobody's business but the king's and he could even pass them on to the wardrobe, as for instance Henry IV did, to the tune of £5,455 in 1405 and 1406, when the wardrobe was finding it desperately hard to get cash.[22] But in general we know very little about chamber expenditure. Some of its money was certainly spent on jewels and plate, and the jewels, plate and spare cash remaining would be hoarded by the receiver of the chamber, to be used as pledges for loans, or passed back to one of the other departments when cash there ran out. However, although we know so little about the details of chamber finance in the fourteenth century, it would be very unwise to under-estimate either its wealth or its importance.

There are two periods in particular when there is evidence suggesting that the chamber was extremely wealthy: the 1360s, and the late 1390s. Edward III's personal wealth in the 1360s came principally from the French ransoms won at Crécy, Poitiers, and elsewhere, most notably of course the ransom of the French King John himself (set at £500,000, of which over half was probably paid). The amount of money which Edward received from these ransoms, and the uses to which he put it, have recently been analysed by Dr Harriss.[23] Between 1357 and 1364 Edward seems to have received about 25,000 marks from the ransom of Charles de Blois, 20,000 marks from the ransom of the Scottish King David, £40,000 from the ransom with whch the duke of Burgundy bought off the English in 1359–60, and £166,666 from King John's ransom. This totals £236,666. Of the French king's ransom, £4,000 was paid into the chamber, £64,437 was spent very largely on military needs (over half of this went to the Black Prince in Gascony), £46,154 was spent by the exchequer in other ways which are not traceable with certainty (although in fact most of this seems to have been spent on military activities, too), and £47,171 was left in the Tower, which was in effect acting as a subsidiary chamber at this time. Most of the money accruing from the other three ransoms was also devoted to military purposes, partly to pay off war debts from before 1360, and partly to subsidise English occupation in Brittany, Normandy and Gascony. As Dr Harriss points out, the king regarded these ransoms as his personal wealth. But that does not mean that he used them selfishly. 'Up to the end of 1364,' remarks Dr Harriss, 'the king's expenditure of the ransoms was very largely controlled in his own interest.' This depends on whether one regards 'establishing his son in Gascony' as paternal benevolence or as a necessary element in the English war effort—and the same is true of the payments made to Breton and Norman commanders.

Little further was received from the ransoms in 1365, but between 1366 and 1369, Dr Harriss estimates that Edward received at least a further £84,103 from these and similar sources. In addition there was still the unspent residue of £47,171 from the French ransom, and in 1368 Edward received at least a further £12,400 from the duke of Milan, given to him as a marriage-portion when his son Lionel married the duke's daughter, Violante. As the renewal of the war became inevitable, however, Edward soon showed himself willing 'to commit his gains of war once more to the hazard, to lose all or to win again'.[24] Between November 1368 and June 1369, the exchequer receipt rolls record a total of over £133,400 received from these sources, of which £12,400 came from the Milanese marriage-portion, and the rest from the chamber or directly from the ransoms (this includes the residue of £47,171). During the previous year (November 1367 to November 1368), the chamber had loaned a further £8,046 to the exchequer, and between August 1369 and July 1371 there followed another £6,380. After this, loans from the chamber to the exchequer slowed down, although further substantial sums were sometimes transferred, like the £4,766, which was no doubt used to finance the king's own abortive expedition from Sandwich, handed over on 28 September 1372.[25] Between 1368 and 1377, Edward in fact transferred a total of more than £160,000 of his personal wealth, from the chamber, the Tower hoard, and the ransom instalments which continued to accrue, into the exchequer, the vast majority of which was spent on military needs. Some of the smaller sums were marked with repayment dates, but the larger sums were not even marked as loans, and it is unlikely that even as much as ten percent of this total was ever repaid to the chamber. Combining this with the evidence which Harriss has compiled from the exchequer rolls between 1357 and 1368, it becomes clear that Edward had actually committed something in the order of £300,000, and probably more, of what he was perfectly entitled by the *mores* of the day to regard as his personal wealth, to the English war effort (it is impossible to be absolutely clear as to the amount because it is not always possible to trace how the money was spent, although the assignments are often verifiable from the issue rolls). How much that left him with, we do not know, but relatively speaking it may not have been a great deal.

Of course it may not have been Edward's original intention to part with his money in this way. In the mid 1360s he was spending lavishly in the wardrobe, great wardrobe, and the Royal Works, and it may well be that royal ministers were worried by the king's domestic extravagance. Yet whatever Edward's original intentions may have been, he was prepared, once the prospect of war loomed again, both to cut back substantially on his domestic expenses, and to prop up the ailing exchequer with his own money—probably realising full well that it was unlikely that he would see most of it again. The history of the chamber in the 1360s (insofar as it can be written) demonstrates just how important a part it could play in national finance. In effect, it acted as a storehouse of great wealth during the halcyon days, and a vital source of ready cash once those days were over. During the first two years following the renewal of war in 1369, the exchequer was finding it desperately difficult to get money with which to finance English expeditions, partly because it took time for a grant of taxation actually to be converted into cash in the exchequer.[26] Without the chamber money, it is difficult to see how it might have coped.

Not until the last few years of his reign does Richard II seem to have acquired any sizeable store of personal wealth in his chamber. Between 1377 and 1386 chamber receipts from the exchequer averaged only about a quarter of Edward III's *certum*, and some at least of Richard's jewels and plate were transferred to the exchequer so that they could either be used as pledges for loans, or even sold off to pay creditors. The transfer occurred on 11 May 1378, and the transactions involving the king's treasure were supervised by the royal clerk John Bacon, an intimate of the young king, who was both chamberlain of the exchequer and receiver of the chamber, and was later to become Richard's secretary.[27] Between this date and September 1382, Bacon sold off jewels to a total value of £17,390; the sale was recorded in September each year, but presumably they were sold off gradually through the year as needs pressed and only entered at the end of the year, once Bacon's account had been audited by members of the council.[28] In addition, between these years Bacon regularly pledged several thousands of pounds' worth of jewels and plate as security for loans, and on at least one occasion the jewels could not be redeemed, so that the lender (Robert Knolles) was allowed to keep them. The jewels kept by Knolles were valued at over £2,000.[29] This policy of selling and pledging the king's jewels ended in September 1382—although by then nearly £20,000 worth of them had been disposed of permanently. Presumably Richard, by now taking a more active personal role in government, put his foot down and demanded the return of his jewels to the chamber to prevent them from being used to pay off his or his grandfather's debts.

By the late 1390s, there is some evidence to suggest that the chamber was once again very wealthy, although this evidence is largely incidental in nature and it is impossible to·quantify the sum. There were certainly rumours about Richard's personal wealth. The commons in Henry IV's first parliament claimed (correctly) that in his will Richard had bequeathed the first £20,000 of his gold (*sic*) for the payment of his household debts, and demanded an enquiry into the whereabouts of the former king's treasure.[30] One chronicler reported Richard's personal wealth at the end of his reign as £300,000 in cash and at least as much again in jewels and plate.[31] Verifiable facts are less easy to come

D

by, and Richard's reckless extravagance during his last years may have meant that much of the wealth that he should have been able to accumulate was dissipated. But exchequer liveries to the chamber were certainly generous after 1392, averaging just over £7,000 *per annum*, and from 1396 onwards the king also had his new bride's dowry; this had been set at 800,000 francs (£133,333), and, according to Dr Palmer, the first three instalments were paid 'promptly and in full' by Charles VI. From this, Richard would have acquired £83,333 between 1396 and 1399, and it is quite clear (and quite reasonable) that he regarded this as his personal money, even if he might use it to make loans to the exchequer.[32] More specifically, there is the acquittance given to John Ikelyngton, a trusted royal clerk at the end of Richard's reign, by Henry IV in November 1400. This stated that Richard had committed to Ikelyngton the sum of 65,946 marks (£43,964), together with many goods and jewels 'ad magnam summam se extendentia', out of which Ikelyngton was only to make gifts or payments with the special warrant of the king. Ikelyngton had in fact deposited this cash and treasure at Holt castle (Clwyd), and, according to the acquittance, had indeed made certain payments out of it (quantity unspecified), and he now handed over the residue to Henry and received acquittance.[33] It is very unlikely that the payments made by Ikelyngton on Richard's instructions had been substantial, for the real reason why Ikelyngton had been given the money was in order to fulfil the cash bequests stipulated in Richard's will (of which he was an executor). These cash bequests amounted in total to 91,000 marks, and the king's will states that, in addition to the money given to Ikelyngton, a further 24,000 marks had been deposited with Thomas Holand, duke of Surrey, to be used for the same purpose.[34] All this certainly suggests that Richard was not short of ready cash for his personal use at the end of his reign, but if he had hoped that it might be of use to him in his hour of need, he was disappointed. In the end it seems to have been his supplanter who benefited from Richard's cash hoard.

Under Henry IV, the king's chamber money was put to rather different purposes, although this was not because the king willed it, but because the chronic shortage of cash in the exchequer (and hence in the wardrobe) enhanced the value of the chamber as a source of ready money. In effect, it seems that Henry was frequently forced to use his chamber money as a back-up for the household when he was unable to secure supplies of cash from the exchequer with which to cover the expenses of the wardrobe. There were two periods of the reign when this was particularly necessary: 1399 to 1401, and 1405–6. Between January 1405 and January 1407 a total of £5,445 was passed by the receiver of the chamber (Thomas Ringwood) to the keeper of the wardrobe (Richard Kingston). This money was not marked as loaned (although it was itemised separately from the rest of the wardrobe's receipt); nor was it handed over in large sums, but sporadically, to meet pressing commitments, in some ninety-five small and irregular sums, many of which were clearly just redeeming bills and tallies issued by the wardrobe (as is stated in the preamble to the list of payments).[35] Between October 1399 and March 1401 even larger sums were probably transferred from chamber to wardrobe, possibly amounting in total to something like £10,000, although the exact figure cannot be obtained because the records of the wardrobe's receipt are incomplete.[36] Some of this probably came from Richard II's 'hoard', initially stored by Henry in his chamber, but Henry had other sources, too, to draw on for his chamber; during the first three years of the reign, for example, duchy of Lancaster revenues totalling at least £4,560 were paid into the chamber, and although they never reached the same level after 1402, the duchy continued to contribute approximately £830 on average to the chamber each year.[37]

Between 1401 and 1405, and after January 1407, the chamber transferred less of its wealth to the wardrobe (though there was a loan of £1,207 at Easter 1403), which certainly indicates that it was not Henry's wish to have his personal wealth used in this way, and that the transfers of 1399–1401 and 1405–6 were occasioned only by dire necessity.[38] Nor was Henry keen to loan his chamber money to the exchequer: only £4,676 was transferred to the exchequer over the whole reign, most of it during the early years, and it was usually repaid as rapidly as possible. Like both Edward III and Richard II, Henry naturally preferred to regard his chamber money as his pocket-money, and in fact it seems that for most of the reign the principal items of expenditure continued to be jewels and plate.[39] After 1406 the amount of money passed from exchequer to chamber nearly doubled (from *c.* £4,300 *per annum* in 1399–1406, to *c.* £8,000 *per annum* in 1407–13), and the chamber may have taken on some additional financial responsibilities, such as making payments for some of the king's weaponry. It may also be significant that during the last year of the reign Thomas Ringwood was acting as both receiver of the chamber and keeper of the great wardrobe, which might indicate greater inter-departmental co-operation; but as ever, the absence of chamber accounts makes it impossible to know exactly what these broader responsibilities consisted of. Nevertheless, it does seem clear that in general the chamber under Henry IV was more closely involved in the overall system of household finance than it had been under either of his immediate predecessors, even if this was a consequence of financial difficulties rather than of any change in the way in which Henry viewed his chamber. Ideally, any king wished, quite naturally, to keep his chamber money for his personal expenses.

The importance of the chamber in the late medieval royal financial system has been under-rated in the past. In an age of personal monarchy, it was vital for any king to have a personal hoard of ready money for use in emergencies, and it is abundantly clear that these hoards could reach enormous proportions. The jewels and plate kept in the chamber were vital too: over and over again they were used as pledges for loans to the crown, especially at times when the crown's credit was low. Normally, much of this hoard was probably carried around with the king wherever he went, in the care of his receiver of the chamber, and under the supervision of the king's chamberlain, both usually intimates of the king. When the hoard got too large to be carried around, though, it would be deposited in some stronghold for safekeeping; Edward III used the Tower, Richard II used Holt castle. This did not make it any less 'chamber money' for the chamber, in its financial sense, consisted of the sum total of treasure in the keeping of the receiver and his deputies at any given time, wherever that might be deposited. But what also emerges from a study of the chamber during this period is how important a role the chamber could play as a reserve source of instant cash in times of financial difficulty. This is starkly apparent in the years 1368–71, when most of the money needed to finance the French war was in fact Edward III's personal wealth, but it is also apparent on various occasions during the reigns of Edward's grandsons (1378– 82, 1399–1401, and 1405–6). Whatever might have been the king's true wishes, the operations of the chamber in this period suggest that the dividing line between 'crown income' and the personal wealth of the king was not as clear in practice as it was in theory. Usually the king must have hoped that exchequer loans could be raised from other sources, and that the chamber would only be used as a last resort; but occasionally it may have been the first resort, for it was very handy. Its usefulness at such times made it an important part of the national financial system.

The royal family

Between them, then, these four household departments accounted for the money spent by the king on his *domus*. But apart from the household of the king himself, there were also subsidiary royal households to be financed, that is, those of the queen and the king's children. Theoretically, both the queen and the royal children (once they had been endowed) were supposed to be finan- cially independent of the exchequer. In practice, however, they were often not, and criticism might arise when, for instance, a queen spent much of her time living, with her household, under the same roof as the king, but without mak- ing contributions to the costs of the household, which naturally pushed these costs up, something critics were not slow to point out. A precedent was estab- lished by Edward III and Queen Philippa in the 1360s. Despite the increase in her endowment from the (apparently standard) £4,500 to *c.* £7,000 *per annum*, Philippa had always had problems in making ends meet. So in May 1360 Edward decided to merge her household with his, and in return she would pay £10 a day into the wardrobe to cover the expenses of her servants. The king also paid off many of his wife's debts, amounting to at least £5,851 between 1360 and 1363. From 26 May 1360 (the date of the merger) until her death in August 1369, this £10 a day was paid regularly and in full by Philippa's recei- ver, Richard Ravenser, into the king's wardrobe, and the two households, although retaining an internal distinction between the king's and the queen's servants, were for financial purposes as one.[40] After 1369, there was no queen to support until 1382; Princess Joan, the Black Prince's widow, was supported between 1376 and 1385 by a grant of one-third of the revenues of the duchy of Cornwall.[41] Nor were any of Edward III's children a burden on the exchequer between 1360 and 1377 for the older ones had all been endowed by 1360, while Thomas of Woodstock lived in the king's household until 1373, when he was endowed with lands from the Bohun inheritance.

There were of course no royal children to support under Richard II, but there were two queens. The successful merger of 1360–9 led to the expectation that if a queen were to live under the same roof as her husband, then she should make the same sort of contribution as Philippa had made to her husband's wardrobe. This was after all why she was endowed, to support her lifestyle. Anne, as far as can be gathered, spent most of her time with Richard, although she undoubtedly had her own household servants.[42] She had moreover been endowed soon after her marriage with lands which, in theory, should have provided her with an income of £4,500 *per annum*, and occasional additions were made to this sum. Yet her contributions to Richard's wardrobe were extremely intermittent. Before the financial year 1387–8, she contributed nothing. In the Merciless Parliament there was a petition from the commons that she should contribute £10 a day to the wardrobe as Philippa had done, or else it should be deducted from her revenues.[43] Presumably the £205 received by the keeper of the king's wardrobe some time between September 1387 and September 1388 from the queen's receiver-general, Thomas More, was as a result of this petition. For the remaining six years of Anne's life, her contributions varied: £733 in 1388–9, £347 in 1389–90, £727 in 1390–1, £1,200 in both 1391–2 and 1392–3, and £809 for the truncated year from 1 October 1393 to 8 June 1394, when she died.[44] It seems that after 1391, the agreed annual sum was £1,200 (a little over £3 a day). Whether this was because Anne had fewer servants than Philippa, or was more frugal, or only spent part of the year with Richard, is not clear. Richard's second wife, Isabella of France, made no contributions to the king's wardrobe between 1396 and 1399; it is difficult to know how large a household the child queen would have had, though she certainly had some sort of domestic establishment.[45]

Henry IV came to the throne with four sons but no wife.[46] He acquired the latter in 1403, and in the October 1404 parliament it was requested that, provided she was properly endowed with an income of 10,000 marks *per annum*, she should contribute to the wardrobe in the same way that 'other queens' had done, or else the money should be deducted from her revenues or from what (it was claimed) she received at the exchequer. It was stipulated that Queen Joan's council be sworn to put this into effect.[47] It was not, however, for throughout the reign Queen Joan made no financial contributions to Henry's household. Moreover, she did occasionally draw money from the exchequer, although this seems only to have been when the revenues from her endowment failed to mature, and the sums involved were not large. The king's four sons proved to be rather more of a drain on the exchequer: in May 1402 Prince Henry was granted 1,000 marks at the exchequer for his maintenance (although Prince of Wales, he must have been very hard put to it to derive any profits from his Welsh lands, given the disturbed state of the country at this time); Thomas, John and Humphrey received grants of the same amount in June 1403, before

November 1405, and before 1410, respectively. How regularly and punctually these were paid is not entirely clear, but even if they were not all paid all of the time, some of them certainly were some of the time.[48] It seems clear, therefore, that even if it is difficult to quantify precisely the amount of money which Henry's large family cost the exchequer, the amount was undoubedly greater than the cost to the exchequer of subsidiary royal households between 1360 and 1399, which had been virtually negligible. In considering the overall cost of the king's household during this period, this needs to be borne in mind.

Table 3: *The costs of the household 1360–1413*[49]

Period	Wardrobe	Great Wardrobe	Chamber	Total
1360–3	18,400	5,300	6,700	30,400
1363–7	23,600	9,500	6,700	39,800
1368–77	16,400	3,100	6,700	26,200
1377–86	15,800	3,200	1,700	20,700
1386–9	12,800	—	3,400	—
1389–92	17,300	4,400	3,400	25,100
1392–5	18,900	7,900	7,000	33,800
1395–9	34,000	12,200	7,000	53,200
1399–1403	26,300	11,100	4,300	41,700
1403–6	25,200	2,800	4,300	32,300
1407–13	19,600	2,700	8,000	30,300

The total cost of the household over the period 1360–1413 is summarised in Table 3 above. Because accounts from different departments overlap with each other, and because they are in some cases missing entirely, it is impossible to compile completely accurate figures for the cost of the household, but the table does nevertheless indicate clearly the main trends in household expenditure during this period. It shows that each of the three kings indulged in a (fairly short) period of very heavy domestic expenditure: Edward III between 1363 and 1367 (averaging £39,800 *per annum*), Henry IV between 1399 and 1403 (averaging £41,700 *per annum*), and, outstripping them both by a considerable margin, Richard II between 1395 and 1399 (averaging £53,200 *per annum*). Yet year for year over his whole reign, Henry IV's domestic expenditure was higher than Richard II's, for whereas the first fifteen or so years of Richard's reign had seen fairly modest expenditure on the household, the last ten years of Henry's reign saw continued high expenditure (and higher still if one includes the cost of the subsidiary royal households). In conclusion, the table presents a picture of twenty-five years of relatively low costs (1368–92) sandwiched between two periods of high costs (1360–7, and 1392–1413). The twenty-five years of relatively low costs coincide almost exactly with the second phase of the Hundred Years' War, when naturally less money was available for domestic extravagance.

General problems of the accounts

The chamber's sources of income have already been discussed. The great and privy wardrobes were financed almost exclusively from the exchequer—although the great wardrobe did receive a few rents from the shops around Baynard's castle, and occasionally sold off surplus stock, but the sums received were negligible by comparison with its exchequer income. There are occasional book-keeping entries of some significance recorded in the great wardrobe's receipt, but these are best considered in relation to similar entries in the wardrobe's receipt, which is what really needs to be discussed here.

For accounting purposes, the income received by the keeper of the wardrobe during any single accounting period would be entered under one of three headings: (a) *recepta scaccarii* (exchequer receipt), that is, money received from the treasurer and chamberlains of the exchequer, which would also be entered by the exchequer officials in their issue rolls as having been delivered to the keeper; (b) *recepta forinseca* (foreign receipt)—money or the value of provisions received from any source other than the exchequer; (c) before 1377, *debita* (debts)—debts of the wardrobe for which bills of wardrobe debenture, wardrobe tallies, or other sufficient wardrobe credit instruments had been issued, but which had not been cleared by the exchequer (that is, the exchequer had not yet issued tallies or cash to redeem them) at the time when the keeper's account was audited; the idea was that these debts would be transferred to the exchequer, thus they were reckoned as wardrobe income from the exchequer. After 1377 these were entered under *recepta forinseca*. *Recepta scaccarii* was overwhelmingly the principal source of wardrobe income; of the wardrobe's total income over the period 1360–1413, *c*. seventy-five percent was entered under this head, and in fact, as will be seen, the proportion of its *real* income which the wardrobe received from the exchequer was over ninety percent.

This is because *recepta forinseca* was very largely a book-keeping contrivance. The personal responsibility of the keeper of the wardrobe for all sums received by him is one of the key-notes of the accounting system employed. These are emphatically not budgeted accounts. At the end of each accounting period, it was the duty of the keeper to draw up a list of all the victuals and other provisions remaining in stock in each of the household offices. This list, with a note of its value, was entered under the *prestita* (imprests) at the end of the account and it was known as the keeper's *remanencia*. At the beginning of the next accounting period (i.e. the following day), exactly the same list was then entered under the keeper's *recepta forinseca* for the new account. The value of the stock *remanencia* was almost invariably over £1,000, frequently over £2,000, and sometimes well over that. Exactly the same procedure was followed with any cash which remained with officers of the household at the end of the accounting period. Members of the household's staff involved in purveying often had to be issued with cash in order to carry out their business, and sometimes they had some left in their hands when the accounting period closed. This, like the remaining stock, was entered under *prestita* at the end of one

account, and under *recepta forinseca* at the beginning of the next. The chief but-
lers in particular, who travelled largely independently of the household and
dealt in an expensive commodity, sometimes had a thousand pounds or more
with them, which could swell the *recepta forinseca* considerably. These two
items, the stock *remanencia* and the cash *remanencia*, between them often contributed three-quarters or more of the *recepta forinseca*, and it is abundantly clear
that they are not really income at all, except in the context of the keeper's personal responsibility for whatever passed through his hands during the period of
any single account.

Another book-keeping contrivance which might swell the *recepta forinseca*
was the practice of entering the wardrobe's outstanding debts under this head.
After the death of Edward III the practice of entering debts under a separate
head (*debita*) was abandoned, and instead each keeper waited until the end of
his whole period of office and then entered all his accumulated debts under
recepta forinseca. Thus, for instance, after Richard II's deposition, it was found
that the debts accumulated by Richard's last keeper (John Carp) over his nine-
year tenure of the office amounted to £12,438, partly for victuals not yet paid
for, and partly for arrears of wages and allowances to members of the household. The entire sum was simply entered under *recepta forinseca*.[50] The idea was
that these debts would be paid by the exchequer. But responsibility must fall
on the right shoulders: in one sense Carp had indeed 'received' this sum, for he
had 'received' the victuals and cash allowances which it represents, inasmuch as
he had not paid for them. Thus, when the time came to pay the debts, the
exchequer would have to reckon the payments it made against the value of the
goods and services which the keeper had received. Technically it can be argued
that they should really have been entered under exchequer receipt rather than
foreign receipt, but evidently the system employed was considered more appropriate and, as can be seen, there was a certain logic in reckoning debts as assets.
Under Henry IV in particular, with frequent changes of keeper, these debts frequently pushed up the nominal *recepta forinseca* enormously.

Thus the income 'received' under *recepta forinseca* is quite useless as a source
for reckoning the real income of the wardrobe unless each item under that head
is analysed individually. In fact, it does include a few items of real income: contributions from the queen's receiver-general between 1388 and 1394 and, more
significantly, between 1360 and 1369, were entered here; so were the profits of
the court of the verge and the assizes held by the clerk of the market, which
brought in about £150 *per annum* on average; the butler's profit from the
king's *recta prisa* on wine at English ports, often worth several hundred
pounds, and the profit made from exacting the right to twenty-one quarters of
corn for every twenty paid for by purveyors, were also genuine income; old or
broken dishes and goblets might be sold off and the profit entered under *recepta
forinseca*, and occasionally forfeits were passed directly to the household too,
such as the rather pathetic quantities of victuals forfeited by William Grindcob
and some of his fellow rebels in 1381.[51] Finally, inter-departmental transactions
were recorded under *recepta forinseca* too, such as the sums passed by the chamber

to the wardrobe in 1405–6, or the £2,387 worth of cloth, wax and spices passed from the great wardrobe to the wardrobe in 1366–7, or the £1,447 transferred from the late Edward III's chamber hoard in July 1377 to help cover the cost of his funeral.[52]

So it can be seen that the *recepta forinseca* contributed very little to the real income of the wardrobe in most years, and if inter-departmental transactions are excluded (they may have been new income for the wardrobe, but they were not for the household as a whole), it was even less. The wardrobe was almost totally dependent on the exchequer for its receipts, and this was a situation with which the king was entirely in accord. Even when the wardrobe's income from the exchequer was curtailed by would-be reformers, such as the Commissioners in 1386–9, there was no attempt by the king to make the wardrobe independent of 'exchequer control'. The apparently large total of £5,380 for *recepta forinseca* in 1386–7, for example, was made up from a stock *remanencia* of £2,314, and a cash *remanencia* of £2,694 in the hands of butler John Slegh, leaving less than £400 of real income—from the usual sources (verge court profits, *recta prisa*, and corn *incrementum*).[53] The days when wardrobe independence from exchequer control might be the aim of the king were long gone—if indeed they had ever been.

Recepta scaccarii forms the first item in almost all wardrobe account books. It consists of a chronological list of all sums, whether in cash or by tallies of assignment, handed over by the exchequer to the wardrobe or to the wardrobe's creditors, which were intended to cover expenses incurred by the wardrobe during the period of the account. There are several problems involved in the interpretation of the *recepta scaccarii*, principally because there were several ways in which the wardrobe might 'receive' money, and it is not always easy to distinguish them. These problems are discussed in more detail in Appendix II, but essentially what is important is to distinguish those entries which represent an actual acquisition of cash by the wardrobe from the exchequer, from those which represent credit pledged by the wardrobe and redeemed by the exchequer. When the exchequer was able to pass on to the wardrobe sufficient sums to enable the household to pay its way on a day-to-day basis, this meant that those who provided goods or services for the household stood a reasonable chance of being paid promptly, in the counting-house. But when the wardrobe was not receiving enough cash from the exchequer to cover its daily expenses, it was left in the position of having to issue creditors with bills of wardrobe debenture, which they were then supposed to redeem either at the exchequer or with a local exchequer accountant (such as a customs collector). The problems which they might encounter in doing so were considerable, to say nothing of the delay and inconvenience.[54] Thus the ratio of 'direct' payments (those in which the wardrobe actually received cash) to 'indirect' payments (those in which it was running up debts which the exchequer was then expected to pay off) recorded in the *recepta scaccarii*—inasfar as this ratio can be determined—is one of the most important indications of the household's solvency during any given accounting period.

This point is best illustrated by comparison of the *recepta scaccarii* for 1366–7 and 1383–4. During William Gunthorpe's account from 1 February 1366 to 31 January 1367, his exchequer receipt totalled £18,472. Of this, £13,966 was received personally by Gunthorpe either in cash or tallies at the exchequer, at regular intervals between 8 February and 13 November 1366, on eleven different occasions, in sums ranging from £4,000 to 350 marks. A further £3,400 of this total was received in two payments by chief butler William Street, again directly from the exchequer, making a total of £17,366 in thirteen direct payments, an average of £1,336 per payment. A further £614 was received from the king's chamber for the use of the royal goldsmith Thomas Hassey, and £26 worth of honey came from the Windsor castle bees, leaving three 'indirect' payments totalling less than £500.[55] The clear inference to be drawn from this is that the exchequer was able to keep the wardrobe supplied with a steady flow of cash during the year, thus presumably facilitating transactions in the wardrobe and enabling creditors to be paid in the counting-house.

The 1383–4 account presents a very different picture: William Packington's exchequer receipt for his account covering the period from 1 October 1383 to 30 September 1384 totalled £14,899.[56] This was made up of no less than 302 separate payments (compared with Gunthorpe's eighteen). Because of the problem of interpreting some entries, it is not possible to be absolutely sure how much of this was received directly and how much consisted of creditors being paid at the exchequer, but in most cases there are strong indications one way or the other. Many were specifically said to be *per billam*, while others are clearly direct handovers *apud Wyndesore* or *in moneta*, or *in pecunia numerata*. But while acknowledging that complete accuracy cannot be hoped for, it seems that direct payments can be analysed as follows: to Packington himself, £767 in five payments; to butler John Slegh or his sergeant Thomas Brounfleet for making purchases for the buttery, £4,236 in nineteen payments; to cofferer John Carp, £2,847 in thirteen payments, and to other members of the household receiving on behalf of the keeper, £956 in eighteen payments. This makes a total of £8,807 in fifty-five direct payments, an average of £160 per payment. Only two really large individual payments were made: 2,000 marks to John Carp on 8 October 1384, and £2,100 to John Slegh on 22 December 1384. However, the really significant feature of the *recepta scaccarii* in 1383–4 is not the size of the direct payments from exchequer to wardrobe, but the fact that less than three-fifths of the total was received directly. The remaining £6,092 'received' was made up of some 247 relatively small sums paid out to about 200 different individuals (some creditors appear more than once, such as the London grocer Robert Reson, clearly a regular household supplier). The great majority of these payments consisted of wardrobe debts being cleared by the exchequer. Such a high proportion of indirect payments provides a striking contrast with the situation in 1366–7, and again there is a clear inference to be drawn: in 1383–4 the exchequer was quite unable to keep the wardrobe supplied with enough cash to meet its expenditure on a regular basis, so that instead the wardrobe officials were reduced to issuing numerous bills and passing their ceditors on to the exchequer; given the problems at the exchequer, the creditors probably had little more success there.

There is a further point of significance about the 1383–4 *recepta scaccarii*, namely, that it was not received coterminously with the period of the account, October 1383 to September 1384, but between April 1384 and March 1385. Of the total receipt of £14,899, only £5,495 was received during the Easter 1384 term, while £9,404 was received during the Michaelmas 1384–5 term. Thus Packington did not even begin to receive any money to cover his household expenses for the year until he was over half-way through the year. In effect, the exchequer had imposed a six-month 'stop' on payments either to the wardrobe or to its creditors, refusing either to hand over money to the wardrobe officials or to honour wardrobe bills arising out of the current period of account until the beginning of the Easter term. Moreover, this six-month stop did not operate only in 1383–4, but throughout the years 1382–90, and this is clearly another factor which must have frustrated wardrobe creditors.[57] Before going on to analyse the accounts in more detail, some further problems involved in their interpretation need to be considered.

Whether the keeper (or his deputies) received his direct payments from the exchequer in cash or in tallies was probably not of great concern to him. No doubt he preferred cash because it involved less bother, but as far as can be gathered household officials did not encounter great difficulties in cashing their tallies, at least during the reigns of Edward III and Richard II. Steel has analysed the level of fictitious loans (replacements for 'uncashable' tallies) in which each of the household departments was involved for the period 1377–1413.[58] Between 1377 and 1389, fictitious loans on 'bad' tallies issued to the wardrobe totalled £6,270, from 1389 to 1399, only £428, and from 1399 to 1413, £17,378. The number of fictitious loans created on tallies issued to the chamber and great wardrobe also rose markedly during Henry IV's reign; for Richard II's chamber, they totalled only £900, while for Henry IV's they jumped to £10,990, for Richard's great wardrobe they totalled £4,877, while for Henry's they totalled £20,466. Thus, fictitious loans totalled nearly £49,000 over the whole reign for the three principal departments of Henry's household. As is now well known, Steel attached an altogether excessive importance to the level of fictitious loans. The fact that a high number of fictitious loans was created for the household is an indication, not that Henry's household departments were 'practically bankrupt', but that they remained consistently high on the exchequer's list of preferential creditors and almost invariably managed to have their 'bad' tallies renewed promptly with good ones. However, fictitious loans are not without significance for even if a fictitious loan is to be interpreted as a successful operation of reassignment rather than a symptom of departmental bankruptcy, from the household's point of view the result of the initial failure to cash the tallies might mean delay and inconvenience, and consequently a shortage of ready cash in the wardrobe. They do indeed reflect, as suggested by Steel, a chronic shortage of cash available to the crown.[59] Yet since the household managed to secure reassignments without much delay, it would be unwise to over-emphasise the effect of those 'bad' tallies which it did receive.

Given therefore that direct payments, whether in cash or tallies, nearly always represent a genuine acquisition of cash by the wardrobe, how easy is it to distinguish direct from indirect payments? The best indicator as to the nature of the payment is the person *per manus* of whom it is made. In many cases this is quite easy to establish: where they are creditors it will often be fairly obvious, for example, *per manus N. cives et grosser Londiniensis* or, *per manus constabularii de N*—the latter very probably indicating purveyance of victuals from the inhabitants of a village where the constable had acted as intermediary between the purveyor and the villagers (as he was by statute required to do). Some names are unfortunately quite untraceable and in such cases the probability must be that they were household creditors, although again it is impossible to be certain. Members of the household often received quite small sums in the name of the keeper, and these are not easy to interpret. Were they receiving money on behalf of the keeper, or were they really creditors of the wardrobe who had been sent to the exchequer armed with a wardrobe bill for (for example) arrears of wages? The probability is the latter. Direct payments from the exchequer to the keeper seem unusually—though by no means always —to have been in fairly large sums, and usually only specified persons (the cofferer, or the personal clerk of the keeper) were deputed to receive them at the exchequer on the keeper's behalf. In general, it must be said that it is impossible to categorise with complete certainty all entries in the *recepta scaccarii* into direct and indirect receipts, but with the great majority of them one can be fairly sure as to the category in which they fall.

Where wardrobe account books survive, it is relatively easy to establish a complete breakdown of payments from exchequer to wardrobe during the accounting period. Enrolled accounts are less useful, for they only give abridged lists of the *recepta scaccarii*, often rolling two or three payments on the same day into one (for example, the 302 payments listed in the *recepta scaccarii* of the 1383–4 wardrobe account book are reduced to 114 payments—totalling the same, naturally—in the corresponding enrolled account).[60] Yet the records of payments contained in the enrolled accounts can be useful, for the simple number of payments made—where they can be compared over a reasonable period —is often an indicator of the exchequer's inability or ability to pass cash to the wardrobe; hence Gunthorpe's eighteen 'parcels' of receipt in 1366–7, compared with Packington's 302 'parcels' in 1383–4. Naturally such figures have to be used with caution, but it was inevitably true that when the exchequer was not under pressure it was able to hand over large sums (or tallies for large sums) to the keeper, which he preferred because it obviated the need for him and his deputies to make repeated journeys to collect money. When it *was* under pressure, the reverse was true. Analysis of the number of payments made within each accounting period (working on the enrolled accounts) in fact produces a pattern which fits quite well with other evidence concerning the wardrobe's solvency during this period.

Turning away now from analysis of the *recepta scaccarii*, there are various other items in the account which can be used to help determine the extent to which the keeper was meeting his obligations. These too need to be interpreted with care. Take, for example, the balance recorded at the end of each accounting period.[61] What this balance represents is the deficit or surplus of the keeper, with reference to income received and expenditure incurred during the period of that particular account, on the day on which the account was actually audited, which might be several years, and was invariably several months, after the accounting period ended. The problems involved in using these figures incautiously are illustrated by the nominal deficit and surplus recorded during the last two years of Richard II's reign. For the year 1397–8, John Carp had a nominal deficit of £11,605. Carp's real income for this period totalled just under £25,700 (exchequer receipt of £25,373 plus a little over £300 of real foreign receipt).[62] Yet his *dieta* totalled £29,834, and his foreign expenses came to £7,926, so his total expenses for the period, at £37,760, exceeded his real income by over £12,000. However, he 'received' on 1 October 1397 a stock *remanencia* of £3,634, and left on 30 September 1398 a stock *remanencia* of only £2,064, so his real deficit for this period was probably closer to £10,500. This is important when considering the next account, for 1398–9, which includes under *recepta forinseca* an entry of £12,438 for outstanding debts *totius tempora eidem Johannis*.[63] These were indeed the outstanding debts accumulated by Carp during the whole period of his keepership (July 1390 to September 1399), but in reality the vast majority of these debts had been incurred during a single year, 1397–8. His account for 1398–9 shows a nominal surplus of £9,850, but of course this includes the £12,438 of debts. In fact Carp's real income for this, his final account, was about £41,000, while his expenses (including war wages) totalled £40,101, and his imprests, including stock and cash *remanencia* as well as numerous advances on war wages for the Irish campaign, came to £6,116, which puts his nominal surplus of £9,950 into a very different perspective.

Thus it can be seen that while the level of deficit recorded in 1397–8 is in fact quite a good guide to the degree of wardrobe insolvency during this period, the surplus recorded in 1398–9 is totally misleading. There are other occasions (1369–74, for instance) when the recorded deficits reflect genuine problems for the keeper, but without proper analysis of the accounts concerned these balances are of no use at all. Of considerably greater significance were the debts entered under foreign receipt by each outgoing keeper at the end of his period of office. These can be taken as reliable statements of the level of debts run up, but it is important to note that they cover the whole period of office of the keeper, and do not relate simply to the period of account under which they were entered (for example, Carp's £12,438 worth of debts entered under 1398–9, but in fact very largely incurred in 1397–8). What this means is that when there were frequent changes of keeper, as under Henry IV between 1399 and 1406, it is possible to work out the level of debt in the wardrobe on an almost annual basis—hence the swollen foreign receipt totals in the early years of Henry IV's reign, which reflect nothing more than the vast debts run up by the wardrobe during these years. Where keepers acted over a long period, however, it is not so easy to establish when the debts were accumulated. So once again, the figures have to be used with caution, but they can help to determine the degree of wardrobe solvency. Bearing all these factors in mind, the accounts themselves now need to be discussed.

The accounts 1360–1413

Where wardrobe account books survive in full, it is not difficult to gain a fairly clear idea of the level of indirect as compared with direct receipts from the exchequer. These figures do not provide a 'barometer' of wardrobe solvency; only by analysing and collating a number of different factors can a true picture of wardrobe solvency be achieved. They are however an indicator. The account books of the later years of Edward III's reign show that the percentage of exchequer receipt which was passed directly from exchequer to wardrobe was normally very high, ninety-six percent or more. This picture is substantiated from both the issue rolls and the enrolled accounts for the same period, which frequently show large cash sums or assignments being passed directly from exchequer to wardrobe, especially in the 1360s. In the 1370s, however, cash was not quite so easy to come by, and this is refleced in the greater number of individual handovers (averaging between thirty and forty a year) in the 1371–3 and 1376–7 accounts. It will be remembered that expenditure too dropped sharply from 1368 onwards, and these figures reflect the shortage of revenue occasioned by the pressure of war. The evidence relating to debts incurred by the various keepers points in the same direction.

In the 1350s, when the wardrobe keepers had been acting as paymasters to the royal armies, enormous debts had been allowed to accumulate. In 1360, the exchequer estimated that the still unpaid debts of keepers John Buckingham (1353–7), Henry Walton (1358–9), and William Farley (1359–60) stood at £4,906, £8,665, and £31,432 respectively (Farley had financed the 1359–60 campaign which culminated at Brétigny): a total of £45,003.[64] In the immediate post-war years great efforts were made to pay off these debts and by Michaelmas 1363, at least £26,206 of these debts had been repaid, and during the next two years at least the efforts were continued.[65] During the 1360s, despite the high level of expenditure, immediate needs were less pressing because of the peace, and the debts run up by the keepers of the wardrobe were not allowed to get out of hand in this way. Even during the first year or two following the renewal of the war in 1369, the new keeper Henry Wakefield (who had taken over in June 1369) seems to have been able to get sufficient cash from the exchequer with which to meet his obligations, despite the fact that already by 1370 the exchequer was having to resort to widespread borrowing in order to finance the war. Wakefield's two accounts covering the period from June 1371 to September 1374 tell a rather different story, however. His nominal deficit of £2,563 for the period June 1371 to June 1373 can be checked from the wardrobe account book, which in fact shows an excess of real expenditure over real income of at least £3,600, while the enrolled version of his 1373–4 accounts reveals a similar real deficit of about £3,000.[66] Between July 1374 and September 1375 this situation was remedied as from 12 to 22 July 1374 Wakefield received from the exchequer a total of £4,397, all of which was specifically said to be for repayment of debts run up by him during the last few years. In addition, in April 1375, chief butler William Street was issued with tallies reassigning £873 worth of 'bad' tallies originally issued to him in January 1371 to purchase wine for the household.[67] This suggests that Wakefield's debts between June 1371 and 1374 must have reached something like £7,500. During his final (1374–5) account, however, his real income passed his expenses by about £5,000 which (allowing for the fact that he had already begun to pay off some of his debts before October 1374), meant not only that he could pay off the rest, but that at the end of his period of office, in October 1375, he was actually left with a small surplus in hand of £1,199, 'which,' as the enrolled account states, 'he paid at Worcester in the 50th year'—that is, he restored it to an exchequer official (he became bishop of Worcester on retiring from the keepership).[68]

Excluding the military debts carried over from the 1350s, it was only during the years 1371–4 that the wardrobe was really failing to meet its obligations during the later years of Edward III's reign. Moreover, many of these creditors were probably satisfied fairly rapidly in 1374–5. No doubt this was facilitated by the fact that there was no English campaign to finance in 1374—although there was one in 1375, but it was brought to a rapid (some thought too rapid) halt by the truce agreed at Bruges in June 1375, which lasted until the end of the reign and no doubt allowed the financial recuperation to continue. Some debts were indeed permitted to accumulate in 1360–2 and 1376–7, but they never reached alarming proportions. When in 1380 the commons requested that Edward III's debts, both for victuals taken for his household and for cash loaned to him, should be discharged, the government was able to reply that 'it has been done in large part' and the remainder would follow shortly.[69] Thus the evidence suggests that, despite the higher level of expenditure, wardrobe finances were more healthy in the 1360s than in the 1370s, but that even in the 1370s they were by no means disastrous.

William Packington acted as keeper of the wardrobe throughout the first thirteen years of Richard II's reign, until his death in office in July 1390, and during these years the level of expenditure remained fairly low. Despite this, Packington experienced considerable difficulties in securing sufficient quantities of cash from the exchequer to allow him to pay his way, so instead he was forced to resort to the issuing of bills redeemable by creditors at the exchequer. The *recepta scaccarii* for the 1383–4 account shows a pattern of receipt quite different from any other surviving wardrobe account book apart from that of 1402–3. Only about sixty percent of it was received directly, and the number of individual payments was much greater. Moreover, it was not just in 1383–4 that this occurred for fragments of both the 1382–3 and 1384–5 account books also survive, including in each case the list of *recepta scaccarii*, and they tell a very similar (though not quite as accentuated) story of a relatively low level of direct handovers accompanied by a high number of small payments to creditors.[70] For example, during the exchequer's Michaelmas term 1383–4 (covering wardrobe expenses incurred during the 1382–3 account), a total of £8,002 was nominally 'received' by Packington of which about £6,391 was received directly (in thirty-nine 'parcels'), while the remainder was paid to creditors (in 106 'parcels')—making a direct receipt percentage of about eighty percent.[71] The enrolled accounts provide further evidence of this trend, and although the abridged type of entry used in the enrolled accounts needs to be treated with caution, they indicate that for much of the period 1381–90 the pattern of substantial indirect receipts was maintained.[72]

It is difficult to believe that this was a situation which was appreciated by either the wardrobe's creditors or that department's officers—or indeed by the young king himself, for monarchs presumably liked whenever possible to avoid the sort of odium which became attached to their households when too many bills were left unpaid. Yet the cash-flow situation in the wardrobe was aggravated still further by the six-month stop imposed on the wardrobe for much of this period. It seems to have been the increase in expenditure in 1381–2 (occasioned in part by Richard's wedding and Anne's coronation) which led to this further deterioration in wardrobe finances—although over the two years and three months of his previous (1379–81) account Packington had a real deficit of well over £2,000, so 1382–3 was not going to be an easy year in any case. In 1381–2, expenditure rose quite sharply, reaching nearly £19,000. During the period covered by the account, however, the exchequer was only able to make £13,058 available to the wardrobe, which meant that in order to pay off these debts Packington continued to draw money on his 1381–2 account during the exchequer Michaelmas 1382–3 term, to the tune of £4,656. This in turn meant that during this term the exchequer could not provide him with any cash to cover the current term, so that it was not until 2 April 1383 that the keeper was able to start drawing cash to cover his 1382–3 account. For the next three years this situation continued, with the keeper's cash allowance (and tallies paid to his creditors) always six months in arrears. Then in 1385–6 the situation deteriorated further when, even allowing for the six-month stop, the exchequer only provided Packington with £13,992, although his expenses reached £16,948. Thus, to cover his 1385–6 debts he had to go yet another term ahead, drawing £4,570 during the first two months of the Easter 1387 term. Once again, this meant that hardly any money could be made available for current expenses, and in fact during the whole period of the 1386–7 account (which lasted until 30 September 1387) only £1,718 could be provided for current expenses, which totalled £11,922. So it can be seen that throughout the period from *c.* 1381 until 1386 the cash flow in the wardrobe was getting steadily worse, with debts continuing to mount (by October 1386 they stood at over £13,000), and creditors being left longer and longer before securing repayment.[73] So despite the fact that expenditure was not particularly high, it is understandable that the Commission of Government which came to power in November 1386 felt obliged to do something about it.

Debts of this magnitude could not be wiped out in a year or two, especially as the Commissioners had come to power at least partly as a result of the anti-taxation stand taken by the parliament of 1386 and it would have been humiliating to have had to raise taxation levels. In fact the six-month stop on the wardrobe continued in operation until 1390, although at least the threat that this would have been converted into a one-year stop (which must have seemed very likely in 1386) was averted. This partial success was achieved because the king was forced to moderate his household expenditure throughout the years 1386–9 (wardrobe expenses averaged *c*. £12,800 *per annum* at this time), and by the end of 1389 the exchequer was once again in a position to start making payments to the wardrobe on its current account. The first such payment was made on 30 December 1389, although a total of only £1,264 was handed over to Packington for his current account during the whole of this term. By the time he died on 26 July 1390, Packington had in fact received no more than £8,465 to cover his 1389–90 account, although his expenses during this period were £13,346.[74] Following his death, his final account was immediately frozen, and it was another two and a half years before many of the wardrobe's 1389–90 creditors were paid. On 25 January 1393 a further 7,000 marks were issued from the exchequer to the new keeper John Carp and wardrobe clerk John Stacy, which effectively covered the 1389–90 debts (this brought the total *recepta scaccarii* for the 1389–90 account to £13,132, which, together with a few items of genuine foreign receipt totalling about £770, in fact left a small surplus of *c*. £550 on the account).[75]

Packington's total debts at the time of his death are difficult to estimate with certainty. Apart from the deficit of over £4,000 which was not made good until January 1393, he also acknowledged in his *recepta forinseca* an obligation of £2,413 to 'divers knights, clerks, esquires and valets' of the household for accumulated arrears of fees, robes and wages over the whole period of his keepership but the entire household agreed to take a one-third cut in the arrears owed to them, thus reducing the debt by £804.[76] On paper, then, his debts would seem to amount to between £6,000 and £7,000, most of which had apparently been repaid by April 1393 (when the account was audited). The problem lies in knowing how many of the wardrobe's creditors who had been sent to the exchequer with bills of debenture during the 1380s had actually been able to secure tallies from the exchequer which they had consequently been able to cash. Given the difficulties at the exchequer, and given that the wardrobe had been forced to send a very considerable number of its creditors there (particularly in the early-to-mid 1380s), the actual level of wardrobe debt may have been considerably higher than can be shown from the evidence. But things seem to have improved by the middle of the decade, for a higher percentage of receipt was coming in direct payments by 1389–90, and the virtual twelve-month stop of 1385–6 had once again been reduced to six months.[77] This much, it seems, had been largely the doing of the Commissioners.

John Carp, a wardrobe clerk of great experience who had been cofferer since 1376, became keeper on Packington's death in July 1390 and retained the post until Richard's deposition in September 1399. Although he acted for a substantially shorter period than had William Packington, far greater sums of money passed through his hands, partly because of Richard's increased expenditure on his household (particularly from 1395 onwards), and partly because Carp also acted as paymaster to the two Irish expeditions of 1394–5 and 1399. On the whole, he does not seem to have had great difficulties in securing sufficient cash or tallies from the exchequer to cover his expenses. The surviving wardrobe account books for 1392–3 and 1395–6 show direct receipts averaging about ninety-two percent and ninety-eight percent respectively of the total *recepta scaccarii*, and this picture is supported by a study of the issue rolls from 1397–9, and by the (incomplete) list of *recepta scaccarii* for the 1393–5 account.[78] It is clear that throughout the 1390s, the percentage of its *recepta scaccarii* which the wardrobe received in direct payments was on average well over ninety percent. The French war had now ceased, which always eased the financial pressure considerably, and after 1389 Richard re-established his personal control over the exchequer, which meant that he could insist on the priority of the household in securing assignments there (as Edward III had clearly done too).

Yet there are sure signs that during the last two or three years of the reign Richard's extravagance was beginning to bite. As noted above, Carp's real deficit for the 1397–8 account was approximately £10,500. Up till this point he had usually had money in hand, for although he ran up a few debts in 1390–2, he recovered these fully in 1392–3 (when his real surplus was *c*. £4,500) and probably continued to have cash in hand until 1396–7. In this year his real deficit was around £1,600, followed by the £10,500 of 1397–8.[79] This was carried over into his 1398–9 account, when he acknowledged total debts of £12,438 for the whole period of his keepership, but these had in reality largely been incurred the previous year. They were said to be owed 'to various creditors both for various victuals bought from them for the expenses of the household and to various knights, clerks, esquires, valets and others of the said household for their wages and robes, for the whole period of the keepership of John Carp, their names and the sums owed to them being stated in the book of particulars.' It is a great pity that the wardrobe account book does not survive, for it would be of great interest to know whether these were mainly purveyancing debts, or mainly arrears of wages and robes to servants of the household. Certainly there were complaints in Henry IV's first parliament about the purveyancing debts still outstanding from Richard's reign, and if, as seems likely, Carp had once again begun to run up sizeable debts of this kind during the last two years of his reign, this would help to explain the unpopularity of Richard's household.

The wardrobe accounts of Henry IV's reign exhibit a new degree of financial chaos. Five men acted as keepers of the wardrobe under Henry: Thomas Tutbury (1399–1401), Thomas More (1401–5), Richard Kingston (1405–6), John Tiptoft (1406–8), and Thomas Brounfleet (1408–13). Every one of them except Tiptoft was obliged to run up very substantial debts during his period of office, and because of the frequent changes of keeper the accounts present us with regular 'up-dates' of those debts. The greater degree of chaos is certainly to be associated with the first rather than the second half of the reign, and not surprisingly this coincides with the period of highest expenditure (an average of *c.* £25,800 *per annum* between 1399 and 1406, compared with *c.* £19,700 *per annum* between 1407 and 1413), but a fair degree of chaos remains discernible throughout the reign. Unfortunately only two wardrobe account books survive from Henry's reign (covering the exchequer years 1402–3 and the period from 1 October 1405 to 8 December 1406), but this is partially compensated for by the massively detailed study of Henry's household finances by Dr Alan Rogers in his thesis. Dr Rogers undertook an extensive study of the issue and receipt rolls of the exchequer as well as documents relating more directly to the household departments, so that he was able to build up a very comprehensive picture of household finance during the reign. Much of what follows is based on his research.

Analysis of the *recepta scaccarii* listed in Thomas More's wardrobe account book for 1402–3 shows the lowest percentage of direct receipts from the exchequer (just under eighty percent), and the highest number of individual handovers from exchequer to wardrobe (163), of any account book since 1383–4. The account book for 1405–6 shows a much higher percentage of direct receipts (about ninety-six percent), but this is misleading because exchequer receipt fell so far short of expenses during the time of Kingston's account. As noted above, this shortfall had to be made up in part by the transfer of £5,445 from the king's chamber at various stages during the two years.[80] This introduces a new possibility: when it was short of cash, the exchequer might continue to make direct payments to the wardrobe, while at the same time imposing in effect a stop on wardrobe creditors by declining to issue tallies redeeming bills of wardrobe debenture. This is very probably what happened in 1405–6, and it may well be what had happened in 1397–8 as well. This only reinforces the fact that in trying to estimate the solvency of the household at any given time, it is impossible to use any set of figures in isolation as a barometer of its ability (or willingness) to meet its obligations. The various pieces of evidence need to be taken in conjunction. Thus, while in 1405–6 the proportion of direct handovers was high, this fell so far short of meeting the wardrobe's obligations that many creditors were undoubtedly being left unpaid, and so unsure were the exchequer's officials of their sources of revenue that they would not even issue tallies.

The evidence of chronic insolvency in the wardrobe revealed by these two accounts is supported and amplified by Rogers's use of the issue and receipt rolls. He suggests that Thomas Tutbury may have been incompetent to manage the wardrobe's finances, and this is why he was dismissed from office during the parliament of 1401. At any rate, under Tutbury's management (1 October 1399 to 8 March 1401) the new king's wardrobe got off to a disastrous start. The exchequer was quite unable to make enough money available to cover the wardrobe's (somewhat excessive) expenditure, and a high proportion of indirect receipts, accompanied by a substantial number of fictitious loans on tallies issued to the wardrobe, culminated in Tutbury having to acknowledge debts amounting to *c.* £10,300 at the time of his dismissal. This is partly why his nominal *recepta scaccarii* was so great, but it was also swollen by several substantial loans from magnates, prelates and others, which was only storing up trouble for the future.[81] Tutbury was replaced by Thomas More, an experienced wardrobe clerk who had been cofferer of Richard II's household 1395–9 (and before that Queen Anne's receiver-general). No doubt it was hoped that his experience might help to rectify the situation. More's period of office lasted nearly four years, until 6 January 1405, and although for most of this time the percentage of direct receipts from the exchequer was not as low as in his 1402–3 account, this is not necessarily a sign that things were better at other times. In fact, it seems that wardrobe insolvency under More reached its peak during his final accounting period (October 1403 to January 1405), when his expenses passed his real receipts by about £7,000. The year 1404 saw a considerable amount of borrowing by the wardrobe, as well as a number of fictitious loans on tallies issued to More. As in 1405–6, a partial or complete stop on wardrobe creditors seems to have been in operation at the exchequer for at least part of the time.[82] Unfortunately the folio containing More's *recepta forinseca* for his final account is badly damaged, but it totalled £16,151 (compared to £2,940, £3,326, and £1,936 in his first three accounts), and there is no doubt that this consisted largely of debts entered in the usual way.[83] Over the whole period of his keepership, his real receipt had fallen approximately £12,000 short of his expenses, and the burden of debt which he acknowledged must have been roughly of this magnitude. His successor, Richard Kingston, a long-serving Lancastrian follower who had been Henry's treasurer before he became king, fared no better. His account covered nearly two years, from 7 January 1405 to 7 December 1406, when he was dismissed in one of the last acts of the long parliament of that year. He too suffered from several uncashable tallies, was reduced to extensive borrowing from the chamber, and was probably obliged to accept a stop on the wardrobe's creditors at the exchequer for much of his accounting period. When he left office, he left debts of £10,730.[84] The speed with which debts were accumulated in the wardrobe at this time was remarkable: it took Tutbury eighteen months, More less than four years, and Kingston less than two years, each to amass debts of over £10,000. Remembering that Carp's acknowledged debts of over £12,438 had been incurred mainly in 1397–8, the full extent of the wardrobe's insolvency between 1397 and 1406 becomes apparent. It coincides almost exactly with the highest level of expenditure (excluding war-burdened accounts) ever seen in the wardrobe.

Nor was it only in the wardrobe of the household that debts were allowed to accumulate. When William Loveney, who had been keeper of the great wardrobe since the beginning of the reign, came to present his final account (for the period 1 October 1407 to 30 April 1408), he acknowledged debts of £4,077 *de toto tempore Willelmi Loveney nuper custodis magni garderobi*.[85] Exactly when these had been incurred is impossible to say, but the first four years of the reign saw the highest amount of spending in the great wardrobe, and there must be a strong possibility that this was the time when it had not been able to meet its obligations. After 1403, spending in the great wardrobe dropped, although spending in the wardrobe did not.

After 1406, however, expenditure in the wardrobe did fall, and things now improved. How much of this was due to the organisational ability of the new keeper John Tiptoft is not entirely clear, but Tiptoft was undoubtedly one of the prime figures behind the move for reform. Despite the fact that he was one of Henry's chamber knights, he was a forceful and critical speaker of the commons in 1406, and when he retired from the keepership of the wardrobe in July 1408 it was in order to take up the office of treasurer of England. Later he was to be one of Henry V's most trusted councillors, steward of the royal household 1426–32, and a peer of parliament while his son became earl of Worcester. Tiptoft's abilities are beyond question. During his keepership (8 December 1406 to 17 July 1408) wardrobe finances were put on a much sounder footing: expenditure was reduced to an annual average of £20,446, the ratio of direct to indirect receipts was very high, and his real receipt and expenditure were balanced almost exactly at just under £33,000 each. Thus, he acknowledged no debts in his *recepta forinseca*, and indeed the exchequer in 1407 was even able to step up its repayment rate on debts incurred by Tiptoft's predecessors.[86] Tiptoft's successor, Thomas Brounfleet, was a wardrobe official of long standing. He had become chief butler of Richard II's household in 1394, and was controller to Thomas More from 1401 to 1403. Brounfleet's keepership lasted from 18 July 1408 until the end of the reign (Henry IV's household was actually disbanded on 11 April 1413, some three weeks after the king's death, to allow time for the funeral to take place. This was normal: Edward III's household did not disband until over a month after his death). During this time he managed to keep expenses down to an even lower level than had Tiptoft, averaging £19,272 *per annum*. The year 1410–11 was particularly cheap, perhaps because of the king's illness and Prince Henry's assumption of power.[87] Nevertheless, Brounfleet could not help running up debts and the *recepta forinseca* of his final account shows the customary inflation, to £14,575. Unfortunately the folio is again too damaged to show the figure entered for debts, but even allowing for the fact that it included a few substantial items of genuine receipt (such as the 500 marks transferred to the wardrobe from the Duchy of Lancaster revenues to help cover the cost of the king's funeral), there can be no doubt that this sum was made up largely of debts, probably to the tune of at least £10,000.[88] Most of these debts seem to have been incurred during the first (1408–9) and last (1411–13) periods of his keepership, when his expenses exceeded his real receipts by about £3,600 and £5,300 respectively. But despite the debts incurred in 1408–9, it seems that in general Brounfleet's problems increased rather than diminished as his period of office continued. The year 1410 was a bad one for the exchequer, with low receipts, and in the summer a stop on annuities had to be imposed and the low level of receipts continued into 1411.[89] Between 1408 and 1410 the percentage of direct payments from exchequer to wardrobe remained high, but after this it declined steadily until the end of the reign. The period of real improvement, therefore, did not last very long; although after 1406 matters never again got as bad as they had been before that, by the end of the reign the wardrobe was once again failing to meet its obligations.[90]

The debts entered by each outgoing keeper in his final *recepta forinseca* were supposed to be paid off by the exchequer. The question arises, therefore, how rapidly was the exchequer able to redeem them (or at least to issue tallies for them, which may very well not be the same thing at all, but was at any rate the first step on the road to redemption, and is as far as the evidence will normally permit us to go)? Most of the debts run up by Henry Wakefield between 1371 and 1374 seem to have been redeemed in 1375; between 1381 and 1393 there were probably some very long-standing wardrobe debts, but by the end of 1393 it seems that most of Packington's outstanding obligations had been cleared. There is unfortunately no way of knowing when John Carp's debts were paid off, as they were supposed to be dealt with by a fund set up under the terms of Richard II's will, and no documentation concerning its operation appears to have survived. Under Henry IV, however, the regular changes of keeper make it easier to work out whose debts were being paid off when, and Rogers has analysed the information as follows: of Thomas Tutbury's debts of £10,300, nearly £9,000 had been redeemed by the end of Henry IV's reign; of Thomas More's debts (*c.* £12,000), only about £1,800 had been cleared by the end of the reign; of Richard Kingston's debts of £10,730, only £696 had been paid by the end of the reign; Tiptoft left no debts, while Brounfleet's in 1413 were probably around £10,000.[91] Thus, at the time of his death, the outstanding debts of Henry IV's wardrobe stood at a minimum of £31,500, and in reality they may have been considerably higher (depending on how many exchequer tallies issued on these debts had been found to be cashable). Henry's goods and chattels at his death were valued at 25,000 marks, and Henry V agreed to sell these in order to establish a fund for the payment of as many as possible of the debts of his father's household. By 1422, however, the debt had only been reduced by about £4,000. Not until 1433 was the account more or less cleared. It had taken twenty years, but what is perhaps more remarkable is that it had at least been done.

COMPLAINTS AND REMEDIES

During the 1360s there were few complaints about the financial (or any other) activities of the royal household,[92] but from 1371 onwards all this changed. Throughout the 1370s and 80s, and then again from 1397 until the end of

Henry IV's reign, complaints of various sorts about the household were a feature of almost every parliament. These related mainly to two grievances: firstly, that the household was failing to pay for its provisions, and secondly that the overall size and therefore cost of the household was excessive. To remedy this situation, various expedients were proposed, some by the king and his advisors, others by his critics. Again, these can be divided into two principal categories: firstly, attempts to ensure that the control of household finance was placed in the hands of men other than the king's nominees, men who (it was hoped) would take a more responsible attitude to the problem and who would be more 'publicly' accountable; secondly, attempts to establish those sources of revenue which should or should not be made available to the household, so that regular supply to the wardrobe could be maintained from those which should, and the king would be discouraged from encroaching on those which should not. This process involved a number of conflicting priorities. The aim of this section is to investigate the intensity and direction of the complaints made against the household during this period, and the various currents of thought which lay behind the remedies proposed, as well as the degree of success with which they were implemented.

Abuse of power and the problem of control

Abuse of the royal right of purveyance was the field of activity through which the household normally touched upon the lives of the greatest number of people, and not surprisingly it featured continually as a cause of complaint.[93] At the beginning of this period, in 1362, the king had conceded what came to be known as the Great Statute of Purveyors, a comprehensive series of regulations dealing with all aspects of the problem, from non-payment and petty corruption to a request that in future 'the hateful name of purveyor' should be replaced with 'buyer'.[94] It was the culmination of a series of petitions dealing with the subject which had been presented to parliaments throughout the first half of the fourteenth century, and although it seems to have achieved some success in reducing the level of petty corruption among purveyors, there remained the problem of non-payment and under-payment for provisions. This was something which neither the purveyors themselves nor, quite frequently, the officials of the wardrobe, could do very much about: their ability to pay for goods depended on their ability to secure money from the exchequer, and as seen above, this was not always forthcoming. After 1362, complaints about purveyance frequently took the form of requests that the statute should be enforced, which makes it difficult to know whether the real grievance was corruption by individual purveyors, or non-payment, or some other aspect of the subject. However, there is a clear correlation between periods when complaints were made, and periods when the supply of money to the wardrobe was poor, which does suggest that non-payment was probably the real grievance for much of the time. Petitions were submitted to the parliaments of 1371–3,

1376, October 1377, 1378, 1380–1, February and October 1383, 1384–5, 1399 (relating to Richard II's household), 1401–2, 1404, 1406, 1407, and 1410.[95] Frequently, these went no further than requests for the enforcement of the statute; in 1384, the Great Statute of Purveyors even took its place alongside Magna Carta and the Forest Charter as one of those hallowed charters of liberties automatically confirmed at the opening of parliament. On occasions, however, the commons clearly believed that the sanctions written into the 1362 statute did not go far enough, and tried to strengthen them. In January 1380 they requested that justices of the peace be given the power to try purveyors who contravened the statute. On this occasion the request was refused, but when the same point was made in the parliament of October 1383, the king conceded that 'the damaged party have recourse to the common law if he wishes'. Clearly this was ineffective, however, for when in 1385 the commons yet again asked that justices of the peace should have the power to enforce the statute, the king once again refused.[96]. The king's refusal to tolerate interference with his household servants only served to increase their unpopularity and early in 1387 the Commissioners advised the king in strong terms that in future he should ensure that provisions purveyed for the household were paid for.[97]

At the beginning of Henry IV's reign complaints about purveyance intensified. In February 1400, when the reign was less than five months old, the council strongly advised him to stop abusing his right, while Thomas Walsingham declared that the main grievance against Henry in 1401 was that 'accipiens victualia, nihil solvit'.[98] When convocation made a grant to the king in 1404, it was only on condition that the goods of the clergy should be exempt from purveyance; in Archbishop Scrope's 'manifesto' of 1405, the only article concerning the household was one about the abuse of purveyance.[99] Some of the complexities of the problem are revealed in the request from the commons of 1402 that household purveyancing debts should take precedence over assignments for annuities on sheriffs' farms and it is worth remembering that several members of the commons held such annuities themselves.[100] After further bitter petitions on the subject during the long and difficult parliament of 1406, the commons in 1407 found one way of dealing with the matter. Thomas Chaucer, the speaker, presented the usual complaint that purveyors were not paying for the goods they took; the steward and keeper made the reply that any individual charges against purveyors would be heard, a device frequently used by the government, and usually sufficient to close the discussion. Chaucer was prepared this time, however, and promptly produced a petition brought by Sir Thomas Broke against William Wydycombe who presumably (though he is not listed in the account book for 1405–6) was a household purveyor. The details of the charges are not clear, but once the articles had been examined the commons 'prayed judgment' against Wydycombe; he was instead mainperned on pain of £1,000 to appear before the king in chancery next Hilary term. This occurred at the very end of the session (2 December) which might indicate that there had been something of a wrangle over what was to be done with Wydycombe and what happened to him following his appearance in chancery is, unfortunately, not known.[101] But the case highlights the difficulty of securing redress against the king's purveyors for cases concerning them were often heard in the household's own court, the court of the verge, and naturally it was far from easy to win judgments against them. Yet purveyors themselves could hardly be blamed for the non-payment which seems to have been the main grievance against them at this time (as compared to the 1340s and 50s, when charges of petty corruption were most frequent). They were not given the money to pay with, and when their creditors came into the counting-house to try to secure payment, there was probably little money there either. As seen above, the most persistent complaints against purveyance were in the years 1371–3, 1376–85, and 1399–1407; this fits well with the evidence concerning the wardrobe's level of indebtedness discussed earlier.

Associated with complaints about purveyance were petitions which claimed that the overall cost of the household was excessive and should be reduced. There were no complaints in these terms about Edward III's household during the later years of his reign, but the early years of Richard II's reign witnessed several vehement attacks on the young king's household, with phrases such as the 'grantz et excessifs coustages de dit Hostiel', and 'outrageouses nombre des familiers esteantz en dit Hostiel' being bandied around parliament with apparent impunity. This was bitterly resented by Richard. By 1385–6 he was clearly exasperated at the repeated criticisms of the commons, and replied very tetchily to the complaints made in those years.[102] In November 1381 the king was asked to draw up an ordinance regulating the size of the household (the commons claimed that its expense had been one of the main factors behind the rebellion of that year), and in 1383 he agreed to issue a new series of household regulations. None survive, however, although when a similar complaint was made in the parliament of 1385, Richard declared that he would in future try to abide by the regulations governing the household, by which he may have meant regulations which he and his ministers had drawn up since 1383.

The repeated criticisms of the commons during his minority help to explain Richard's over-reaction to Haxey's bill in February 1397. Since 1388, there had been no complaints in parliament about the way in which the king ran his household. From 1395, however, expenditure in the household had escalated rapidly, and the bill which Thomas Haxey presented (on behalf of the commons) in the first parliament of 1397 was all too reminiscent of the petitions of the king's minority: the size and expense of the household were outrageous, and bishops and ladies were being maintained in grand style at court when they ought to have been living at home at their own expense.[103] Richard was furious. He was determined that he would not brook again the temper of the parliaments of the 1380s. The commons were told that to discuss such matters was to infringe the king's regality, and were forced into abject apology. Haxey was convicted of treason, though spared his life at the request of the prelates (he being a clerk). There were no complaints about the household in the last parliament of the reign.

The early years of Henry IV's reign present a picture similar to that of Richard's minority. Once again, a highly critical series of parliaments directed their attacks against the government in general and the household in particular, and Henry could hardly react as Richard had done in 1397. The parliaments of 1401, January 1404 and 1406 were especially critical. In 1404 the embattled king, having been forced to expel four named persons from the household as a token gesture to reduce expenses, invited the lords to draw up guidelines for the size and cost of the household. In 1406 speaker John Tiptoft launched another violent attack on the household and demanded that forty-three named aliens be removed from it. It was agreed that the newly-appointed council should take in hand the whole question of household finance, and at a council meeting held at the end of the parliament this was done: the council declared that a 'suitable sum' should be set aside for household expenses over the Christmas period, after which king, council and household would retire to 'some suitable place' and make long-term provision for 'moderate government in the said household, so that it can in future exist to the pleasure of God and the people.'[104] Despite the reforms inaugurated at the council meeting (in March 1407, discussed below),[105] there were further complaints about the household's failure to pay its debts in the parliament of 1410.

Once again, it can be seen that criticisms of a general nature about the cost of the royal household fit into the pattern of insolvency suggested by the evidence of the wardrobe accounts: the years 1380–8, and 1397–1406, witnessed frequent such attacks. So how did critics of the household think that the situation could be remedied?

One method by which it was hoped that reform in the household could be achieved was by securing the appointment of key officers of the household in parliament. This was not of course a new idea; it went back to the reign of Henry III, and had emerged on several occasions since then, usually at times of political crisis (1258, 1311 and 1341 are the obvious examples). Nor was it restricted to officers of the royal household, but usually embraced the three chief officers of state as well (chancellor, treasurer, and keeper of the privy seal), and sometimes lesser royal officers such as the chief justices, chief baron of the exchequer, and keepers of the king's forests. What is noticeable, however, is that at times when the household in particular was under attack, the number of household officers whose appointment in parliament was demanded tended to increase. The first parliament of Richard II's reign made such a request, which included all the royal officials mentioned above, as well as the steward, keeper of the wardrobe, and king's chamberlain. This was probably prompted more by the age of the king than by any intended criticism of his household at such an early stage of the reign, but when in January 1380 the commons requested that the 'Cynk principalx Officers' of the realm (defined as the chancellor, treasurer, keeper of the privy seal, steward and chamberlain) be chosen and sworn in parliament, a degree of criticism was clearly implied. The request was repeated in November 1380, and then in 1381 a variation on the theme was attempted when the chief officers of the household (only) were made to swear in parliament that they would enforce the regulations of the household newly-established by the commission set up a few days earlier.[106] Further similar requests followed in 1383 and 1385, by which time Richard was becoming exasperated with them. He was eighteen now, and resented the constraints which successive parliaments had tried to place on his powers. To the request in 1385 he replied curtly that the king 'will change them (his officers) when he pleases', and a further request that the household should be 'viewed' once a year by the three chief officers of state was met by Richard's retort that he would do it when it pleased him to do so. It was not until the parliament of 1386 that the commons had any success on this front. On this occasion when a similar request was made, it was backed up with the impeachment of chancellor Michael de la Pole, and on 24 October all three principal officers (de la Pole, treasurer John Fordham, and Walter Skirlaw, keeper of the privy seal) were replaced. However, the commons had also asked that a new steward of the household be appointed in parliament, but this Richard specifically refused to do, saying that he would appoint his steward by the advice of his council. In fact, early in 1387 he appointed as steward the thoroughgoing courtier John Beauchamp of Holt, who within little more than a year had lost his life at the hands of the Appellants. At the beginning of 1388, the Appellants replaced Beauchamp with John Devereux, and appointed Peter Courtenay as king's chamberlain in place of Simon Burley (the king was 'well pleased' to accept Courtenay, who was already a chamber knight, according to the Westminster chronicler).[107] This was the only occasion in Richard's reign (after 1382, that is, when he began to rule as well as to reign) when the king was forced—and forced is clearly the right word—to accept as chief officers of his household men who were not his own nominees.[108]

Following his resumption of power in May 1389, Richard immediately implemented wholesale changes in the personnel of his chief officers of state, but he seems to have been quite content with his chief household officers, and there were no further requests during his reign for either household or other officers of the king to be appointed in parliament.[109] Predictably, such requests were renewed early in Henry IV's reign, and met with more success. The question of the appointment of royal officers first raised its head in the parliament of January-March 1401, when the commons attempted to secure the dismissal of the three chief officers of state and the three chief officers of the household, whom on this occasion they defined as the steward, the keeper of the wardrobe, and the controller of the household.[110] On 8 March, at the very end of the parliament, all three chief household officers were duly replaced. This was a striking success for the commons (although the three chief officers of state were not replaced quite so promptly). What is also of significance here is that the demands for changes in household personnel concentrated more on the financial officers, such as the keeper and controller, than on the political officers such as the chamberlain. Criticism of Richard's household during his minority was politically as well as financially inspired.[111] Criticism of Henry IV's household was largely restricted to its finances.

Although there were further requests (notably in 1404) for household officers to be appointed in parliament, not until 1406 did the commons again succeed in bending the king to their will in this matter. In this year they asked
that the king's councillors, the three chief officers of state, and the steward,
keeper, controller, and king's chamberlain should all be sworn to adhere to the
common law, and that the latter four be sworn to observe the regulations of
the household (particularly in respect of purveyance) and to answer for it at
their peril at the next parliament.[112] At the end of the parliament the commons
scored a further success when they persuaded the king to accept John Tiptoft as
keeper of the wardrobe for he had been speaker, and was a declared reformer.
At a meeting on 8 December 1406, the day on which Tiptoft took up office,
the council also tried to persuade Henry to accept either Thomas Brounfleet or
Arnold Savage (speaker in the parliament of January 1404, and another avowed
reformer) as Tiptoft's controller, but Henry declined to remove John Straunge
from the post, and in fact Straunge continued to act until the end of the
reign.[113] Brounfleet did however become keeper in July 1408, when Tiptoft
moved from the wardrobe to the exchequer, and the backing which the council
gave him in 1406 probably helped him to secure this appointment. He was evidently trusted by the commons too, for in March 1401 it was he who had
replaced Robert Litton as controller.

After 1406 there is no evidence of further requests for the appointment of
officers of the household in parliament, and there was considerably more stability in the top echelons of the household as a result. In 1401 and 1406, Henry
had been persuaded to accept something which Richard had never accepted
(until forced to, in 1388), namely that the chief officers of the royal household
were men of very considerable public responsibility, and as such it was not
entirely reasonable of the king to regard their appointment as a purely personal
matter. They handled enormous sums of money, and should be expected to
shoulder some of the blame when things went wrong. The commons in Henry
IV's reign had a clear idea of the type of man who should be in charge of
household finance: the appointments of March 1401 all saw the replacement of
a long-standing Lancastrian servant with little or no experience of handling
crown finances by an experienced royal administrator who had held high
office in Richard II's household.[114] For a year or two, the new officers did
manage to reduce expenses in the household quite considerably; it was not
until the period of his last account (1403–5) that the financial pressure on
Thomas More really caused him to run up large debts.[115] Richard Kingston,
the keeper replaced in December 1406, was another long-serving Lancastrian
with little experience of high financial office in the service of the crown. Tiptoft, who replaced him, may not have had any more financial experience than
Kingston, but he had made his views on household finance known in no uncertain manner, and presumably the commons trusted him to carry through his
promises of reform; they were not to be disappointed. It may well be true,
then, that the officers replaced in 1401 and 1406 were incompetent, and in a
sense contributed to the financial chaos of 1399–1401 and 1405–6. In this

context, it is worth noting that there were no attempts to replace Richard II's keeper William Packington either in 1386 or in 1388. Packington's problems were in some ways similar to those faced by Henry IV's keepers, but there was a crucial difference too: expenditure on the household in the 1380s was far from excessive, whereas between 1399 and 1406 it was. There was at least one direct road to financial solvency between 1399 and 1406, and that was by slashing expenditure; Packington's major problem, on the other hand, stemmed from the exchequer's inability to provide the wardrobe even with quite moderate amounts of money. There was little that any keeper could do about this.

Richard's reluctance to take advice concerning the appointment of royal officers led to the adoption of another device by the commons, that is, the attempt to secure an all-embracing commission of reform, established and sworn in parliament, with a mandate to root out waste and effect economies wherever possible. Again this was not a new idea (the Ordainers of 1311 are the obvious example), and again such commissions were not suggested solely in order to deal with the household. It is clear, however, that at times it was the household in particular to which the commissioners were supposed to turn their attention. The most famous and effective of these commissions was of course the one appointed in the 1386 parliament, but the success of 1386 was the culmination of a series of attempts to set up such a commission, all of which had previously proved ineffective. The continual council established in the Good Parliament of 1376 can be regarded as a sort of precedent for such bodies, although it was not established so much to effect economies as to fill the political vacuum caused by Edward III's senility (and was as such totally ineffective). Moreover, it is clear that the existence of a continual council did not exclude the possibility of a separate commission, for the first attempt to set up a commission in Richard's reign occurred in the Easter 1379 parliament, when the third continual council was still holding power. On this occasion, and again in January 1380, a body of commissioners was sworn in parliament and accepted by the king, but they seem to have been unable to translate their appointments into reality once parliament had ended. In November 1381 the commons were more determined: another commission was appointed, and the commons refused to resume parliamentary business until they had ascertained that it was actually meeting. The commissioners did meet and one of their first acts was to recommend the dismissal from the household of Thomas Rushook, the king's unpopular confessor, and they probably even got as far as drawing up regulations on the size and expense of the household.[116] Once again, though, the commissioners seem to have been ignored as soon as parliament had ended, and not until 1385 did the commons return to the idea when the same procedure was repeated, and again it is clear that the commission did meet, for in the parliament of 1386 de la Pole was accused of ignoring the recommendations which it put forward.[117]

Hence the anger of the commons in October 1386. Having seen their wishes flouted on so many occasions, this time they both impeached de la Pole and made their grant of a subsidy conditional upon the continued efficacy of the Commission of Government for one year. The emphasis on reform of the household was stronger in the 1386 commission than in any previous one, although naturally their terms of reference comprised a thorough overhaul of crown finances.[118] Richard had no option but to hand over control of the chancery and exchequer to the commissioners, but in early February 1387 he removed his household from the London area and spent most of the next nine months in the midlands and north of the country, largely it seems in order to avoid the scrutiny of the commissioners. Thus when, after Radcot Bridge, the Appellants entered the royal household at Westminster and (according to some chroniclers) effected a wholesale purge of the king's servants, they could with justice claim that they were only doing what the commissioners had been charged with doing, but prevented from effecting, in 1386–7.

The Commission of Government of 1386–7 shaded into the Appellant regime of 1387–9, so that for about two and a half years (November 1386 to May 1389), Richard exercised little real control over his principal departments of government. The reforms initiated by Richard's opponents between 1386 and 1389 were extensive and, in some areas at least, met with considerable success. For a start, expenditure in the wardrobe was cut substantially, especially during the first year of the commission (1386–7), when it was only £11,922. What is important to note, however, is that the commissioners made a real attempt to clear some of the backlog of household debts. In fact, during the financial year 1386–7, the exchequer actually passed *more* money to the wardrobe (£15,067) than it had in 1385–6 (£14,634). The difference was that creditors on earlier accounts were given priority over current expenses. Of this £15,067, only £1,718 was made available for current expenses, while the remaining £13,349 was used to pay off debts incurred before the 1386–7 accounting period began. Naturally this created further debts in 1386–7, but over the next two years the reduced level of expenditure did ease the situation, and by the time Richard resumed power in May 1389 the danger that the six-month stop might become a twelve-month stop had been averted.[119]

Yet the commissioners were well aware that this was only part of the problem, and that what was really needed was the maximisation of the revenues of the crown so that there would actually be more money coming into the exchequer which could be passed on to the spending departments. To this end a committee was set up in February 1387 to investigate the profits derived from royal lands, feudal casualties, and the alien priories in each county, to try to ensure that they were being properly valued and that the king's claims were not being evaded.[120] One result of this was that more stringent conditions came to be attached to grants of these revenues: from the spring of 1387 onwards, those who held farms of royal lands, customs, alien priories, and feudal casualties were obliged to enter into recognisances for double the amount of the annual farm, to be levied in case the farm was more than one month in arrears; alternatively, they could be expelled. It also became usual in 1387 to attach to such grants a clause stipulating that 'if in future some other person shall be willing to render more for the keeping, then the said N. may render such larger sum and have the keeping in preference to others' (sometimes this clause was qualified by 'genuinely willing to render more'). Similar clauses had only occasionally been employed for royal farmers during the first decade of the reign but now they became systematic, and can sometimes be seen in operation.[121] For a year or so after his resumption of power in May 1389 Richard II continued the practice of attaching these clauses to grants, but gradually between 1390 and 1392 they ceased to be used. Occasionally in 1391–2 the king even allowed the attachment to grants of a clause stating that even if someone else did offer more, the grantee was not to be asked to pay more or to be expelled.[122]

There are various indications that during the years 1386–9 more importance was attached to the principle of trying to maximise profit from crown assets, and less to the view that such assets were there to be distributed as rewards for political support. In February 1389, for example, offers were invited from any who wished to purchase lands forfeited by the 'traitors' convicted in the Merciless Parliament, the clear implication being that they were to be sold to the highest bidder.[123] This contrasts markedly with Richard II's treatment of the estates forfeited by his opponents in 1397, which were rapidly granted out to a small group of royal favourites. When James Berners was granted the marriage of the son and heir of Robert Lord Poynings for 500 marks in November 1387, it was 'on condition that he ask no pardon of the said sum or any portion of it; if he has obtained any such pardon he is to derive no advantage therefrom, nor mitigation of the sum'.[124] In this case it may well be that the condition imposed was inspired by personal as much as financial reasons, for Berners was an intimate of the king who was to lose his life at the hands of the Appellants within five months.

There does, however, seem to have been an attempt to reduce financial corruption generally. In February 1387 a proclamation was issued to the effect that all those 'who have since the king's coronation given or paid ought to his officers or others to have or procure assignments or payments by tallies levied in the receipt of the exchequer, shall hasten to the great council in order to sue and declare in particular how much they so paid or gave, to whom and how.' Where such payments could be proven, those who sued were to have one-third of any sums recovered.[125] For much of the time, this process of (in effect) discounting exchequer tallies seems to have gone on unchecked and, as with the similar charges laid against John Lord Nevill and others in the Good Parliament, there was no doubt a degree of political vindictiveness involved in initiating such a process. Nevertheless, it was a step in the right direction.

The Westminster chronicler claimed that on the last day of 1387, the Appellants began a drastic purge of the royal household: 'they came to Westminster, where they discussed the persons who stood about the king, considering whether or not they deserved to remain in attendance on him; and inquired into the horde of officials ensconced in every department. The buttery was found to contain a hundred office-holders; and in the kitchen and all the other departments they likewise discovered superfluous numbers, whose excess they pruned, while still leaving those departments adequately staffed.'[126] It is impossible to verify this statement from wardrobe account books, as none survive between those of 1383−4 and 1389−90, which record household staff levels of 396 and 454 respectively.[127] As is well known, many of the king's chamber knights and royal clerks were either executed or told to absent themselves from court in 1388. There is some evidence from the early months of 1388 that a few minor figures in the household were also pensioned off. In April, for example, two palfreymen of the king were granted annuities of 2*d.* each 'provided that [they] do not henceforward reside in the household nor receive wages or robe therein', but this is hardly sufficient to support the idea of a wholesale purge as suggested by the chronicler.[128] On the other hand, the chronicler should have been in a good position to know what was happening at Westminster, and he is on the whole a reliable source for this period of the reign. That some sort of reduction in the size of the household occurred at this time, and as a result of action taken by the Appellants, is very probable. It did not however make a major contribution towards reducing expenditure in the wardrobe, since this was actually higher in 1387−8 than it had been in 1386−7.

Critics of the Appellants have often pointed to the £20,000 which they awarded themselves at the end of the Merciless Parliament; this, they claimed, was to enable them to pay their expenses for the Radcot Bridge campaign. Whatever the rights and wrongs of this grant, their financial motivation should not be judged by one act alone. There were indeed some serious attempts to bolster up royal finances between 1386 and 1389. What was plain to all, however, was that it was only by securing virtually complete control of the major government departments that the king's critics had eventually forced him into financial retrenchment, both in relation to his household and in other spheres of government spending. This had entailed a major political upheaval which brought the country to the verge of civil war, and was an experiment born of desperation. The fact that on as many as five occasions between 1379 and 1386 the commons had requested such commissions shows just how uneasy they felt about the household and the financial policy of the government generally during these years.

After 1389, there were no more requests for all-embracing commissions during Richard's reign, nor was it an expedient resorted to in Henry IV's reign. The commissions demanded between 1379 and 1386 could be justified by reference to the king's age, an argument which could hardly be used about Henry IV. Perhaps, too, the eventual successful establishment of a commission in 1386 had proved too traumatic an experience in the political history of the country for it to be repeated so soon. Instead, the commons under Henry preferred to try to secure the appointment of the king's councillors in parliament, a move which, if successfully carried through, could have an effect very similar to the transfer of governmental control from the king to the commission of 1386. The history of the king's council in Henry IV's reign has been exhaustively studied. For long periods, notably in the years 1407 and 1410−11, it really did exercise extensive powers independently of the king, and can thus be closely equated with the commission of 1386, except that no time limit to the exercise of its power was set. It is also worth emphasising that although it was the commons who complained most loudly about government finances, they preferred on the whole to leave it up to the council (in whom they thus showed a similar faith to that shown by the commons in the magnate commissions of 1379–86) to draw up the detailed arrangements for financial reform.[129] These proposals for reform now need to be discussed in greater detail.

The war-treasurers

In general terms, the aims of those who tried to reform the finances of the royal household were threefold. Firstly, they wished to see expenditure reduced; secondly, they wished to see a steady supply of direct payments into the wardrobe, so that expenditure could be met, and purveyancing debts would not be allowed to accumulate; thirdly, they wished to ensure that only those sources of revenue which ought to be used for the household were in fact used for it, so that other sources of supply could be devoted to the purposes for which they had been properly granted.

From the mid 1370s, the question of which sources of revenue could properly be used to supply the household became a matter of frequent discussion in parliament, and during the minority of Richard II the attitude taken by successive parliaments was very stringent. To begin with parliaments' requests were usually made in fairly general terms, as in October 1377 when the commons asked that the king's household be financed solely from the 'revenues du roialme et de les autres droitz de sa corone et seigneuries.' Naturally this excluded both direct and indirect subsidies, but what else did it exclude? In 1381 they asked that the king should 'vivre honestement de son propre desoreenavant.' What they meant by this was made clearer in the parliament of February 1383, when the king was asked to 'vivre deinz les revenues de votre roialme', so that the wool subsidy, together with all wardships, marriages, escheats and 'autres commoditees' could be applied entirely to the war. Richard replied that he would ordain good government in his household by the advice of his council, 'salvant son honeur'.[130] If feudal casualties, together with all kinds of subsidies, were to be used exclusively for the war, what did this leave for the household? Strictly speaking, only the ancient custom, the farms of alien priories, and the traditional crown revenues such as farms of the shires, profits of justice, the mint, the hanaper and so forth. But what in practice could the commons do about it? With regard to feudal casualties, they could do very little, and there are in fact numerous examples of profits from wardships, marriages, and temporalities *sede vacante* being reserved specifically for the household during this period.[131] Indeed it seems that, despite the requests of the commons, feudal casualties were generally regarded as one of the principal sources from which the household might derive its cash, and when the king's opponents were in power between 1386 and 1389 they seem to have had no objection to this policy.[132] The other main sources, apart from traditional crown revenues, which were sometimes reserved for the household were the ancient custom and the farms of alien priories. In December 1377 it was actually stipulated that the ancient custom should be paid directly into the wardrobe, rather than into the exchequer; for much of the reign, some or all of the alien priories too were specifically reserved for the household.[133]

Large assignments for the household were in fact generally drawn on the permissible revenues during the 1380s, but the use also of feudal casualties demonstrates one fact of which the commons were acutely aware, namely that once money had actually reached the exchequer, there was very little that could be done, short of establishing a commission of the type that took office in November 1386, to stop it being used in whatever way the king decided. Therefore, as far as the subsidies were concerned, and it was after all the commons who granted the subsidies, about the proper use of which they consequently felt particularly strongly, more stringent controls were necessary. It was for this reason that the system of war-treasurers was developed. It was a system which was to have a disastrous effect on household finance.

The first request by the commons for the establishment of separate treasurers for war revenues came in the last parliament of Edward III's reign, in January 1377. They asked that two earls and two barons be appointed to supervise the spending of the first poll-tax, granted here, so that none of it should be paid into the exchequer but that it should be spent solely and entirely on the war. These four should also, it was suggested, supervise the spending of the clerical tenth and the wool subsidy (but not of course the ancient custom). A memorandum inserted into the *Rotuli Parliamentorum* states that when the commons were informed how much these four lords would have to be paid in fees if made to undertake the task, they dropped their request and agreed that the treasurer should receive the taxes 'en manère acustumee'.[134] This sounds distinctly like a piece of sharp thinking on the crown's behalf. In a sense, though, the system of having separate war-treasurers was one which emanated from the crown itself. The traditional channel through which war wages were paid was the wardrobe, and with the renewal of the war in 1369 this procedure was once again adopted. Between June 1369 and June 1371, Henry Wakefield as keeper of the wardrobe accounted for war wages totalling £74,934. From June 1371 until December 1372 there was no official treasurer for war, although Wakefield continued to receive much of the money spent on the war, and not all of it was for arrears.[135] By the end of 1372, however, following the dismal failure of Edward III's final attempt to lead an expedition in person, it must have been clear to all that the king would take no further active part in the military prosecution of the war, and the wardrobe was thus deemed inappropriate as a channel for war revenues. A separate war-treasurer was appointed, Adam Hertingdon, who was also Beauchamp chamberlain of the receipt, and he accounted personally for all monies spent on the war between 1 December 1372 and 31 January 1374.[136] In fact he continued to receive large sums for the war through until December 1374, although most of what he received after January was for arrears.[137] For the 1375 campaign there seems to have been no official war-treasurer, the sums being delivered directly to the commanders by various clerks of the exchequer, and no separate account of military expenses being compiled.

There was thus a precedent for the request made by the commons in January 1377, at least a precedent of a sort. At any rate, there was a vacuum to be filled, for it would obviously be several years before Richard was old enough to lead a campaign in person, and not until that time would the wardrobe of the household again be the appropriate channel for military expenses. On the other hand, what the commons were asking for was clearly something rather different. Hertingdon had been an exchequer official. What the commons wanted was a system of independent officials receiving these war-grants directly from the collectors, specifically to ensure that none of it went into the exchequer, whence it could easily be diverted to non-military purposes. Dr Sherborne has shown recently that it is highly probable that in the years before 1377 quite a lot of money granted for the war was in fact diverted to other purposes, hence the demand made in January 1377. After 1377, he suggests, very little money from war-grants was used for other purposes. Nevertheless, the commons remained suspicious, and thus continued to request the appointment of war-treasurers.[138] But it was not simply because the commons remained suspicious that they continued to make such requests: it was precisely because the use of war-treasurers proved so successful.

In the parliament of October-December 1377, the commons repeated their request for separate war-treasurers, and this time it was granted. The London merchants John Philpot and William Walworth were duly appointed as joint war-treasurers on 14 December; they were personally to receive all revenues granted for the war (the double tenth and fifteenth, the clerical tenth granted in convocation, and the wool subsidy) and to ensure that they were spent solely and entirely on military expenses; special lists of 'war receipts' were to be drawn up and itemised separately from other revenues on the exchequer receipt rolls.[139] In fact the system of drawing up separate lists of war receipts was not adopted until a year later, but there is no doubt that the new system was effective from the start. On 2 February 1379 Philpot and Walworth were formally acquitted for a total of £145,651 received and disbursed by them between 14 December 1377 and 4 February 1379, which they had spent entirely on the war. In the parliament held at Easter 1379, a petition was submitted requesting that these two should now be relieved of their office, and that all subsidies should in future be received at the exchequer in the normal manner, and not surprisingly the king readily agreed to the request.[140] This is rather strange, for it was quite contrary to the normal attitude of the commons during this period, nor indeed (despite the indication to the contrary in the official parliamentary record) was it acted upon. It may be that the request came from Walworth and Philpot themselves and their acquittance for sums received in February 1379 may be an indication that they did not particularly enjoy their job, for the responsibilities were very considerable and it is probable that they were subjected to pressure from both sides. They continued to act as war-treasurers, however, and from Michaelmas 1378 their special receipts were itemised separately on the exchequer receipt roll, which makes it easy to work out the precise total received by them as compared with the amount received through the normal channels. During the Easter 1379 exchequer term they received a total of £55,235 out of a real receipt of £56,931 recorded on the roll.[141] On 18 November Walworth and Philpot were personally acquitted for all sums received by them up to the end of the Easter 1379 term, but this did not signal the end of the system.[142] Either Walworth and Philpot continued to act (which seems probable), or new treasurers of war were appointed to cope with the grants received for Buckingham's expedition in 1380, in accordance with the request made in the parliament of January 1380.[143] During the Michaelmas term 1379–80, special war receipts totalled £51,754 out of a real receipt total of £71,591, while in the Easter term 1380 the special receipts amounted to £118,990, which actually exceeded the real receipt total of £114,011.[144] This introduces a cautionary note, suggesting as it does that some of the special receipts for the war could be book-keeping entries. There were indeed some, but they were very few; on the whole—as would be expected, given the nature of the revenues they were receiving—the special receipts itemised by the war-treasurers consisted largely of cash, with book-keeping entries occurring mainly among the 'normal' receipts brought to the exchequer in the accustomed way.

Unfortunately there is no surviving exchequer receipt roll for the Michaelmas term 1380–1, but since the commons, when they granted the fateful third poll-tax in the parliament of November 1380, again specifically requested that it should be received separately, there must be a good chance that this was done.[145] It is worth noting just how much crown revenue had been diverted from the exchequer during the first three years of the reign. Steel has calculated that between September 1377 and September 1380 the real receipt of the exchequer (i.e. excluding book-keeping entries) amounted to £497,538; special receipts by the war-treasurers during the same period accounted for £371,632 of this, almost exactly seventy-five percent. The significance of this as far as the household was concerned is that it left only about £125,000 over a three-year period to cover all extra-military expenses of the crown. It also meant that the items of revenue most likely to be received in large individual sums were removed from the household's grasp. Not surprisingly, therefore, household assignments during this period tended to be made up of a host of tallies spread around a number of sources each of which was not capable of producing a great deal of revenue, which was hardly likely to be conducive to efficient financial management in the household.[146] So although taxation was running at a high level during the early years of Richard's reign, the success of the commons in enforcing the principle that it should not be used for purposes other than the war was making it very difficult for the government to find adequate sources of supply for recurrent expenses such as the household.

After the events of 1381, the level of taxation dropped considerably, but when subsidies were granted the commons continued to try to ensure that these were spent only on the war. Such requests nearly always accompanied the grants.[147] Evidence from the receipt rolls suggests however that the system was not being operated between 1381 and 1385 as successfully (from the point of view of the commons) as it had been during the opening years of the reign. There are no lists of special receipts during these years, and revenues from subsidies seem to have been treated—for the purposes of receipt—like any other sort of revenue. Whether they were in practice reserved for war expenses only, as was promised by the king and his advisors in successive parliaments, is impossible to say. There are examples of subsidies being misappropriated (for example, a household assignment of £600 on the clerical tenth in August 1383) but they are few and far between.[148] Most of the evidence for the continued efficacy of the war-treasurers system during this period relates to tunnage and poundage, which the commons clearly regarded as appropriated supply to be used primarily for the defence of the seas. In the parliament of May 1382 Thomas Beaupyne and John Polymond were appointed to receive the wool subsidy and tunnage and poundage from the western ports, and John Philpot and Hugh Fastolf to receive it from the northern ports, and in their letters of appointment it was always said that this should be spent only on the 'garde du mer'. In the October 1383 parliament the system was changed, so that instead the money from tunnage and poundage was to be paid directly to the two admirals of the western and northern fleets; the admirals, as well as the king and his ministers, were sworn in parliament not to put these revenues to any other purpose.[149] But it was difficult for the commons to maintain such strict vigilance, and general orders such as these were often countermanded by special mandates from king or council. In December 1383, for example, all collectors of tunnage and poundage were ordered to bring any money they had straight to the exchequer 'any command of the king to the contrary notwithstanding'; in June 1383 Thomas Beaupyne (a Southampton merchant) was himself allowed the first 500 marks from the wool customs and subsidies in his native port, in repayment of a loan given by him to the household, which was in fact a rather roundabout way of using the wool subsidy for the household.[150] In general there do seem to be grounds for suspicion that between 1381 and 1385 appropriation of supply was not enforced quite as strictly as it had been between 1377 and 1380. It was not a practice approved of in any way by kings, who much preferred to have all revenues brought into the exchequer so that they could determine the order of priorities for disbursement, and it may be that while the lords of the council between 1377 and 1380 had felt constrained to accede to the full rigours of the system, Richard II, once he began to exercise power in person, felt less obliged to do so.[151] But with the level of taxation well down after 1381, and appropriation of supply still, it seems, enforced to a considerable degree, the household was not finding it any easier to secure the cash that it needed.

The angry parliament of October 1385 returned to the question of misappropriation once more, and insisted that more decisive steps be taken for its enforcement. Three war-treasurers were appointed: William Gunthorpe, baron of the exchequer (who in fact did not act) John Hadley and Nicholas Exton, both prominent citizens of London. They were to be 'controlled' (i.e. their receipts were to be supervised) by the former treasurer Thomas Brantingham, bishop of Exeter, and John Lord Cobham; they were to receive the one and a half tenths and fifteenths voted in parliament, which were to be spent only on the war or the defence of the sea; each payment was to be authorised by the council under letters of privy seal; Hadley and Exton were to notify the exchequer weekly of their receipts, and each was to receive a fee of £20 for his labour.[152] The receipt roll for the Michaelmas 1385–6 term records special receipts for the war of £43,484 with a further £25,445 received in the Easter 1386 term.[153] Steel has calculated that real receipts at the exchequer during these two terms totalled £134,412, so the special receipts accounted for about forty-four percent of this total. (The acquittance given to Hadley and Exton in August 1387 gives slightly different figures, but they were not the only persons who acted as war-treasurers during these two terms.)[154] Once again, this proved disastrous for the household; it was in 1385–6 that the six-month stop which had been in effect since 1382 almost became a twelve-month stop.

In the Merciless Parliament the commons again insisted that subsidies be used only for the war yet there is no evidence in the receipt rolls for either 1386–7 or 1387–8 that a war-treasurers system was in operation. At the Cambridge Parliament in September 1388, however, Nicholas Exton (again) and John Hermesthorpe were appointed as new war-treasurers to be replaced in May 1390 by John Hadley and William Fulbourne, who continued to act until they were acquitted in December 1390.[155] Between them, they received a total of £67,393 out of real receipts totalling approximately £145,000 at the exchequer between March 1389 and November 1390, just over forty-six percent.[156] Shortly before Christmas 1390, the system of separate war-treasurers came to an end, for Richard II's reign at least. From late 1390 through until the end of the reign there is no evidence of special receipts at the exchequer, and it is clear that subsidies of all kinds were now being received there in the normal way, along with other sources of revenue. Gradually, but noticeably, the attitude of the commons softened. In the parliament of November 1390 they were still insistent that the wool subsidy be used for the war only, while a year later they made the treasurer of England swear in parliament, under pain of impeachment in the next parliament, that the one and a half tenths and fifteenths granted should be put to no use other than the defence of the realm or the king's pro-jected visit to France. Conditions were again attached to the grant voted in January 1393, although no provision was made for their enforcement, but when the half tenth and fifteenth granted here was confirmed in January 1394, the commons allowed that it 'soit mys en disposition de nostre Seigneur le Roi et de son Conseill, pur estre dependuz sur les busoigns du Roialme, soit il Pees, Trieves, ou Guerre.'[157] Further grants made in the parliaments of January 1395 and January 1397 paid only lip-service to the idea of appropriation of supply, while in the 1397–8 parliament the king was granted the wool subsidy and tunnage and poundage for life, as well as one and a half tenths and fifteenths, with no conditions at all attached (although it was suggested that the money might be used by the king to reward some of his political supporters in 1387 and 1397, an invitation which Richard graciously accepted).[158] This was the first time in the fourteenth century that a lay subsidy had been granted in England without any stipulations at all as to how it should be spent.

Before 1390, then, appropriation of supply granted for the war was undoubtedly a subject on which the commons felt very strongly, and concerning which they were to a large extent able to enforce their will. One of the impeachment charges against chancellor Michael de la Pole in 1386 was that he had misappropriated the grant voted in the parliament of 1385 (although the evidence of the receipt rolls suggests that any such misappropriation was not on a large scale).[159] There can be no doubt that this was one of the principal factors behind the inability of the household to find sufficient sources of cash during this period. The problem with the 'traditional' revenues of the crown was that they were slow to come in, and were frequently heavily assigned with annuities and so forth; feudal casualties were unpredictable and there were sometimes objections to them being used for the household—as witness, for example, the wrangle over the March inheritance.[160] To meet its obligations, the household needed to have access to larger and quicker sources of revenue, but this it was for the most part denied. Hence the chronic shortage of cash in the wardrobe, the six-month stop, and the inevitable abuse of purveyance. Richard had some cause to feel aggrieved when the commons rounded on the household and accused it of not paying its way. In the parliament of April 1384 he protested (through the mouth of de la Pole) that he could hardly maintain a household at all, and begged to be granted some money so that he would not be put to shame by the king of France when he went to ratify the (projected) treaty between the two countries.[161] All the indications are that he was not exaggerating.

Evidence already discussed here shows clearly that the supply of cash to the wardrobe improved markedly after 1390, and it is difficult to avoid the conclusion that this was at least in part a result of the softening of the attitude of the commons towards appropriation of supply. Thomas Walsingham stated that as early as the parliament of January 1390, the commons had agreed that one-quarter of the proceeds of the wool subsidy should be given to the king to be spent as he pleased.[162] This is not mentioned in the *Rotuli Parliamentorum*, but it is not unlikely for such 'special grants' were quite often made in Henry IV's reign. The idea was that the sums allocated should be used to clear household debts, and it may be that the commons were increasingly aware that in order to achieve solvency in the household more constructive measures needed to be taken. To what extent the king used his new-found freedom after 1390 to supply his household with cash drawn from subsidies voted for the war is impossible to say: assignments for the household were not usually made on these sources (although some were),[163] but there is no way of knowing what was done with cash once it reached the exchequer. What is clear is that the king was now able to determine his own order of priorities for the disbursement of cash, and that the wardrobe benefited considerably from this. In November 1389, for example, the collectors in the twelve major English wool ports were ordered not to honour any tallies until the wages of the garrison at Calais had been paid, because wages there had fallen so badly in arrears that the soldiers were 'purporting to withdraw thence'. One exception was specified, however, with the treasurer of Calais to have preference over all other creditors, 'excepting our household'.[164] But the wardrobe also benefited from other, often short-term, but very useful, sources of cash during the 1390s. The March inheritance, for example, was regularly tapped between 1390 and 1394, and yielded at least 2,500 marks a year.[165] Queen Anne's contributions to the household increased after 1389, and after her death in June 1394 her estates continued to be administered by her former receiver-general, Thomas More, who was also now cofferer of the household, and who paid regular sums from the profits into the wardrobe. The murdered duke of Gloucester's estates yielded £1,000 to the wardrobe in 1398.[166] Not until 1397 did the flow of cash to the wardrobe begin to deteriorate once more; by this time, the problem was not the king's inability to regulate disbursements from the exchequer, so much as the level of expenditure in the household. By the end of the reign, Richard had a virtual *carte blanche* to spend his revenues as he pleased, but his reckless extravagance in the household was once again creating serious problems of supply.

From the beginning of Henry IV's reign, appropriation of supply and the definition of the sources upon which the household might draw again became thoroughly contentious issues, and again the steps taken to restrict the king's freedom to use his revenues as he pleased had a major effect on household finance. The evidence has been fully discussed by Dr Rogers, and what follows is more or less a summary of his conclusions.[167] During the first four years of the reign, the council seems to have been of the opinion that revenue for the household should normally be drawn from the following sources: tunnage and poundage, the alien priories, feudal casualties (including temporalities *sede vacante*), forfeitures, and of course the traditional crown revenues. Various experiments were tried, such as (in February 1400) using the forfeited estates of the Ricardian earls to establish the nucleus of a special fund for the household, or (in May 1401) reserving the entire proceeds from tunnage and poundage for the household for two years, but these experiments failed to attain either of their objectives, which were, firstly, to supply sufficient cash to the wardrobe, and secondly, to discourage the king from using subsidies for his household. In fact there was no effective check during these years on the king's ability to use his revenues as he pleased, and he frequently used both the lay subsidies and the clerical tenth to provide assignments for his household between 1401 and 1404. Despite this, the high level of expenditure in the household created massive debts, and by January 1404 the commons were in an angry mood.

In this parliament the commons made two suggestions concerning household finance, both of which were most unwelcome to the king. Firstly, they backed up the demands which they had made during the first four years of the reign (for subsidies to be used for the war only) with a demand for the re-appointment of war-treasurers. Four war-treasurers were duly appointed (John Oudeby, clerk, and three London merchants, John Hadley, Thomas Knolles and Richard Merlawe), and they acted in this capacity through most of 1404. Moreover, the system was renewed in the parliament of October 1404, which granted two full tenths and fifteenths, the wool subsidy for two years, and tunnage and poundage for two years, but only on condition that they should all be spent on the war. New war-treasurers were appointed, in the person of Thomas Lord Furnivall (who was also treasurer of England) and the chamber knight John Pelham. They were to 'responderont et accompt rendront a le Commune du Roialme a proschein Parlement'; the grants were not even to be used to pay off war debts outstanding, but only for its future prosecution; anyone who received any of this money for any purpose other than the defence of the realm in time to come was to be regarded as a traitor.[168] According to Rogers, the appointment of war-treasurers from January 1404 led to 'a complete breakdown of government finances'.[169] Between 1404 and 1406 appropriation of supply granted for the war was enforced with considerable success, and the result once again was that there was insufficient cash going to the wardrobe, so household debts once again mounted rapidly.[170] The second idea propounded by the commons in January 1404 was that a *certum* should be established for the wardrobe. This was probably not a new idea, for the council seems to have suggested a *certum* of £16,000 *per annum* for the wardrobe in 1401, but if so it was never implemented.[171] The *certum* proposed by the commons in January 1404 amounted to only £12,100, which was thoroughly unrealistic, and it was to be taken on those sorts of sources which the commons in the 1380s had regarded as appropriate for the household: customs, alien priories, and the traditional revenues.[172] Thus the attitude of the commons had hardened considerably since the beginning of the reign: tunnage and poundage was now excluded from the household's grasp, subsidies were to be protected from misappropriation by the war-treasurers, and Henry was given to understand in unequivocal terms what the commons thought his wardrobe's annual expenses should amount to— which was in fact about half of what it was spending at this time.

With regard to its size, the *certum* was totally ineffective, for Henry's wardrobe expenses during the three years following the January 1404 parliament continued at a level of more than double the proposed £12,100. The various measures imposed in 1404 did achieve something, however, for during these three years there were far fewer assignments for the household on the 'prohibited' revenues, and many more on the 'legitimate' ones. The chaos which this created caused the commons to launch their fiercest attack yet on the household in the long and bitter parliament of 1406. In future, they demanded, all the 'revenues of the kingdom' should be reserved for the household until its debts had been paid off. By this they meant traditional revenues, the ancient custom, feudal casualties, and alien priories.[173] As noted above, it was also in this parliament that they secured the appointment of Tiptoft as keeper of the wardrobe. There are signs, however, that despite the hard line taken by members of the commons in both 1404 and 1406, there was a growing realisation that the problems of household finance were not going to be cured by the sort of drastic strictures put forward in these parliaments. The whole question of crown income and the uses to which it could be put needed to be examined from a more realistic angle: which was more important, to achieve effective appropriation of supply, or to make proper provision for the household so that a start could be made in paying off its debts and restoring some sort of solvency? No doubt different members of the commons would have answered this question in different ways, but already in January 1404 there had been the beginnings of a shift in attitude when it was agreed that a sum of £12,000 should be set aside out of the newfangled tax on landed property, to be earmarked for the payment of household debts.[174] This remedy was repeated in 1406 when the council, meeting towards the end of the parliament, recommended that £10,000 should be reserved out of feudal casualties accruing to the crown over the next two years, again to be used to pay off household debts, and only after these had been met could feudal casualties be used to pay fees or annuities. At the same time, parliament agreed to submit the whole question of household finance to the council, and it was agreed that after Christmas the king, the council, and the household should retire to 'some suitable place' and hammer out an agreement on the matter.[175] In other words, the commons had in effect given *carte blanche* to the council to reach its own solution, as long as it worked.

Annuities, grants and the settlement of 1407

The proposed council met in March 1407, and, perhaps under the guidance of Tiptoft, made one vital recommendation that in future *all* sources of revenue, including the wool subsidy and other subsidies voted for the war, should be made available to the household. An indication that this was the direction in which the council might move had already been given when in December 1406 parliament had agreed to allow the king £6,000 out of the wool subsidy with which to cover Christmas expenses and pay off pressing creditors. This was followed in March 1407 with the council's decision to assign £7,000 out of the lay subsidy to the wardrobe and chamber, and £3,000 out of the wool subsidy to the wardrobe.[176] The new policy of making all revenues available to the household was ratified by the council again in February 1408, and during the last six years of the reign the three main household spending departments all continued to draw on the lay subsidies when necessary. This freedom to use all revenues marked the effective end (under Henry IV) of the campaign against misappropriation of supply, but from November 1408 it was accompanied by another demand less welcome to the king which was the imposition of a *certum*, an attempt to stop the household from abusing its access to large quantities of ready cash. Tiptoft had succeeded since 1406 in reducing expenditure considerably, and no doubt this, and the fact that he had made the wardrobe pay its way, helped to make the new policy acceptable, but there were evidently still those who considered £20,450 *per annum* for the wardrobe excessive.

The new *certa* were set at £16,000 for the wardrobe (of which £10,000 was to come from the lay subsidies), and £4,000 for the chamber (the chamber *certum* was raised to 8,000 marks in September 1410). These *certa* were ratified by the parliament of January 1410, and remained officially in force until November 1411, when the king, resuming control of government after a period of nearly two years when Prince Hal had effectively dominated the council and the government, abolished them. They had not really been effective in any case, for wardrobe expenditure had never been kept to £16,000, and the chamber was receiving about £8,000 a year from the exchequer after 1406. Moreover, special grants still had to be made on occasions to try to clear household debts: for example, in the parliament of January 1410 it was agreed that 20,000 marks from the lay subsidy, the wool subsidy, and tunnage and poundage, spread over three years, should be given to the king 'pur ent disposer et faire a vostre plesir,' and in November 1411 this was followed by the grant to the king of a special land tax of 6s. 8d. for every £20 worth of lands and rents, 'pur ent disposer et ordeigner a la frank volunte de nostre dit Seigneur le Roi'.[177] Nevertheless, the last six years of the reign did witness considerable improvements in the financial position of the wardrobe and this was partly because of the reduction in expenditure, but it was also a consequence of the household's ability to draw on those sources of revenue which were capable of providing large quantities of cash. A principle may have been sacrificed, but most of those concerned seem to have considered that it had been worth it.

The campaign which the commons had waged during the years 1377–90 and 1399–1406 to uphold and enforce the principle of appropriation of supply was in one sense contrary to their own interests. Many of the commons, and indeed of the lords, were crown annuitants with their annuities frequently being assigned on the traditional crown revenues (farms of the shires, crown lands, and so forth). When the king was unable to use extraordinary income to help cover recurrent expenditure such as the household, this naturally put greater pressure on the traditional sources of income, and could lead to substantial delays in the payment of annuities, or sometimes even complete stops on all assignments on sources of crown income. Naturally, therefore, there was another strand to the commons' criticism of government financial policy: in order to preserve his sources of income as much as possible, the king was asked to restrict his generosity, particularly, of course, if the recipients of his generosity were at the same time regarded as political undesirables. Yet it was always recognised that the distribution of grants, annuities and offices was both the right and the duty of any king. The problem, therefore, was a complex one, a question not only of balancing the demands of, for example, the household, against the demands of annuitants, but also of balancing the demands of different claimants to royal favour.

These crown annuities were often subject to delay. The exchequer issue rolls for the years 1372–4, for instance, clearly reveal that many annuities were unpaid in 1372–3, but that in 1374 payments were renewed and arrears often included for the previous year.[178] But despite the fact that Edward III was by nature both a generous and extravagant king, there is very little evidence to suggest that royal patronage became a politically contentious issue to any serious degree during his reign. In the mid 1360s it may be that the king was advised to cut back on his rapidly escalating domestic expenditure, but any 'financial crisis' at this time seems to have been putative rather than actual, and did not extend to Edward's distribution of rewards.[179] In the Good Parliament, however, Peter de la Mare asked that wardships and marriages be granted only to those who deserved them, and with the advice of the newly-appointed continual council. Whether this was intended as an attack on the unpopular court clique, or primarily as a financial expedient to preserve revenues, it heralded a new era in which such demands became frequent and vociferous.[180]

Dr Tuck has emphasised that royal patronage was a major political issue in Richard II's reign.[181] It was always a double-sided issue. Firstly, there was the 'political' problem that the wrong people were being patronised and secondly, there was the more strictly financial grievance that revenues ought to be preserved. There is clear evidence for both types of complaint during Richard's minority. The commissions requested in both the 1379 and 1380 parliaments were supposed to examine all annuities and grants distributed by the crown, but as seen above they were never given the power to do so.[182] In November 1381 the commons were more specific, requesting that in future no grant whatsoever of land, rent, wardship, marriage or escheat be made to any person until the king's debts had been cleared and the war ended. The royal reply to this was that this was altogether too drastic an undertaking to give, but that he promised not to make any grants without the consent of his councillors. In February 1383 the commons asked that all feudal casualties be reserved for the war, and in 1385 they petitioned that 'touz les revenuz notre Seigneur le Roi, si bien en l'escheqer come aillours' be reserved solely for the war, 'sanz estre donez a nully par null grant'. The king was invited to charge all his officers and councillors to abide by this, openly and in full parliament to which Richard agreed, and presumably it was done.[183] Naturally, the commissioners appointed in 1386 were given the power to review annuities, fees and grants, and there is plenty of evidence to suggest that they did so. They promptly advised the king not to make any grants out of his crown revenues or feudal casualties without their consent, or to appoint officers without consulting them. They also took upon themselves the task of issuing individual writs of *liberate* for the payment of fees and annuities, the implication being that those who did not receive such writs would not be paid.[184]

It is impossible to quantify the level of royal patronage as there are far too many occasions on which it is impossible to know the true value of, for example, a farm, or an office in the king's gift. Richard's patronage in the years 1382–6 does indeed seem to have been distributed to a rather narrow circle of favourites, and increasingly so in the years 1384–6 (Robert de Vere and Simon Burley in particular received large numbers of grants at this time), but in general Richard was far from profligate at this time, for the simple reason that he had very little

to give. Like any other king, Richard was hampered by the actions of his predecessor. During the first year of his reign, the council confirmed or granted annuities totalling £14,325 *per annum*; of this total, £8,189 consisted of confirmations
of annuities granted by Edward III; £2,927 consisted of confirmations of annuities
granted by the Black Prince (but these were, so to speak, self-supporting, for they
were on sources of revenue which had belonged to the Prince, and which now
fell in to the crown; nevertheless, they deprived the crown of the ability to use
these revenues for other purposes); and £3,208 consisted of new grants, which
were on the whole few in number but large.[185] There was really no option but
to confirm Edward III's grants. Life-grants were, after all, life-grants, not for
the life of the grantor but of the recipient, but naturally it reduced enormously
the new king's scope to reward his own supporters. There are numerous indications that throughout his minority Richard found it extremely difficult to
find sufficient sources of revenue with which to reward his own supporters on
even a modest level. In December 1380, for example, the king's chamberlain
William Beauchamp had to content himself with a promise of '200 marks yearly
so soon as the king shall be relieved of the payment of such a sum by the death
of those to whom annuities or rents to that amount have been granted, or so
soon as lands of that value come into his hands.' Similarly, in May 1383 the
chamber knight Sir Peter Courtenay was granted £40 at the exchequer 'until
the custody of a castle or some office falls vacant, when he is to have 100 marks
yearly.' The earl of Cambridge, the king's uncle, was finding it so difficult early
in 1380 to secure the 500 marks which he was supposed to receive annually at
the exchequer that he had to be granted the farm of part of the Despenser
wardship during the minority. When the commons requested that feudal
casualties or other types of revenue be reserved for the war, they sometimes
seem to have been taking little account of the government's other commitments. In July 1380 John of Gaunt was granted the marriage of Mary de
Bohun, whom he intended to marry to his son Henry; the marriage was said to
be worth 5,000 marks, but it was given to Gaunt for nothing in lieu of war
wages owed to him by the exchequer. In January 1383, the king acknowledged
a debt of £7,000 to John Lord Nevill for arrears of war wages and various
annual sums from the wool customs and subsidies were granted to him, plus
the promise of an assignment of £1,000 at the beginning of each financial year,
backed up with a promise of wardships and marriages falling in to the king
should any of his assignments fail.[186] There simply was not enough money to
go round.

No doubt this explains why Richard was eager to seize on whatever sources
he could, and in doing so he indeed seems to have acted outside accepted laws
or customs on some occasions, notably in relation to the lands enfeoffed for the
performance of Edward III's will, and in relation to the March inheritance.[187]
Before 1385, however, the number of new grants made by the king was very
limited. In 1385, one important new source of patronage became available to
the king when his mother died and her dower lands in the duchy of Cornwall
were used to reward several of the rising stars of the king's chamber.[188] In 1385

and 1386 there is a noticeable increase in the number of new grants calendared in the patent rolls, and not surprisingly it was the king's close friends and political supporters who were the principal beneficiaries (as had also been intended when Richard tried to use the resources of the March inheritance and the lands enfeoffed in Edward III's will). Richard had (or thought he had) at last found some room for manoeuvre, and was doing exactly what Edward III had done in the 1330s, that is, using the king's power of patronage to reward those closest to him. Richard seems himself to have been aware that some of these grants were controversial for on two occasions, firstly when granting the castle and lordship of Queenborough to Robert de Vere in the spring of 1385, and secondly, when granting an annuity of £1,000 at the exchequer in early 1386 to Leo, the deposed king of Armenia ('until he recovers his lost kingdom'), he concluded the grants with the phrase, 'the curse of God and St Edward and the king on any who do or attempt aught against this grant!'[189] These grants were probably unwise and so, it seems, was the restriction of royal patronage to a relatively limited number of men. But in the circumstances it is not easy to see what else Richard could do. Charity began at home, and the problem in the 1380s was that there was not enough to allow it to go much further.

Between 1386 and 1389 Richard had virtually no room for manoeuvre, and there is no doubt that grants made during this time would have had to have the approval of, in the first place, the commissioners, and in the second place the Lords Appellant. After 1389 there is evidence to suggest that conciliar supervision of grants remained normal for several years. Nearly all grants were made 'with the assent of the council', and up until *c*. 1393–4 the council remained a fairly independent and broadly-based body.[190] After 1393, however, the council gradually changed in composition, so that by 1397 it was heavily dominated by men who were closely associated with the court clique and unlikely to oppose the wishes of the king. Nevertheless, for much of this period, even up to 1397, Richard's distribution of patronage remained quite restrained. During the early 1390s it seems that the king and council were working to some sort of established guidelines when distributing grants. Apart from the multitude of grants made 'with the assent of the council' there were also some which were qualified with the phrase, 'as long as it does not contravene the ordinance of king and council'. This ordinance does not survive, but there are various clues as to what it might have said. William Pirie, the clerk of the king's private wardrobe, was told in November 1390 that he would be promoted to some benefice in the king's gift 'which he can enjoy to the yearly value of the amount limited by the statute of the household'. In March 1391 William Podmour was appointed marshal of the king's justice in South Wales, but only on condition that 'the said office is not one of those excepted by the king and council'. It seems to have been accepted policy too that the crown lands should not be granted out: when the king's esquire Nicholas Lond was granted the manor of Sevenhampton (Somerset) in December 1390, it was 'provided that the manor be not parcel of the crown'. Equally, when John Beaufitz was granted in February 1391 custody of the ferry between Sandwich and Stonor, it was 'on condition that it is not an office heretofore demised at farm for the king's pro-fit'.[191] Whether all this really adds up to a consistent policy of trying to keep crown lands in the king's hands, maximising profits from farms and offices, and restricting grants and annuities to fixed levels, is very doubtful indeed. But at least the intention to act along these lines seems to have been there, and may have been effective in some cases.

Such phrases as these disappear from grants calendared from 1392 onwards and as noted above, so do the clauses attached to royal farms calendared in the fine rolls.[192] From this time onwards, the pressure on crown income receded rapidly. There was no French war to pay for, the Irish campaign of 1394–5 was not particularly expensive, and not until 1395 did household expenditure really begin to rise. Moreover, there were various windfalls for the crown at this time. The Westminster chronicler said that following the Mortmain legis-lation of November 1391 there was a rush to buy licences before Michaelmas 1392, as a result of which 'the chancellor and the treasurer had by Michaelmas (1392) accumulated untold sums of money to fill the royal treasury to over-flowing.'[193] The corporate fine of £10,000 imposed on the Londoners reached the exchequer in February 1393.[194] In the following year Queen Anne died, and (despite the fact that Richard confirmed many of the annuities payable on her revenues, which reduced their value to himself) they nevertheless yielded substantial profits to the exchequer over the last five years of the reign.[195] The king's generosity expanded accordingly and in 1391–3, for example, he embarked on a new burst of retaining, which naturally pushed up the annuities bill at the exchequer.[196] Yet even as far as the king's new courtier clique of the 1390s was concerned, Richard, as Dr Tuck has pointed out, was initially far from indiscreet in his distribution of patronage.[197] Not until 1397 did the king's generosity to his political supporters really become excessive. Early in 1397 several of the leading figures in the court clique began to receive signifi-cant new favours.[198] In late 1397 and early 1398 Richard embarked on another burst of retaining, much more extensive and expensive, but at the same time more politically narrowly-based, than in 1391.[199] The forfeited estates of the magnates convicted in the 1397–8 parliaments, together with the profits from the March and Lancaster inheritances in 1398–9, were rapidly parcelled out to a small group of favourites. At the same time, household expenditure was soar-ing. When the commons in 1399 accused Richard of having dissipated the crown's revenues, and as a consequence having to raise exorbitant taxes which he then spent on his 'ostentation and pomp and vainglory', then with regard to the last three years of the reign they were undoubtedly right.[200] With regard to the earlier part of the reign, they were very probably wrong.

A few weeks later, the same point was made to Henry IV. The commons asked the new king to take care when making grants, and that he should only do so with the advice of his council and after making sure that he knew exactly what each grant was worth.[201] Henry, however, was in a difficult position for naturally, he must reward his own supporters, but at the same time he must be careful not to alienate too many of those who had been the recipients of Richard

II's generosity, for fear of provoking a backlash against the new regime. Rogers has estimated that during the first year of his reign Henry promised annuities totalling £22,351 on the crown revenues, divided almost equally between new grants and confirmations of grants made by Richard II. This accords well with the estimate of the council in July 1401 that the total annuities bill was in the region of £24,000.[202] Moreover, this excluded annuities assigned on duchy of Lancaster revenues; throughout the reign, the duchy revenues were burdened with approximately £8,000 worth of annuities, which largely nullified their usefulness to the crown as a source of ready cash.[203] It might be argued that such a heavy annuities bill was the price which a usurper had to pay for his crown, but it was also in part a consequence of Richard's extensive retaining policy in the 1390s.[204] By the time of his deposition, Richard's annuity bill must have topped £20,000. Even though Henry did not confirm all these (the annuities to Richard's Cheshiremen, for example, costing over £5,000, were not continued), this was a heavy burden to assume.

Nevertheless, the commons in successive parliaments were evidently convinced that there was no need for Henry to be as generous as he was. It was during Henry's reign, amid the general aura of financial crisis, that the question of annuities really came out into the open. For the first seven years of the reign, the commons adopted a highly critical but generally consistent attitude to the problem. They begged Henry to be less generous with his grants, and tried to create the machinery through which this might be achieved while at the same time they tried to ensure that annuitants did actually receive payment. But, and this was the crucial point, when it came to a choice between household creditors and crown annuitants, they consistently stipulated that household creditors should have preference.[205] Because there was so much pressure on all forms of crown income, what this meant was that in practice fees, wages and annuities were disastrously in arrears. In 1404, with the reintroduction of effective war-treasurers, the situation got even worse and in July, the king had to order a stop on all crown annuities, which seems to have remained in force for some two years.[206] This must have affected directly too many of the class from which the commons were drawn, for in the parliament of 1406, when they asked that certain types of revenue be set aside for the household, they also stipulated that any grants made out of these sources should nevertheless continue to be paid. From this time onwards, they reversed their priorities. In both 1408 and 1409, when sources for household assignments were specified, it was stated that these were to take second place to annuities charged on the same source.[207] Naturally, this was all part of the financial settlement worked out during the latter half of the 1406 parliament and in the March 1407 council. The crucial decision made then, it will be remembered, was to allow the household henceforth to draw on all sources of revenue, including the subsidies voted in parliament. One of the main reasons for doing this, undoubtedly, was to relieve the pressure on traditional revenues so that annuitants would in future be paid. And after 1406, the prospects for annuitants do seem to have improved. This was partly because the king was more circumspect about making grants. Dr Wolffe has asserted that 'royal grants which diminished the revenue do seem to have shown an appreciable drop from October 1406.'[208] But it was principally because annuitants now had preference over the household on these sources. In 1409 there was a concerted attempt to pay off arrears of annuities. But unfortunately the improvement did not last long. Within a year the pressure had once again become too great, and in the summer of 1410 another virtual stop on annuities had to be ordered.[209] A few months earlier, the speaker of the commons, Thomas Chaucer, had yet again begged the king to be less extravagant, and only to make grants to people 'if it is to the profit of the realm'.[210] Henry said he would try. He always did.

In this equation of household sources and annuities, there emerged also the question of the crown lands and the uses to which they were put. Dr Wolffe has argued that the origins of the expression that the king should 'live of his own' are to be found in the expressed desire that the king should stop abusing his right of purveyance, and that it was only with the accession of such a great landholder in his own right as Henry IV that it came to refer specifically to the idea that the crown lands should be reserved to form the basis of a fund from which the royal household could be supported.[211] Much of what Dr Wolffe says seems to be indisputable but with regard to Richard II's reign he has overstated his case a little. There do seem at this time to be clear indications of a movement towards the idea that traditional crown lands should be retained in the king's hands so that they could make a more substantial contribution towards recurrent expenditure. Dr Wolffe himself admitted that the idea seems to have been in some people's minds in 1340, and, as he again noted, the commons in 1377 and 1378 were at pains to point out to the young king that he had inherited the lands of both his father and his grandfather, and that this should have helped him to become rather more self-sufficient. Moreover, at the time of his deposition, Richard was condemned because he had been unable, 'without oppressing his people, to live honourably from the issues of the kingdom and from the patrimony belonging to the crown, when the kingdom was not burdened with the expense of wars.'[212] The idea also surfaced in 1388. Following the convictions and forfeitures in the Merciless Parliament, the commons requested that all lands and goods forfeited by the 'traitors', together with all other lands, feudal casualties, 'and other profits whatsoever' which fell in to the king for any reason, should be kept in the king's hands for as long as the war lasted, so that his debts could be paid off. This in itself was not much different from what had often been requested before, but the commons then stipulated one condition on which such lands might be granted out, namely

'that if any man has lands, tenements or possessions by grant of the king or of any of his predecessors, which were parcel of the crown, that by good agreement between the king's council and the holders of such lands and tenements, the same lands, tenements and possessions can be re-united to the said crown, to the king's profit; granting other lands, tenements or possessions out of the said forfeitures, in exchange for the said lands, tenements and possessions of the crown'.

The petition went on to say that no-one was to be forced to make such an exchange; also that the forfeits (but not the crown lands) could be sold off, as indeed some of them were. This certainly does not suggest that at this stage anyone thought that the king should be able to support his household solely out of the revenues of the crown patrimony, but it does suggest that there was a fairly clear idea of what the crown patrimony consisted of, and that there were those who thought that it should under no circumstances be alienated, but on the contrary attempts made to reassemble it.[213]

Even under Henry IV, it seems that the idea that the household should be supported principally from the crown patrimony was restricted to a fairly small and radical element among the commons. Even the most stringent of the arrangements agreed in parliament for the financing of the household, the £12,100 *certum* on specified sources in January 1404, envisaged a mixture of sources including substantial assignments on the alien priories, the cloth subsidy, and the wool customs.[214] Indeed it is difficult to detect any great difference between the attitude of Richard II's and Henry IV's parliaments (before 1407) on the question of which sources should be used for the household. Nevertheless, the idea that the crown lands should make a greater contribution to the exchequer was clearly gaining ground from the 1370s onwards. The clear expression of this attitude early in the fifteenth century which could be detected in some quarters was not solely a consequence of Henry IV's personal endowment; it represented also a gradual hardening over twenty-five years. The irony, of course, was that the 'settlement' of 1406–7 reversed this train of thought in one of its essential points, and allowed the subsidies to be used for the household.

CONCLUSION

The financial history of the household is one element—and often a major one— in the general history of royal finance. Throughout the period from 1360 to 1413 all the household departments except the chamber were almost entirely dependent for their funding on the exchequer. What this means is that the ups and downs of household finance will tend to reflect the more general strengths and weaknesses of the crown's financial position.

In the 1360s, the financial position of the household was on the whole very healthy. Despite the fact that Edward III, particularly in the middle years of the decade, was indulging in a domestic spending spree which some of his ministers, and apparently some of the commons, thought somewhat excessive, nevertheless the signs are that the exchequer was able to support this burden without great difficulty—the cash supply to the wardrobe was good, substantial debts left over from the war were paid off, and few new debts were allowed to accumulate. It is probable, however, that the vital factor in this equation was the personal wealth of the king, which was enormous at this time. Without this, it is unlikely that domestic spending could have reached the level it did, for much of Edward's chamber money was used to support the continuing military commitments in France, thus releasing 'ordinary' income for the household, the department of works, and the other domestic spending departments.

Once the threat of war loomed again, however, Edward quickly cut back on his domestic expenditure, spending much less on his household from the winter of 1367–8 until the end of the reign. Between 1368 and 1371 the king poured over £140,000 of his personal wealth into the exchequer, mainly to subsidise the renewed war effort. This, combined with an extensive and unpopular programme of borrowing,[215] was just about enough to tide the exchequer over the first two years of the war, but the enormous demand for money created by the intense military and diplomatic activity in 1369–70 caused the cash supply in the wardrobe to deteriorate (though not excessively), and debts began to mount.[216] The gravity of the crown's financial predicament led to the political crisis in the parliament of 1371, in which the three principal officers of the king were dismissed. By 1371 the king's personal wealth was probably more or less exhausted, though by this time substantial amounts of taxation were coming in. For the household, however, the years 1371–4 were difficult ones and by 1374, wardrobe debts amounted to at least £7,500, and the complaints against purveyance were renewed. Nevertheless, during the last three years of the reign these debts were largely paid off, partly because of a reduction in military activity, and partly because of another round of royal borrowing, especially in 1374.[217] This extensive borrowing, however, meant that although the household's financial situation may have improved, the exchequer's obligations did not decrease; the criticisms of the government's financial policy in the Good Parliament are evidence of this.

During the first three or four years of Richard II's reign the level of taxation was extremely high, but the successful introduction of the system of war-treasurers from December 1377 meant that the government was unable to divert much of this money away from the war effort. The continued employment of war-treasurers for much of the period from 1377 to 1390 was probably one of the main reasons why the finances of the household deteriorated steadily during the first decade of the reign. The cash flow from exchequer to wardrobe was meagre, creditors found themselves subjected to longer and longer delays, and by late 1386 wardrobe debts amounted to at least £13,000. As has been shown this led to repeated and angry criticism of the household in parliament, in relation both to purveyance and to its over-all size and cost. Allied to this was increasing pressure on the king to restrict his grants and annuities. Richard became thoroughly irritated with such criticisms, and with some reason perhaps, for his household was not particularly costly, and his grants and annuities were far from excessive. From 1384, however, he did begin to spend a little more on his household, and to reward his friends more generously which caused criticism to escalate further and finally to explode in the parliament of 1386.

During the next three years (1386–9) the commissioners and the Appellants instituted various financial reforms aimed at cutting royal expenditure, paying off creditors, and trying to maximise royal revenues, and they enjoyed a certain amount of success. Expenditure in the wardrobe during these years was lower than at any other time between 1360 and 1413, and many earlier creditors were now paid. In 1390, however, wardrobe debts still stood at £6,000 or more. It was only with the cessation of the war in 1389 that real recuperation could come and during the early 1390s the financial situation at the exchequer steadily improved, helped along by a number of windfalls. This is reflected in the lack of parliamentary criticism of household finance, and the softening of the commons' attitude on appropriation of supply, which in turn helped to improve the cash flow to the wardrobe. In 1392–3 particularly, many household debts were paid off. It was from this same year, however, that Richard's domestic expenditure began to increase significantly, as it continued to do until the end of the reign, especially after 1395. The Irish campaign of 1394–5 had little effect on royal finance; rising costs in the wardrobe, the extravagance of the festivities at Calais in 1396, and the king's increasing generosity to his supporters from early 1397 were more significant. The last two years of the reign provide unmistakable signs of renewed financial difficulties, with the cash flow to the wardrobe deteriorating and debts of over £10,000 accumulated in 1397–8 alone. Richard, however, showed no signs of moderating his expenditure. Some of the more unpleasant acts associated with the 'tyranny' of 1397–9 may well have been motivated by financial as much as political or personal considerations, in order to enable the king to go on living in the style to which he was becoming accustomed. Thomas Haxey complained of royal extravagance in February 1397, but Richard's reaction to his petition was sufficient to stifle any further criticism for the rest of the reign.

Henry IV's income from traditional revenues throughout his reign was very probably lower than his predecessor's, partly because the customs yield declined with falling wool exports, and partly because the disturbed state of the country, with rebellions in England, anarchy in Wales, and serious problems on the Scottish border, probably made it difficult for local officers actually to get revenue collected and delivered.[218] And although Henry was not involved in warfare with France to any serious degree until the last two years of his reign, the Welsh, Scottish and Irish problems all consumed substantial amounts of money.[219] But financially speaking, Henry did little to help his own cause. His grants, particularly during the first few years of the reign, were over-generous. And his household, until 1403, cost little less than Richard's had done at the end of the previous reign. This led to bitter recriminations against the household in parliament, as well as to a growing demand that the crown patrimony should make a more substantial contribution to domestic expenditure, an idea that had been around during Richard's reign too, but which was now more clearly and forcefully articulated. The first crisis came in the parliament of 1401 which had some effect on household finance, but this proved to be both temporary and insufficient. Not until the winter of 1403–4 was there any marked improvement in terms of expenditure, with great wardrobe spending reduced substantially. By this time, however, the commons were exasperated and introduced much stricter controls on the king, notably the reintroduction of war-treasurers and the imposition of a drastic *certum* on the wardrobe. The *certum*, which was quite unrealistic, was also quite ineffective, but the effect of war-treasurers on household finance was catastrophic: only by extensive borrowing, and by channelling substantial funds from his chamber into the wardrobe, could Henry maintain even a semblance of solvency in his household.[220] By the end of 1406, though, the accumulated debts of the household during the first seven years of the reign were at least £25,000. But equally catastrophic was the effect on annuities payable by the king; because the household was in such dire straits, it had usually been given preference over annuities during the first half of the reign. Already by 1404, therefore, annuities were badly in arrears, and between 1404 and 1406 they virtually ceased to be paid altogether.

The culmination of this financially disastrous period came in the long parliament of 1406, which witnessed a more sustained and unequivocal attack on royal finance than had yet been seen in any English parliament. Not surprisingly, it was accompanied by a political crisis too, the main effect of which was to remove many of the king's principal councillors and to usher in a period of five years (until November 1411) during which power was increasingly in the hands of Prince Henry.[221] It was at a council meeting in early 1407 that an agreement was finally hammered out. The crucial decision taken at this meeting was that parliamentary subsidies were now to be made available to the household. This marked the end of the campaign for appropriation of supply under Henry IV and the commons were forced, out of dire necessity to sacrifice a principle for which they had fought long and hard for decades, indeed for centuries. There were two reasons why they did so: to improve the cash flow to the household and thus allow it to pay both its way and its debts, and to release traditional revenues from the clutches of the household so that annuitants too would be paid. For the next two or three years, the prospects for both the household and annuitants improved considerably. This was not simply because of the reallocation of assignments agreed in 1407, it was also because household expenditure dropped significantly at the same time, and continued at a more moderate level through until the end of the reign, even if the *certum* proposed in 1408 was not fully effective. The years 1407 to 1409 were the best, financially speaking, of the reign. After 1409, however, the pressure began to build up again. Receipts at the exchequer fell in 1410–11, military intervention in France was renewed, and with the king's recovery of power in late 1411 domestic expenditure began to rise again. In the end, Thomas Brounfleet's debts after nearly five years as keeper were close to those of Thomas More after nearly four years, despite the fact that Brounfleet's average annual expenditure was about £5,000 less than More's. Financial instability was chronic under Henry. At the time of his death the accumulated debts of his household stood at over £30,000, and it took twenty years to clear them.

CHAPTER III

The Courtiers

EDWARD III

The king's mistress

ON 22 December 1377, almost exactly six months after Edward III's death, his mistress Alice Perrers was brought into parliament to stand trial for her alleged misdeeds.[1] It was the second time in eighteen months that her conduct had been the subject of parliamentary discussion. During the Good Parliament of 1376, while Edward still lived, the commons had drawn back from presenting detailed charges against her, and had contented themselves with an ordinance forbidding women in general, and Alice in particular, from pursuing quarrels in the king's courts, under pain of forfeiture and banishment from the realm. The chroniclers, however, make it perfectly clear that discussion of her activities during the Good Parliament must have been much more wide ranging than this ordinance suggests.[2] Trading on the king's infatuation with her, Alice had survived and was soon back by his side. With Edward dead, however, there was to be no escape.

Sitting in judgement on Alice were five of the greatest lords of the realm: John of Gaunt duke of Lancaster, and the earls of Cambridge, March, Arundel and Warwick. The charges against her were presented by Richard Lescrope, lord of Bolton in Wensleydale, steward of the royal household. She was accused on two counts. Firstly, that after the council had ordered Sir Nicholas Dagworth to go to Ireland with a view to investigating the charges against William Windsor, Alice persuaded the king to countermand the order on the grounds that Dagworth was an enemy of Windsor's and would not do justice to him; this incident was alleged to have occurred at the king's manor of Havering-atte-Bower (Essex) in early November 1376. Windsor, as was well known by this time, was Alice's husband and he had been lieutenant of Ireland between 1369 and 1372, and 'governor and keeper' of Ireland between 1373 and 1376. On each occasion his misrule had resulted in a plethora of complaints and accusations against him from the king's Irish subjects.[3] Secondly, it was alleged that after the merchant-courtier Richard Lyons had been impeached and convicted of malpractice in the Good Parliament, and his lands had been seized into the king's hands and some of them given to Edmund of Cambridge and

Thomas of Woodstock, the king's sons, Edward III took pity on Lyons and restored some of his lands and chattels to him. Alice was accused of persuading the king not only to take back the lands given to his sons and restore them to Lyons, but also to pardon Lyons £300 of debts owed by him at the exchequer, and to make him a gift of 1,000 marks; this incident was alleged to have occurred at Sheen, in May 1377.

Naturally, Alice replied that she was not guilty, and would prove so by testimony of John d'Ypres, William Street, Alan Buxhull, Nicholas Carew, and others who had been about the king at the time. D'Ypres and Street had been steward and controller of Edward's household during the last year of the reign, Carew had been keeper of the privy seal, and Buxhull had been a chamber knight for the last twenty years of the reign. They were all men whom she must have known well. D'Ypres and Buxhull had granted lands to her in the past, John of Gaunt, who chaired the trial, had made her a gift of a goblet of beryl garnished with silver and gilt.[4] But if she hoped that these men would speak up for her, Alice was to be disappointed. Although d'Ypres seems to have played no part in the trial, the other three all gave evidence, as did a number of other men. First to give evidence was Roger Beauchamp, chamberlain of the household from June 1376 to January 1377. Beauchamp said that he had been at Havering one day when Alice came to him and gave him a bill asking the king not to send Dagworth to Ireland because he was an enemy of Windsor's. When he discovered what the bill contained, Beauchamp said that he did not dare to give it to the king because it contradicted the order of the council. At this point, however, the king heard them arguing and came out to ask what the matter was and on seeing the bill, he agreed to stop Dagworth. Beauchamp now reminded the king of the council's order, only to be reminded in turn by Edward that he was king and sole judge of such matters, and that the bill seemed quite reasonable to him. As for the Lyons affair, Beauchamp declared that he had not been chamberlain at the time and knew nothing of the matter.

John of Gaunt now abandoned the chair for a while to testify. He too had been at Havering and had seen the bill, and had suggested to the king that Windsor and Dagworth be brought before the council to determine whether or not there really was enmity between them. The king agreed to this 'pur le heure', but as soon as he had left the room, Alice went straight to Gaunt and begged him on no account to allow Dagworth to go to Ireland. Gaunt refused, and Alice left him. But next morning, when Gaunt went to speak with his father, the king told him that Dagworth's mission was to be countermanded, which was duly done. As to Lyons's pardon, Gaunt said 'en sa consience' that he was sure that Alice had been the prime mover in the affair, but that he had not been present when it was done. Next to give evidence was Philip la Vache, a knight of Edward III's chamber. He testified that he had not actually heard Alice ask the king about the Dagworth affair, but that he had heard her talking about it around the household, saying that Dagworth must be stopped. He had been at Sheen, however, at the time when Richard Lyons was brought before the king, and he had been called into the king's chamber to hear what was to be done; also present were Alice, Carew, Buxhull, Walter Walsh (esquire of the chamber), and several others. When la Vache heard what was being discussed he 'ne voudroit demurer', and soon left, but, he said, it was commonly spoken about the court that Alice was behind the whole thing.

The evidence given by Carew and Buxhull was even more damning. Nicholas Carew said that one day at Sheen he had been called before the king; there he found Lyons, and he and Lyons were then told to go into the king's bedchamber, where they found Alice 'sitting at the head of the bed'. The king told Carew that he had decided to pardon Lyons his £300 of debts at the exchequer, and to give him 1,000 marks of his treasure, as well as to restore to him the lands which had been granted to Cambridge and Woodstock. Edward then asked Carew to inform his sons of his decision. Carew asked for witnesses to be brought in 'behind the curtains' (dedeinz les curtyns), so Buxhull and various other knights and esquires were summoned, and the king repeated his wishes. Carew's story was corroborated by Alan Buxhull. Buxhull said that one day at Sheen he had been called to the king's presence, where he found Alice, Carew, and various other knights and esquires. Carew explained to him that the king wished to pardon Lyons and Alice then asked Buxhull to inform the king's sons of the decision which Buxhull said he would do if ordered to by the king himself, whereat Edward 'a l'instance de dite Alice', did so. As for the Dagworth affair, Buxhull knew nothing about it except that he had heard Alice on several occasions say that Dagworth should not be sent to Ireland because he was an enemy of Windsor's and would not do justice to him.

William Street also gave evidence, as did John Beverley, another esquire of Edward's chamber. Street also swore that Alice had been 'principale promotrice' in the Dagworth affair, but he knew nothing of the Lyons affair. Beverley said that he had not actually heard Alice speak to the king concerning either matter, but that she did not normally plead such matters when he was present; evidently he and Alice were not on the best of terms. But he believed 'en sa consience' that she had been behind the whole business, because he knew of no-one else who could have pursued the matter. A jury of seven knights (including four of Edward's chamber knights) and nine esquires of the household was then asked whether they believed Alice to be guilty of the charges (interestingly, the jury included most of those who had given evidence: Beauchamp, Buxhull, la Vache, Carew, Beverley, and Street). They replied that they believed her to be guilty on both counts. The lords then reminded Alice of the ordinance passed against her in the Good Parliament, and sentenced her, on account of the 'damages et vilenyes par ele faitz au Roi et au Roialme', to be banished from the realm, and to forfeiture of all her lands and chattels, including those held by others to her use. This last clause, however, was not to be regarded as a precedent, but was enacted here solely 'pur sy odiose chose en se cas especial'.

The record of Alice's trial affords a remarkable, almost unique, insight into the sort of 'chamber politics' which must have been a feature, to a greater or lesser degree, of every royal court. Alice, of course, was exceptional. The feeble, senile Edward, the merest shadow of the king who for forty years had ruled England with vigour and astonishing success, had, during the last few years of his life, degenerated in both mind and body to the extent that he had become little more than a plaything of the courtiers. And pre-eminent among those courtiers was the king's mistress, who seems to have been able to bend him at her will. In the affairs of both Richard Lyons and Nicholas Dagworth, Alice was meddling in politics at the very highest level. William Windsor's activities in Ireland, and Richard Lyons's activities at the English court, were both *causes celèbres* of the first order in the scandalous politics of the 1370s. But it was not only in national politics that Alice's influence was felt. A lawsuit recorded by the chronicler Thomas Walsingham (no friend to Alice), in which his own abbey of St Albans was involved, reveals further aspects of court politics, and shows once again the importance of being able to call upon friends who had the king's ear. The case concerned a moiety of the manor of Oxeye Walrond (Herts.), which was disputed between the abbey and one Thomas Fitzjohn.[5] Having once entered on the premises, and promptly been ejected by the abbot and convent, Fitzjohn re-entered on 9 July 1374 and, on the same day, drew up a charter enfeoffing the lands to Alice Perrers. Clearly, this was an attempt by Fitzjohn to win powerful support for his claim, and as such it succeeded for 'this Alice Perrers,' recorded Walsingham, 'was of such power and eminence in those days, that no-one dared to prosecute his case against her. And therefore all those who were then of the abbot's council advised him that it would be better to desist from prosecuting his claim against her, and to wait until kinder fortune smiled upon him.' The abbot only had to wait two years and following Alice's discomfiture in the Good Parliament, he was encouraged to re-enter, and the abbey remained in peaceable possession of the manor from 1376 until 1381. In March 1380, however, Alice's husband William Windsor had been granted all the estates forfeited by Alice in 1377, which included Oxeye Walrond, and in July 1381 he took possession of the manor and ejected the abbot's servants. For three years Windsor remained in possession of the premises, but meanwhile the abbot had not been inactive; now it was his turn to use the influence of friends who had the king's ear. He enlisted the support of three knights, and brought them to St Albans in June 1384 to hear his version of the case. The names of the knights are instructive: they were Lewis Clifford, a knight of Richard II's chamber, John Worth, a close associate of the new king's court circle who was to be expelled from court in 1388, and Thomas Morwell, steward of Richard's queen, Anne of Bohemia. The three knights were evidently impressed by what they heard, and issued a letter testimonial, 'as being [the abbot's] friends in whom he has great trust, and in his hardships hope of succour', declaring their belief in the righteousness of his cause. Duly fortified, the abbot now took out an assize of novel disseisin against Windsor. At this point (September 1384) William Windsor died, but the abbot promptly took out another assize of novel disseisin against his nephew and heir, John Windsor. Unfortunately for the abbot, John Windsor was an esquire of the royal household, and now used what influence he had to secure a protection under the great seal against the assize. This, however, availed him little (apart from a delay of a year or so), for by now the abbot had enlisted even more powerful support. He secured from the king, 'at the prayer of your most dear uncle the duke of Lancaster . . . , an especial assize of novel disseisin', and succeeded in having Windsor's protection quashed. Eventually, in March 1386, John Windsor was forced to submit to the arbitration of the dukes of Lancaster and Gloucester, and of Thomas Percy (brother of the earl of Northumberland). The abbot agreed to pay £50 to Windsor, and Windsor agreed that, regardless of the outcome of the assize, he would release all his rights in the land to the abbot.

The assize, held at Hertford a few months later, in fact found in favour of the abbot, and that was the end of the matter. That it had taken twelve years to settle the dispute satisfactorily was not because the legal principles involved were especially complicated (although they are certainly interesting), but because, at every turn, influence at court had proved more decisive than legal right. The ability to influence affairs, at both the local level and the national level, was what made courtiers both popular and unpopular; popular in the eyes of those men who sought their favour and benefited from their influence, unpopular in the eyes of those who suffered from their influence, or who simply thought they had too much influence. Every king had his courtiers. Often they were men who held posts in the king's chamber or chapel, the inner and personal enclaves of the royal household, sometimes they were privy councillors, sometimes they held no formal position in the king's service, but were simply men (or sometimes women) with a strong personal attachment to the king. These were the king's friends, companions, and trusted advisors. Their recruitment, employment and behaviour were crucial factors in the politics of any reign, and their personalities were every bit as important as their policies. This chapter is very much concerned with personalities. Its aim is a simple one: to ask who were the courtiers in the period 1360 to 1413, and how did their behaviour affect the politics of the time?

The Good Parliament and the court covyne

Quite early on during the proceedings of the Good Parliament, the speaker for the commons, Peter de la Mare, made his views on Edward III's courtiers perfectly clear,

> My lords, we have declared to you and to the whole council of parliament various trespasses and extortions committed by various people, and we have had no remedy; nor is there anyone about the king who wishes to tell him the truth, or to counsel him loyally and profitably, but always they scoff, and mock, and work for their own profit; so we say to you, that we shall say nothing further until all those who are about the king, who are false men and evil counsellors, are removed and ousted from the king's presence;

and until our lord the king appoints as new members of his council men who will not shirk from telling the truth, and who will carry out reforms.[6]

There were many in the Good Parliament, among the commons certainly, among the lords very probably, who shared Peter de la Mare's view of the court. What this parliament witnessed was, manifestly, an attack by the commons on the court clique which had come to dominate the king during the last decade or so of the reign. The eye-witness account of the proceedings which survives in the *Anonimalle Chronicle* makes it perfectly clear that it was the commons who took the lead throughout, instigating the impeachments, drawing up the charges, cross-examining both victims and witnesses, and demanding judgment on those convicted. Indeed, the very process of impeachment which they used (for the first time in parliament) testifies to the central role of the commons in the trials. The role of the lords was secondary; the fact that, as judges in parliament, they passed judgments of guilty on the accused, certainly suggests that there were many among them who sympathised with the commons' view of the court, but to ascribe to them the leadership of the anti-court party is to undervalue the achievements of Peter de la Mare and his fellows.[7] This was not a clash of magnate factions, as for example in 1309–11, 1387–8, or 1450. Nor was it an attack upon the household, even if some of those accused held high office in the royal household. There was indeed criticism of the household in the Good Parliament, but it was criticism along quite traditional lines (purveyance, the court of the verge), and in no sense an attack on any household system of government. The word which the commons continually used to describe the courtier group was *covyne*. Thus, then referring to Richard Lyons, 'ceux qi y sont de la dite covyne entour la roi', when referring to William Latimer, 'autres malx faitx par luy et autres des soens et de sa covyne'. At other times they talked of 'aucuns privez entour le roi', or 'aucuns du Prive Conseil nostre seigneur le roi'.[8] What they were talking about was a court clique.

There is little difficulty in identifying the leading members of this clique. Alice Perrers was certainly one of them. Alice was of quite humble parentage, very probably the grand-daughter of Sir Richard Perrers of Hertfordshire. She came to the king's notice because she was lady-in-waiting to his queen, Philippa of Hainault, and by 1376 she had been Edward's mistress for a dozen years or more.[9] Among the mistresses of the medieval English kings, Alice was unique, unique in that her behaviour became a national scandal, and unique in that after her lover's death she was publicly tried and convicted in parliament. Her power over the king has already been amply demonstrated. What made her behaviour even more abhorrent to contemporaries was that she was a greedy and very capable businesswoman. By the time of Edward's death she had acquired, partly through royal favour, and partly through her own commercial acumen, a large fortune in cash and jewels, as well as a landed estate which extended into seventeen counties.[10] There were few who would have disagreed with the comment passed by Thomas Brinton, bishop of Rochester, preaching on 18 May, in the middle of the Good Parliament, 'it is not fitting or safe that all the keys should hang from the belt of one woman'.[11] The extraordinary power and influence of Alice was, to contemporaries, perhaps the most notable characteristic of Edward III's court during his later years, notable especially because it was so unusual in medieval England.

Also among the leading members of the court circle were three men who were personally attacked in the Good Parliament: William Lord Latimer of Danby, John Lord Nevill of Raby, and Richard Stury. Latimer, born in 1335, was a banneret of the royal household by 1359, steward of the household from 1368 to 1371, and the king's chamberlain from 1371 to 1376. Tout described him as a 'violent, self-seeking and unscrupulous man'.[12] This he may have been, but he also had a long and distinguished record of service in the war, and between 1369 and 1375 he was perhaps the man most intimately involved in the organisation of the renewed war effort from England. The exchequer issue rolls of these years contain numerous references to his visits to Westminster 'to expedite the king's secret affairs'. He was frequently travelling about the country, inspecting forces, overseeing the payment of wages, as well as campaigning in person and spending several months at the conference table in Bruges in 1374–5. Closely associated with Latimer was another northern lord, John Nevill (he was to marry Latimer's daughter early in Richard II's reign, even though he was slightly older than his father-in-law). Nevill was retained for life by John of Gaunt in 1370, and was steward of the royal household from 1371 until 1376. Thus for four and a half years before the Good Parliament, these two held the two highest offices in the household. After Alice Perrers, the Latimer-Nevill dyarchy was probably the most powerful influence at court at this time. Nevill might well have escaped impeachment in the Good Parliament had he not sprung to the defence of Latimer: Thomas Walsingham records that he was only impeached because he uttered 'verba grossa et ampullosa' at Peter de la Mare's audacity in accusing a peer of the realm (Latimer), whereupon he was abruptly told to keep quite as his turn would come next.[13]

Richard Stury was a man who had worked his way up from quite humble beginnings in the service of Edward III. Born in 1330, he had become a valet of the king's chamber by 1349, an esquire of the chamber by 1359, and a knight of the chamber by 1365.[14] He remained a knight of the chamber under Richard II, and a trusted diplomat and councillor until his death in 1395. His promotion was rapid, and he was clearly a favourite of the old king's. In 1371, it was said he 'stays continually with the king', in 1365, the king 'would show especial favour to the said Richard, who is abiding continually in his service' and he was described by Walsingham as 'regi familiarissimus'.[15] He was also very extensively rewarded by Edward with lands, offices, wardships and marriages, and so forth, perhaps because he had inherited little.[16] As an undoubted member of the court clique, he was a natural victim in 1376. Nevertheless, he was not formally impeached, and the *Rolls of Parliament* make no mention of the attack on him. The *Chronicon Angliae*, however, states that he was 'eliminatus . . . a curia et praesentia regis' because he had been acting as go-between from king to parliament, informing each of the wishes and replies of the other, and, having been bribed, he was passing false information. The *Anonimalle Chronicle* states that Richard Stafford was removed from the council, but it is virtually certain that this is an error, and that Stury is the man to whom the chronicler refers.[17] It is worth noting that when the time came to set up the continual council, it was agreed that all reports of the council's activities should be delivered to the king by the councillors themselves, 'et nemye par autres par nulle voie', which may have been a reference to Stury's alleged misrepresentations.[18]

Another undoubted leader of the court clique was a man with a very different background, Richard Lyons. Lyons was a Fleming, and a bastard, who had settled in London. Although described as a vintner, he in fact traded in a large variety of commodities, and by the mid 1370s his principal activity was almost certainly money-lending.[19] His rise to prominence was extremely rapid. The earliest indication that he was in any way involved with the court was in 1364, when he was ordered to stop molesting Alice Perrers and to allow her to go about her business unhindered.[20] Despite this unpromising beginning, he and Alice were later to become close associates, as revealed in her trial. Although he was acting as deputy to Robert Ashton, admiral of the western fleet, in 1371, it was only from *c.* 1373 that Lyons began to make his mark in a big way. In this year commenced his money-lending activities to the crown, and during the next three years he was involved, either personally as a lender, or as a middleman capable of raising large sums at short notice from the city merchants and others, in loans totalling over £46,000. It was no doubt this ability to find cash at short notice which won him a place on the privy council, perhaps as a sort of financial advisor to the government.[21] What is certain is that in the last two or three years before the Good Parliament he reached a position of influence of which men from his background can hardly have dreamed. He also had numerous business and personal connections with other members of the court circle, and from 1374 he began to hold high office in the municipal government of London.[22] In addition, he was warden of the London Mint, and farmed the London petty custom from 1372 to 1375. Lyons was intensely unpopular; five years after his impeachment in the Good Parliament, his manor of Overhaul on the Suffolk-Essex border was one of the first properties to be ransacked by the rebels, and a few days later he was lynched and executed in Cheapside by the London mob.[23]

Latimer, Nevill and Stury, Alice Perrers, and Richard Lyons: these were probably the five leading members of the group around the king in the 1370s, those whose voices carried most individual weight with the ageing monarch. But the circle spread wider than this. The activities and personnel of the *privata familia* can be traced in a number of ways, most obviously perhaps in a series of land and money transactions recorded in the Patent, Close and Fine Rolls, which demonstrate the close personal and business associations of these people and their friends. Members of the group were frequently granted land together, stood as mainpernors for each other, owed money to each other, petitioned the king jointly for grants or favours of various sorts, acted as attornies or witnesses for each other, sat on commissions together, or granted each other lands.[24] The other prominent members of the group were Nicholas Carew, a household esquire who had acted as lieutenant to the steward in the court of the verge through the 1360s, and was keeper of the privy seal from 1371 until the end of the reign;[25] John d'Ypres, a life retainer of John of Gaunt and president of the duke's council by 1376, but also controller of the royal household from 1368 until 1376, and steward in 1376−7;[26] Alan Buxhull, a chamber knight from at least 1358, constable of the Tower of London from 1366, and under-chamberlain of the household 1369−71;[27] Robert Ashton, the man who had been sent to Ireland in 1372 to investigate the charges against William Windsor, but who by 1375 was clearly reconciled to the court; he was treasurer of England from September 1375 until January 1377, and the king's chamberlain from then until the end of the reign;[28] William Street, the king's butler from 1361 until July 1376, when he replaced d'Ypres as controller of the household;[29] and John Beverley, an esquire of Edward III's chamber who was greatly favoured with gifts by the king, whose hunting he organised and who was married to Amice, the daughter of Alan Buxhull.[30]

Many of these men were precisely of the sort that one would expect to belong to a courtier clique, that is members of the staff of the king's chamber, and holders of high office in the household and the other government departments. But investigation of the charges levelled against the leading members of the group in the Good Parliament reveals further ramifications of the influence of the courtiers, the names of yet more of their associates, and further examples of the way in which the tentacles of the court reached out to interfere in what often seem to be purely local matters. Many of the specific charges laid against the courtiers are probably incorrect in detail, but to expect them to be too well-researched is at least partially to miss the point.[31] What the commons were out to do in 1376 was to destroy the influence with the king of the courtier clique. Although they were obviously deeply concerned about the mismanagement of both the war and the nation's finances, they were just as concerned with personalities as they were with policies. What seems to have happened in the Good Parliament is that, initially, the commons set out to destroy Latimer and Lyons. These two were the most notorious figures around the king (excluding Alice Perrers), and the attention devoted by the chroniclers to their trials makes it clear that their impeachments were very much the centrepiece of the proceedings. Thus a number of charges against them were devised, relating to their joint mercantile malpractice in relation to the Staple, their unnecessary and usurious loan of 20,000 marks to the king, and their brokerage of royal debts for their own profit. Lyons was also accused of fraud in his dealings at the Mint, and Latimer was charged with various extortions and derelictions of duty arising out of his part in the war, notably as king's lieutenant of Brittany in the 1360s. Latimer and Lyons did not go down without a fight, however. The commons were forced to provide detailed evidence for their accusations, more detailed perhaps than they had anticipated, for ultimately both Latimer and Lyons only seem to have been convicted on a minority of the charges brought against them. For the commons, however, the provision of more detailed evidence did have its compensations, for as the charges gradually unfolded, so more evidence came to light, more associates of the original victims were unearthed, and consequently more impeachment charges were framed.

Apart from those already mentioned, we know the names of six further persons impeached in 1376: William Ellis, John Pecche, Adam Bury, Hugh Fastolf, John of Leicester, and Walter Sporier. In the last three cases there are no records of the charges brought against them, and we only know of their impeachments because of the petitions for their pardons submitted to the parliament of January 1377.[32] Of Walter Sporier virtually nothing is known,[33] but with both Leicester and Fastolf there are at least clues as to their alleged misdemeanours. John of Leicester was described in January 1368 as 'the servant of Adam of Bury' but more to the point, perhaps, in April 1374 he was appointed Exchanger and Assayor of monies in the Tower of London. He still held this post when Lyons was appointed Warden of the Mint in September 1375, and six months later (only three days before the opening of the Good Parliament), he and Lyons were jointly commissioned to investigate falsities and deceptions arising out of the coining of money in the Tower. One of the charges against Lyons, as noted above, concerned his activities at the Mint; according to the *Chronicon Angliae*, the reason why Adam Bury was impeached was because he had acted fraudulently in connection with the money arising from the ransom of King John of France, which had been sent to the Tower.[34] There is little doubt, therefore, that the impeachment of John of Leicester arose directly out of the investigation of either the charges against Lyons or those against Bury, most probably the former.

The impeachment of Hugh Fastolf also probably arose, indirectly, out of investigations made into the conduct of Richard Lyons. The man who provided the link between them was William Ellis, though Fastolf was himself a man with strong courtier connections. His brother John was an esquire in Edward III's household, and Hugh himself was deputy-admiral of the north under John Nevill in 1370, and 'constantly attendant upon divers of the king's affairs'.[35] For some fifteen years before the Good Parliament, Fastolf and George Felbridge, an esquire of Edward III's chamber, had been jointly farming the petty custom in all the East Anglian ports for a down payment of £200 *per annum*.[36] Both Fastolf and William Ellis were members of the Great Yarmouth merchant oligarchy, and Ellis was a business associate of Richard Lyons. Indeed, one of the charges against him related to alleged extortions during the time that he was Lyons's deputy for the farm of tunnage and poundage in Great Yarmouth. The details of the case are complicated, and have already been summarised elsewhere, but what does emerge clearly from the records is how closely associated Lyons and Ellis were in the whole affair, and it is more than likely that it was investigation into their behaviour that implicated Fastolf as well.[37]

The same is almost certainly true of John Pecche. Pecche was a London fishmonger who had been active in the municipal government since *c.* 1350. He too had court connections. In 1367 Richard Stury and Helming Leget (an esquire of Edward III's chamber) acted as his attornies, and in 1376 Stury was still prepared to stand as mainpernor for his release from the Tower following his impeachment. He was accused of having, with the help of Richard Lyons and 'autres privez entour le roi', procured from the king a monopoly on the retail of sweet wine within the city of London, and of having made a substantial profit out of his monopoly. The charge was probably unfair as it stands, but more interesting are the details of how it was to be enforced:[38] it was in fact exercised through three taverns, one in Cheap, one in Walbrook, and one in Lombard Street. In August 1365, when Adam Bury was mayor, Richard Lyons leased these three taverns from the city government for an annual rent of £200. He was still leasing them at the time of his arrest in 1376.[39] Moreover, at the time when the monopoly was granted, in November 1373, Adam Bury was once again mayor of the city. Thus, both Lyons and Bury were deeply implicated in the establishment of the monopoly, and again it was very probably through investigation of their activities that Pecche was brought to trial. Indeed, it may well be that he was little more than a front man, and that the real profiteer was Lyons.

Finally, there is the case of Adam Bury, a London skinner who like Pecche had been a frequent office-holder in the city government for twenty-five years before the Good Parliament. Bury had been in trouble before: in January 1366 he was dismissed from the mayoralty of London by order of the king, either for murdering another skinner, or for defrauding the king in some way in connection with King John's ransom money.[40] He must also have been well-known by several of the courtiers for he had sat on commissions with both Latimer and Ashton, and had frequently made himself useful to the Black Prince. He was a long-time business associate of Richard Lyons. In 1370, for example, the two men jointly petitioned Chancellor William Wykeham for permission to purvey 1,000 quarters of grain in East Anglia for the town of Calais, since the land around the town could no longer support the people living there.[41] The accusations against Bury concerned both his behaviour when he was mayor of the Calais staple, and certain alleged deceits at the time when he was involved with the king's exchequer in London.[42] Whether there was much truth in the charges is impossible to say, in fact they were never brought to the test, for he fled to Flanders as soon as he heard he was likely to be tried, but once again it seems very likely that it was the tightening of the knot around Richard Lyons that led to charges being brought against Bury.[43]

The process, then, seems a fairly clear one. Beginning with the charges against Latimer and Lyons, the commons gradually began to unearth a whole series of impeachable offences involving not only their principal victims but also lesser members of the court clique such as Bury, Pecche, Ellis and Fastolf. These lesser men were then brought to trial, and the evidence against them not only helped to spread the commons' net wider, but also to heap further opprobrium on Latimer and Lyons. The same process may well have occurred in the case of both Stury and Nevill. As noted above, Stury's alleged deceits arose directly out of events occurring while the Good Parliament was actually in session. The charges against Nevill concerned the brokerage of royal debts for profit and the accusation that his retinue had plundered around Southampton on its way to Brittany in 1372. Furthermore, it was said that Nevill had taken a seriously under-strength retinue to Brittany once he did sail. The accusation concerning plunder at Southampton was based on a petition submitted to the Good Parliament by the men of Southampton although it is not at all clear why they had not complained of this in the parliament of 1373. It is worth remembering that Walsingham thought that Nevill was impeached because he spoke out in favour of Latimer and the other two charges, relating to brokerage of royal debts and conduct in Brittany, may well have arisen out of investigation of similar charges against Lyons and Latimer. So, even though there was probably quite a lot of truth in the accusations made against Nevill, it is likely that his impeachment too was something of an afterthought.[44] The ordinance against Alice Perrers, we may be sure, did not arise out of the charges against Latimer and Lyons; Alice was in a class of her own.

The presence of merchants such as Lyons, Pecche and Bury either in or on the fringes of the court circle highlights another characteristic of the royal court at the end of Edward III's reign. The association of merchants with courtiers was nothing new, but it does seem to be particularly marked at this time, and it may be doubted whether any merchant before Lyons had come to a position of quite such influence in government circles. Other London merchants were also closely involved with the court clique, John Pyel, for example, a friend of John of Gaunt, with whom he went to Bruges for the peace negotiations of 1374.[45] It was Pyel who had, jointly with Lyons, arranged the loan of 20,000 marks for which Lyons was impeached in 1376, though when called to give evidence in the Good Parliament Pyel had no hesitation in disowning his part in it.[46] Adam Francis, William Walworth, Nicholas Brembre and John Philpot were all associated with the courtiers too, though the last three were to win greater fame (or notoriety) in the next reign. It was, perhaps, the dire financial situation in the 1370s which led to the prominence of merchants at court. It was Richard Lyons's ability to raise money which was chiefly responsible for the favours shown to him. In return, the merchants got financial favours—at the Mint, in the collection of customs, or in relation to trade. Holmes's analysis of the financial and commercial charges levelled against the courtiers and their associates in 1376 has made the nature of such favours clearly apparent.[47] Both the number of, and the importance attached to these charges is readily by the prominence of certain merchants at court.

The courtiers, then, were a close-knit group, and during the last few years of the reign they had come to exercise a disproportionate amount of influence over the king. What is more, their policies—military, financial, and ecclesiastical—had met with a striking lack of success, so that they were surrounded by an aura of failure and had clearly alienated substantial numbers of both lords and gentry, the political classes. Some of the circumstances which had allowed

F

them to acquire such power have already been mentioned. Firstly, there was the smallness of the court: Edward III's increasing separation from his household through the 1360s and 70s turned the court into a rather isolated and exclusive, perhaps somewhat introverted, little gathering, diminished the channels of communication to the king, and probably left him more vulnerable to the small group that surrounded him.[48] Secondly, the senility of Edward, and his infatuation with Alice Perrers, clouded his judgement. Thirdly, the financial problems of the 1370s forced the government to open its arms to the sort of man who could raise cash quickly (Richard Lyons), but whose activities were clearly not beyond suspicion.

Lords, bishops and councillors, 1360–1377

Another very striking feature of the court at this time was the decline of aristocratic influence. This was simply a matter of death. The lords who were of the same generation as Edward, who had been his cherished war-captains and close friends in the early campaigns of the Hundred Years War, and who, whether in England or on campaign, had regularly been about the court and active in government, were almost all dead by this time. Of the six earls created by Edward in 1337, for example, not one lived beyond 1369. Salisbury and Huntingdon died in 1344 and 1354 respectively; Henry of Grosmont and William de Bohun both died in 1361, Warwick and Suffolk in 1369, Oxford in 1371, Ralph of Stafford in 1372, and Humphrey de Bohun, heir to the comital inheritances of both his father and his uncle, in 1373. Of the king's real friends among the earls, only Richard Fitzalan of Arundel was left, and he died in January 1376. Thus the last decade of the reign witnessed the rise of a new generation among the aristocracy, a generation which, while it may have longed to repeat the glories of Crécy and Poitiers, lacked that essential sympathy with Edward which its fathers, uncles, and grandfathers had had. No longer did the king count many of the nobles among his closest friends, and this fact is reflected in the composition of the court. Even some of the king's sons were beginning to disappear from the scene. Lionel of Clarence, Edward's second surviving son, died in 1368. The Black Prince, the heir to Edward's throne, returned from Aquitaine in 1371, war-weary and sick in body, and handed his continental principality back to his father because he was too feeble to govern it. This signalled his virtual retirement from public life. Over the next five years, he only witnessed three royal charters, one in 1373, and two in 1375. On 8 June 1376, he died. That the Black Prince disassociated himself from his father's court after 1371 is indisputable, though whether it was from inclination or from ill health is not entirely clear. Probably it was the latter, but it is also true that, like the king, he had few friends left at court, and at the time of the Good Parliament there were certainly rumours circulating to the effect that he cared little for those who were now about the king.[49]

The witness lists to the charter rolls are not without their problems.

Individually, they are not necessarily reliable guides either to the royal itinerary or to the royal entourage, and because they rarely list those below the rank of banneret they are of little use for discovering the knights and esquires who were active in government. Collectively, however, they do give a general picture of those lords who were about the court and at Westminster, and on this score they offer some interesting information.[50] Those of the king's sons who were still alive and healthy, when they were not out of the country, were frequently at court. For much of the time, however, they *were* out of the country: John of Gaunt was abroad, either campaigning or negotiating, from mid 1370 until November 1371, from July 1373 until March 1374, and for most of the year from March 1375 until March 1376. During the last year of the reign, however, he remained almost permanently at court, and was clearly the guiding hand behind the government now. Edmund of Cambridge was abroad for much of the period 1369–72, and again from late 1374 until early 1376. Edward's youngest son, Thomas of Woodstock, first appears on the witness lists in 1375, when he was nineteen, and from then until the end of the reign he was frequently at court. Of the other magnates, however, the only one who was regularly at court was the earl of Arundel, who remained close to the king's side until shortly before his death in January 1376. The witness lists of the 1370s generally have a very different aspect from those of the 1360s, when nearly all charters were witnessed by half a dozen or more earls, and men like Oxford, Suffolk, and Warwick, as well as Arundel, were regularly about the court.

Holmes has recently emphasised the importance of the clerical grievances against the court in the years leading up to the Good Parliament, in particular the concordat with the papacy in 1375 which allowed Pope Gregory XI to begin taxing the English clergy again after a break of nearly forty years.[51] It is possible that some members of the clergy also felt rather left out of things at this time, for although the court circle included few magnates after *c.* 1370, it was by and large dominated by laymen. The only clerks who had close associations with the courtiers were Henry Wakefield, keeper of the wardrobe from 1369 to 1375, and subsequently bishop of Worcester until his death in 1395, and the indomitable William of Wykeham, bishop of Winchester from 1367 to 1404.[52] During the 1360s Wykeham was the dominating influence in the royal administration, and perhaps at court too. Already in 1363 he was described by Edward as 'his secretary, who stays by his side in constant attendance on his service'.[53] From 1364 to 1367 he kept the privy seal, and from 1367–71 he was chancellor. 'All things were done by him,' said Froissart, 'and without him nothing was done'.[54] This was perhaps a little unfair to Alice Perrers, but what does seem clear is that there was no enmity between Wykeham and Alice. The bond which they presumably established at court was to stand both of them in good stead later: according to the *Chronicon Angliae* it was through Alice's influence that Wykeham's temporalities were restored to him on 18 June 1377, following his disgrace in October 1376.[55] This is far from improbable. Wykeham remained a good friend to Alice after her own disgrace in 1377, corroborating her story in 1389 in what sounds like a distinctly suspicious case concerning the whereabouts of some of Edward III's jewels, and in 1397 granting her the manor of Compton (Warwicks.).[56]

Wykeham's continued friendship with Alice is perhaps surprising in view of his apparent antipathy to the courtiers expressed in the Good Parliament. Wykeham was clearly at no pains to save Latimer, even suggesting that he should not be allowed time to prepare his defence, and his own mock-trial in October 1376 was said to have been 'par abetement del duk de Loncastre et le seignur de Latymer'.[57] It was in 1371 that Wykeham had first fallen from grace, when he, along with the clerical treasurer and keeper of the privy seal, was dismissed from office at the request of lords and commons in parliament, and all three posts were placed in the hands of laymen. The obvious antagonism between Wykeham, the dominant courtier of the 1360s, and Latimer, the dominant courtier of the 1370s, perhaps reveals something of the undercurrent of faction attending the dismissals of 1371. But although the clerics must have lost ground at court in 1371, they were not entirely inactive in government after this. Before 1371, Wykeham as chancellor and Thomas Brantingham, bishop of Exeter, as treasurer (and his episcopal predecessors in that office) were normally the only bishops who regularly witnessed charters. Immediately after the 1371 parliament, there was actually an increase in the number of bishops witnessing charters and Wykeham clearly remained very much about the court, and continued to witness charters frequently until the autumn of 1376, when his clash with Gaunt and Latimer sent him away to lick his wounds. Simon Sudbury (bishop of London, and after 1375 of Canterbury), and William Courtenay (bishop of Hereford from 1370, and of London from 1375) were also frequent witnesses during these years. Moreover, in January 1377 the chancellorship and treasurership were restored to the bishops of St David's (Adam Houghton) and Worcester (Henry Wakefield) respectively. Thus the prelates were not entirely excluded from government after 1371. Nevertheless, the court during these years was very much a laymen's court and both Wykeham and Courtenay had bitter quarrels with the court in the winter of 1376–77.[58] It can safely be inferred both that there was little clerical representation in the court circle between 1371 and 1377, and that there was little clerical sympathy for its policies—which made the concordat of 1375 even harder to take.

Some other men seem voluntarily to have disassociated themselves from the court. Guy Lord Brian is one example. By 1370 Brian had passed his fiftieth birthday and was now a distinguished elder statesman; he had spent a lifetime in the king's service, rising from an esquire of the household in the 1330s to become steward of the household (1359–61), a banneret, and a peer of parliament.[59] He was both a soldier and a diplomat in whom the king had shown the utmost confidence, frequently sent on important diplomatic missions, and as late as 1372 he acted as the king's spokesman in parliament.[60] By this time, however, he seems to have been becoming disillusioned with the court. Brian had never been a time-server; he had disagreed with the king twice already, in

1362 and in 1365, over questions of ecclesiastical patronage, but clearly remained in favour with Edward, respected, perhaps, for his honesty as well as for his ability.[61] Until about 1367, Brian was a regular witness to royal charters, both at Westminster and elsewhere; after 1367, however, he witnessed fewer and fewer, until July 1373, when he ceased to witness them entirely. The reason is hardly likely to have been ill-health, for as will be seen he remained an active man and did not in fact die until 1390. What is perhaps more telling is that Brian seems to have found favour with the commons: in 1373, and again in 1376, he was a member of the inter-communing committee of lords which discussed business with the commons and he was also on the council of nine set up in the Good Parliament to advise the king.[62] But even more telling is Brian's behaviour in February 1377, when the London mob, incensed at Gaunt's treatment of their bishop and at his attempts to extend the marshal's jurisdiction in the city, were thirsting for vengeance against the duke. According to the *Chronicon Angliae*, it was Lords Brian and Fitzwalter who told the Londoners (on 20 February) that Henry Percy (the marshal) was illegally detaining a prisoner in his London house, whereupon the Londoners sacked Percy's house, released the prisoner, and went in search of Gaunt and Percy, who had to escape by barge to Kennington.[63] It is difficult to avoid the conclusion that Guy Brian had little love for the courtiers, and that he preferred not to be too closely associated with them. The same is probably true of Roger Beauchamp, another respected elder statesman who had been high in the king's confidence during the middle years of the reign but who also seems to have shunned the court in the 1370s. Beauchamp too found favour with the commons, and was appointed to the council of nine. Moreover, by 28 June 1376 he was acting as king's chamberlain, a post which he retained until January 1377.[64] This means that he was appointed to the office before the end of the Good Parliament, which might suggest that he was regarded as a man acceptable to the court's critics. His removal on 11 January 1377 was one of a number of ministerial changes that day which bear all the hallmarks of John of Gaunt's influence. As his evidence against Alice Perrers in her trial demonstrates, there was evidently little love lost between her and Beauchamp either.

John of Gaunt's role in the years leading up to the Good Parliament is difficult to fathom. Tout suggested that the courtiers of this era were 'identical with the followers of John of Gaunt'.[65] Some of them were certainly closely associated with the duke (John Nevill and John d'Ypres especially, also William Latimer, Alan Buxhull, and John Pecche), but a number of factors make it improbable that Gaunt was really the mentor of the court circle before 1376. For a start, he was out of the country for over half the time between the summer of 1370 and the opening of the Good Parliament—though that does not necessarily mean that he lost touch with affairs in England, particularly when he was as close as Bruges, for example. Until June 1376, however, the presence of his elder brother the Black Prince must have restricted Gaunt's ability to appear too dominant at court; even if he was sick and not much in evidence, the Black Prince was still the heir to the throne. Nor does Gaunt seem to have exercised any striking influence over the king's ministerial appointments. Richard Lord Lescrope of Bolton (treasurer 1371–5) was one of his feed retainers, but when Lescrope was called to give evidence in the Good Parliament he was aparently at no great pains to save Latimer or Lyons, and his sympathy with the court is to be doubted.[66] John Knyvet (chancellor 1372–7) was a former royal justice and a member of the Black Prince's council who had no apparent association with Gaunt. The appointment of Ashton as treasurer in 1375, and the ministerial appointments of January 1377, can be more obviously linked to the court circle, but before that time the hand of Gaunt is far from evident. It would perhaps be demeaning to men like Latimer, Nevill and Stury, and to Alice Perrers, to suggest that they needed John of Gaunt behind them to ensure their positions at court. They were powerful and influential enough in their own right not to need to be any man's tools. What can perhaps be suggested is that those who held the chief ministerial offices of the crown in the years from 1371 to 1376 were, by and large, not men of great individual weight or authority, which probably meant that the courtiers had a free hand to do more or less as they liked. It is worth noting that neither the chancellor, nor the treasurer, nor the keeper of the privy seal was dismissed in 1376.[67] As to the king's council, it seems to have been a rather informal body at this time, and this too probably played into the hands of the courtiers. Latimer, Nevill, Stury and Lyons were all described in the Good Parliament as being of the 'prive conseil du roi', from which they were duly removed. Naturally, the three chief officers of the king were also on the council (thus including another courtier, Carew). Guy Brian was described as 'the king's councillor' in May 1371, but he was certainly not active in government during the last four or five years of the reign. Simon de Neylond, a bachelor in civil law, was retained to be of the king's council in January 1372, and may well have remained on it until the end of the reign, for in February 1378 his attendance fee of £20 *per annum* was confirmed 'provided that he constantly attend the king's service'.[68] As a lawyer, however, his role on the council was presumably to offer legal advice rather than to involve himself in policy decisions. Beyond this, the membership of the council is impenetrable. If there was a formally-constituted council, it seems to have been unable to restrain those about the king. All in all, the sources of executive authority from *c.* 1371 until 1376 seem to have remained firmly within the court clique. This was why the commons in 1376 were so keen to establish a formal, and continual, council.

But if John of Gaunt's leadership of the court circle before the Good Parliament is unproven, there is no doubt that he was the man who seized the reins of government immediately after the Good Parliament, and for the last year of his father's life he was very much in charge, 'gubernator et rector' of England, as Walsingham put it.[69] Gaunt now espoused the cause of the courtiers in a way that he had not done before. He made no attempt to conciliate those who had opposed the court. The continual council, if it ever sat at all, was rendered totally ineffective within a matter of weeks, if not days, of the ending of the parliament. At a great council which met at Westminster on 13 October (when the king was gravely ill and seemed about to die at any moment—the timing was clearly not coincidental), Gaunt set in motion the process of formally pardoning those who had been impeached and punishing those who had attacked them.[70] Peter de la Mare was arrested and imprisoned in Nottingham castle, and William of Wykeham was publicly tried and disgraced. By the time of the next parliament, in January 1377, many of the courtiers had already been pardoned, and the appointment of Adam Houghton and Henry Wakefield to the chancellorship and treasureship had placed two Lancastrian sympathisers at the head of the administration. This parliament seems to have been seriously divided: petitions were submitted, for example, for both the release of Peter de la Mare and the pardon of William Latimer. There was clearly opposition to Gaunt from some of the prelates, but from the lay lords there is no hint of disaffection.[71] These divisions seem to have played into Gaunt's hands for he secured the subsidy that he required for his projected expedition to France, calmed any fears relating to his treatment of Prince Richard by having him formally acknowledged in parliament as Prince of Wales and heir to the throne, and gained at least tacit approval for the actions of the October council. During the spring and early summer the remaining victims of the Good Parliament received their formal pardons, and the humiliation of Wykeham was compounded in March by the conferment of his temporalities on Prince Richard.[72] Right through until the end of the reign, John of Gaunt remained in charge of the government. And there by the old king's side when he died, at about seven o'clock on the evening of 21 June 1377, at his favourite manor of Sheen, was Alice Perrers.[73]

Beyond any doubt, Peter de la Mare and his fellows had failed in what had been their primary aim in the Good Parliament—to destroy the influence of the court *covyne*. Nevertheless, some notable victories had been scored: after the parliament, the government was forced to reconsider its pro-papal stance;[74] moreover, the parliament had ended without any grant of direct taxation. Even in terms of personalities, some minor successes had been gained for Latimer never became chamberlain again, and Nevill's dismissal from court seems to have been permanent. But the real problem remained unsolved, and was, for the moment, insoluble, that is, a senile king, no longer able to feel the pulse of his kingdom, past clear thinking or rational judgement, was incapable of controlling the greedy little group of men and women who gathered round him in his dotage. Only with the king's death could the clique be dispersed, and that, in the end, was how it happened. There was, however, another problem waiting around the corner. The commons in 1377 affected great faith in Richard of Bordeaux, but nothing could disguise the fact that the new king was going to be a minor and a teenage king was, arguably, just as likely to be subjected to evil influences as a senile one. In the long run, it may be that some hard lessons were learned as a result of the events of 1376–7. There is no doubt that the behaviour of Edward III's courtiers during the 1370s greatly shocked contemporaries and during the early years of his grandson's reign, real efforts were made to prevent a repetition of such events. As it turned out, these efforts proved fruitless, and within less than a decade of his accession, Richard II's courtiers had acquired a reputation little better than those of his grandfather. The result was the political crisis of 1386–8, and the bloodshed of the Merciless Parliament. Part of this, surely, was a hangover from Edward III's reign: the events of the early 1370s bred a deep distrust of courtiers—all the worse for following thirty or more years of strong personal rule—and it would be surprising if some of this distrust had not carried over into the next reign. But another lesson learned in 1376 was that to imprison, dismiss, or fine the offending courtiers was not enough. Parliaments came and went, but the court was always there, and so was the king, and sooner or later, the courtiers would find their way back to court, and very probably the king would be there beckoning them. To have any real hope of ousting a court clique, more drastic measures were necessary, the offenders had to be physically eliminated. By 1388, this had become all too obvious to Richard II's opponents: there is indeed a certain sense in which the events of 1376 merely form a prelude to the altogether more bloody affair of 1388.

RICHARD II

Knights of the chamber: personnel

Of those who can be clearly identified as members of the court clique of the 1370s only Richard Stury and Alan Buxhull were knights of Edward III's chamber. Chamber knights were, almost by definition, natural courtiers, and one of the reasons why more of them do not figure as members of the court circle is because Edward had very few chamber knights in the later years of his reign. Apart from Buxhull and Stury, only five other men were described in the wardrobe account books of the period 1360–77 as chamber knights: Thomas Beauchamp, Richard Pembridge, Peter de Brewes, Esmond Everard, and Philip la Vache.[75] Philip was the son of Richard la Vache, a former under-chamberlain of the king who died in 1365; although he was much about the court during the last year or two of the reign, he only became a chamber knight *c.* 1374 and was too young to make his mark under Edward III.[76] The others were all really men of the 1360s rather than the 1370s. Thomas Beauchamp was the younger son of the earl of Warwick. Following the death of his elder brother he became his father's heir, and succeeded to the earldom in 1369 and he was to be a noted opponent of the court in the 1380s. Peter de Brewes was a knight of Edward's chamber from at least 1360 until the end of the reign, but he played little part either in government or in affairs at court; both he and Esmond Everard, who was listed as a chamber knight only in 1369, were unremarkable men, and politically insignificant, though presumably the king counted them among his friends. Richard Pembridge is more noteworthy. He was a knight of the king's household as early as 1353, and a knight of the chamber from 1360 until 1372. During the 1360s he was a close associate of Wykeham's, and undoubtedly high in the king's favour; he held several of those posts so often reserved by kings for their chamber knights, such as Constable of Dover castle and Warden of the Cinque Ports, keeper of Southampton castle, and keeper of the New Forest.[77] But just a few months after his friend Wykeham's dismissal from the chancellorship in March 1371, Richard Pembridge's career collapsed in ruins. The king, by now well aware of the shortcomings of William Windsor's administration in Ireland, offered the Irish lieutenancy to Pembridge. Pembridge was an experienced soldier (he had fought at Crécy), but he evidently had no desire to go to Ireland. He 'utterly refused' to accept the appointment, whereupon the king was infuriated: he deprived Pembridge of all his offices, and dismissed him forthwith from his post as chamber knight.[78] Pembridge left court at once, and never returned; he died three years later, still in disgrace, a sad end to a distinguished career. His dismissal, however, throws some light on the kind of service which kings expected from their chamber knights for they were the king's servants, very much bound to his person, and bound to do his will. That Edward III had so few chamber knights in these years is perhaps symptomatic of his withdrawal from active involvement in government. But when considering the experiences of Richard II's much larger body of chamber knights, the case of Richard Pembridge is worth bearing in mind.

Through the twenty-two years of Richard's reign, a total of thirty-five men were described at one time or another as knights of the king's chamber. A further fourteen men held one of the three senior lay offices in the household (under-chamberlain, steward, or controller), thus bringing the total number of men of the rank of knight or above who belonged to the household almost to fifty.[79] Any discussion of Richard's courtiers should properly begin with an investigation of his chamber knights and household officers, for it is abundantly clear that they played a major part in the politics of the reign.

Prominent among the king's chamber knights were some cadets of very distinguished families as well as men who owed their eminence almost entirely to the king's favour. They may be divided into three broad chronological groups. Firstly, there were the chamber knights of the period from 1377 to c. 1383–5, many of whom were not really Richard's own friends but inherited by him from his father or grandfather. Secondly, there were the king's 'new men' of the early and mid 1380s, achieving rapid prominence and notoriety before being cut down with equal rapidity between 1388 and 1391. Thirdly, there was the new group of chamber knights of the 1390s, a less controversial group on the whole than those of the 1380s, and more dominated by a few outstanding figures such as William Lescrope and John Holand.

Those who served as knights of the chamber during the first six or seven years of the reign were mainly former servants of the Black Prince: Richard Abberbury snr., Baldwin Bereford, Nicholas Bonde, John and Simon Burley, Lewis Clifford, Peter Courtenay, John del Hay, Nicholas Sharnesfeld, Aubrey de Vere, and Bernard van Zedeletz had all been primarily servants of the king's father. The dominant figures in this group were Abberbury (who was Richard's 'first master' in 1376–7), Bereford, Simon Burley (a lifelong intimate of the Black Prince who was Prince Richard's chamberlain in 1376–7, and subsequently under-chamberlain of the king from 1377 until his execution in 1388), and Aubrey de Vere, Robert de Vere's uncle, who became earl of Oxford in 1393. Of the other ten chamber knights during this early part of the reign, six were former servants of Edward III: Guy Brian, John Harleston, Nicholas Dagworth, Thomas Murrieux, Robert Rous, and Richard Stury. Dagworth and Stury were both highly-experienced diplomats and soldiers, the sort of men who, despite some questionable episodes in earlier times, almost any king would have been glad to employ. William Beauchamp, John Holand and William Nevill (brother of John Nevill and of Alexander Nevill, archbishop of York) were all three of very high birth and probably owed their positions to this factor as much as anything. The only real 'new man' among these early chamber knights was William Murreres, who came from Yorkshire but was by this time settled in Suffolk; he was marshal of the household through the 1380s and emerged unscathed from the traumas of 1388, but he never cut much political ice.

Many of these early chamber knights soon began to disappear from court: Bonde, John Burley, Rous, Hay and Murrieux all died between 1381 and 1387, while Zedeletz (who was probably Netherlandish) played no real part in English affairs after about 1383. William Beauchamp's close association with the court seems to have ended soon after he surrendered the chamberlainship to Aubrey de Vere early in 1381. The others, however, remained at court. What is more, they formed a substantial group among those who were attacked by the Appellants and their followers in 1388 with Simon Burley being executed, and Abberbury, Bereford, Dagworth and de Vere all ordered to absent themselves from court. Thus the attack on the court in 1388 was not directed solely at Richard's new friends who had joined the court in the 1380s. It included this solid group of well-established and experienced men, most of them former servants of the Black Prince, who had successfully made the transition to the new king's court, and who were evidently regarded as undesirable influences on Richard. Those who would criticise the courtiers of the 1380s must also wonder whether the Black Prince was a better judge of men than his son.

In the place of those who disappeared from court during the 1380s there arose a new group of chamber knights, clearly men of the king's own choice, many of them roughly the same age as Richard. Not all of them were young men, however; Robert Bardolf, an Oxfordshire esquire who had been in Edward III's household in 1372–3, was first described as a chamber knight in 1386, while John Clanvow, a chamber knight from 1381, had been retained as a knight by the earl of Hereford before 1373, when Richard was only six. The real 'new men' of the 1380s were on the whole younger men, however, and they rose fast. James Berners from Surrey had been a king's esquire in 1378, but he only came of age in 1382 and was a chamber knight in the same year.

The Westminster chronicler described him as 'regi summe familiaris'. Thomas Lord Clifford (of the Westmorland Cliffords) was 'the king's young knight' in 1382, and still described as a 'young knight' at the time of his death in 1391.[80] The Scottish campaign of 1385 provided a fund of newly-dubbed young knights upon which Richard drew for his chamber staff: John Golafre, John Beauchamp of Holt, and John Salisbury were all knighted on this campaign, all became knights of the chamber, and all were attacked in 1388 (Beauchamp and Salisbury had both been esquires of Edward III's household in 1376–7). Thomas Blount was first described as a chamber knight in 1384, when sent to escort various French ambassadors to Calais.[81] The rapidity with which some of these men became unpopular must have surprised them as well as the king. Already in the parliament of October 1386 threats were made against Berners, Beauchamp and Salisbury, as well as against Simon Burley, and it may well be that they were strongly advised to abjure the court. Perhaps this is why these four were singled out for execution in 1388.[82] Yet not all the new chamber knights of this period became objects of attack in 1388. Thomas Peytevyn, for instance, a Herefordshire knight who had been usher of the king's hall since 1377 and a chamber knight before 1383, was left untouched by the Merciless Parliament.[83] So was George Felbridge, who had also been knighted on the Scottish campaign of 1385. Most of the others, however, became victims of the Appellants' wrath. Beauchamp, Berners and Salisbury were beheaded, an order was issued for Golafre's arrest (but fortunately he was in France at the time, and Richard was later able to pardon him)[84] and Thomas Blount and Thomas Clifford were ordered to leave court.

Of the twenty-three known chamber knights in 1387–8, twelve were regarded by the Merciless Parliament as undesirables. The reasons why they were so hated are not hard to find. They were the most prominent members of a household which had been constantly criticised during the first decade of the reign. They were closely associated with a government which was conducting an expensive and unsuccessful war. Some of them had risen very fast, particularly Simon Burley, to whom the king had tried to grant large estates in Kent, and whom he probably hoped or intended to create earl of Huntingdon, and John Beauchamp of Holt, who had risen from an esquire in 1385 to 'Lord Beauchamp and Baron of Kidderminster' as well as steward of the household, in 1387.[85] If Beauchamp really had been threatened in 1386, his rapid promotion in 1387 seems almost deliberately provocative. As personalities, they attracted little praise (although the Westminster chronicler said that Beauchamp 'acquitted himself well in the post' of steward).[86] Walsingham described them as 'more knights of Venus than of Bellona, more potent in the bedchamber than on the battlefield, stronger with the tongue than with the lance, always ready to talk, but never to perform acts of war.' Walsingham's prejudices are well-known, and he was to make some equally deprecating remarks about Henry IV's knights in 1403, but even so Richard's chamber knights seem to have made little effort to improve their public image.[87] As early as 1379, the commons complained in parliament that 'certain knights and esquires of the king's court' had been using unsavoury methods in an attempt to raise loans for the crown.[88] Several of them were involved in the gruesome torture of the Carmelite friar John Latimer during the Salisbury Parliament of April 1384, and early in 1385 John of Gaunt publicly complained of the company kept by the king.[89] The Kirkstall chronicler singled out Simon Burley for his ostentatious lifestyle, while the commissioners of 1386 pointedly advised the king to attach to himself men of estate, property and honour.[90] Regular attempts were made to place in the household men who, it was hoped, would have a better sort of influence on the king: Richard Waldegrave in 1377, John Lord Cobham in 1379, the earl of Warwick in 1380, Michael de la Pole and the earl of Arundel in 1381.[91] As a result de la Pole threw in his lot with the court, while the others seem to have become increasingly disillusioned with it. Richard continued to ignore the unpopularity of his court, and the result was the Merciless Parliament.

The aim of the Appellants and their supporters in 1388 was to destroy the influence of Richard's inner circle, and although this included a large group of chamber knights it included many others too. Three of the five Appellees had themselves been closely involved with the court since the early 1380s: Robert de Vere (chamberlain since 1382), Michael de la Pole (placed in the household in 1381, chancellor 1383–6, and created earl of Suffolk in 1385) and Robert Tresilian, chief justice and retained for life to be of the king's council in February 1385.[92] Alexander Nevill had witnessed royal charters regularly between 1385 and 1387.[93] Nicholas Brembre's crimes were more specific, although he too seems to have been personally disliked: in the 1386 parliament several of the city guilds had submitted complaints about oppressions which he was alleged to have committed while mayor of London.[94] Apart from these five, however, there were numerous other knights, many of whom were closely associated with the court, who were attacked too. William Elmham and Thomas Tryvet, neither of whom were ever described as chamber knights, were arrested along with Dagworth and the four executed chamber knights, and only released at the end of the parliament on condition that they would stay away from court. They had both been involved in the 1383 Flemish 'crusade' bribe scandal, Elmham was also one of those who had tortured the Carmelite friar in 1384, while according to the Westminster chronicler Tryvet had tried to ambush the Lords Appellant on their way to a meeting with the king in November 1387.[95] A further six knights (John Worth, John Lovell, Hugh Burnell, Thomas Camoys, John Beaumont, and William la Zouche), as well as several clerks and ladies of the court, were ejected from the king's entourage.[96] It is clear that all of them were members of that group, centred in the chamber, which populated the court and was thought to lead the king astray. The Appellants spread their net wide: they were not leaving anything to chance.

Between 1388 and 1391 there was a high degree of turnover of staff among the knights of the chamber. This was partly a result of the action taken by the Appellants in 1388, and partly a result of a spate of accidents during the next few years. Apart from the four who were executed in 1388, the court career of Aubrey de Vere seems to have been effectively ended in 1388. Although 'restored' to the earldom of Oxford in 1393, he played little part in the politics of the 1390s, and by 1397 he was 'incurably infirm'.[97] In 1391 William Nevill and John Clanvow went on crusade and died within two days of each other in a village near Constantinople, while in the same year Thomas Clifford went on crusade too and died 'on an island on the way to Jerusalem'.[98] Richard Abberbury remained Queen Anne's chamberlain until her death in 1394, but after this he was hardly at court at all while Lewis Clifford and Nicholas Dagworth seem to have retired from active politics at much the same time, along with William Murreres and Thomas Peytevyn. Sharnesfeld died in 1395, Golafre in 1396. Robert Bardolf and Richard Stury, who were not listed as chamber knights in any of the wardrobe account books of the 1390s, also died in 1395. George Felbridge, though described as a chamber knight in 1393, was not listed in any of the wardrobe account books of the 1390s. By the end of 1396, then, only Baldwin Bereford remained. The fact that he had been ordered to abjure the court in 1388 is sufficient testimony to the failure of the Appellants to secure more than a partial destruction of the court clique. Natural forces (death and retirement) had in the end proved just as effective as execution and eviction.

The new chamber knights of the 1390s were William Arundel, Simon Felbridge, William Lescrope, Stephen Lescrope, Thomas Percy, John Russell, Arnold Savage, Benedict Sely, William Lisle, Philip la Vache and Robert Witteneye. The dominant figure among them was undoubtedly William Lescrope, although John Holand, the king's half-brother, made earl of Huntingdon in 1388 and duke of Exeter in 1397, and Thomas Percy, brother of the earl of Northumberland, made earl of Worcester in 1397, were also prominent during this period. Arundel, Simon Felbridge, Stephen Lescrope and Witteneye probably joined the chamber mainly through family connections. William Arundel was the second son of John Lord Arundel (d. 1379), and thus nephew to the truculent Earl Richard, though this did not deter him from accepting the castle and town of Reigate from the king after his uncle had been arrested in July 1397.[99] Simon Felbridge was the son of George Felbridge, and he became the king's standard-bearer after Nicholas Sharnesfeld's death in 1395. He demonstated his reliability by petitioning for the trial of the Appellants in 1397 (as did Baldwin Bereford and Philip la Vache), and lived until 1442.[100] Robert Witteneye was almost certainly related to Perrin Witteneye, damsel of the queen's chamber and daughter-in-law of the former chamber knight John Clanvow.[101] Both Witteneye and Clanvow came from Herefordshire.

Stephen Lescrope (of Bolton) was the younger brother of the notorious William and succeeded William as under-chamberlain of the household in the last year of the reign. John Russell, retained for life by the king in 1387, having formerly been retained by the earl of Warwick, was a thoroughgoing courtier and an active councillor during the last years of the reign. He was trapped with Lescrope, Bussy and Green in Bristol Castle in late July 1399 by Bolingbroke's invasion force, and only released after feigning insanity. Benedict Sely's background is obscure, but he was clearly a strong Ricardian: a Sussex knight who became marshal of the household at the end of the reign, he joined the earls' rebellion against Henry IV in January 1400 and was executed. Arnold Savage was an active administrator from Kent whose mother had been Richard's nurse. He had been an esquire of the household in 1383–4, and was listed among the chamber knights in 1392–3 but not in 1395–6. He made a name for himself with his fierce criticism of the government when chosen as speaker of the commons in the parliaments of January 1401 and January 1404. Philip la Vache must have been a well-known face at court by the time he joined Richard II's chamber as he was the son-in-law of Lewis Clifford, and had been a member of Princess Joan's household. In 1399 he was Queen Isabel's chamberlain.[102] In all there were probably thirteen chamber knights between 1396–9.

The only one of these chamber knights executed in 1399 was William Lescrope. The others who died in 1400 (Sely, John Holand and Thomas Blount, the chamber knight from the earlier part of the reign) brought their deaths upon themselves by rebelling against Henry in January 1400. They were spared in 1399 partly because of Henry IV's general policy of leniency towards Richard's supporters, but also, and this is worth noting, because there was a general lack of criticism of the new group of chamber knights during the later years of the reign. They were, quite natually, strongly Ricardian for the most part in their sympathies, but they were not lampooned by the chroniclers in the same way that the chamber knights of the 1380s had been, and it is clear that they were not, as a group, thought to exercise the same sort of influence over the king as had their predecessors. Some of them found little difficulty in switching their allegiance to the new regime and Arnold Savage and Thomas Percy both accepted high office in Henry IV's service. Yet the relative (and 'relative' should be emphasised) obscurity of many of the chamber knights of the 1390s is really to be explained by the concentration of power and influence in fewer and greater hands towards the end of the reign. By the end of 1397, Richard had succeeded (just as Edward III did in 1337) in effectively creating his own nobility, and it was principally among this new aristocratic cabal that the real powers at court were to be found, particularly Lescrope (made earl of Wiltshire in 1397) and the king's cousin Edward, made earl of Rutland in 1389 when he was only fifteen, and duke of Aumâle in 1397. The honours heaped on the latter two men were astonishing: Rutland became constable of England, admiral of England, constable of the Tower of London, constable of Dover castle and warden of the Cinque Ports, keeper of the king's forests south of the Trent, and was granted the lordship of the Isle of Wight and Carisbrook castle. Lescrope was made keeper of numerous castles (including Bamburgh, Queenborough, Pembroke, and many in North Wales), and justiciar of Ireland 1395–7, justice of Chester and North Wales, treasurer of England 1398–9, under-chamberlain of the household 1393–8, and was granted the 'whole county and lordship of Anglesey' together with Beaumaris castle in 1397. Between them, these two shared out about half of the fifteen or so really important and lucrative posts in the king's gift, posts which in times past had often been spread around among the king's household or chamber knights. Rutland's appetite was insatiable. In May 1399 he paid 2,800 marks down for the Beaumont, FitzWaryn and Lestrange wardships, which must have been three of the most valuable wardships available in England at the time.[103] As is well known, both he and Lescrope also benefited from the forfeiture of the Appellants' estates in 1397 as well as from the partition of the Lancaster and March estates in 1387–9. Richard had a lot to give in 1397–9, but he gave it to few.

Knights of the chamber: rewards and duties

The rewards granted to Richard's chamber knights throughout the reign consisted for the most part of temporary grants such as wardships, the custody of royal lands or castles (with attached fees), life annuities, and salaried posts in the king's gift. The chamber knight whose service to the king opened up a route to permanent landed wealth, let alone the peerage, was a rare creature. This was because, firstly, for much of the reign there was little to give, and considerable pressure from both the commons and the lords to keep what there was in the king's hands, and secondly, because by rewarding men with such temporary sources of wealth Richard ensured that they remained bound to the king. When new sources of patronage did come on the market, they were often used to reward chamber knights. After his mother's death, for instance, Richard granted many of her Cornish and other lands to the new knights he had created on the Scottish campaign of 1385.[104] This was an important new source of patronage for Richard, for up until this time he had had little opportunity to reward the rising stars of his court (with one exception, Simon Burley). The only chamber knight in Richard's reign whose service brought him to the peerage was John Beauchamp of Holt—and his peerage lasted less than six months. Even in his case, his elevation was not marked by the acquisition of much permanent landed wealth and that was precisely why his was a 'barony by patent'. Simon Burley, as noted above, had probably acquired enough land (mainly in Kent and South Wales) by 1387 to support a peerage, but although Richard may have intended to give him one, it never quite happened. The other six chamber knights of Richard II's who received individual summonses to parliament did so not because they achieved promotion through service, but because of their birth, or in the case of William Beauchamp Lord Bergavenny, because of a fortunate and skilful arrangement and an accident of death.[105] Thomas Clifford, Aubrey de Vere, William Lescrope, Thomas Percy, and John Holand were all born into the peerage (Lescrope's and Percy's earldoms, and Holand's dukedom, were certainly the fruits of royal favour, but these did not make them peers, for they were that already). It was Edward III, not Richard II, who created peerages for his knights: William Montague, Robert Ufford, William Clinton, and William Bohun, are the most obvious examples, and there were many more who became peers but not earls. It is true, however, that the more fluid peerage of the early and mid fourteenth century no doubt made it easier for Edward to grant peerages to new men; the more rigid (almost closed) peerage of the later fourteenth century made it a harder climb for Richard's courtiers.

Allied to the question of peerages is the territorial pattern of grants made to Richard's chamber knights. The geographical provenance of Richard's chamber knights will be discussed in conjunction with that of the other 'king's knights',[106] but as to the grants made to them, there are few cases in which the king seems to have made a deliberate attempt to establish one of his courtiers as a leading landowner in a particular part of the country. The clearest exception to this is the series of grants made to William Lescrope in North Wales, especially the 'whole county and lordship of Anglesey' in February 1397. Lescrope was also keeper of the king's castles of Beaumaris, Conwy and Caernarfon, justice of Chester and North Wales from January 1398, keeper of the March Lordship of Denbigh from August 1398, and purchased the Isle of Man from the earl of Salisbury for 10,000 marks, so there was undoubtedly a pattern of territorial aggrandisement here, clearly allied to Richard's own entrenchment in his Cheshire principality.[107] If he hoped to make Lescrope ruler of North Wales in the late 1390s, Richard had tried equally hard to make Robert de Vere ruler of Ireland in the mid 1380s, but this was a short-lived dream. His grant of extensive Kentish lands to Simon Burley was equally short-lived, but his attempt to make John Holand a power in the west country bore more fruit, and it may well be that here Richard made a major contribution to the long-term decline of the Courtenay earls of Devon as the dominant power in that county.[108] Whether this was intended as a deliberate attack on the earl of Devon is debatable: the original grant of lands in the west country to Holand, made in 1384, was the foothold which enabled Holand to develop his power in the region, but the reason why these lands had been granted to him was because they were (or at least Richard treated them as if they were) available, and the king was looking around for suitable estates with which to endow his half-brother.[109]

The case of John Stanley is rather different. It has been said that Edward IV made Lord Stanley 'undoubted ruler of Lancashire' in the 1470s,[110] but the Stanley power in this area had been growing for well over half a century before this time, and it was the grandfather of Edward IV's Lord Stanley who really set his house on the road to glory. John Stanley was not a chamber knight, but he was closely associated with the court from 1389 onwards, and was controller of the household in the last two years of the reign. So well did he accustom himself to the change of dynasty in 1399 that he was also steward of Henry IV's household from 1405–13. As Bennett has pointed out, he is the classic example of a man who rose through royal service to become the dominant lord in an area where there were no great resident magnates. But it was a long, slow process.[111] Not until 1455 did the Stanleys actually receive the peerage which befitted their power in the region. It needed the favour not of just one king, but of several, and it needed both skill and fortune in good measure.

In general, then, Richard had no desire to transform his chamber knights into territorial magnates. He wanted them at court, because he had jobs for them to do. There were certain types of jobs which chamber knights were customarily given, and in general these reflect both the trust which the king had in them and their own special skills. They acted as keepers of castles, as diplomats, as soldiers, and as the king's special commissioners. Of those who acted as the king's ambassadors to foreign courts, six of Richard's chamber staff can be singled out as particularly skilled (judging by the number and/or importance of the missions entrusted to them).[112] Nicholas Dagworth was sent on at least seven diplomatic missions between 1381 and 1391, twice to the Pope, once to Scotland, once to Aquitaine, and three times to France. He was involved in the important French peace talks in 1383 and again in 1391, and was clearly a thoroughly accomplished diplomat (he was even sent to France in December 1388, during the Appellant regime, despite the fact that they had only released him from prison six months earlier). Richard Stury undertook at least four missions, one to Germany, and three to France (including French peace talks in 1380 and 1394), while Nicholas Sharnesfeld went twice to Germany and to France with Dagworth in 1391. George Felbridge, while still an esquire of the chamber, was sent to Germany in 1380, Bohemia in 1381, Flanders in 1382, and Guelders in 1385 and after he was knighted he again went to Guelders in 1387 and 1393 and to Bohemia in 1391. Perhaps the most delicate missions were those concerning Richard's marriages, and it is not surprising to find that the two men consistently involved in these two series of negotiations were, in 1380–1, for the Bohemian marriage, Simon Burley, and in 1395–6, for the French marriage, William Lescrope (Rutland, John Lord Beaumont, and the earl of Nottingham frequently accompanied Lescrope on these missions). Although these six seem to have been the most experienced of Richard's diplomats (among the laymen, that is), many other knights and esquires of the chamber were used occasionally: Richard Abberbury, John Burley, William Nevill, John Clanvow, Lewis Clifford, and Robert Witteneye among the chamber knights, and William Brauncepath and Janico Dartasso (twice) among the chamber esquires, all served as the king's ambassadors at various times during the reign. It was primarily to his chamber knights, and to the clerks who brought their legal training to bear, that the king turned when foreign negotiations needed to be conducted.

It was also to his chamber knights that Richard entrusted the most important castles in the realm.[113] By this time many of the king's castles were in a severe state of disrepair, and most of them had long since ceased to have any serious military importance. But there remained a hard core of strategic defensible strongholds up and down the country such as Dover, Nottingham, Bamburgh, Portchester, Queenborough, Southampton, the North Welsh castles, the Tower of London, and Windsor. Although during the early years of the reign several of these were held by men to whom they had been granted by Edward III, from the mid 1380s onwards they were nearly always entrusted to the keeping of men closely attached to the court, usually chamber knights.[114]

Nottingham, for example, the major royal stronghold in the midlands, was kept successively by John Burley (before 1381), William Nevill (1381–91), John Golafre (1391–6), and William Arundel (1396–9), all chamber knights. Dover castle, which was always held jointly with the wardship of the Cinque Ports, was held by Simon Burley (1384–8), John Devereux steward of the household (1388–93), John Beaumont (1393–6), Rutland (1396–8) and John Beaufort marquess of Dorset (1398–9). Queenborough was held successively by the king's esquire Thomas atte Lee, Robert de Vere, William Lescrope, Arnold Savage, and then Lescrope again; Southampton by Thomas Holand the king's half-brother, and then by his son Thomas duke of Surrey; Portchester by Robert Bardolf (1381–95), and then jointly by the king's clerk Roger Walden (later archbishop of Canterbury) and his brother, the king's esquire John Walden; Windsor by Simon Burley (1377–88), then for a short time during the Appellant regime by the king's butler Thomas Tyle, and from January 1390 by the chamber knight Peter Courtenay. Various other castles, whose importance to the king lay primarily in the fact that they were desirable and lavish residences rather than military strongholds, together with several of the king's favourite manors, were also normally entrusted to chamber staff. Berkhamstead, Wallingford and Hadleigh castles, and Kennington, Chiltern Langley, and Havering manors are examples.

There were often lucrative fees and perquisites attached to the custody of these castles and manors. There was, for instance, a £300 *per annum* fee attached to the constableship of Dover castle and wardenship of the Cinque Ports, but the value of the post was undoubtedly greater than this: in 1370 Richard Pembridge purchased these offices from Ralph Spigurnell for a down payment of 400 marks and a promise of £100 *per annum* for life thereafter, which gives some indication of what (in addition to his fee) he hoped to make from the office.[115] Yet it should not be thought that the king handed out these castles simply by selecting courtiers whom he wished to reward. The idea, particularly in regard to the truly defensible castles and favoured residences, was to make sure that they were kept by men whom the king could trust to do the job properly, and not surprisingly there were certain men who seemed almost to collect keeperships and constableships of castles, in the same way that other men were regularly employed as diplomats. John Golafre was one. He held Wallingford castle from 1387 to 1396 (when he died), Flint and Pembroke 1390–6, Nottingham 1391–6, and Cherbourg 1390–3. Simon Burley held Windsor, Dover and Carmarthen castles during the 1380s, while William Arundel held both Nottingham and Rochester castles during the last few years of the reign. At various times in the last decade of the reign John Holand held Berkhamstead, Conwy, Rockingham, Carlisle, Trematon and Tintagel castles, but it was above all William Lescrope to whom Richard entrusted royal castles at this time. In North Wales he held Beaumaris from 1394, Caernarfon from 1396, Holt from 1398, and Conwy, which was transferred to him from Holand in February 1398, and in South Wales he held Pembroke from 1396, while in England he held Bamburgh, Queenborough, Marlborough, and Richmond in Yorkshire.

Castles in occupied France and on the Scottish border were generally entrusted to men of proven military ability, and that included many of Richard's chamber knights or other close associates. The vital bridgehead of Calais, for instance, was held successively by John Devereux, Edmund de la Pole (brother of the chancellor), Philip la Vache, Henry earl of Northumberland, Thomas earl of Nottingham, and John Holand from 1389 until its surrender to the duke of Brittany in 1397. Cherbourg was held by Thomas Holand earl of Kent, William Lescrope, and John Golafre. Numerous other castles in Aquitaine and in the marches around Calais, such as Fronsac, Guines and Oye, were held by king's knights (these lesser castles were rarely held by chamber knights). The most important castles on the Scottish border were Berwick, Roxburgh and Carlisle. Berwick was held for most of the reign by various members of the Percy family apart from a brief period between 1388 and 1391 when it was held by John Stanley and Thomas earl of Nottingham, which apparently pleased the earl of Northumberland not a bit.[116] Carlisle was in the hands of, successively, John Lord Nevill (the former steward of Edward III's household), Ralph Nevill his son and a king's knight, Henry Percy (Hotspur), John Beaumont, and then John Holand during the last three years of the reign. Attached to these two castles were the wardship of the east and west marches of Scotland respectively, and the northern border families such as the Percies and the Nevills tended to be very sensitive over the question of these appointments, so the king did not have too much latitude to appoint his own men in these castles even if he had wanted to.[117] One man whom he clearly did regard as a capable soldier was John Stanley (and quite rightly so, as far as can be gathered), for apart from his brief tenure of Berwick castle, Stanley also held Roxburgh and Newcastle during the later years of the reign. Stanley also served as lieutenant or deputy lieutenant of Ireland on various occasions from 1386 onwards and under Henry IV, and there can be no doubt that he was a man highly valued by both kings for his military expertise.

There were other appointments in the king's gift, more or less exacting but almost invariably well-paid, which traditionally went to chamber knights and other close associates of the king. The keeping of the king's mews at Charing, for example, where the king's hunting birds were reared and trained, carried with it a wage of 12*d.* a day, and was held successively by the chamber knights Simon Burley (1377–88), Peter Courtenay (1388–90, while he was chamberlain), and Baldwin Bereford (1390–9).[118] The masters of the king's horse were, successively, Nicholas Bonde (1377–81), Thomas Murrieux (1381–6, when he went to Spain with his father-in-law John of Gaunt), Baldwin Bereford (1386–7), Thomas Clifford (1387–91), John Russell (1391–7), and Richard Redman (1397–9), all chamber knights apart from Redman who was a king's knight.[119] Simon Burley, John Beauchamp of Holt, Robert de Vere, Thomas Percy, Richard Stury, Thomas earl of Nottingham, and William Lescrope all acted at various times as justices of either North or South Wales (with a fee of £40), while the keeping of the forests south of the Trent was held successively by Thomas Holand and the earl of Rutland, and of those north of the Trent by

William Nevill, Thomas Clifford, and Ralph Lord Nevill. Each post carried an annual fee of 100 marks. All these posts were lucrative, prestigious, carried considerable responsibilities, and were no doubt much sought-after. It was the king's duty to share them around among those whom he trusted and whom he wanted to reward. There can be no doubt, however, that in the last two or three years of the reign a high proportion of them were concentrated in the hands of a very small group of persons, Rutland and Lescrope especially, but also John Holand (chamberlain of England from 1390, keeper of Carlisle and the west march from 1397, captain of Calais 1398–9, as well as various other castles as noted above), and John Beaufort, who seems to have risen very rapidly during the last two years of the reign (marquess of Dorset in 1397, admiral of England and Ireland in 1398, constable of Dover castle and warden of the Cinque Ports in the same year, and appointed king's lieutenant in Aquitaine, also in 1398, although he never actually went there). Such concentration of power and wealth in a few hands may well help to explain why men, supposedly close associates of the king, and including chamber knights, were prepared to desert him in 1399. It does not help to explain why Rutland and Beaufort deserted him, but both these men were faced with conflicts of loyalty: Rutland was young and ambitious, and his father the duke of York had already made his peace with Bolingbroke, which put him in an invidious position; Beaufort was of course Bolingbroke's half-brother (but even so, he didn't desert Richard quite as rapidly as is sometimes thought).

Besides acting in regular, salaried posts such as those mentioned above, the chamber knights were frequently used as special commissioners by the king, when a specific job needed to be done, often in a hurry. In 1377, for instance, Nicholas Dagworth was sent 'to survey Ireland', while in May 1385 John Clanvow was sent to South and West Wales 'with special mandate to act on behalf of the king in examining the conditions of those parts'.[120] Foreign dignitaries of sufficient rank were usually escorted from their port of embarkation to wherever the king was by one or more chamber knights. In June 1384, for example, Thomas Blount escorted the king of France's ambassadors back to Calais, while John Holand, Simon Burley, and John Montague (steward of the household) were sent in December 1381 to meet Richard's bride Anne of Bohemia and bring her to the king.[121] Special commissions often involved the inspection of defences in strategic areas as, for example, when William Nevill (in 1383) and Richard Stury (in August 1389) were sent to check on the state of the Calais garrison.[122] During the French invasion scare in the autumn of 1386, William Nevill and John Clanvow were sent to examine the defences of Orwell (Suffolk), while Nicholas Sharnesfeld and Thomas Holand were sent to do the same at Portsmouth, with the household esquire Robert Chalmely. In March 1394, William Lescrope was appointed to survey all the king's castles in Cheshire and North Wales, and repair their defences if necessary.[123] Detachments of household men might be sent to garrison a particular town or castle in an emergency. Thus, again during the invasion scare of 1386, the Westminster chronicle reports that 'orders were given this year by the king's council that certain members of his establishment, that is those who were superfluous to the needs of the household, should go to Sandwich and, at the king's expense, devote the whole summer to guarding the neighbouring coastal districts against assault by the enemy.' The garrison was in fact commanded by Baldwin Raddington, controller of the household, and the king's privy wardrobe provided considerable quantities of weaponry.[124]

The value of the king's chamber knights, therefore, lay primarily in the fact that they formed a reliable and capable group of men, closely bound to the king and in turn well rewarded by him (apart from the offices they held, most of them were in receipt of life annuities at the exchequer ranging between about £60 and £100), who performed a variety of administrative, military and diplomatic functions for which reliable and capable men were needed. Their service to their monarch was never closely defined. They might go off for months or even years on end (campaigning, crusading, or on embassies, for instance), and although there were probably always a certain number of them with the king, they were certainly not obliged to remain permanently at court. Like good servants, however, they were probably more or less obliged to accept the duties which the king asked them to perform. Edward III certainly took this line with regard to Richard Pembridge.[125] Richard II, as far as can be gathered, never dismissed any of his chamber knights, indeed he showed a high degree of loyalty to them through the crises of 1386−9. As a group, they certainly gained a bad reputation in the 1380s, and some of them were no doubt greedy and perhaps violent men, but in the circumstances of that decade, with failure in war, financial crisis, and a teenage monarch, it was almost inevitable that those closest to the king would have to take their share of the blame for the country's misfortunes.

Moreover, the image which the court presented to the public was not a good one. There were a number of unpleasant incidents at court which seem to have made an impression on the public mind (or at least on the minds of the chroniclers), such as the Hauley-Shakell murder, the affair of the Carmelite friar, the dismissal of Richard Lescrope from the chancellorship in 1382, and Richard's violent (and very personal) quarrels with his uncles, with the earl of Arundel, and with Archbishop Courtenay.[126] The chamber knights got a bad name. Walsingham accused them of being immoral and militarily inactive. It is quite possible that some of them were (in Walsingham's terms) immoral. There were one or two such scandals at court, such as John Holand's seduction of Gaunt's daughter Elizabeth and Robert de Vere's seduction of Queen Anne's lady-in-waiting Agnes Lancecrona (Walsingham also hints at a homosexual relationship between the king and Robert de Vere),[127] but to accuse Richard's chamber knights of military inactivity was hardly fair. Many of them had long records of active service under Edward III or the Black Prince, and continued to campaign during Richard's reign, despite the fact that both the opportunities and the attractions were now considerably reduced.

Apart from the knights of the chamber, there were also esquires of the chamber, some of whom were clearly as high in the king's esteem as were his knights. I have only discovered twenty-eight men described as esquires of the chamber throughout the reign, but this is undoubtedly an under-estimate and the true figure is probably nearer fifty (they were never listed separately from the esquires of the household, so there are only incidental references to rely on). Their careers in many ways parallel those of the chamber knights, except that esquires tended on the whole to receive the custody of less important castles, hold fewer and less lucrative offices, and so forth. It was from their ranks that the knights of the chamber were sometimes drawn: Robert Bardolf, George Felbridge, John Beauchamp of Holt, John Golafre and John Salisbury had all been esquires of the chamber before they became knights of the chamber. At the beginning of the reign they were nearly all drawn either from the household of the Black Prince or from that of Edward III. Of the nineteen identifiable esquires of the chamber during the first decade of the reign, seven had been esquires in Edward III's household, and nine had been the Black Prince's esquires (all of whom had passed into Richard's household when he was Prince of Wales in 1376–7).[128] Some of these esquires received offices, commissions and annuities little different from those given to chamber knights. Philip Walweyn, for example, who had been usher of the Black Prince's hall and acted as usher of Richard's chamber when he was Prince of Wales, became constable of Corfe Castle in 1380 and was the leading member of a Herefordshire family at least five of whose members were employed in the household. Roger Coghull acted as sheriff of Flintshire and constable of Flint castle 1386–90, while the Gascon Janico Dartasso, a soldier of considerable repute who joined Richard's household around 1390–2, received an annuity of 100 marks at the exchequer and was twice sent by Richard on important diplomatic missions, to Italy and Germany in 1392, and again to Germany in July 1397.[129] Dartasso demonstrated both his courage and his loyalty to Richard by refusing to take off the livery badge which the king had given him when told to by Bolingbroke in August 1399. This irritated Bolingbroke so much that he ordered Dartasso to be imprisoned in Chester castle, but before long he had been pardoned and was soon clearly high in the new king's confidence.[130] Another chamber esquire of interest is Richard Hampton, the former feodary of the Black Prince who was havenor of Devon and Cornwall and keeper of Tintagel castle during the 1380s, and was clearly much favoured by Richard. In 1383–4, however, he forfeited his offices because of certain 'rebellious words' spoken by him in the presence of some of the king's ministers, and was only pardoned and restored to his offices at the intercession of Simon Burley.[131] As well as Dartasso and Walweyn, the other esquires of the chamber who seem to have been especially close to the king (apart from those who became chamber knights), were Adam Ramsey (to whom the king gave £4 when his son was baptised),[132] John Rose, who was described, most unusually in this period, as 'king's esquire of the body',[133] and John Worshippe, one of the very few members of the chamber staff who acted as sheriff of his county (Buckinghamshire) in this period.

The king's clerks

From the chamber came the majority of the laymen who formed the inner circle of the king's companions. It was the king's chapel which provided his clerical intimates. The essential distinction between the king's lay and clerical courtiers was in the type of work which they did. Unlike the knights and esquires of the chamber, the king's clerks were nearly always employed to do specific jobs within specific departments. They were clerks of the chancery, of the exchequer, of the judicial benches, or, if they were in the household, of the privy seal office, the chapel, and the various offices of the household (buttery, marshalsea, etc.). Altogether, about 240 men were described as 'king's clerks' during Richard's reign, of whom 90–100 were clerks working in the household, though there were never more than fifty in the household at any one time.

Few, if any, of the clerks of the offices were of political importance. Those clerks who were associated by the chroniclers and critics of the court with Richard's inner circle of advisors were usually chaplains or clerks of the chapel, or occasionally clerks of the privy seal office working within the household (most of the privy seal clerks remained at Westminster, but some of them were usually with the court). Certain general remarks can be made about these clerical intimates of the king. They were pluralists, if not to a man, then almost so, and they frequently held rich prebends or canonries in, for instance, the king's free chapels (St George's at Windsor, St Stephen's at Westminster, Hastings, Wolverhampton, Bridgenorth, St Martin-le-Grand, and so forth), or in the great cathedrals. Needless to say, they were frequently absentees too. Unlike the king's knights and esquires, they provided only a small drain on the crown's financial resources, for the king only gave them annuities until such time as they were found suitable livings, and the wealth of church patronage available to the king was such that these annuities rarely had to be taken for long. Several of them, particularly in the later years of the reign, became bishops. Some of them had a legal training, and one point which they had in common with the chamber knights was that they might be sent on diplomatic missions together. Several of them became just as notorious as some of Richard's chamber knights, and like the chamber knights they can be broadly divided into the clerks of the 1380s (several of whom were attacked in the Merciless Parliament) and those who rose to favour in the 1390s. With one or two exceptions, however, the Appellants clearly failed to destroy the clerical court clique in 1388.

At the head of the group of courtier clerks in the 1380s stood Nicholas Slake. His origins are obscure, but he seems to have joined Edward III's household at the very end of that king's reign.[134] By 1382 he was a clerk of Richard II's chapel, and already in 1384 he was singled out by Walsingham as one of two clerks from whom the king was accustomed to take his counsel, rather than from the 'pares regni' and Walsingham attributes Richard's rash behaviour over the affair of the Carmelite friar to the fact that he was too fond of taking Slake's advice. Walsingham took another swipe at Slake at the time of the latter's arrest in January 1388, when he described him as 'dean of the king's chapel, whose words were much relied on at court'.[135] If Slake was indeed dean of the chapel, he had only attained that office recently, for Thomas de Lynton, dean since 1377, was still acting in that capacity early in 1386.[136] That he was arrested and imprisoned by the Appellants is, however, beyond any doubt. Three of his companions in the king's chapel, Richard Medford, Richard Clifford, and John Lincoln, were imprisoned at the same time. No specific charges were preferred against them, but it was clearly believed by the Appellants and their followers that all four of them had acquired too easy an intimacy with the king and had been in a position to influence him unfavourably.

Like Slake, Clifford and Medford had been the recipients of special royal favours in the early 1380s. Richard Clifford, who was probably a member of the Westmorland family which included the chamber knight Thomas Clifford, was already prebendary at St Stephen's, Westminster, in 1383, and in January of that year the king granted him a house and garden within the confines of the palace of Westminster—of which there can have been few. Medford and Slake were granted special rights to hunt in the king's forests in 1384, and both held prebends at St George's (Windsor).[137] Medford was the senior member of the group, having been a clerk of the royal household as long ago as 1366, and he acted as the king's secretary (keeper of his secret seal, or signet) from 1385 until his arrest in January 1388. In 1386 Richard II tried to secure the see of Bath and Wells for him, but instead it went to Walter Skirlaw. John Lincoln, by contrast, had arrived on the scene more recently, and was first described as a clerk of the king's chapel in January 1386.[138] He rose fast, however, and in November 1386, at a time when the king badly needed reliable friends in the principal government departments (his own nominees as chancellor, treasurer and keeper of the privy seal having been ousted in the Wonderful Parliament), he appointed Lincoln as chamberlain of the receipt of the exchequer in succession to Thomas Orgrave.[139] John came from Grimsby and may have been related to the Robert Lincoln who was clerk of the chapel throughout Richard's reign; unlike John, Robert avoided controversy and was still a clerk of the chapel in Henry IV's household in 1402–3.[140]

These four were not treated with the same barbarity as were the chamber knights, largely no doubt because of their cloth. All four were kept in confinement throughout the Merciless Parliament (a sobering experience, one would have thought), and released on bail on 4 June. It was stipulated that they should answer for their crimes at the next parliament, and that under no circumstances were they to return to court.[141] In fact they were never brought to trial in any subsequent parliament, but their expulsion from court does seem to have been effective for a short while, for none of them was listed as a clerk of the chapel in the 1389–90 wardrobe account. Within the next year or two, however, they gradually crept back. Richard Clifford was appointed keeper of the great wardrobe in November 1390, which post he held until February 1398. Meanwhile in late 1397 he became keeper of the privy seal and was thus a member of the council during the final period of the reign. The king demonstrated his trust in Clifford by appointing him one of the executors of his will. He was one of only two of Richard's inner group of household clerks who found favour with Henry IV: he retained his post as keeper of the privy seal until November 1401, and was then successively bishop of Worcester (1401–7) and London (1407–21). Given his strong curialist attachment during Richard's reign, the fact that he was able to survive the revolution of 1399 with such apparent ease speaks highly for his ability. Nicholas Slake and John Lincoln were both back in the king's chapel by 1392, and both remained closely attached to the king through the last years. Lincoln was Richard's secretary from 1395–9, while Slake was appointed dean of St Stephen's in April 1396, and in 1399 he was singled out by the Londoners as one of three royal clerks considered to be King Richard's 'special counsellors', and imprisoned by them to await the arrival of Bolingbroke.[142] Although soon released, he was once again arrested on 4 January 1400, which can only have been in connection with the earls' rebellion against the new king. Eel-like, however, he wriggled free once more, and by September 1401 was actually described as a king's clerk, though he never regained his old influence.[143] Richard Medford, too, continued to be favoured by Richard II after 1388: having tried in vain to secure his election to the see of St David's in 1389, the king finally succeeded in 1390 in winning the see of Chichester for him, whence he was translated to Salisbury in 1395. He clearly remained active in government, and frequently witnessed royal charters during the last three years of the reign.[144]

The other two royal clerks attacked by the Appellants in 1388 were John Fordham and Thomas Rushook. Fordham had been the Black Prince's secretary both in Aquitaine and in England, and acted as Richard's receiver-general and keeper of his privy seal when he was Prince of Wales. He rose high in Richard's administration, as keeper of the privy seal (1377–81), and treasurer of England (January-October 1386). In 1381 he became bishop of Durham. He was already unpopular, the rebels demanded his head and plundered his wine cellar in the Strand, and in 1386 he was forced to resign the treasurership on the same day that de la Pole resigned the chancellorship.[145] In 1388 he was expelled from court and translated (demoted, in effect), to Ely. Although he lived until 1425, Fordham was clearly not as active in the politics of the 1390s as he had been before 1388, although he did witness a good number of royal charters between 1396 and 1398.[146] At the beginning of the parliament of November 1390, Richard announced that all those who wished to proceed with any of the charges brought against either Fordham or 'others who had been accused on various counts' in the Merciless Parliament should do so now, but no one availed himself of the opportunity, and Fordham lived out the remaining thirty-five years of his life in peace.[147] This was a sensible and necessary move by the king. The Appellants' aim was no doubt to keep dangling these charges over the heads of those they had expelled from court in 1388, but Richard effectively removed the threat, and it heralded the return of several of them to court.

Thomas Rushook was a Dominican friar who had been the king's confessor since the beginning of the reign, and was thoroughly disliked. Gower described him as supple, flattering, an evil influence on the king.[148] He earned the distinction of being the first of Richard's intimates to be chosen for expulsion from court, when the commons rounded on him in the parliament of November 1381.[149] He took no heed of their criticism, for he clearly remained at court and became bishop of Llandaff (1383–5) and Chichester (1385–8). He was an obvious target for the hatred of the king's enemies in 1388, and the proceedings against him were taken much further than those against the other five clerks already discussed. He was impeached for treason: the charges were not specified in detail, but among other things he was said to have threatened and cajoled the king's judges into answering the famous questions put to them in 1387, and to have uttered verbal threats against the lives of the 1386 Commissioners. He escaped with his life, just, but was found guilty of treason and sentenced to forfeiture of his temporalities, demotion from the see of Chichester, and exile to Ireland. The pope was persuaded to translate him to Kilmore and although the king granted him an annuity of £40 in March 1390 (because he 'has but a modest bishopric'), he played no further part in English politics, and died in 1392.[150] He was the only cleric in the king's inner circle whom the Appellants succeeded in destroying.

These six were the most prominent of the king's clerks attacked in 1388. But also among those individually exempted from the general pardon at the end of the Merciless Parliament were the king's clerks John Ripon, Henry Bowet, William Monkton and Geoffrey FitzMartin. None of them were household clerks, and it is not clear what their crimes were. Ripon had been responsible for negotiating Robert de Vere's divorce at Rome in 1387, which may have been seen as a crime by the Appellants, and at least demonstrates his close association with the king's principal favourite. He was caught in disguise near Tutbury in June 1388 and imprisoned, but pardoned in 1393. Monkton was pardoned in 1390. Bowet was the king's proctor at the Roman court, and had been in prison once before, in November 1383, but whether this was connected with his unpopularity in 1388 is not clear.[151] At any rate, he survived to rise high in Henry IV's favour and became bishop of Bath and Wells (1401–7) and archbishop of York (1407–23) and was also treasurer of England briefly in 1402. Also exempted from the general pardon were Robert de Vere's confessor, Thomas Roughton, who had escaped with his master from Radcot Bridge, and Roughton's brother Richard, who was the queen's confessor.[152] It was a bad year for confessors.

Finally, there were two other clerks who were clearly high in the king's favour during the early 1380s. John Bacon, receiver of Richard's chamber when he was Prince of Wales, chamberlain of the exchequer 1377–85, and king's secretary 1381–5, died in 1385 on a diplomatic mission for the king to Rome.[153] Richard had a requiem mass said for him in Westminster Abbey, which the king attended in person.[154] Secondly, Walter Skirlaw, doctor of laws and chancery clerk under Edward III, was keeper of the privy seal from 1382 until October 1386, when he was forced into resignation along with chancellor de la Pole and treasurer Fordham. Skirlaw was clearly very able. He undertook more diplomatic missions for the king (eleven) than any other person during the reign, particularly between 1377 and 1386. He was made bishop of Coventry and Lichfield (1386), then Bath and Wells (1386–8), and eventually replaced Fordham at Durham (1388–1405). Although seemingly regarded as a curialist in 1386, his relations with the court seem to have cooled after this. Perhaps the king resented the fact that he had been preferred to Richard Medford for the see of Bath and Wells in 1386. By January 1388 Skirlaw was considered sufficiently trustworthy by the Appellants to be appointed as one of those who was to be placed in the household for the day-to-day guidance of the king.[155] In 1389–90 Skirlaw had what was evidently a bitter dispute with the new rising star of the court, William Lescrope, as a result of which Lescrope was obliged to donate a jewel worth at least £500 to the shrine of St Cuthbert in Skirlaw's cathedral.[156] However, his relations with the king clearly remained good for a few years yet: he was a regular member of the council in late 1389, he was witnessing royal charters with frequency in 1391–2, he was one of the king's ambassadors to the crucial French peace talks in 1393, and in January 1394 the king held a great feast in Skirlaw's London house. After this, however, he was little in evidence at court. He was certainly not a prominent Ricardian during the last few years of the reign, and when the king asked him for a loan in 1399 he declined to give one.[157]

Thus with the exception of Thomas Rushook, the clerical element of the 1380s court circle was, in the long term, virtually untouched by the events of 1388; by 1392 at the latest they were all back at court, and all those clerks of the chapel who had been imprisoned and dismissed in 1388 continued to be prominent and active until the end of the reign. They were joined at court by a new group of clerks, some of whom were to win great favour with the king during the last few years of the reign, and were to prove themselves strikingly loyal to him in 1399–1400. Most notable among them were Alexander Bache, John Burghill, William Ferriby, John Ikelyngton, Richard Maudeleyn, Thomas Merks, Guy Mone, Ralph Selby, Roger Walden and Tideman of Winchcombe. Bache and Burghill followed successively in Rushook's footsteps as the king's confessors. Bache was Richard's confessor from at least February 1389 until his death in 1394, and bishop of St Asaph from 1390. In November 1390 he secured from the king various privileges for the clergy of his diocese, an interesting example of how a courtier might use his influence.[158] However, the Westminster chronicler for one did not like him, and described him as arrogant.[159] Burghill, a Dominican friar, and described by Adam of Usk as 'a covetous man', succeeded Bache in 1394, and became bishop of Llandaff (1396–8) and of Coventry and Lichfield (1398–1414). Richard spent Christmas 1398 in great splendour at his confessor's episcopal palace at Lichfield.[160]

By 1392 Guy Mone and Roger Walden were both already clerks of the chapel, while Tideman of Winchcombe, a Cistercian monk, had been the king's surgeon since at least 1390, and Ralph Selby, doctor of laws, was retained to be one of the council in October 1393, and remained one of the king's councillors until the end of the reign.[161] All these four, then, were trusted and intimate royal clerks for most of the decade, and all were regarded as closely associated with Richard's regime. Mone and Walden both rose to high office in the administration as well as the church. Mone was keeper of the privy seal 1396–7 and treasurer from January to September 1398. When replaced as treasurer by William Lescrope, he was still retained to stay on the council. He was also bishop of St David's 1397–1407 though at his death, Walsingham remarked that 'while he lived he was the cause of much wrongdoing'.[162] Roger Walden was the king's secretary from 1393 to 1396, then treasurer of England until January 1398. In 1397 he was exalted—excessively, some thought —to the archbishopric of Canterbury. He and Ralph Selby were arrested (along with Nicholas Slake) in July 1399, because they were thought by the Londoners to be the king's 'special counsellors'.[163] Walden was promptly demoted from his archbishopric but despite the fact that he was implicated in the earls rebellion of January 1400, he was later (1404) allowed the bishopric of London.

Also involved in the earls' rebellion were Tideman of Winchcombe, Richard Maudeleyn, Thomas Merks, William Ferriby and John Ikelyngton. Winchcombe was made bishop of Llandaff (1393–5) and of Worcester (1395–1404) and on the latter occasion the king personally attended his installation.[164] The other four only really came to prominence at court during the last three or four years of the reign. Merks was a monk of Westminster Abbey; he was a clerk of the chapel by 1395, the king's proctor at the French court in 1397, and bishop of Carlisle in 1397–9.[165] Of him and Tideman of Winchcombe, the author of the *Vita* remarked that they were 'privati viri et maximi consiliarii cum rege Ricardi . . . adeo ut maiorem partem noctis per annum cum illo in somprem ducerunt.' Merks was one of that little band of followers who remained with Richard right through the desperate days of the summer of 1399; he made a famous, and courageous, speech condemning Henry's usurpation in the parliament of October 1399, and was deprived of his see for his pains. Despite their involvement in the earls' rebellion, both of them were allowed to live, but the author of the *Vita* noted that Winchcombe 'numquan postea in curia regis visus est', which is hardly surprising.[166] He died in 1401, Merks in 1410, both peacefully.

Richard Maudeleyn and William Ferriby were not so fortunate. Ferriby was appointed as the king's chief notary in November 1397.[167] Maudeleyn was said to resemble the king greatly, and so favoured was he by the king that there were even rumours that he was Richard's illegitimate son, although these do not seem to be contemporary. He was a king's scholar at Cambridge in 1386, and had been described as a king's clerk as long ago as 1387, which makes it impossible that he could have been the king's child.[168] In 1395 he was a clerk of the chapel, in 1396 he was granted a prebend at St Stephen's, and during the next eighteen months he received a great number of benefices from the king.[169] Both Maudeleyn and Ferriby were nominated as executors of Richard's will, as was John Ikelyngton. John Ikelyngton held a special position as 'clerk of the king's treasure at Holt', that is, Holt castle in Clwyd, forfeited in 1397 by the earl of Arundel and converted by Richard in 1398 into a stronghold for the safeguard of the king's treasure.[170] Ikelyngton had been entrusted with 65,946 marks together with many goods and jewels 'ad magnam summam se extendentia', out of which he was to pay the bequests nominated in the king's will (these very generous bequests amounted to 91,000 marks; Richard's will stated that a further 24,000 marks was in the hands of Thomas Holand).[171] Moreover, the king made sure that his treasure was well defended. In September 1398 Ikelyngton received 200 hauberks, 60 hatchets, 300 bows, 200 arrows, 30 crossbows, 2,000 quarrels and 80 pounds of gunpowder from the privy wardrobe to help him to discourage intruders.[172]

Ferriby and Maudeleyn both remained loyal to Richard in the summer of 1399, but were not initially punished by Bolingbroke. There followed a curious episode in the parliament of October 1399 when after Richard's deposition, a scroll with some magic words, said to have belonged to the king, was found in Maudeleyn's possession yet when asked about it in parliament, Maudeleyn declared that he had no idea what the writing foretold. Nevertheless, King Henry decided to keep the scroll himself. Whether or not Maudeleyn was telling the truth, the secret of the scroll was soon lost for good, for he and Ferriby joined the earls' rebellion in January 1400, and both were executed as a result.[173] Ikelyngton also seems to have become implicated in the rebellion, for on 4 January 1400 an order was issued for his arrest, along with Maudeleyn, Nicholas Slake, John Lufwyk (a king's esquire who was another executor of Richard's will), and the former king's almoner, Richard atte Felde. Either Ikelyngton was found to be innocent of any complicity in the plot, or the king decided to pardon him, and in fact he soon passed into Henry IV's service. In November Henry acquitted him of any outstanding sums from the 65,946 marks entrusted to him, and he subsequently served as chamberlain of the exchequer and treasurer of the household of the Prince of Wales.[174]

During the last few years of the reign, the number of clerks among the king's closest companions and advisors was considerably greater than the number of chamber knights. In the 1380s the reverse had generally been true. They were clearly thoroughgoing Ricardians. Many more of the clerks of his chapel than knights of his chamber were involved in the plot to murder Richard's supplanter and restore him to the throne in January 1400, while eight of them were nominated by the king as executors of his will, usually a sign of personal trust (Merks, Winchcombe, Medford, Mone and Clifford, as well as Maudeleyn, Ferriby and Ikelyngton. Edmund Stafford, keeper of the privy seal 1389–96 and chancellor 1396–9, was also nominated, but he does not give the impression of a courtier so much as an able administrator; he became chancellor again under Henry IV). The only chamber knights nominated as Richard's executors were William Lescrope and John Holand (Rutland and Thomas Holand were also executors, together with the esquires of the chamber John Lufwyk and William Serle. Both Lufwyk and Serle were undoubtedly close to the king during these last years of the reign, and both remained loyal to him. Lufwyk's involvement in the rebellion of 1400 has been noted. Serle escaped to Scotland after Richard's capture in 1399, where he apparently forged the royal signet, and began sending letters to various Ricardian sympathisers in England claiming that Richard was still alive and inciting rebellion. He was eventually captured on the northern border in 1404 and executed barbarously by Henry IV, at which time it was also claimed that he had been implicated in the duke of Gloucester's murder in 1397.)[175]

It was normally among the clerks that the greatest continuity in household personnel was to be found, but apart from Clifford and Ikelyngton (who was switched to the exchequer), they were all discarded by Henry. Like the chamber knights of the 1380s, the household clerks of the 1390s had clearly earned themselves a degree of collective unpopularity. This collective unpopularity, moreover, must have spread to the episcopal bench (which no doubt accounts for Haxey's dig at the 'multitude of bishops' hanging around the court in 1397) for by the end of the reign Richard had secured bishoprics for so many of his household clerks that the episcopacy must almost have come to resemble an extension of the household. During the last few years of the reign the sees of Canterbury (Walden), Ely (Fordham), Salisbury (Medford), Worcester (Winchcombe), Carlisle (Merks), St David's (Mone), Lichfield (Burghill), Durham (Skirlaw) and Exeter (Edmund Stafford) were all held by men who had at one time been clerks in the household, while those of York (Robert Waldby, the king's former physician, 1396–8, and Richard Lescrope, king's councillor, 1398–1405), Chichester (Robert Reade), Llandaff (Thomas Peverell, the queen's chancellor),[176] and Norwich (Henry Despenser, one of the few men actually to take up arms in Richard's cause in 1399),[177] were held by men who were certainly to be counted among the king's friends. Despite the fact that many of these Ricardian bishops were at no pains to disguise their opposition to the new regime, Henry IV was, with the exceptions of Walden and Merks, prepared to treat them with considerable leniency in 1399 and 1400. He was then prepared to execute clerks, but not bishops; by 1405, he was prepared to execute an archbishop. Henry has frequently been criticised for his execution of Richard Lescrope, but his patience must have been sorely tried by the persistent opposition which he encountered from senior members of the church establishment during the early years of his reign. Churchmen of all kinds were very prominent in the conspiracies and rebellions of 1400–5. Besides the household clerks and bishops noted above, the abbot of Westminster was one of the ringleaders of the earls' rebellion of January 1400, the prior of Launde and several friars planned another revolt in 1402, and the abbots of Beeliegh, St Osyth, and St John's (Colchester), along with several monks, attempted to stir up a rebellion in Essex in 1404, encouraged by the countess of Oxford.[178] Lescrope's rebellion in 1405 must have been the last straw. No doubt this persistent disaffection goes a considerable way towards explaining the anti-clerical sentiments expressed by the knights at Henry's court (also it should not be forgotten that many of Henry's knights had been followers of his father, and some of Gaunt's anti-clericalism may have rubbed off on them), but it also highlights the support which Richard received from the church. The Westminster chronicler described him as guarding the church's liberties more zealously than any bishop, while his generosity to and concern for the church were almost the only virtues in Richard which sprang to the mind of the author of the *Vita*.[179] Richard clearly saw the value in cultivating church support, and in a way his policy bore fruit.[180]

The final point to emphasise about the king's household clerks is that their political importance was, like that of the chamber knights, personal, not institutional. Some of them certainly wrote under the signet, but the political and administrative importance of the signet, particularly in the years 1383–6, has been greatly exaggerated. It is certainly true that the number of warrants to the chancery which were sent under the signet increased greatly between mid 1383 and November 1386, and then, when the Commission of Government assumed power, stopped abruptly.[181] This was a direct consequence of Richard's personal involvement in government from 1383 onwards, but its significance is limited to that fact. If, as has been suggested, Richard during these years was using the signet as a special 'instrument of prerogative', it seems to have been a singularly pointless exercise, for with Michael de la Pole at the chancery (as well as Skirlaw at the privy seal office and Segrave and Fordham at the exchequer), surely Richard could rest assured of his ability to control the principal departments of government. In fact the conditions under which the king might have wanted to create a more 'personal' alternative administrative instrument occurred in the two and a half years *after* November 1386, not preceding that date, for this was the period during which he could not feel assured of co-operation within chancery and exchequer. Moreover, it would have been as an instrument of original force, not as a warrant to chancery, that Richard might have used it. If it was so used in this period, the evidence for its use has certainly not survived.[182] The king's clerks were not attacked because they wrote under the signet. There was no mention of the signet in the Wonderful Parliament of 1386. There were indeed complaints about the signet in other parliaments, but it is worth noting, firstly, that these were not confined to Richard's reign, let alone the period 1383–6, and secondly, that they all deal with a specific problem, that is, the use of the signet to interfere with actions at common law. Moreover, there were complaints about both the great and privy seal interfering with the common law as well.[183] Richard II's use of the signet in 1383–6 was for practical convenience, the consequence of the king's personal assumption of power (rather than the means by which it was effected), and the culmination of the long process by which the privy seal had moved 'out of court'.[184] His non-use of it after November 1386 was similarly a consequence of the fact that political circumstances were abnormal for the next two and a half years, not a cause of that abnormality.

The royal council

The king's chamber and his chapel were the obvious departments into which the king could place his close advisors and friends, his *familiarissimi* as the chroniclers liked to call them. It would have been surprising if he had not also tried to keep a certain number of his *familiarissimi* on the council, and there is indeed a considerable overlap of personnel between the council and both the chamber and chapel. The council, however, met largely independently of the king, and it was a place for tried and tested administrators as well as for courtiers—which is not to suggest that some of the courtiers were not able administrators, but that a place on the council should not necessarily be seen as a sign of favouritism. Unfortunately, our knowledge of the composition of the council during Richard's reign is, with the exception of three brief periods, limited. The first of these periods is 1377–80, the time of the continual councils. They were occasioned by Edward III's failure, a clear dereliction of his duty, to provide for his grandson's minority. Little need be said about them, except to reiterate that they consisted on the whole of a mixture of well-established royal servants and followers of the Black Prince, and that, although frequently criticised both by contemporaries and historians, they can in fact be credited with having done a difficult job quite well.[185] The second period is 1386–7, when the commissioners appointed in the Wonderful Parliament acted in effect as the king's council. Even if they were not all hostile to the court, they were certainly not the king's nominees.[186] Between 1380 and 1386, virtually nothing is known of the composition of the council, but one point about this period is worth making. In the 1390s, there are quite frequent references to men being 'retained to be of the king's council', or 'appointed to attend the king's council', for which they received a standard fee of 100 marks *per annum*. In other words, men were formally appointed to the council. Between 1380 and 1386 I have found only one such reference, when the chief justice Robert Tresilian was 'retained for life of his (the king's) council', in February 1385.[187] The apparent absence of such formal appointments certainly supports Tuck's view that the composition of the council may have been very fluid at this time, resulting perhaps in the removal of a possible check on the influence of the king's favourites.[188] Certainly, if the general tenor of the accusations made against the courtiers in 1388 is to be believed, then if there was a formally-constituted council at this time, either it was dominated by the courtiers themselves, or they were in effect able to ignore it. In other words, the situation was very similar to that preceding the Good Parliament.

The Commission of 1386–7 shaded into the Appellant regime of 1387–9, so that throughout the two and a half years from November 1386 to May 1389 the council consisted of men basically opposed to the court. The months following Richard II's resumption of power in May 1389 provide the third period during which the composition of the council is fairly well documented.[189] Apart from the three principal officers of state (chancellor Wykeham, treasurer John Gilbert of St David's, and privy seal keeper Edmund Stafford; they were always *ex officio* members), those in frequent attendance were Walter Skirlaw bishop of Durham, the duke of York, the earls of Northumberland (Percy), Nottingham (Mowbray), and Huntingdon (John Holand), and the knights William Nevill, John Devereux, Nicholas Sharnesfeld, Lewis Clifford, Richard Stury, Edward Dalyngridge, and John Lovell. The household, then, was very well represented on the council at this time, but the presence of Northumberland, Devereux (appointed steward of the household by the Appellants in January 1388, which post he retained until his death in February 1393), and Dalyngridge (a knight from Sussex who was experienced in local administration and probably supported the Appellants in 1387–8)[190] certainly gives it a balanced look, and the only one of these knights who had been dismissed from court in 1388 was John Lovell. They were the 'politically acceptable' chamber knights, and no doubt this was one reason why they were councillors.

For the next four years or so the composition of the council changed little, but from late 1393 onwards there were more significant changes.[191] William Nevill died in 1391, while Devereux, Dalyngridge, Stury and Sharnesfeld all died between 1393 and 1395, so changes were inevitable, but what is perhaps of more significance is that the men who replaced them were not household men. Within a month of each other in October and November 1393, three new councillors were appointed: Laurence Dru, Ralph Selby and Richard Waldegrave.[192] Dru and Selby both remained on the council until the end of the reign, and both were clearly members of that inner circle of the king's advisors who acquired such intense unpopularity between late 1397 and 1399. Dru was an esquire who held land in Berkshire and Wiltshire, a lawyer who had been made king's attorney in the common bench as early as September 1381, but who only really became prominent among the curialists after 1393. He remained loyal to Richard in 1399, and refused to join Bolingbroke, but was not apparently punished.[193] Selby too had a legal training, though he was a clerk (and archdeacon of Buckingham), and was one of those arrested by the Londoners in 1399 as the king's special councillors.[194] Richard Waldegrave, however, was a man in a rather different mould. A Suffolk knight who had sat as member of parliament for his county in almost every session between 1376 and 1390, was speaker of the commons in 1381, and was constantly active in local administration, he had been a king's knight since the beginning of the reign and had, with the advice of the council, been placed in the household before December 1377.[195] By this time he was already aged about forty. Although he acted as steward of Queen Anne's lands for a brief period after 1382, he was never really a courtier and by the time he became a king's councillor in 1393 he gives the impression more of a respected elder statesman than of a thoroughgoing Ricardian. He remained on the council for at least four years, but seems to have either been discharged or discharged himself early in 1398, for there is no evidence that he continued as a member during the last eighteen months of the reign, and he was not one of those hounded by the supporters of Bolingbroke in 1399. Indeed he seems to have kept a low profile during the revolution, and subsequently retired to his estates in Suffolk, where he died in 1410.[196]

These three, together with the three chief officers of state, Thomas Percy (steward of the household), and John Holand (chamberlain), formed the nucleus of the council in the years 1394–7. Waldegrave's departure in the winter of 1397–8 was one element in a radical change in the composition of the council. By this time the chief officers of state were (with the exception of chancellor Edmund Stafford) unequivocal Ricardians. Walden, Mone and William Lescrope acted successively as treasurers between 1395 and 1398, while Mone again and Richard Clifford kept the privy seal from 1396 onwards. The king's confidence in Guy Mone was reiterated when he was retained to stay on the council for a further year after leaving the treasury in September 1398.[197] On 1 August 1397 John Bussy and Henry Green were appointed to the council, and although there is no record of his formal retention to the council before March 1399, William Bagot had since late 1397 been a member, along with Bussy and Green, of that special tribunal before which those who wished to purchase pardons from the king had to appear.[198] The other members of the council in 1397–8 were Richard Lescrope archbishop of York (though he was abroad for much of this period),[199] John Holand (duke of Exeter from 1397), the chamber knight John Russell, Edward duke of Rutland and William Lescrope. Lescrope had been a member of the council on and off since 1393, when he became king's under-chamberlain, but he had been abroad, both as justiciar of Ireland and on embassies for the king, for much of the period 1394–7. Tuck is almost certainly correct in identifying him as the dominant influence on the council during the last two years of the reign, and by July 1399 he was greatly detested.[200]

It is probable, then, that there were three broad stages in the composition of the council during the period 1389–99. Firstly, from 1389 to *c.* 1393, when there was a good sprinkling of independently-minded lords and bishops in regular attendance (Northumberland, John Gilbert, the successive chancellors William Wykeham and Thomas Arundel, as well as Edward Dalyngridge and John Devereux), and those knights of the chamber who attended were the ones who had not been attacked in 1388. The independent line adopted by the council at this time is amply demonstrated by its quarrel with the king over the terms on which the earl of Nottingham was to hold the wardenship of the east march of Scotland, and it is worth noting that almost all new grants made by the king during these years were made 'with the assent of the council'.[201] After 1393 the council has a decidedly more Ricardian look about it, and from late 1397 it is unashamedly so. By early 1398 all the men who might have acted as a moderating influence between 1393 and 1397 (Thomas Arundel, John Gilbert, Richard Waldegrave) had been removed, and the council was almost entirely dominated by men who were closely associated with the tyranny of the last two years (Edmund Stafford being the sole exception). The unpopularity of Richard's councillors in 1399 is not difficult to explain. Richard and his friends made many mistakes after 1397, but perhaps the greatest was that he attacked not only those who had clearly been his enemies, but also those whom he merely suspected might have been. His vengeance touched not only the militants, but numerous moderates, too. The so-called 'blank charters' demanded from the home counties, the pardons which those who had supported the Appellants in 1387–8 were forced to sue for in person, the attempted censorship of foreign correspondence, and all those other arbitrary acts of government which are associated with Richard's tyranny, were largely instigated and controlled by the council.[202] In 1399, three of Richard's councillors were executed (Lescrope, Bussy and Green), while another four were arrested (Bagot, Selby, Dru and Russell), though later released.[203] The only two who were to find any favour with the new regime were chancellor Stafford and privy seal keeper Clifford. As a group, they were as hated in 1399 as the chamber knights had been in 1388.

This study of the personnel of Richard's court has so far omitted one crucial factor, namely the character of the king himself. It was the king who chose the king's companions (although not exclusively so in the early years of the reign), who decided whose advice to take and whose to reject, whom to employ and whom not to. Richard's character has long fascinated historians, but there is one clear message which emerges from contemporary comment on his court: his contemporaries believed that Richard was far too impressionable. That is particularly true of the 1380s, when he was still a boy, but it is also true of the 1390s. It is of course this belief which explains the importance attached both by the chroniclers and by the Appellants to the personnel of the court. It is true, admittedly, that once they had decided on the impracticability of deposition (in late December 1387), the Appellants really had no option but to couch the charges which they brought against the king's friends in 'evil councillor' terms.[204] But it is equally true that throughout the reign Richard was thought to rely far too much on the advice of a few intimates, and that he (and perhaps his father too) was not a good judge of whose advice to rely on. It was the prevailing vice of Ricardian rule.

Yet how many men could be *familiarissimus* with the king at any one time? In 1388, for instance, the Appellants executed, arrested, exiled or dismissed from court more than forty individuals (excluding the judges sent to Ireland). Some of these men were punished for specific crimes (Nicholas Brembre, for example, and some of the minor figures exempted from the general pardon), but the general charge against the great majority of them was manifestly that they had used their influence with the king in an undesirable way, either to feather their own nests, to distort government policy, or simply to the exclusion of those who (in their own opinion) might have advised him better. It is obviously impossible to believe that each of these individuals personally had great influence with Richard. There were leaders, men upon whose backs other men climbed, and there is no real difficulty in identifying them. Among the laymen were Robert de Vere and Simon Burley certainly, and John Beauchamp and Michael de la Pole probably, while among the clerks, Nicholas Slake and Thomas Rushook. Some of the others no doubt did have personal influence with the king, but in practice their guilt, in contemporary eyes, was guilt by association. They were a clique, a *covyne* as their enemies put it. They were friends (though not always), business associates, companions in royal service. They certainly were not all evil men, and some of them were probably very able (Dagworth, for example, or Richard Clifford), but as a group they were far too reminiscent of the courtier clique of the 1370s, and even if most of them were not in fact benefiting very much from the king's patronage, they were thought to be doing so.[205] Both the thoroughness and the ferocity of the parliament of 1388 testify to the popular feeling about Richard's court in the 1380s.

In their attempt to destroy the inner circle of the king's court, the Appellants were only partially successful. However, they did succeed in removing all but one of the ringleaders (Slake is the exception), and this was probably about as much as they could have expected. Nevertheless, many of the others were back at court by the early 1390s, and the fact that by 1395 the group of chamber knights of the pre-Appellant period had almost entirely disappeared from court was due as much to natural forces as to the strictures of 1388. It may have been the deep feelings aroused by his chamber knights before 1388 which induced Richard both to reduce their number in the 1390s and probably to rely less on their advice. With the exception of William Lescrope, John Holand and Thomas Percy (all of whom had been born into the peerage, and all of whom by 1397 had clearly become something rather more than chamber knights), the *familiarissimi* of the 1390s were nearly all royal clerks, or councillors with no official place in the household. Most of the chamber knights of the 1390s were men who attracted little contemporary comment, adverse or otherwise, few of them exerted much influence with the king. The powers behind the throne during the last years of unfettered Ricardianism were, among the laymen, William Lescrope, Edward earl of Rutland, and probably John Holand and John Bussy, and among the clerks, Roger Walden, Guy Mone, Merks, Selby and Richard Maudeleyn. Henry of Lancaster rejected them just as decisively as the Appellants had rejected their predecessors.[206]

Henry IV

The king's friends

The atmosphere at Henry IV's court was very different from that of the previous reign. That this was so was due primarily to the character of the king. Henry was much more sensible, more level-headed, less volatile or prone to outbursts of temper than Richard. Though a compassionate man, he seems to have been quite unemotional. He was also much less easily led. In part, this was due to his age as he was already thirty-three when he came to the throne, whereas Richard had been but ten. But this difference in ruling age can be exaggerated and at the time when he committed the worst of his tyrannies, Richard was almost exactly the same age as Henry was at his accession. In fact less than a year separated the two cousins in age, but in temperament, there was a massive gulf between them.

As a result, Henry's court was almost entirely free from the scandals, rumours of intrigue, and 'incidents' which had characterised court politics

during the last thirty years of the fourteenth century. This was probably deliberate policy on the king's behalf. He must have been as aware as anyone that
the sort of attention which had been focused on the court since *c.* 1370 was
deeply harmful to the reputation of both king and government. He sought, in
little ways as well as big ones, to remove any likelihood of criticism on this
score. One point, perhaps quite insignificant really, is nevertheless instructive:
the patent rolls for Henry's reign do not contain a single reference to a knight
of the king's chamber, even though all the men whom we know from other
sources (wardrobe accounts, mainly) to have been knights of the chamber
figure frequently in them. By contrast, both Edward III and Richard II often
issued letters patent in which men were specifically described as knights of the
chamber. Henry, it seems, neither wished nor needed to emphasise the fact that
they were chamber knights. Much more importantly though, Henry tolerated
criticism of his court, even from men who were very much a part of it. His
courtiers were certainly not his puppets. It is striking to note that three of the
fiercest parliamentary critics of the king's household were themselves closely
associated with it. Arnold Savage, speaker in the parliaments of 1401 and 1404,
was steward of Prince Henry's household from 1401–3, and a regular councillor from 1402 to 1406 yet in both parliaments he launched major attacks on the
household and royal administration. John Tiptoft was even closer to the king.
He had been an esquire in Henry's comital household in the 1390s, and was
knighted by the king on the eve of his coronation. By 1402 he was a knight of
the king's chamber, and remained one until December 1406, when he became
the first lay keeper of the wardrobe. Yet it is the remarkable and obviously very
talented Tiptoft who, as speaker of the commons in the long 1406 parliament,
spearheaded the most violent and persistent attack of the reign on the royal
household, which, he claimed, was full of 'de raskaille'.[207] The speaker in the
parliaments of 1407, 1410 and 1411 was Thomas Chaucer, son of Geoffrey and
despite the fact that he held the post of chief butler from 1402 to 1413, he too
was a forthright critic of the household. That Henry tolerated such criticism
was partly due to his weakness—his financial weakness, that is, not his weakness of character. Nevertheless, the fact that such criticism could come from
within the court itself indicates a healthy independence of mind among those
who were about the king. Unlike his predecessor, Henry was neither blinded
to reality nor unduly swayed by his closest friends. Although he may not always
have seen it that way, it was actually one of the great strengths of his rule.

After long years of neglect, Henry IV's court has recently been studied quite
fully, by Professor A.L. Brown especially, but also by K.B. McFarlane and
Rogers.[208] For this reason, and because the history of the court during Henry's
reign is less dramatic, less subject to personal attacks and political vicissitudes
than under Richard, it can be dealt with more briefly. There certainly was criticism of Henry's court, but the criticism was directed largely at its extravagance, not at its personnel. There were dismissals from court, too: the three
chief officers of the household were replaced in the 1401 parliament; four named

members of the household were expelled at the insistence of the commons in the spring of 1404; and some forty aliens were dismissed during the 1406 parliament. But these dismissals were not for corruption nor because those involved were thought to exercise too much influence over the king. The dismissals of 1401 were almost certainly for incompetence, while those of 1404 and 1406 were, quite explicitly, to reduce costs.[209] Nevertheless, Henry did have friends, and on one occasion at least in the reign, in late 1406, when the composition of the council was changed quite radically, there seems to be quite a clear suggestion that he was relying too heavily on them. Henry's friends, and the part they played in the politics of the reign, deserve some investigation.

Among the intimate associates of the king during the early years of the reign, eight names stand out: the knights Thomas Erpingham, John Pelham, Hugh Waterton, Peter Bukton, and Thomas Rempston; the esquires John Norbury and Robert Waterton; and the clerk Philip Repingdon. Every one of the seven laymen was a long-standing servant of Henry's, and each figures prominently in his surviving household accounts of the 1390s. Five of them (Bukton, Erpingham, Rempston, Pelham, and Norbury) went into exile with him in 1398, while the other two were among the first to join him on his return. Hugh Waterton had acted as Henry's attorney during his exile, and was thus involved at first hand in the sequestration of the Lancastrian inheritance following John of Gaunt's death in the spring of 1399. He and his cousin Robert met Henry almost as soon as he had landed at Ravenspur while in the meantime John Pelham was sent with a detachment to capture Pevensey castle and hold it for the invader.[210] Erpingham seems to have acted as Henry's right-hand man during the revolution. He accompanied Northumberland to Conwy for the famous interview with Richard, made himself useful in a number of other ways, and was later publicly commended in parliament for his role in the events of 1399. Thomas Rempston and John Norbury were similarly commended for their actions at the time.[211] With all three of them, Henry rather jumped the gun: Erpingham and Rempston were actually described as 'king's knights' on 21 and 31 August respectively (and they certainly were not Richard's knights), while on 3 September Norbury was made treasurer of England.[212]

It was to these men, who had proved their undoubted loyalty to Henry through the bad times as well as the good, that Henry entrusted several of those posts which normally went to chamber knights and other intimates of the king. Within a month of the coronation Erpingham had been appointed under-chamberlain of the household, constable of Dover castle, and warden of the Cinque Ports; he became a knight of the garter in 1401, served as steward of the household for some nine months in 1404, and was commended a second time by the commons, in the parliament of 1406, for his outstanding service to the king.[213] He witnessed the king's will in 1409, and was again to serve as steward of the household under Henry V, from 1413–17. Thomas Rempston, who had been Henry's standard-bearer on his Prussian crusades, was made steward of the household and constable of the Tower in October 1399. By 1401 he was also keeper of Nottingham castle and Sherwood forest, and admiral of the south and west, as well as a knight of the garter. As a soldier, councillor (in 1404), ambassador, and administrator, he served Henry constantly until his death (by drowning in the Thames) on 31 October 1406.

John Pelham had been an esquire in John of Gaunt's household in the 1390s, but was knighted by Henry on the eve of his coronation and appointed sword-bearer to the king and a knight of his chamber. It was to Pelham that Henry initially entrusted the custody of the deposed Richard II, immediately after the usurpation.[214] He was evidently a reliable gaoler, for in 1405 he was also made custodian of the duke of York (the former earl of Rutland) when the latter was under suspicion of treasonable activities, and in 1406 he was given care of the young earl of March and his brother after an attempt had been made to abduct them. Pelham was very active in both local and national administration. He was appointed to numerous commissions in his native Sussex and elsewhere, sat as MP for his county in several parliaments, acted as treasurer for wars between 1404 and 1406, and was treasurer of England from November 1411 until the end of the reign. He was an executor of the wills of both the king and Archbishop Arundel, and received further positions of trust under Henry V.

No family stood higher in Henry's esteem than the Watertons (of south Yorkshire and north Lincolnshire), especially the cousins Hugh and Robert Waterton. Sir Hugh had been prominent in Henry's service for twenty years before the revolution, and was entrusted by Henry with the guardianship of his children during the exile of 1398–9.[215] In July 1402 he was again given care of two of the king's younger children, as well as the two March minors, during the king's campaign to Wales, and in 1405 he replaced Sir Peter Courtenay as constable of Windsor castle.[216] Hugh Waterton was also chamberlain of the duchy of Lancaster from 1399 until his death in 1409. He may have been ill for some time before his death, for in 1403 he wrote to the king apologising for not joining him, explaining that he was ill and that he feared to travel in case he caught cold—and this was in July![217] Yet the personal nature of the responsibilities entrusted to him leave no room for doubt as to his high standing with Henry. Robert was equally close to the king: he was master of the king's horses throughout the reign, and master of the royal hart-hounds, too, after the death of Edmund duke of York in 1402. Although never knighted, he received fees and robes in the wardrobe as a knight of the chamber. He was Richard II's gaoler at Pontefract castle over the winter of 1399–1400; in 1408 he seems to have been deputed by the king to issue pardons to and collect fines from those involved in Northumberland's final rebellion.[218] In the following year he was made one of the executors of the king's will.

It is these indications of personal trust, and friendship with the king, which distinguish this small group of men who were really close to the king from those who, though loyal servants, did not have the same sort of personal relationship with Henry. Sir Peter Bukton, who had been steward of Henry's comital household before 1399, became the king's standard-bearer in 1399. He was described by the Kirkstall chronicler as a particularly loved confidant of Henry's, and although he spent much of his time in duchy administration he was also high in the king's confidence.[219] In May 1404 he was made governor of all the lands of Maud, countess of Oxford, at the time when she was involved in organising a rebellion against Henry, and in the same year Bukton was heavily engaged in the delicate negotiations with Northumberland's supporters in the north, who were still holding out for terms from the king.[220]

The remarkable career of John Norbury has been described elsewhere.[221] He was a mercenary from Cheshire, though it was in Hertfordshire that he acquired lands and was usually involved in local administrative duties after his return from exile with Henry in 1399. He was undoubtedly very talented, as both a soldier and a councillor. A frequent diplomat throughout the reign, he was also a regular member of the council before 1406, and treasurer of England from 1399 to May 1401. In June 1401, a month after leaving the exchequer, he was still 'in continual attendance on the king'. In June 1405 he was summoned to the king's side because Henry 'considered that his presence would be necessary for good counsel and advice on the king's actions touching the governance of Wales and otherwise.' The king stood as godfather to Norbury's son (called Henry, perhaps after the king), and made him a grant 'of the king's special grace', a rare phrase in the formal documents of Henry IV's reign, though much more common under Edward III and Richard II. As Thomas Walsingham pointed out, Norbury was not afraid to speak his mind, and his words evidently carried weight. In the parliament of 1410, which like so many of Henry's parliaments voiced strong anti-clerical sentiments, Norbury spoke out in favour of the church and advised Archbishop Arundel to launch a counterattack against those who were demanding its despoliation.[222] John Norbury was, without doubt, a man of influence and personal stature in government circles throughout the reign; Ralph Nevill, earl of Westmorland, recognised the fact, and retained him in November 1399 with an annuity of £60.[223]

The only clerical member of this inner circle of royal confidants during the first half of the reign was Philip Repingdon (or Repton). Although he had Lancastrian connections, his personal friendship with Henry cannot be traced back to before 1399, which makes him the exception to the group. An Austin canon and a former Lollard, he had apparently been confident of winning support from John of Gaunt against Archbishop Courtenay's clampdown on Oxford heresy in the summer of 1382, but in this he had been disappointed.[224] He was forced to recant, therefore, and from this time onwards Repingdon stuck to the orthodox path. Yet Gaunt evidently did not regard him with disfavour. In 1394 he became abbot of St Mary's, Leicester, of which Gaunt was patron. After 1399, his career really blossomed, and this was clearly at the instance of the new king. In 1400 he became chancellor of Oxford university, and was described in the same year by one contemporary as 'clericus specialissimus regis'.[225] In May 1401 Repingdon wrote a long letter to the king (preserved in Adam of Usk's chronicle), in which he claimed that Henry had asked him, when he last left court, to report to him on the state of the country, and this he now intended to do. The country, he declared, was torn apart by divisions, misrule, and a general contempt for law and justice, and it was time that the king did something about it.[226] The letter is remarkable not only for the close relationship between Henry and Repingdon which it clearly demonstrates, but also because it is yet another example of Henry's ability to take criticism without bearing grudges. It is hard to imagine any of Richard II's courtiers writing to him in such terms.

An anecdote preserved in the register of charters of Leicester Abbey shows that Repingdon's friendship with the king was not jeopardised by his outspokenness. Immediately after the battle of Shrewsbury, the king enquired of his soldiers if any one of them was a servant of Repingdon's. On finding one, Henry gave him a ring from his finger and 100s. and told him to go with all haste to Repingdon, give him the ring, and reassure him that the king was alive and well and had triumphed over his enemies.[227] Within a year, Repingdon had become Henry's confessor, and through the summer of 1404 he was closely involved in the negotiations with Northumberland and his adherents in the north.[228] By March 1405, the king had succeeded in securing the see of Lincoln for his confessor, and Repingdon remained bishop of Lincoln until (most unusually) he resigned in 1419. After becoming a bishop, Repingdon seems to have had less time to spend at court, and although his day-to-day influence with the king probably diminished during the second half of the reign, there is nothing to suggest that personal relations between the two men deteriorated.

Taking the reign as a whole, Philip Repingdon was probably the only churchman to be on the same sort of terms with Henry as, for example, Thomas Rushook, Nicholas Slake, or Richard Maudeleyn had been with Richard II. It is possible that there was an element of reaction here from the very clerically-dominated court of the 1390s. The convocation of October 1399 (taking its cue from Haxey) had admonished the 'clerici curiales' for spending too much time at court and not enough in their dioceses.[229] The involvement of numerous churchmen in the rebellions of 1400–5 was hardly calculated to win the sympathy of the new king for the first estate, and in any case so many of the bishops in 1399 were so closely associated with Richard's regime that Henry probably placed little trust in them. There may well have been a streak of mild anti-clericalism in Henry himself which was unlikely to have been discouraged by his father. Though he rejected the extremist demands sometimes put forward by groups of knights in parliament or at court, Henry seems to have done little really to stamp out such sentiments. Perhaps he found them quite useful.

Changes at court and council

Not only was the episcopal bench largely untrustworthy, but, in the aftermath of the traumatic events of 1397–1400, factions among the magnates were shifting dangerously and, from the king's point of view, largely uncontrollably (as witnessed by the rebellions of 1403–8), so it is far from surprising that, initially at least, Henry relied very heavily on this small group of proven supporters.[230] As the reign progressed, however, some of them of course died (Rempston in 1406, Hugh Waterton in 1409) or disappeared from court (Repingdon from *c.* 1405). It is only possible, however, to point to two men who came to replace them as intimates of the king. One who certainly did, from about 1404, was Richard Lord Grey of Codnor. Grey's intimacy with the king, and his role in Henry's government, have been consistently under-valued. He was a peer by birth, and as much at home on the battlefield as in the council chamber. He had accompanied Richard II to Ireland in 1394, and although he received an annuity of 80 marks from Richard, he was never retained by him. His first major appointment under Henry was as admiral of the north, in 1401. In 1403 he became a knight of the garter, and in February 1404 he replaced Thomas Erpingham as the king's under-chamberlain. He held this post until the end of the reign. From 1403 onwards he was also heavily involved in the Welsh wars, and in the parliament of 1406 he was especially commended by the commons for his outstanding service. In the same year he succeeded Rempston as constable of Nottingham castle.[231] Henry's confidence in Grey is revealed by the fact that he was given custody of two vitally important prisoners, King James I of Scotland, and the son of the Welsh rebel leader Owen Glendower. He was also used frequently as an ambassador by the king, and was a regular member of the council between 1404 and 1407. In 1409 he witnessed the king's will, and was granted a remarkably large life annuity at the exchequer of 400 marks. In 1410 he was the only person outside of the royal family whose grants were specifically declared (in parliament, and at the instance of the king) to be eligible for compensation when the sources on which they were assigned were reserved for the expenses of the household.[232] Despite his many other duties, however, he was still campaigning in France in 1412–13, and continued to do so under Henry V until his death in 1418. Richard Grey was certainly one of the foremost members of the court during the second half of the reign.

The other man who probably grew closer to Henry as the reign progressed was Thomas Arundel, archbishop of Canterbury, but the relationship between king and archbishop is difficult to decipher.[233] Richard II's treatment of him and his brother is probably sufficient to explain his part in the events of 1399, but despite his crucial involvement in the revolution, Arundel seems to have put some distance between himself and the court during the early years of the reign.[234] In 1405 there was even a suggestion that he might have been plotting against Henry, and the execution of Archbishop Scrope of York in that year, against which Arundel had pleaded desperately, but had apparently been duped, must have driven a wedge between them. From the winter of 1406–7, however, he came more to court, and for three years from January 1407 he held the chancellorship, until dismissed, presumably by Prince Henry, in favour of Sir Thomas Beaufort. It may well be, as McFarlane suggested, that the increasing challenge to the king's power represented by Prince Henry and his faction from 1406 onwards served to push Arundel into closer association with his ailing master. He quite possibly resented, or mistrusted, the pushing, younger men who followed the prince. Nevertheless, there are no real signs of personal intimacy between the king and Arundel, and it is equally possible that, while realising the need to involve himself more closely in government during the second half of the reign, he maintained his earlier aloofness from the court.

One point to notice about Henry's inner group of confidants is that they were not as closely associated with the household as had been the case under either Edward III or Richard II. Rempston and Repingdon were only formally attached to the household for quite short periods (eighteen months and about a year respectively), while Norbury, Bukton, Hugh Waterton and Thomas Arundel never were. Spreading the net a little wider, the same general argument holds true. There was a further group of loyal and often long-serving Lancastrians, men who served Henry faithfully and were often rewarded by him with high office or lucrative grants, but who are not really to be counted among the king's close friends. Naturally some of the chamber knights and clerks of the household fell into this category (see below), but so did several men who had no apparent household connections. Of those who were principally involved in government administration, the most notable were Lords Roos, Willoughby and Furnivall, Sir John Cheyne, and the esquires John Doreward, John Frome, and John Curson. All these men were regular members of the council before 1406.[235] Among the king's knights, valued more for their service in local administration and in war than in central government, those who seem to have been especially highly regarded by Henry include John Blount, John Cornwall (who married the king's sister Elizabeth), Ralph de Euyr, John Greyndour, Henry Lord FitzHugh, and Edward Charlton, lord of Powys. Among the king's clerks, John Leventhorpe, Laurence Allerthorpe, Henry Bowet (bishop of Bath and Wells 1401–7, and archbishop of York 1407–23), and Robert Hallum (bishop of Salisbury from 1407), all held high office under Henry, but none were clerks of the chapel or other departments of the household.

Those from within the household who fall into this category naturally included several of the knights of the chamber.[236] Only two lists of chamber knights survive from Henry's reign, in 1402–3 and 1405–6, and few further names can be gleaned from other sources. As far as the picture can be seen, however, there seems to have been a high level of stability and continuity among them. Eleven names figure in both lists: Richard Arundel, Robert Chalons, Francis de Courte, John Dalyngridge, Richard Goldesburgh, Nicholas Hauberk, John Pelham, Ralph Rochefort, John Straunge, John Tiptoft, and Payn Tiptoft.[237] In addition, Robert Corbet and John Littlebury were both described as chamber knights in 1401 (but do not appear on either list),[238] and Thomas Swynford (the son, by her first marriage, of the king's stepmother Katherine Swynford) was included on the 1402–3 list, but not in 1405–6.[239] Finally, Hugh Stafford was a knight of the chamber from late 1406 until the end of the reign.[240] It will be noted that not one of these men had been in Richard II's household for the choice of a king's chamber knights was a very personal matter. To these fifteen names can be added those of nine men who held the post of steward, chamberlain or controller during the reign: Rempston, Grey, and Erpingham, together with Thomas Brounfleet, William Heron Lord Say, Roger Leche, Robert Litton, John Stanley, and Thomas Percy, earl of Worcester.

This makes a total of twenty-four laymen holding high office in the household during the reign. The most obvious characteristic which many of them shared in common was that they had been in Henry's service for many years before he became king and were, therefore, old friends or trusted servants. This was true of Chalons, de Courte, Dalyngridge, Erpingham, Goldesburgh, Leche, Litton, Rempston, Rochefort, both the Tiptofts, and Swynford.[241] Others, such as Pelham, Straunge, and Corbet, were retainers of John of Gaunt before 1399. Arundel, Grey and Stafford all came from powerful magnate families, while William Heron married into one and became a peer of the realm *jure uxori*. The remaining three had all been king's knights under Richard II. John Stanley, despite being controller of Richard's household from 1397 to 1399, came over rapidly to Henry in 1399.[242] So effortlessly did he accustom himself to the new regime that in November 1404 he was made steward of the household, and held the post until the end of the reign. Many favours came his way from now onwards, partly it seems because he had finally proven his loyalty during the rebellion of 1405. In that year he became a knight of the garter, and in 1406 he was granted, 'to him and his heirs', the Isle of Man, said to be worth £400 *per annum*. Then in 1409 he replaced Hugh Waterton as constable of Windsor castle.[243] John Stanley had the ability to impress his masters.

In contrast to Stanley, both Nicholas Hauberk and John Littlebury seem to have remained loyal to Richard in 1399, which perhaps makes it surprising that they should have become knights of Henry's chamber.[244] In Littlebury's case it is doubly surprising, for he was quite closely associated with some of the more notorious characters of Richard's later years, such as John Bussy and William Lescrope, and in the September 1397 parliament he was one of four knights who formally petitioned for the trial of the Appellants.[245] By 1408, Littlebury was receiving a grant of 50 marks from Henry for his 'great expenses about the king's person', but he remains the most unlikely of the king's chamber knights.[246]

As a general rule, Henry's chamber knights certainly seem to have been more militarily active *while they were chamber knights* than Richard II's had been, but the real reason for this was probably because there was more military action to be involved in during Henry's reign, and because the king himself was a more active campaigner (until 1407, anyway) than his predecessor. Many of Richard's chamber knights had long years of military service behind them, but with a king who was relatively inactive militarily, it was perhaps inevitable that they would be less personally involved in the warfare of the reign. Thomas Walsingham had castigated Richard's knights for being knights of the bedchamber rather than of the battlefield. The fact that several of them were probably Lollard sympathisers, and that at least three of them (John Montagu, Lewis Clifford, and John Clanvow) were poets, might have contributed to the slightly effete public image projected by Richard's court. But Walsingham was not especially impressed by the company that Henry kept either. The king's knights and esquires, he declared *sub anno* 1403, were more like Dionysis (god of drunkenness) than Mars, more like Laverna (goddess of gain) than Pallas (goddess of wisdom).[247] What Walsingham really objected to, it seems, was the anti-clericalism of some of those who populated Henry's court (this remark was interposed in Walsingham's discussion of a suggestion by some of Henry's knights to despoil the church). Moreover, his resentment of Henry's knights was not apparently shared by other chroniclers, nor by the commons in parliament. In general, there seems to have been a widespread feeling that Henry was a good enough judge of character to be left to choose his own associates.

As already noted, Richard II had become heavily dependent on a group of household clerks, especially during the last few years of his reign. Henry IV's household clerks can be discussed much more briefly. Very few of them became 'favourites' of the king, and very few of them became bishops. And as with the laymen who moved in court and government circles during the reign, so with the churchmen: they were drawn as much from outside the household as from within it. Thomas Arundel, Henry Bowet, Robert Hallum and Laurence Allerthorpe were all closely involved in government affairs at the highest level, but not one of them was ever attached to the household. Not one of Henry's clerks of the chapel became a bishop, although two of his confessors did, Philip Repingdon and Robert Mascall. Mascall was a Carmelite friar who preceded Repingdon as Henry's confessor from 1399 to 1404. He was dismissed from the household at the request of the commons in the January 1404 parliament, and became bishop of Hereford later in the same year. He seems to have been close to the king, but it is difficult to establish quite why he was dismised from the household.[248] Although the four dismissals at this time were said to be for financial reasons (and as such, very much a token gesture), it is possible that there was an element of personal unpopularity involved, too.[249] Otherwise it is difficult to see why four people were singled out like this. And king's confessors were often thought, perhaps rightly, to be in a position of undue personal influence with the king.

The only other clerks who held positions in the household and who became bishops were three successive keepers of the privy seal: Richard Clifford, who had been expelled from Richard II's household back in 1388, and who became bishop of Worcester in 1401; Thomas Langley, an executor of John of Gaunt's who was the king's secretary from 1399–1401, keeper of the privy seal 1401–5, chancellor 1405–7, and bishop of Durham in 1406; and Nicholas Bubwith, who became bishop of London in 1406. Thomas Langley and Nicholas Bubwith were both very much men of the Lancastrian regime, and rose rapidly early in the reign. Indeed by about 1406, with Arundel, Bowet, Repingdon, Mascall, Langley and Bubwith all holding bishoprics, the episcopal bench must have seemed much more to Henry's taste. Generally, though, the list of clerks among the king's friends is not a long one. It is possible to point to one or two other churchmen who had long records of service in either Henry's or Gaunt's service before 1399, such as Thomas Tutbury (Gaunt's receiver-general, and keeper of the wardrobe 1399–1401), or Richard Kingston (Henry's treasurer for wars in the 1390s, dean of the king's chapel 1399–1402, and keeper of the wardrobe 1405–6), who might have been expected to rise to the episcopacy under Henry. That they did not is possibly due to Henry's desire to avoid the charge of 'clerici curiales' which had been levelled at Richard's bishops. On the whole, though, Henry preferred the company of laymen to the company of clerks. He was not a 'priest's king', as Richard was, or indeed as Henry V was, at least by reputation.[250]

Despite the fact that Henry was by and large considered to be a reasonable judge of his own friends, there were nevertheless two occasions on which several of his friends were replaced, almost certainly against his wishes, in high government offices. Immediately following the revolution of 1399, Henry entrusted many senior posts to men who had virtually no experience of the royal administrative machine, even if some of them had long experience in his or his father's administration. Thomas Tutbury became keeper of the wardrobe, Thomas Remptson and Robert Litton became steward and controller of the household and John Norbury became treasurer. Between March and May 1401 all of them were dismissed, almost certainly at the insistence of the commons, who evidently believed them to be incompetent. The financial chaos of the first eighteen months of the reign was intense, and the commons were very probably right to believe that the inexperience of Henry's officers contributed to it. The officers apparently failed to understand the workings of the royal administration, which had its own rules and conventions with which it no doubt took newcomers some time to get acquainted.[251] Henry's Lancastrian 'outsiders' failed to master the system.[252] One has only to look at the men who replaced them in 1401, all men with many years of experience in the royal administration, to get an idea of the sort of qualities that the commons were looking for in such officers.

Although the old Lancastrian servants were never to be so prominent in the administration again, Henry did not take the lesson of 1401 completely to heart. In January 1405 he appointed his old friend Richard Kingston, who again had virtually no experience of royal administration, to be keeper of the wardrobe; once again the financial chaos accelerated, and at the end of 1406 Kingston was replaced, almost certainly at the insistence of the commons, by John Tiptoft, who although he had no more experience than Kingston of high administrative office, was at least dedicated to reform. But the replacement of Kingston in December 1406 was a relatively minor occurrence compared with the changes in the composition of the privy council effected in the same month.[253] Although the loss of most of the council records from 1407 onwards makes it difficult to be certain about it, it seems fairly clear that many of those 'lesser' men who had been regular members of the council since early in the reign without apparently hitherto incurring the censure of the commons, now disappeared from it. Men such as John Cheyne, Hugh Waterton, John Pelham, John Norbury, Arnold Savage, John Doreward, John Curson, Henry Bowet and Lord Willoughby, all men upon whom the king had relied heavily during his early years, were now in effect dismissed from the council.[254] Their places were taken by Prince Henry and his followers, the three Beaufort brothers, the young earls of Arundel and Warwick, Bishop Henry Chicheley of St David's, Hugh Burnell, and Henry Lescrope of Masham (who was later to lose his life for plotting against Henry in 1415). From early 1407 until late 1409, and even more so in 1410–11, the council was largely dominated by Prince Henry's men. Yet there was no suggestion in 1406 that the king's councillors had been corrupt, or that they had been evil influences on the king. It was a quiet revolution, as bloodless as that of 1388 had been bloody. In essence, it was simply a consequence of a substantial shift in power at the very highest level, from the king to the prince, whereby the confidants of the one faded into the background, and the confidants of the other came to the fore. There was no question of hounding the ex-councillors; many of them remained at court, and continued to receive important appointments.[255] And not surprisingly, once the king regained full power late in 1411, some of those who had been dropped in 1406 began to re-appear on the council, as did Henry Bowet, for example, and William Lord Roos, and John Pelham, who was treasurer of England for the last sixteen months of the reign.[256]

CONCLUSION

The principal factor in determining the atmosphere at court, and the extent to which those about the king were able to impose their personalities on the politics of the time, was the character of the king; in this sense Henry IV succeeded where Richard II, and Edward III in his last years, had failed. Yet allied to the question of the king's character was the question of his age, an important factor in the politics of the 1370s and 80s. The last thirty years of the fourteenth century were of course far from unique in medieval English history. One has only to think of the hatred directed at the courtiers of Henry III, Edward II and Henry VI to realise how much depended on the king himself. It is greatly to Henry IV's credit that despite the overwhelming financial and political problems which he faced, there was very little criticism of the company he kept. And it serves as a reminder that medieval English kings were not deposed because they failed to manage their budgets, but because, innately, they lacked the ability to manage other men.

There were other factors, however, which increased the possibilities for courtiers. The highly centralised nature of English government placed a vast store of patronage in the hands of the king, and there were very few checks on the way he dispensed it. In some other European countries, such as France, Germany, or Scotland, the local power of great princes tended to act as a natural check on the monarch's ability to bestow lands and offices on those whom he favoured, and thus on his ability to influence local affairs. Equally, there was a lack of well-established or effective alternative sources of executive authority, which also placed tremendous power in terms of political decision-making in the hands of the king. To have the king's ear was to have the ability to influence such decisions. The obvious alternative source of executive authority was the council, but it was very difficult to make the council into an effective check on an adult king. Nevertheless, it was to the idea of a more powerful council (which might on occasions masquerade as a commission of reform) that critics of the government repeatedly turned in this period, largely as a remedy against courtiers.

The serious financial problems which plagued the government for much of the period from *c.* 1370 to 1413 also led to opportunities for greedy and influential men to make profits. Whether or not the details of the charge relating to Latimer's and Lyons's loan of 20,000 marks to the crown in 1374 are true, they certainly reveal the scope for profit. Indeed the whole system of government finance was a preferential one, in which personal influence was paramount.[257] In May 1376 Latimer, Lyons and Nevill were accused of making profits from the brokerage of royal debts, that is, buying up discounted tallies and then using their personal influence to cash them at the exchequer for their full value. Yet five months later, at his trial in the October 1376 council, William Wykeham was charged on the grounds that, at the time when he was keeper of the privy seal, he had been allocated 20,000 marks from the treasury with which to buy up tallies at a discount for the king's profit. He had bought £100 tallies for £25, £500 tallies for £200, and so forth, but the profit to the treasury had only amounted to 2,500 marks and should have been much greater.[258] There was a difference of course in that Latimer, Lyons and Nevill were supposed to have made a personal profit from discounting tallies, whereas Wykeham was supposed to be doing it for the profit of the crown, but it is perfectly clear that discounting tallies was not only widespread but officially sanctioned by the crown (which is hardly surprising), and the opportunities which such a system placed in the hands of those with influence are plain to see.

In times of financial stringency there was also considerable pressure on the king not to be over-generous with the resources at his disposal. Here again, the king was in a difficult position. Naturally, he wished primarily to reward those whom he regarded as his most loyal and useful servants, but when the resources were limited, those few who were the recipients of his favour were bound to be envied. Patronage was not really a politically contentious issue under either Edward III or Henry IV, or at least not in relation to individuals. It seems to have been more of an issue under Richard, particularly in the years leading up to the parliament of 1386, but even then its importance seems to have been rather exaggerated by recent historians. The charges in 1376 are really about corruption. The charges in 1386 and 1388, while touching on patronage in a broad sense, are again largely concerned with corruption, as well as evil influence over the king, political manipulation (the questions to the judges, the distribution of livery badges), and treasonable dealings with the

French.[259] Even in the detailed list of deposition charges drawn up against Richard in 1399, patronage plays a very small part. The word 'patronage' needs much tighter definition than it has received hitherto. Did a simple failure to receive sufficient rewards from the king really incite men to violent opposition to the government? The evidence from this period suggests that it was a relatively minor consideration, and that suspicions of corrupt financial dealings, or major policy blunders, such as the Irish question and the fiasco of the 1374–5 Brittany expedition (in the Good Parliament and in relation to Alice Perrers's trial), or the 'double foreign policy' occasioned by Richard II's secret negotiations with the French in 1386–7 (in 1388), were much more important.[260]

The word 'courtier' is a difficult one to use, often seeming almost by definition to imply criticism, corruption, unwarranted influence. This has not been my intention in using the word: every king had his courtiers, and what made the difference between acceptable and unacceptable courtiers was the ability of the king to discriminate between them, between the self-seeking, the sycophantic, or the foolish, and the more public-spirited or (in a whole variety of ways) more capable. Among the forty and more courtiers executed or dismissed from court by the Appellants in 1388, there were surely some at least who were thoroughly capable, even outstanding, royal servants. Even men like William Latimer and John Nevill, greedy as they may have been, had risen to high office because of their hard work and ability in the royal service. Latimer and Nevill both had quite brief careers as courtiers, taking advantage of the rather exceptional combination of circumstances prevailing in the early 1370s (an ailing king, lack of magnate leadership, and grave financial problems), but other men, whom one might almost describe as professional courtiers, spent their lives in the service of a succession of monarchs. The remarkable career of George Felbridge illustrates many of those aspects of a courtier's life which made the royal court so attractive to all classes of men. Felbridge came from northern Norfolk, and was probably born *c.* 1335. By 1360 he was already an esquire of Edward III's chamber, and he remained one until the end of the reign, passing from there into Richard II's chamber in 1377. He was closely involved with both the court circle of Edward's last years and that of the 1380s, and as early as 1362 he used his influence at court to secure for himself and his friend William Ellis (the Yarmouth burgess impeached in the Good Parliament) the farm of the customs on all merchandise except wool, in all the East Anglian ports. These two continued to farm these customs until the end of the reign.[261] But despite his associations with the courtiers, Felbridge was left untouched in both 1376 and 1388. He took part in the Scottish expedition of 1385, was knighted during the campaign, and thus became a knight of the chamber. His main talent seems to have been as an ambassador rather than as a soldier, however, for between 1380 and 1393 he was sent on at least seven embassies by the king, mostly to Germany and the Low Countries. It was on the last of these missions, to Guelders in 1393, that he was described as a knight of the chamber, even though he was never actually listed as one in the wardrobe account books.[262] He accompanied Richard II to Ireland in 1394, but not in 1399[263] and by this time he seems less active in the king's service. Possibly this was due to his age, but Felbridge was a man with many other commitments, and by now there were other Felbridges at court to make sure that his interests were not neglected. His son, Simon, was already a chamber knight and the king's standard-bearer by 1395, and he remained a chamber knight until the end of the reign. Also listed among the household esquires from 1395 were George Felbridge the younger and Robert Felbridge, perhaps younger sons of Sir George.[264] Like those other servants of Richard's chamber, Simon Burley and Philip Walweyn, George Felbridge had made sure to secure good positions at court for his family.[265] But the services of a man like Felbridge were not required only by the king. He was also granted an annuity of £20 from the earl of March in July 1397, acted as attorney for the duke of Norfolk when he was sent into exile in October 1398, and was closely connected with the duke of Gloucester, who saw to it that Felbridge's soul was catered for in the statutes which he drew up for his collegiate foundation at Pleshey.[266] All three of these families were badly treated by Richard II during the last two years of the reign and this may help to explain why Felbridge, a thoroughgoing courtier for forty years, was less closely associated with the court at the end of the reign when the conflict of loyalties was becoming acute. He seems to have kept a low profile during the revolution, but this is not quite the last we hear of him and by September 1400, he had become a 'king's knight' of Henry IV, and had had all his grants from Edward III and Richard II confirmed.[267] Within another year he was dead.

Not only had three successive kings employed and rewarded Felbridge, so had three of the greatest magnates of the realm. There seems little doubt that he was a thoroughly accomplished and widely respected man who could have found a position of trust and responsibility with any great lord of his time. That he chose to devote himself primarily to the service of the king is hardly surprising; the rewards, as all men knew, were much greater. In the Middle Ages, nothing was more likely to succeed than success in the king's service. This was another attraction of being a courtier, for to rise high at court, to gain the king's ear, also brought you to the notice of other great men prepared to pay for your goodwill. Ralph Nevill, earl of Westmorland, invested nearly £300 annually in retaining John Norbury, Nicholas Aldrewich and John Peryant (both esquires of Henry IV's chamber), and Anthony Ricz, who was Queen Joan's secretary.[268] There can have been few men of substance who did not aspire to the role of courtier in late medieval England.

CHAPTER IV

The King's Affinity

THE affinity, that is, the servants, retainers, and other followers of a lord, was the most important political grouping in medieval society. Much work has recently been done on the affinities of great lords in late medieval England, and some of the ideas which have emerged from these studies will be taken up in the conclusion to this book. What is surprising, however, is that, despite a positive embarrassment of sources, no attempt has yet been made to elucidate the extent, structure, and *raison d'être* of the greatest of all these affinities, that of the king.[1]. The aim of this chapter is to make a start in this direction.

The king's affinity, like that of any other lord, is best envisaged as a series of concentric circles. At the centre, naturally, stood the king himself, the focus of service and loyalty. The inmost circle comprised those most intimately attached to the king, men of the type described in the preceding chapter: they were often great officers of state, royal councillors, chamber knights, clerks of the royal chapel, or magnates, but what distinguished them was their status and/ or their personal relationship with the monarch. The second circle may be defined as those who were bound to the king by ties of service, and by the fact that he paid them a regular wage (or other full-time remuneration) and expected them to serve him on a regular basis. The great majority of the 400 to 700 (in this period) members of the household fall into this category; so do the lesser officials in the chancery, exchequer, and other government departments, and less specialised royal servants such as the sergeants-at-arms. Most of these men were of no individual political importance at all. The sergeants-at-arms are discussed above.[2] The lesser officers of the main departments of government probably numbered around 250 at any one time.[3] They performed thoroughly routine jobs in return for standard rates of remuneration, and survived even revolutions as if they had hardly occurred.

What this chapter is really concerned with is the third and outer circle of the king's affinity, including the king's retinue. King's knights, king's esquires, archers and yeomen of the crown fall into this category. The chief characteristic distinguishing members of the 'second circle' from members of the 'third circle' was the independence of the latter. Although they might be retained, or even sometimes paid, by the king, they were not employed by him on a full-time basis.

They were not bound by close ties of service to the king (as were members of the household and the government departments), but lived their lives largely independently from the court and were often retained by the king for essentially personal reasons rather than for any broad type of service which they might collectively perform. Naturally, this distinction is not always as clear as it might sound. There was constant overlap and movement between the two groups and yet there is an unmistakable difference between the two groups, a difference, really, in what the king's expectations of them amounted to, and it is a difference which is identifiable in magnate affinities, too. After 1377, there is no doubt that pride of place within this outer circle of the king's affinity went to those men who were described as the 'king's knights' (*milites regis*). Before discussing them, however, something must be said about the meaning of certain other terms such as 'knights of the household', 'knights of the chamber', and *bachelerii*.

Household knights and chamber knights

The existence of a group of knights attached to the royal household, known generally as *milites de hospicii* (or *de familia*) *regis* is a well-documented fact for at least 150 years before 1360.[4] For the reign of Henry III, their number, their duties, and their rewards have been established by Dr R.F. Walker.[5] Their primary duty to the king was military. They received robes from the king at Christmas and Whitsun, and fees at the exchequer ranging between £5 and £100 (the majority of the 117 tabulated by Walker got £15 or less, only eleven got £30 or more, and £100 was quite exceptional). The number receiving fees in any one year varied considerably, but it was 'seldom less than thirty', and never surpassed seventy. The fluctuations in numbers are clearly related to military activity, or to intense political activity in which the king evidently deemed military activity to be likely. Thus the numbers rose noticably, for example, in 1228–30, 1253–4, and 1261. Some of them were foreigners, some were members of baronial families in England, and others were humbler men, but what they all had in common was that they were soldiers. They served as military commanders, recruiting agents, and captains of castles; sometimes they would serve a probationary period in the royal army before being formally retained (by *conventionem*) by the king, and being granted their fees. Henry referred to them as '*milites domini regis*' or as '*milites de familia nostra*'. When they came to join the army, they frequently brought at least one other knight with them. They were, in fact, the core of the king's retinue, his nucleus of shock-troops, a force in itself, and capable of rapid expansion when necessary.

Edward I's household troops are even better-known.[6] As Dr Prestwich pointed out, their 'main duties were military', their main activity was 'of course, fighting'. They now received their fees as well as their robes in the wardrobe (rather than at the exchequer), as knights of the household continued to do until 1360. Table 4 on page 205 gives examples over the whole period of the numbers who received these fees. As the table shows, they were now divided into two groups, essentially a recognition of military status: the bannerets, and the simple knights (the term *milites simplici* was frequently used to differentiate the latter from the former). Again there is considerable fluctuation in the numbers, but in general they seem to be a little higher than under Henry III, especially during the first half of the reign. These fluctuations can for example be studied in quite close detail in the years 1284–6, and can be seen to be clearly related to the king's activities: in 1284–5, immediately after the second Welsh war, the combined total of bannerets and knights stood at 101, but during the next (peaceful) year it dropped steadily to fifty-two at Easter 1286. There were other considerations too, however, and although the last ten years of the reign saw almost continuous warfare, on the whole the number of knights and bannerets in the household was rather lower than during the early part of the reign. This may well have been, as Dr Prestwich points out, for financial reasons. It is always important to remember that household knights cost money.

Table 4:[7] *Bannerets and knights of the household as recorded in wardrobe accounts, 1284–1360.*

Date	Bannerets	Knights
1284–5	14	87
Michaelmas 1285	20	56
Christmas 1285	23	48
Easter 1286	13	39
Whitsun 1286	21	41
1288–9	16	27
1289–90	23	35
1297	10	46 (20 newly-created)
1299–1300	30	47
1300	23	40
1301	18	36
1303	23	31
1306	17	28
1312–13	5	32
1314–15	32	89
1315–16	7	45
1316–17	6	52
1317	11	51
1317–18	14	49
1322–3	5	28
1327–8	15	30
1330–1	29	43
1334	9	27
c. 1335	23	39
1338	12	32
1340	17	45
1347	14	66
1353–4	7	12
1359–60	10	37 (11 'of new creation')

Edward I's household knights were not purely military men, even if it was for their military service primarily that Edward retained them. They were occasionally used by the king as commissioners, or as diplomats, and a small number of them were royal councillors 'but such tasks as these,' according to Dr Prestwich, 'were not part of the normal role of the household knights'. Edward II's household knights have not been studied in as much detail as those of his father, but in general their role seems to have been very similar: the enormous increase in numbers for the Bannockburn campaign, for example, suggests strongly that it was still their military value which the king rated most highly. And for Edward III's reign, the reduction in numbers between 1347 and 1353, followed by another expansion for the campaign of 1359, leads to much the same conclusion.[8]

Throughout these three reigns, therefore (up to 1360), the picture is a reasonably consistent one: a body of bannerets and knights, basically fighting men, was attached to the household, but it varied very considerably in size (from between about 20 to 120), and the main reason why it varied is to be found in the military activity of the king. At the same time, however, there was a new development, which was for a small inner group of these men to be described as knights of the chamber. It is difficult to say when the term 'knight of the chamber' was first used, but its use is clearly associated with what Tout called the 'revival of the chamber' in the first half of the fourteenth century, and with the increasing importance attached to the office of king's chamberlain (or under-chamberlain) at this time.[9] Under Edward I, the chamber was generally staffed by about eight or ten *camerarii* and ushers of the chamber, who were of equivalent rank to the esquires of the household, together with a number of clerks and lesser servants.[10] From *c.* 1292, however, a single chamberlain, of the rank of knight, emerged at the head of the chamber staff (Peter de Champvent seems to have been the first man to hold this post under Edward).[11] A list of chamber staff which survives from the later years of the reign notes twenty-two names, of whom one is John Botetourt, generally described as a banneret of the household at this time but he is the only man of knightly rank on the list.[12] Sir John Sudley is described as king's chamberlain in 1306; it is possible that Botetourt held this post in 1301, or that of steward of the chamber.[13] There is reference to the latter post during Edward II's reign, under whom the real revival of the chamber occurred, and to knights of the chamber. The author of the *Annales Paulini, sub anno* 1320, described Edmund Darel, who was suspected of being implicated in a plot to seize the queen, as 'miles de camera domini regis', and official confirmation of the term is found in the king's chamber journal for 1322–3, which refers to 'monsire Giles Beauchamp chivalier de la chambre le Roi', and to 'monsire Johan Lesturmy seneschal de la chambre le Roi'.[14] This was at the time when Hugh Despenser the younger's tenure of the office of king's chamberlain (1318–26) must have greatly enhanced the importance of the chamber and its staff. The references are very scattered, however, and the number of knights of the chamber at this time was probably only two or three.

During Edward III's reign references to the king's chamber knights become more frequent, and their number increased. When the king took his household to Antwerp in July 1338, for example, rooms were hired 'pro militibus camere domini regis', one of whom was John de Molyns.[15] Finally, in the roll of liveries of the great wardrobe for the years 1347–9, there is a list of *milites camere regis*, numbering twelve. Another great wardrobe livery roll, this time for 1364–5, again lists twelve.[16] The term 'knight of the household' was now rapidly disappearing and its replacement by 'knight of the chamber' is confirmed by the four surviving wardrobe account books from the last twelve years of Edward III's reign, which list between three and five knights of the chamber receiving fees and robes in the wardrobe, but make no mention of knights of the household.[17] To complete the story, the three surviving wardrobe account books for Richard II's reign down to 1393 list between eight and eleven knights of the chamber receiving fees and robes in the wardrobe; Richard's 1395–6 account book, and the two surviving books from Henry IV's reign (for 1402–3 and 1405–6), describe them as 'knights of the king's chamber and hall', and they number between eight and twelve.[18] The difference between 'knights of the chamber' and 'knights of the chamber and hall' is not significant and the fuller description from 1395 onwards simply recognises the fact that some of these men had duties in the hall as well as in the chamber. William Murreres and Thomas Peytevyn, for example, described simply as knights of the chamber in the wardrobe accounts of the 1380s, were in fact respectively knight marshal and knight usher of the hall during this period.[19] Finally, it is worth noting that the terminology continued to evolve during the fifteenth century; by Edward IV's time, those knights who received fees and robes in the wardrobe were generally known as 'knights of the body', but their duties were still in the chamber and hall; the Black Book assumed that there would normally be sixteen of them, but more 'yf hit please the king'.[20]

The change in style from 'knights of the household' to 'knights of the chamber' was thus a very gradual process, but it occurred most decisively in the years *c.* 1350–65. So what significance is to be attached to the change? To a certain extent, it obviously relates to that more general trend in late medieval royal and noble households, the increasing preference of the lord for the privacy of his chamber rather than the bustle of the hall.[21] It was logical that those who were the king's companions should be formally attached to the chamber rather than to the household in general. Before 1360, however, the distinction was quite blurred. Comparison of the names of those men who were on occasions called 'knights of the chamber' with those also listed as 'knights of the household' reveals considerable overlap: Guy Brian, Roger Beauchamp, and Robert de Mauley, all described as *milites camere regis* in 1348, were also described as *milites hospicii regis* in 1353–4.[22] During a period of transition, it is hardly surprising that there should have been some uncertainty in the minds of the wardrobe clerks. And other evidence raises further questions. There is for example a list of persons for whom robes were to be provided because they attended the royal court at Christmas 1366.[23] It begins with the king and queen and nine peers of the realm (including four of the king's sons), and then lists twenty-three *bachelerii*. Included among these twenty-three are the four men who received fees and robes in the wardrobe as knights of the chamber in the 1366–7 account book, as well as eleven of the twelve chamber knights listed in the great wardrobe livery roll for 1364–5. Evidently the term 'bachelor' *could* be equated with 'knight of the chamber' but that is not to say that it must necessarily be. Working principally from the registers of John of Gaunt and the Black Prince, J.M.W. Bean has argued that at this time the word 'bachelor' was used to describe 'an inner group within the magnate's household, enjoying a position of closeness to their lord . . . a distinct group of retainers in whom their lord reposed a special trust'; on occasions these men were described as bachelors of the duke's or prince's chamber.[24] Such a description certainly accords well with the list of Edward III's *bachelerii* at Christmas 1366 for apart from those of the twenty-three who were elsewhere described as knights of the chamber, there are a number of men on the list who were clearly close, and often long-serving, knights of Edward's, such as John atte Wode, Gilbert Spenser, Robert Ashton, Roger Elmrugge, and Thomas Tirell.

Should it therefore be assumed that any one of these twenty-three *bachelerii* might just as easily have been described as a knight of the chamber? The answer is probably yes, but we are left with the fact that a total of only seven men are listed as receiving fees and robes as chamber knights in the four surviving wardrobe account books of the period 1366–77, and that among these seven the same names tend to recur (Alan Buxhull, Peter Brewes, Richard Stury, and Richard Pembridge, most notably). To appreciate the significance of this it is necessary to look forward to the reigns of Richard II and Henry IV. A total of thirty-five men were described as knights of the chamber in various sources of Richard's reign.[25] Yet only twenty-one of these are listed as receiving fees and robes in the surviving wardrobe account books; the remaining fourteen did not apparently receive fees and robes in the wardrobe, and are only described incidentally as knights of the chamber in, for example, diplomatic documents, or grants registered on the patent rolls. Henry IV hardly ever used the style 'knight of the chamber' except in the wardrobe account books, but even so two of the fifteen men called chamber knights in the various documents of his reign were not listed in either of the surviving wardrobe account books (Robert Corbet and John Littlebury). There are moreover two 'jewel accounts', so-called, which list the knights who attended the royal court at Christmas 1401 and Christmas 1402. Unfortunately, both documents are in very poor condition and it is not possible to read all the names listed, but that for Christmas 1401 seems to list a total of thirty-three knights divided into three groups: nine who received fees (in lieu of robes) of 10 marks each, six receiving fees of 6 marks each, and eighteen at 5 marks each. The list for Christmas 1402 names only ten knights, with no mention of their fees.[26] Seven of the chamber knights listed in the 1402–3 wardrobe account book also feature on one or other of these lists and once again the remaining names include several men who were closely associated with the king, such as Thomas Picworth, Thomas Pomeray, John

Pomeray, John Littlebury (described elsewhere as a chamber knight, in 1401), John de Etton, and Hortonk van Clux. These jewel account lists, therefore, seem to be very similar to the list of *bachelerii* of 1366.

It is thus clear that throughout the period 1360–1413 the lists of chamber knights in the wardrobe account books do not give us a complete picture of those who might be described as knights of the chamber. In fact they probably include less than half of them. But what is also abundantly clear is that the wardrobe account lists have, in terms of personnel, their own internal consistency so what they represent, therefore, is an inner circle of chamber knights, in the sense that they were almost certainly those among the king's 'bachelors' who actually had regular duties at court, either in the chamber or in the hall, and that they were obliged to remain at court for certain periods of each year (perhaps this was organised on a rotational basis, perhaps it was as other duties allowed, but certainly some of them would have been with the king all the time). During Edward III's later years, this inner group of chamber knights numbered between three and five; under Richard II and Henry IV, it numbered between eight and twelve. It was their proximity to the king which explains why they figured so prominently among the 'courtiers' of these years.[27]. Outside this inner group, however, there were other men who might be described as chamber knights. Perhaps they were under an obligation to attend the royal court on certain occasions, such as Christmas, or the annual Garter ceremonies at Windsor, but they had no specific duties in the household. The term was a flexible one, and is probably best understood (excluding the inner circle) as describing one of that wider body of 'king's knights' who had a more personal relationship with the king than his fellows, one who, perhaps, when he came to court, would normally dine with the king in his chamber rather than in the hall. They were not entitled to fees as the 'real' chamber knights were. The fees paid to his knights by Henry IV at Christmas 1401 were, explicitly, in lieu of robes, and are not to be equated with the fees (in addition to robes) granted to the inner circle of chamber knights.

As to the term 'knight of the household', its demise is quite sudden after 1360. Apart from those described as *bachelerii* in 1366, and of course the knights of the chamber, there are very few references to any knights who were in any sense 'attached' to the king in the last seventeen years of Edward III's reign. The term 'king's knight' which was to become so common after 1377, is not found at all in the records of these years. There are a few references to knights *de retinentia regis* or *de familia regis* but these are associated with military service, nearly all of them relating to the king's abortive naval expedition in 1372.[28] During Richard II's reign there are only two references to 'knights of the household', both in 1385, and both in reality designating knights of the king's retinue on the Scottish campaign of that year.[29] Henry IV, as far as can be gathered, never used the term. It was occasionally used later in the fifteenth century, but what it really meant at this time was apparently either a 'knight of the body', or a member of the king's war-time retinue.[30]

What had happened therefore was that, out of the large and fluctuating body of knights of the household of the thirteenth and early fourteenth centuries, a smaller and more compact group of knights of the chamber had emerged by *c.* 1365. This had been part of the general shift in the centre of gravity of the household from hall to chamber, but there was more to it than this. The service which the king expected from his chamber knights was rather different from that which he had formerly expected from his household knights. For a start, it was more domestic. But it was also more varied. Even if one goes back to the reign of Edward I, it is surely no coincidence that the only knight (apart from the known chamberlains) to be associated with the king's chamber was John Botetourt. Botetourt was doubtless a good soldier, but he was also much more than a soldier for he was a regular member of the council during the later years of Edward's reign, acted as a judge, and was of sufficient stature to be one of those who swore the Boulogne oath of January 1308.[31] The lists of chamber knights from Edward III's reign also include the names of many men who were used by the king in a variety of responsible positions besides military ones: John de Molyns, Guy Brian, Roger Beauchamp, Walter Manny, Richard Stury, Richard Pembridge and Alan Buxhull are only the most obvious. They served their king as councillors, commissioners and diplomats as well as in war. The duties entrusted by Richard II to his chamber knights have already been discussed.[32] These men were, it seems, rather different from the household knights of the thirteenth and early fourteenth centuries. In a word, they were more important.

To say that their service to the king was both more domestic and more varied is not, however, to say that they did not accompany the king when he went to war, or indeed that they did not sometimes campaign independently of the king for this they certainly did. After all, the steward and chamberlain of the royal household, who had even more clearly defined and responsible offices at court, can often be seen to have been absent from the household, usually campaigning or on embassies for the king. But when they did so, they (or the king) probably had to appoint deputies to act in their place in the household. And when the campaign or the embassy was over, it was no doubt to the household rather than to their estates that they would be expected to return. The period from 1360 to 1413 is however one during which the kings of England did not often campaign in person and this is particularly true of the first half of this period: between 1360 and 1385 the only campaign led by the king in person was Edward's brief and futile sortie from Sandwich in the autumn of 1372. This is probably one reason why it was during these years that the system of retaining a large body of household knights, for primarily military purposes, was finally abandoned. Edward's lack of military activity in these years meant also that he was hardly recruiting any new knights to the service of the crown at this time. Most of those receiving annuities from the king towards the end of the reign were men who had been recruited during the heyday of Edward's military career, in the 1330s and 1340s, and as they gradually grew older, or died, or went off to seek their fortunes elsewhere, the number of knights attached to the king dwindled to a handful. Edward was no longer attempting to attach the gentry to his cause nor was he bequeathing to his successor a body of fighting men attached to the crown. With the accession of a new king, both processes had to be begun anew.

The fact that when the king *did* campaign in person between 1360 and 1413, the number of his chamber knights showed no increase, is further proof of the fact that these men were of a different type to the earlier knights of the household. Thus the transition from the sixty or seventy (on average) knights of the household during the first half of the fourteenth century, to the ten or so knights of the chamber during the second half, is much more than a change in style. Although the term was used flexibly, in essence it describes an inner group of high-ranking and trusted royal servants valued by the king for their domestic service and for their brains as much as for their strong right arms. The reasons for this change were, in summary, the king's preference for his chamber rather than his hall, the consequent 'revival of the chamber' in the fourteenth century, and the fact that for twenty-five years after 1360 the king hardly needed a body of fighting knights attached to his service. But there was another reason too, more long-term, but ultimately just as important, and this was because of the spread of lay literacy in late medieval England, and the consequent breaching of the barriers demarcating the work done by clerks and the work done by laymen. The role of the knights in society had gradually changed since the twelfth century; many of them were now as much administrators (either at the county level, or in the service of magnates) as they were soldiers. It is hardly surprising that such an important long-term development should be mirrored in the knights attached to the king. And as we shall see, this applies not only to the inner circle of chamber knights, but also to the wider body of king's knights recruited by Richard II and Henry IV.

From the outset of Richard II's reign we at once meet with a new phrase used to describe this wider body of knights attached to the king, the 'king's knight' (*miles regis*). The change is quite sudden, and it is certainly not just a change in style for although Henry III had occasionally used the terms *miles domini regis* and *miles de familia nostra* interchangeably, to describe his household knights, it was hardly ever, if ever, used by Edward III. Beginning in 1377, however, and continuing through to 1413, some 300 men in all are described in various sources (mostly the patent rolls) as *milites regis*.[33] Sometimes it was applied also to men who were in fact knights of the chamber, but it certainly did not mean 'knight of the chamber' in the strict sense. It is used with considerable consistency and men who were king's knights are usually described as such when they are mentioned in the sources. They did not receive fees from the king like the chamber knights, but they were almost all (if not all) in receipt of annuities at the exchequer (ranging from £20 to £100, but mostly around £40 to £60), and some of them at least received robes from the king when they attended court at, for example, Christmas. In other words, there was a substantial body of knights around the country who were not of the royal household but who were attached to the person of the king. These 'king's knights' were, without any doubt, the most important members of the king's affinity (excluding, naturally, those who were at court, and some of the lords), and they merit detailed investigation.

In addition to the king's knights, there were the king's esquires. 'King's esquire' also takes on a new meaning from 1377. The term is not uncommon during the later years of Edward III's reign, but is used to describe men who were in fact esquires of the household.[34] After 1377, although it is still commonly used to describe esquires of the household, it is also applied to a large number of men who are not listed in the wardrobe account books, and who are clearly not of the household. Individually, some of these king's esquires were just as important as many of the king's knights, but collectively, the superior wealth and status of the knights made them the leaders of the royal affinity in their localities. The king's esquires also received annuities from the king (usually between 20 and 40 marks), but not fees or robes. Both Richard II and Henry IV spent a lot of money on these men, and obviously they set great store by them.

Richard II's retainers

The most satisfactory way to approach the king's knights and esquires is, initially, to take each reign in turn. Excluding the forty-nine men described as chamber knights or who held high office in the household, I have discovered 149 men called king's knights in Richard's reign, and excluding the 360 or so esquires and sergeants of the household, I have discovered 280 king's esquires. This makes a total of 429 members of the 'greater gentry', outside the household, attached to the king.[35] Two points about them present themselves at once. Firstly, that the king's knights and esquires are in different proportions to each other as compared with the knights of the chamber and the esquires of the household. Whereas the household included roughly seven esquires for every knight, the king's knights and esquires are in a ratio of roughly one to two. Moreover, these figures are distorted by Richard's heavy recruitment of esquires during the last two years of his reign. Only 105 'king's esquires' are mentioned before 1397, but after this Richard recruited a great many more, mostly from Cheshire. Thus for most of the reign there were in fact rather more king's knights than king's esquires. The reasons for this seem fairly obvious. In seeking to attach members of the more substantial gentry to himself, the king naturally looked to those who were most 'substantial' first as it made more sense to win the loyalty of a few dominant men in the shire, than that of a greater number of lesser men. On the other hand, to pay a hundred or more knights (who received much higher fees and robes allowances in the wardrobe than the esquires) to perform the duties of the esquires of the household would have made financial nonsense. Thus the senior ranks of the affinity included a greater number of men of higher rank than did the household, although less closely bound to the king's service than the household esquires and sergeants. The second clear point is that these men varied considerably in the degree of their personal attachment to the king. There were some among them who were undoubtedly closely attached to the court, barely distinguishable from the chamber knights. Such men were John Lord Beaumont, William Elmham, Thomas Latimer, John Lord Lovell, Thomas Tryvet, and John Worth (several of whom were in fact expelled from court in 1388).[36] At the opposite extreme were the foreign knights, seventeen of whom Richard either retained for life or described as his knights during the reign. For most of these men this was very much an honorary title (especially as Richard never campaigned outside the British Isles), often associated with diplomatic manoeuvring. Few of them settled in England, although some of the queen's Bohemian knights did, such as Roger Siglem, who in 1389 was described (erroneously) as an esquire 'dwelling with the queen'.[37] The majority of the king's knights fell somewhere between these two extremes. Before discussing the reasons why they were retained, something must be said about the terminology of retaining by a king.

During the first two years of his reign (but principally in March 1378), a total of about 240–50 persons were said to be 'retained' by Richard, of whom sixty were knights, forty-four were esquires, and the remainder were lesser men, many of them valets or other servants of Edward III's entering the new king's service.[38] Nearly all of them were said to be 'retained' at the same time as they secured confirmation of their annuities granted in the previous reign, and it is plain that in this sense the word 'retained' carries no political overtones at all. It means what it means in the modern sense, that is 'kept on'. During the next eight years, up to 1387, Richard seems formally to have retained very few men indeed. Most men simply begin to be described in the records as 'king's knight' or 'king's esquire', without mention of any contract of retainer, let alone a life indenture. It seems, however, that in the late summer of 1387 (for obvious reasons), the king began to adopt a much more positive attitude towards retaining. The Westminster chronicler tells us that it was at this time that Richard, while gyrating through Cheshire and North Wales, 'continually took into his personal service men of the country through which he travelled'. At the same time he sent a sergeant-at-arms into Essex, Cambridge, Norfolk and Suffolk with orders to make the 'more substantial and influential' men of those counties swear to be true to the king to the exclusion of all other lords. They were to be given badges (of silver and gilt crowns), and 'whenever called upon to do so they should join the king, armed and ready.' The response which the sergeant-at-arms met with was, to say the least, lukewarm. He was eventually arrested (by whom is not said, unfortunately) and imprisoned.[39] Article 19 of the Appeal of Treason confirms this, saying that the appellees had persuaded the king to go through his realm and into Wales and summon both members of the gentry and others, 'some by their bonds and others by their oaths', to stand with the king against all people and to help him to counter the commissioners of 1386. In addition article 24 said that the appellees 'caused the king to have *of late* (my italics) a great retinue of sundry people and to give them sundry badges', as none of his predecessors had done. The accusation is also supported in other chronicles.[40]

What emerges from this is that throughout the late summer and autumn of 1387 Richard was making a rather belated and ham-fisted attempt to attach men to himself. Belated, because before this time he had retained (formally) so few men, and ham-fisted because expedients such as sending a sergeant-at-arms to East Anglia to hand out livery badges were likely to be greeted with more suspicion than enthusiasm. Little of this finds support from the evidence of the official records, although it was at this time (16 August 1387) that the king retained the Worcestershire knight (later chamber knight and councillor) John Russell, in terms of considerable interest.[41] Yet this is hardly surprising, since the king was not in control of the chancery at this time, and in any case it was clearly done rather informally and hurriedly. In the winter of 1387–8, Richard paid the price for his bungling: unable to persuade men from the south-east to fight for him, he was forced to fall back on his Cheshire loyalists, led by Sir Thomas Molyneux, who as it turned out were unable to match the army of the Appellants at Radcot Bridge. The Cheshiremen had proved their military useful-ness to the king before, but they were no substitute for a solid basis of retained men throughout the country.[42]

After the events of 1387–8, Richard began to retain men in a much more formal way. This is shown by the figures for the number of knights actually retained *for life* by the king at different stages in the reign. Before 1389, Richard had only retained for life seven knights.[43] Yet during this period (1377–88), some sixty-seven men are described as king's knights (excluding the thirty-four chamber knights and household officers). From 1389 to 1399, a further eighty-two men were called king's knights and/or retained for life (excluding fifteen chamber knights and household officers), of whom only twelve were *not* retained for life. This clearly betokens a change of policy. There were two periods in parti-cular when Richard was actively retaining men for life: between 1391 and 1393 (thirty-six of the eighty-two), and in 1397–8 (a further twenty-five).

This change of policy can probably be ascribed to three factors. Firstly, it dawned rather unpleasantly on the king in 1387–8 that he had not succeeded in winning the support of a sufficient number of the 'more substantial and influ-ential' gentry in the shires, and he determined to rectify that situation. It was definitely towards the top end of the market that the king directed his efforts between 1389 and 1397 and whereas he retained for life more than seventy knights, the number of esquires for whom he did the same was only thirty-nine. Secondly, there is the fact that he was growing up, once again had con-trol of the exchequer, and was thus in a position to use his resources in order to expand his affinity. Thirdly, there was the ordinance on livery and maintenance issued in May 1390. The ordinance was the result of discussions which had been going on for nearly two years before this,[44] and it said that 'no duke, earl, baron or banneret shall give such livery of company unless he (the retainer) is retained with him *for the term of his life* (my italics) in peace and war by indenture', or unless he was a servant dwelling in the lord's household.[45] Evidence has already been given to show that Richard moved rapidly to put the ordinance into effect with regard to his household servants.[46] The evidence given here shows that from 1389, when the subject was already under discussion, the king's knights nearly always did become the king's life retainers as well. It is also interesting to note that several men who before 1389 had been described as king's knights were not formally retained for life until after that date: Robert Bardolf, Thomas Barre, John Lovell, Richard Redman, and Baldwin Raddington, all described between 1386 and 1388 as king's knights, were retained for life respectively in June 1393, November 1390, February 1395, November 1390 again, and June 1393 again.[47]

The evidence concerning esquires is less conclusive, though it points in the same general direction and raises further points of interest. Before 1389, the king hardly retained any esquires for life and of the seventy-two men described as king's esquires between 1377 and 1388 (excluding those who were also esquires of the household), I have failed to discover one who was actually said to be retained for life by the king. A further 208 men were called king's esquires between 1389 and 1399, of whom 125 were said to be retained for life, which certainly suggests that a king's esquire was more likely to be retained for life after 1389. What is perhaps more significant is that before 1397 the number of esquires in the king's retinue was considerably smaller than the number of knights, for 175 of these 208 esquires are only mentioned in 1397–9.[48] Thus while for most of the 1390s Richard was retaining principally the topmost layer of the gentry (i.e. knights), after 1397 he began to recruit more widely, and of course this is also reflected in the archers whom he recruited, mainly from Cheshire, during these last two years of the reign.[49]

It may be that the king saw another advantage in life retaining, that of binding men more closely to himself. The Ordinance of 1390 said nothing explicit about the question of whether or not a man could be granted livery by more than one lord, although it was naturally implicit in the ordinance that any man who wore the livery badge of more than one lord would have to be retained for life by each of them. There was nothing new in the problem of multiple allegiance. Liege homage had been used in twelfth-century France as a way of trying to establish the priority of one lord's claim against another to his vassal's allegiance. Yet despite the silence of the ordinance on the subject, there is some evidence that it was a problem which exercised Richard's mind, especially in the period 1387–9, and again, in rather special circumstances, in 1399. The problem for the king, as for any lord, was to try to avoid throwing good money after bad. If he was going to retain men for life with annuities, then naturally he hoped for some sort of assurance that they would not desert him in a crisis. On occasions, Richard extracted such assurances, though not often. When he retained John Russell in August 1387, he granted Russell a £50 annuity 'in consideration of his having been taken and retained to stay with the king for life, whereby he lost fees which he was wont to receive from his lord, with whom he stayed.'[50] His lord just happened to be the earl of Warwick, by whom he had been retained with an annuity of £20 in 1383,[51] so there is little difficulty in understanding how Russell might have had problems in trying to serve both king and earl at such a time, but the next case is not so clear-cut. When the Yorkshire knight William Elys was retained for life by the king in February 1389, he was granted an annuity of 40 marks 'to compensate for that sum received for his fee when with the king's uncle, the duke of York.' Although York was a commissioner in 1386–7, he has not usually been regarded as following policies hostile to Richard, or indeed any policies at all. Thirdly, in August 1389, the very able and rapidly rising Cheshire knight, John Stanley, was retained by the king 'for life, to serve him above all others'.[52] Stanley's ability was primarily military, which may explain why the king was eager to ensure his loyalty; his previous lord was Robert de Vere, as whose lieutenant he had been sent to Ireland in 1386, so it was perhaps understandable that he should look to the king for patronage.

It is difficult to see how these terms of retaining can be interpreted except as an attempt by Richard to ensure the undivided loyalty of these men, but in Elys's case at least it is difficult to see why he should be singled out. Possibly Richard, in the aftermath of the events of 1387–8, was trying to bind men more exclusively to the crown, but if these three examples do add up to some sort of deliberate policy, it did not last long. There are no further examples of such phraseology during the next nine and a half years.[53] The evidence from 1399, however, is less equivocal. After John of Gaunt's death, Richard, having taken control of the Lancastrian estates, found himself in the position of having to confirm the annuities paid by Gaunt to his servants out of the revenues of those estates. He confirmed about ninety of them, mostly in April 1399, but for thirty-six of the more senior members of his uncle's former retinue, he only confirmed them as long as they agreed to be 'retained to stay with the king *only*' (my italics). Twelve knights and twenty-four esquires, including some of the duke's closest followers, were so retained, while several other esquires and the lesser servants were confirmed in their annuities without having to take any such oath to the king.[54] Even Ralph Nevill, earl of Westmorland, who had already been retained as a king's knight in May 1395, was only allowed to keep his annuity of 500 marks on the Lancastrian estates as long as he took the new form of oath. Many of these annuities had already been confirmed by Henry Bolingbroke shortly before he sailed away to exile in September 1398, presumably in anticipation of his father's death, so whether the king had any right to impose this requirement on his new retainers is questionable. But it was of course a consequence of his sequestration of Bolingbroke's inheritance, which was equally questionable. The reasoning behind it is plain: having done what he had, Richard was hoping to apply pressure on the chief Lancastrian retainers not to render any assistance to his cousin. As for Bolingbroke, he probably viewed the process with as much distaste as he viewed the sequestration of his inheritance, and it may have been an equally powerful incentive to him to take action. Like Richard's attempts to retain men in the summer and autumn of 1387, it gives the appearance of a high-handed and bungled piece of political manoeuvring, but of course that view is tinged with the knowledge that as a piece of political manoeuvring it failed.

A gentry retaining policy—why?

Why did a king have king's knights and esquires? The easy answer is that each man was retained by the king for individual reasons, because he had some skill or influence which the king hoped to turn to his own advantage, and there is nearly always an element of truth in this answer. Yet in addition to this there are probably certain reasons common to a number of men, even if it is often difficult to apply the reason to the man with any degree of certainty. Among the principal reasons why the king retained men were, firstly, because of personal connections, secondly, because he wished to increase his following in certain areas, thirdly, because they were men of local importance and fourthly, because he needed good soldiers for his armies. All these reasons can be subsumed under the one over-riding reason, no doubt high on Richard's list of priorities after 1387–8, i.e. that he wanted to be sure of a loyal core of followers in a crisis.

The importance of personal connections and family tradition in the process by which the king recruited his affinity is readily apparent. For example, the most rudimentary sort of statistical analysis shows that of the 860 or so knights, esquires and sergeants of the king's household and retinue, over 340 shared a surname with another member of the household or retinue. Obviously all those who shared surnames were not related, but most of them certainly were, and in addition there were all those other personal connections, by marriage for example, through friendship, or through service, which are so often hidden from our view. Crude calculations such as this serve to underline what is perhaps better illustrated by a few examples. Simon Burley was in as good a position as anyone to introduce his relatives to Richard's service in the 1380s, and so he did. His brother John served as Richard's chamber knight until his death in 1386 and John's son William was an esquire of the household, while Thomas Burley, probably another of John's sons, also joined the household as an esquire before 1389. The family circle extended further for Baldwin Raddington, controller of the household from 1381 until 1397, was Simon's nephew, while the king's knight Thomas Barre, who like the Burleys came from Herefordshire, was married to the sister of John Burley's wife.[55] Another chamber knight who did well by his relatives was John Clanvow. John was a chamber knight from *c*. 1381 until his death in 1391 and he had either a son or a nephew named Thomas, who was a king's knight by 1395, and Thomas was married to Perrin Witteneye, damsel of the queen's chamber.[56] Perrin was probably either the sister or the daughter of Robert Witteneye, a chamber knight from 1392 to 1399, while Witteneye's son, also Robert, was an esquire of the household in the 1390s. Both the Clanvows and the Witteneyes, like the Burleys, came from Herefordshire. A favoured esquire of the king could be just as successful at introducing his family to court. Philip Walweyn, for example, another native of Herefordshire, had been usher of the hall of the Black Prince and served as usher (or esquire) of Richard's chamber from the beginning of the reign. Philip Walweyn the younger, Richard, and John all became esquires of the household, while Thomas Walweyn was a king's esquire by 1394. Exactly how they were related is not clear, but they certainly were and several of them were also active in local administration in Herefordshire (particularly Thomas and John, and William Walweyn was sheriff in 1411–12). In each case it is probable that one outstanding member of the family (Simon Burley, John Clanvow, Philip Walweyn the elder) rose high in the favour of the king and was thus in a position to act as the trail-blazer of the family's fortunes in the royal service. There were other sorts of personal connections too, which might prove just as rewarding. The chamber knight Arnold Savage, for example, was the son of Eleanor, who had been Richard II's nurse 'in his infancy'. The Yorkshireman John de Routhe had been an esquire in the service of Robert de Vere before the latter's exile, and by 1393 he was a king's knight, retained for life with an annuity of 40 marks.[57] These few examples, from the many which could be cited, reinforce the view that the most important prerequisite for those seeking to become king's knights or esquires was a personal connection of some sort. The same can be said of the lesser members of the affinity, as demonstrated graphically by the Mascy family from Cheshire, at least seventeen of whom were retained (mostly as archers and yeomen of the crown) by Richard in the 1390s.[58]

The ubiquity of the personal connections which bound members of the king's affinity to each other as well as to the king leads inevitably to a further consideration: to what extent did such connections determine the geographical areas from which the king drew his followers? The county of Herefordshire provides an excellent example in Richard's reign. Richard retained an abnormally high proportion of the Herefordshire gentry, that is sixteen king's knights (including six of his chamber knights), and about thirty esquires (the geographical provenance of the king's esquires is not always very clear). There is no very obvious reason why he should have done so. It was not a very large or well-populated shire (its recorded taxable population in 1377 was one of the lowest of the English shires), and the Black Prince seems to have had no special connections with the county, although he may have used Herefordshire gentry to help in the administration of Wales.[59] Nor did it hold any obvious attractions as a strategic royal stronghold. It seems that there are two possible explanations. Firstly, there may have been a lack of leadership from the great magnates to the gentry of the county. The two greatest landholders in the shire for most of the fourteenth century were the Mortimer earls of March and the Bohun earls of Hereford and Essex. The Bohuns died out (in the person of Humphrey, son of William Bohun) in 1373, whereupon their lands were divided between the royal cadet Thomas of Woodstock and Henry Bolingbroke. The earls of March experienced a series of early deaths and subsequent minorities during the second half of the fourteenth century, which may have tended to dilute the quality of their local leadership and disrupt their relationships with the gentry. It was to such great magnates that the gentry of the shire would naturally have turned for 'good lordship', and if that lordship were lacking, there was a greater incentive to turn to the king. There is some evidence that this happened. John Clanvow, for instance, was retained by Humphrey de Bohun before 1373, but when the latter died he entered the service of Edward III and thus passed into Richard's household.[60] John Burley had held the manor of Haresfield (Gloucs.) from the same earl Humphrey, so he too may have been a Bohun retainer before 1373. Yet Burley was certainly a retainer of the Black Prince as well, and was one of Edward III's chamber knights in 1364–5, which was undoubtedly a more decisive factor in ensuring his place in Richard II's chamber.[61] On the whole, the evidence is rather thin. Most of Bohun's retainers seem to have switched to Thomas of Woodstock's retinue after 1373, and the earl of March was clearly retaining some of the Herefordshire gentry in the 1390s.[62] The second possible explanation brings us back to personal connections. The prominence of Herefordshire men among the king's followers is probably explained most satisfactorily as a cumulative process, originating with a small handful of men closely bound to the king (apart from the Burleys, Clanvow, and Philip Walweyn, the chamber knights Nicholas Sharnesfeld and Thomas Peytevyn, and John Devereux steward of the household were also Herefordshire men), and spreading from there to embrace numerous friends, relatives and other local associates of the original group. The same process can be seen operating, though not on the same scale, in the Oxford/Berkshire region (Richard Abberbury, John Golafre, Baldwin Bereford, Thomas Blount, and Robert Bardolf were the chamber knights who hailed from this area).

Thus the geographical provenance of the king's affinity was probably determined as much by personal factors as by any conscious policy of recruitment by regions. Yet it is clear that other considerations were at work too. The naturally court- and capital-oriented area of England, also the area where magnate domination of local gentry was likely to be weakest, was the south-east. Also there were 'special' royal areas, such as Cornwall and Cheshire, where the king had additional powers and additional sources of patronage, and it was logical to retain local men to act for the king in these areas. Furthermore, in general the king would wish to maintain a core of followers throughout the country, in order to keep an eye on 'the disposicion of the cuntries' and to ensure that areas were not ignored.[63] In 1400 the privy council advised Henry IV 'that in each county of the kingdom a certain number of the more sufficient men of good fame should be retained by the king . . . and charged also carefully and diligently to save the estate of the king and his people in their localities', and that each of them be granted an annuity. They also advised that the 'armed esquires and archers' who were to form Henry's bodyguard should be drawn from each county of the realm.[64] Edward IV's household men were used by the king to serve as links between the court and the outlying regions, just as he had been advised in the Black Book.[65] What significance did Richard II attach to such considerations?

Excluding the eighteen king's knights and one chamber knight during Richard's reign who were foreigners, and two further king's knights whose geographical provenance I have been unable to discover, Richard's 177 chamber knights and king's knights break down geographically as follows (I have divided them into regions rather than individual counties for the sake of greater simplicity and because it seems to make more sense):[66] from the south-east (including Hampshire, Wiltshire, Oxford, Northants, Huntingdon, Cambridge, Norfolk, and the counties to the south and east of them) came sixty-four knights; from the west country (including Somerset and Dorset), came eighteen; from the Welsh marches (Hereford and Salop), came twenty-one, all but five of whom were from Hereford; from the west midlands (Gloucester, Warwickshire and Worcestershire) there were twelve; from south Wales came two, and from north Wales two, a surprisingly small number in view of the Black Prince's connections, but Wales was largely administered at the top level by Englishmen; from Yorkshire there were twelve, and from the north midlands (Nottingham, Stafford, Leicester, Lincolnshire, Derbyshire and Rutland) sixteen; from the north-west (Lancashire and Cheshire) came eighteen, and from the four northern counties twelve.

From this evidence certain fairly broad conclusions can be drawn. Firstly, it is evident that no region was seriously under-represented among the king's followers. There were a few counties which, as far as I can gather, did not provide the king with any knights at all (Derby and Rutland, for example), but it is very unlikely that any real significance should be attached to this; equally, there were some counties which provided a noticeably high number of king's knights (Hereford with sixteen, Yorkshire with twelve, Cheshire with eleven, Norfolk with ten, and Devon with nine), but with the exception of Hereford and Cheshire where special circumstances applied, these were all large and well-populated counties and this is hardly surprising.[67] Secondly, about a third of the king's knights were drawn from the south-east, but again this is quite natural, not only because this was the court's obvious 'catchment area', but also because it was by far the largest and most densely-populated of the regions. The third conclusion is more interesting, and relates to the numbers of knights drawn from the northern and southern halves of the country at different periods of the reign. Of the ninety-five king's knights attached to him before 1389, seventy-six came from the southern half of the country (Hereford, Worcester, Warwickshire, Northamptonshire, Huntingdon, Cambridge, Norfolk, and counties to the south of them), whereas only nineteen came from the northern half. Of the eighty-two knights attached to the king in the period 1389–99, however, forty-six came from the north, and only thirty-six from the south. This is partly explained by the king's drive to retain men in the north-west, but it was only during the last two years of the reign that the king really began to recruit heavily in Cheshire and Lancashire and of the eighteen king's knights from the north-west, eleven were retained only in 1397 or later. During the early 1390s, the king was recruiting more knights from other northern counties, such as Lincolnshire and Yorkshire, than from Cheshire and Lancashire.

In Lincolnshire, there were only three king's knights before 1389, by 1395, there were eight. In Yorkshire, there were two king's knights before 1389, by 1396, there were twelve. If Richard's government was as unpopular in the north as has been suggested, then at least after 1388 he was trying to do something about it.[68]

Yet it was not just the number of northern knights that Richard retained in the early 1390s that is significant. It was also the sort of men that he retained, and this leads on to the third broad reason for retaining knights, i.e. because they were men of local importance. Richard has sometimes been accused of packing parliament and the shrievalty with his own men, and perhaps there were times when he did, but it was just as good thinking on the king's part to retain the sort of men who were already prominent representatives of their localities, or whom he judged likely to become so.[69] Many of the men whom the king retained in the early 1390s were of precisely this kind. From Yorkshire, for instance, came John Godard[70] and James Pykeryng.[71] From Lincolnshire came Henry Retford[72] and John Bussy.[73] From Staffordshire came Adam Peshale[74] and the esquire William Walshale.[75] From the southern counties too, the king was frequently retaining men at this time who had already made a local name for themselves such as Edward Dalyngridge from Sussex,[76] William Sturmy from Hampshire,[77] and John Thornbury from Hertfordshire.[78] Before 1388 Richard had sometimes retained similar men, such as John Annesley of Nottingham,[79] but after 1388 he did so much more consistently. It was obviously a sensible policy to try to retain in each county a small number of men from whom there was a good chance that the sheriff or members of parliament might be chosen, and the increasing number of king's knights in the parliaments of the 1390s reflects the (at least partial) success of this policy. After 1397, however, the king more or less stopped recruiting knights from different parts of the country, and concentrated almost all his resources on the northwest. The 'Cheshire phenomenon' (which was also in part a Lancashire phenomenon) is discussed below.[80] First something needs to be said about the fourth reason for retaining knights, that is, to fill the king's armies.

The king's knights were prominent in the armies which Richard led to Ireland in 1394 and 1399; the king's esquires were not. Of the eighty-nine bannerets and knights who accompanied him in 1394 (excluding those in the retinues of other lords, thus counting only those who contracted directly with the king), forty-eight were king's knights, of whom nine were chamber knights. The composition of the king's army in 1399 is not so easy to piece together, but of the forty-nine bannerets and knights who are recorded as having gone with the king, thirty were king's knights, of whom six were chamber knights.[81] Of the 200 or so esquires whom the king took in 1394, 119 were king's esquires, but very few of these (about eight) were not household esquires. Of the sixty-two esquires who are recorded as accompanying the king in 1399 (almost certainly less than half the true total), forty-six were esquires of the household and only three king's esquires. Incomplete as these figures are, they are perhaps suggestive. Service in war is not now normally regarded as a common reason for a lord to retain a man for life; the emphasis is usually placed rather on the life retainer's service in peace.[82] It is of course very difficult to disentangle cause from effect: did the king's knights serve in his Irish armies because they were the king's knights, or had the king recruited them because they were soldiers of reputation and he wished to have a good nucleus of fighting men at his disposal when the need arose? Without suggesting that a conclusive answer can be given to these questions, some points are worth making. Firstly, that there was a high degree of continuity between the knights who went to Ireland with the king in 1394 and those who went in 1399. Of the thirty king's knights who accompanied Richard in 1399, twenty-three had also accompanied him in 1394. Richard had about 130 king's knights at this time whom presumably he could have summoned had he wished to, yet the majority of them either were not summoned or could or would not come. Perhaps this indicates a nucleus of active (that is, fighting) knights in the king's retinue, with a wider body of men whose special skills lay elsewhere. Secondly, that in concentrating on service in peace-time as the principal *raison d'être* of the life retainer, we have perhaps been guilty of neglecting what fourteenth-century writers still saw as the primary obligation to society of the knight, that is to fight, rather than to work or to pray. There were still clearly many knights in fourteenth-century England (and Europe) for whom service in war remained the chief aim in life, some of whom, one must assume, became very skilled at their art. Was it not logical for a king (or a lord) to attach some such men to his retinue? This is not to suggest that a large number of the king's knights were retained primarily for military reasons, but that a certain number may have been. The professional soldier like John Stanley (retained to serve the king 'for life...above all others') was not a man to be ignored, and it seems to have been among the knights rather than among the esquires of his kingdom that Richard found such men.[83]

During the early 1390s, Richard seems deliberately to have broadened the scope of his retinue, retaining more men from the northern as well as the southern counties, bringing in several men who had carved out distinctive roles for themselves in the administration of their counties, and perhaps too not neglecting to include a proportion of real soldiers. From late 1397 onwards, his scope narrowed dramatically and while his retinue increased greatly in size, its composition was from now on determined largely by two criteria: firstly, it was drawn almost exclusively from the north-west (principally Cheshire), and secondly, it was designed for military use, whether within or without the kingdom. Richard's recruitment of Cheshiremen during the last two years of his reign has been exhaustively studied and commented upon, and there is little to add to what has already been said, except perhaps to say that when seen in the context of his retaining policy during the previous eight years, it marks a sudden end to what appears to have been quite a sensible and successful strategy.[84] During the last two years of his reign, the king retained for life twenty-eight knights, seven of them foreigners, which can be explained by his ambitious diplomatic schemes—and of the remaining twenty-one, eleven came from the north-west. Of the 175 esquires retained by the king from 1397 onwards, well over a hundred were from Cheshire and Lancashire. In July 1397, immediately after his arrest of the three leading Appellants, Richard summoned 2,000 Cheshire archers to London, and at the same time he issued an order that no archer from Cheshire was to serve anyone else until 2,300 men had been chosen for the king's retinue. Whether he in fact retained this number of Cheshire archers is open to doubt, but the most complete list of the king's Cheshiremen lists over 760 men by September 1398.[85] Apart from ten knights and eighty-five esquires retained for life, there was also the king's bodyguard of 311 archers divided into seven *vigilia*, which, the chroniclers leave us in no doubt, remained with Richard day and night, 'Dycun, slep sicury quile we wake'.[86] Another twelve esquires were retained during pleasure, while a reserve bodyguard of 101 archers was retained for life, and a further 197 archers retained during pleasure. Including a further fifty-five men whose status and whose terms of retaining are unclear, the list totals 771, but there are a few names which appear twice. This expansion in the king's bodyguard in particular was quite unprecedented. Throughout the fourteenth century there had been king's archers, but in the later years of Edward III's reign the number seems to have dwindled to a handful, and from 1385–95 Richard had retained about forty to fifty of them. Yet these 311 Cheshire archers were in addition to the archers of the crown (who by late 1398 numbered about seventy-five), and moreover they went everywhere with the king.[87] They swelled the already inflated household of 1395–6 to something over 900 persons, and together with the reserve force (which presumably remained in Cheshire until summoned to, for instance, the Irish campaign of 1399), they swelled the king's documented affinity to something in the region of 2,000.[88] The cost was borne by Richard not only financially (his Cheshiremen's annuities cost over £5,000 a year) but politically. It is clear that his obsession with Chester and its people was derided, and his bodyguard despised. Adam of Usk called them the chief cause of the king's ruin, and he may well have been right.[89] It is difficult to see how to interpret Richard's retaining policy after 1397 except as a combination of his strange obsession with his new principality and his fears for his own personal safety. What is perplexing, however, is why he decided to abandon so abruptly the path which he had trodden with considerable success for the previous eight years.

Thus there were probably four principal reasons why Richard retained knights and esquires: for personal reasons, because they were prominent in their localities, because he wished to increase his following in particular parts of the country, and because of their military ability. Yet over-riding and subsuming all these factors was the king's desire for a loyal base of support among the gentry of the kingdom in the event of a crisis. Before 1387, Richard had made little attempt to recruit gentry to his cause, and this was reflected—disastrously for the king—in their reaction to the crisis of 1387–8. Only a group of loyal

Cheshiremen and a small handful of individuals close to the king (such as Robert de Vere, or Thomas Tryvet who apparently tried to ambush the Appellants on their way to London)[90] were prepared to fight for Richard. Most men probably felt much as did Sir Ralph Basset, that he had no intention of getting his head broken for the sake of the duke of Ireland.[91] The next real moment of crisis came in 1399. How did his affinity repay Richard?

Certain points about the revolution of 1399 need to be kept in mind. Firstly, the king had taken about seventy of his knights and esquires to Ireland with him, probably the most militarily capable among them but due to bungling, and perhaps treachery (by Rutland, for instance), at the time of the king's return, they hardly got the chance to put up much of a show of resistance.[92] Secondly, Henry Bolingbroke acted with considerable speed and decisiveness. As late as 20 June York's regency government apparently had no idea that an invasion was imminent for on that day two of Henry's esquires, John Leventhorpe and Richard Ramsey, were permitted to collect from the English exchequer £1,586 in part payment of the £2,000 annually which Richard had granted his cousin during his exile.[93] Yet eight days later York was writing from Westminster to various sheriffs asking them to bring soldiers to meet him at Ware in Hertfordshire with all haste, since the king's enemies were gathering at Calais with malicious intent against the kingdom.[94] Before another week had passed, Bolingbroke had landed, and the snowball had begun to roll.[95] Thirdly, although the real show of resistance came from those who had most to lose, and although there was not a *widespread* opposition to Bolingbroke, there were nevertheless substantial pockets of resistance. Henry's march through England in July and August of 1399 really was not quite the triumphal progress that has often been described. Bearing in mind also those who supported the earls' rebellion of January 1400, some of whom had been prevented by circumstances from bearing arms in Richard's cause in 1399, one might speculate that, had the king's supporters been more effectively organised and directed at that time, they were sufficiently numerous to provide Bolingbroke with a real trial of strength. Unfortunately for Richard, they were never given the chance to do so.

Among the king's knights, his councillors, William Lescrope, Bussy, Bagot, Green and Russell had all nailed their flags so unequivocally to Richard's mast that they had no option in 1399 but to stick with him and hope for the best. Lescrope, Bussy and Green were executed at Bristol, while John Russell was also trapped at Bristol but feigned madness and was released, and William Bagot managed to escape although he was later brought in chains to the new king and subjected to a rigorous interrogation in the parliament of October 1399, from which he barely escaped with his life.[96] There were others who were in a more equivocal position, yet who were prepared to risk (and often give) their lives in Richard's cause. William Elmham, a king's knight of long standing, joined with Henry Despenser, bishop of Norwich, in an armed attack on Bolingbroke's forces.[97] Stephen Lescrope, the king's under-chamberlain, and Walter Bitterley, king's knight, also refused to join the Lancastrian bandwagon, while Benedict Sely, Andrew Hake, Thomas Blount, Bernard Brocas and Ralph Lord Lumley all joined the earls' rebellion, and all lost their heads for it.[98] Of the king's esquires, Laurence Dru (another whose flag was nailed firmly to Richard's mast), John Golafre (son of the chamber knight who had died in 1396), and the remarkable Janico Dartasso (who refused to take off Richard's badge when ordered to by Henry), all refused to desert the king. The king's esquire Thomas Shelley joined the earls' rebellion, while two further esquires of the household, John Pallays and John Seymour, tried to rescue Richard at Lichfield when he was being taken to London. Several other esquires also joined the earls' rebellion, including Richard's executor and receiver of his chamber John Lufwyk, and the king's esquire John Walsh. A substantial group of royal clerks also remained loyal to the king, the most notable of whom were Tideman of Winchcombe, Thomas Merks, Roger Walden, Henry Despenser of Norwich, Richard Maudeleyn and William Ferriby. The king's physician, Master Paul, also refused to desert him, and, in addition to the six clerks mentioned above, John Ikelyngton, Nicholas Slake, the king's almoner Richard atte Felde, and the abbot of Westminster were all implicated in the rebellion of January 1400.

Most of these men were closely associated with Richard, and it comes as no surprise that they stuck by him in 1399–1400. Yet they were only the most prominent of Richard's supporters. On 4 July 1399, the duke of York sent letters to various bishops and nobles, as well as to 'certain knights and esquires of the king's retinue' to join his *comitiva* with all possible haste, and by 12 July more than seventy knights and esquires had responded to the call, bringing with them retinues of ten, twenty, or more archers and men-at-arms. They included, in addition to those noted above, the king's knights Nicholas Hauberk, Roger Siglem, Hugh Despenser, William Hoo, and William Burcester.[99] York also wrote to the sheriffs ordering them to bring their *posses* to join him, to preserve the 'bono statu et gubernacione dicti regni in absencia regis', and at least five of them responded within a week. Tuck's estimate of 3,000 for York's army is perhaps too generous, but it could hardly have been less than 2,000, and it included several magnates (Wiltshire, Suffolk, Dorset, and York himself) as well as several bishops.[100] Why, then, was it left to Henry Despenser and William Elmham to offer armed resistance? There are even indications that the populace may have been less ready to desert Richard than is often supposed. Adam of Usk tells us that the people of the lordship of Usk, led by Sir Edward Charlton and his wife Eleanor, daughter of the duke of Surrey (Thomas Holand), were preparing to resist the Lancastrian army soon after the execution of Richard's councillors at Bristol, and were only dissuaded from doing so by the intervention of the intrepid chronicler in person. According to the author of the *Traison et Mort*, the Welsh were harrying Bolingbroke's troops so effectively in the early days of August that he had to beat a hasty retreat back to, of all places, Chester.[101] Even the Londoners, for long regarded as being among Bolingbroke's firmest supporters during the early days of the revolution, were not apparently as united in their opposition to Richard as was once thought.[102] All in all, it is not really fair to accuse Richard's affinity of wholesale desertion of the king's cause in 1399–1400. It was more a combination of circumstances—the king's absence with many of his leading soldiers in Ireland, the incompetence (perhaps even teachery) of York, the element of surprise skilfully exploited by Bolingbroke—which led to the crumbling of support for the king. Walsingham states that many received wages to fight for the king (as is confirmed by the exchequer records), but then went over to Bolingbroke's side.[103] What he does not say is whether this was as a result of York's agreement with Henry, or whether it preceded that agreement. It is probably true to say, however, that if Richard had entrusted his kingdom to a greater man than his uncle in the summer of 1399, he would have reaped more benefit from the generous retaining policy which he had been following during the previous decade. The affinity came to be led, but nobody was capable of leading it.

Henry IV's retainers

By Richard II's reign, therefore, the practice of attaching to the king a fluctuating body of household knights, whose principal service to the crown was military, had given way to the practice of maintaining a small inner group of chamber knights, numbering about ten, at court, together with a much larger group of king's knights and esquires, numbering over 350 by the end of the reign, whose service to the crown was less military and reflected the growing importance of the 'greater gentry' in both local and national administration. Henry IV adopted his predecessor's practice.[104] Excluding the twenty-four men who either held high office in the household or were described as chamber knights under Henry, I have discovered 142 'king's knights' and excluding the 170 men who were listed as esquires of the household in one or other of the surviving wardrobe account books, there are *c*. 140 'king's esquires'. Bearing in mind that Henry's reign was nine years shorter than his predecessor's, the number of king's knights at any one time was thus very similar during the two reigns (at least after 1389) and bearing in mind that the expansion in the number of king's esquires under Richard only came in the last two years of the reign, then for most of the period under discussion the number of king's esquires was also quite similar. Should we assume, therefore, that the *raison d'être* of the king's knights and esquires under Henry IV was the same as under Richard? Broadly speaking, the answer is yes. There are nevertheless some important differences between the retaining policy followed by Henry and that followed by Richard.

The first question to consider is the geographical distribution of Henry's knights. Including the chamber knights and household officers, Henry's knights numbered 166. Twenty of these were foreigners and for one of the king's English knights (Richard de Langyn) I have failed to discover where his local interests lay, but this is probably irrelevant anyway as Langyn was a doctor of laws and this is almost certainly why Henry retained him.[105] This leaves a total of 145 knights. Using the same regional divisions as for Richard's knights, the picture for Henry's knights is as follows: from the south-east came forty-eight, roughly the same proportion as under Richard, about a third of the total; from the west country came twelve, from the west midlands four, from Wales two, and from the Welsh Marches nine (of whom five were from Hereford, and four from Shropshire); from the north midlands there were twenty-five, from Yorkshire twenty-five, from the north-west eight, and from the four northern counties, twelve. Thus a rough division between north and south reveals that seventy-five of Henry's knights came from the northern half of the country (as compared with sixty-five of Richard's 177 knights), whereas seventy came from the southern half (compared to 112 under Richard). This bias towards the north under Henry and towards the south under Richard is the most striking difference in geographical terms between the knightly retinues of the two kings, but it is far from surprising. The duchy of Lancaster lands were situated for the most part in the north midlands, Yorkshire and of course Lancashire, and it was from these counties that Henry and his father had drawn many of their followers before 1399, so naturally the connections were continued.[106] Certain counties were particularly well represented in the king's affinity, most notably Yorkshire with twenty-five, but also Northumberland and Norfolk with ten each, Lincolnshire with nine, Suffolk with eight, Nottinghamshire with seven, Devon with six, and Derbyshire with five. The figure for Derbyshire may not sound high, but according to Dr Wright there were only eight knights in Derbyshire in 1434, so they were certainly well represented with the king.[107] The ten from Northumberland is also impressive. Eight of these were already king's knights by 1402, probably either because of their connections with the Percies (still loyal at this time, and very influential with the king), or because of the Scottish border warfare, which made it important for the king to favour the local gentry. Robert Umfraville, for example, was a border warlord of renown and (before 1403) a follower of the Percies. He was initially retained by Henry on a temporary basis to defend the border, and having distinguished himself by defeating a Scottish force in September 1400, his temporary contract was cancelled in December 1402, and he became a king's knight with an annuity of £40 at the exchequer. Henry's generosity to Umfraville was repaid when the latter remained loyal to him against the Percies in both 1403 and 1405, and following this second rebellion the king further rewarded him with some forfeited Percy estates in Northumberland.[108]

As to the other counties which provided Henry with a larger number of knights than usual, there are two probable explanations: either they were counties in which the king held extensive estates, or they were counties (like Hereford under Richard II) from which one or more of the king's closest friends came, and these men brought others in their wake. From Norfolk, for example, came Thomas Erpingham and John Straunge (there were also extensive duchy estates in the north of the county); Thomas Swynford and Ralph Rochefort came from Lincolnshire, and two of Ralph's brothers, John and Henry, became king's knights too; Thomas Rempston came from Nottinghamshire, and Richard Grey, Roger Leche and the esquire John Curson were all from Derbyshire; Robert Chalons, the chamber knight, was from Devon; there is no obvious explanation for the high number of Suffolk knights, but it was a large and heavily-populated county.

But it is the twenty-five knights from Yorkshire which is especially striking. The royal affinity in Yorkshire played a vital role during Henry's reign, as has been amply demonstrated by Professor Ross. The king at this time had 'incomparably the greatest affinity in Yorkshire', an affinity based not only on the king's knights but also on the great Yorkshire barons such as Lords Roos and Furnivall.[109] The king's ability to control Yorkshire was the key to his successes against the Percies, for they too had extensive estates in the county, and a number of the Yorkshire gentry were tied to them both by tradition and by indentures of retainer. All three of the 'Percy' rebellions (in 1403, 1405 and 1408) were centred in Yorkshire, the idea being, apparently, that if Yorkshire could be controlled, the northern counties would present no problem, and the rebels would be close enough to strike rapidly towards the south-east and the capital.[110] From the very beginning of the reign, Henry had a substantial following in the county and within six months of his accession, twelve Yorkshiremen were already king's knights, and by the time of the first Percy rebellion in July 1403 the number was seventeen. For several of these men, the rebellion was their moment of decision. Gerard Salvayn had been retained by the earl of Northumberland since 1385; he had also been a king's knight since November 1399. Richard Tempest was also a Percy retainer with an annuity of 20 marks, but he was not a king's knight.[111] Yet it was Salvayn who rebelled, both in 1403 and 1405, and Tempest who stayed loyal and helped the king to suppress the 1403 rebellion. Within a month Tempest was rewarded, becoming a king's knight with an annuity at the exchequer. He also remained loyal in 1405, and was granted lands in Yorkshire by the king.[112] Salvayn was lucky enough to be pardoned both in 1403 and in 1405, and in 1408 he remained loyal.[113] He was not the only lucky one. William Fulthorpe, also from Yorkshire, had been attached to the king since 1399, but he too rebelled and was pardoned in 1403. Like Salvayn, Fulthorpe was a Percy retainer, as was the Cheshire knight William Stanley, who also rebelled. The latter too was pardoned, and became a king's knight soon after the suppression of the revolt. But others were less lucky: the Cheshire knight Hugh Browe, and the Yorkshire knight John Colville del Dale rebelled in 1403 and 1405 respectively, and both were executed. The fact that both of these men had been formally retained for life by the king (which few of Henry's knights were) may have had something to do with this.[114]

Perhaps the most remarkable story, however, is William Clifford's. The Cliffords were really a Westmorland family, but they also had extensive lands around Skipton-on-Craven in Yorkshire. At this time, during the minority of his nephew John (the heir to the Clifford lordship), Sir William was the effective head of the family. He had been retained by Richard II in 1397, but within two months of Henry's accession he was again being described as a king's knight.[115] His first loyalty, however, was to himself, and his second was to the earl of Northumberland. He joined the rebellion of 1403 and after the battle of

Shrewsbury he continued to hold out in the north, as the ringleader of a small but powerful group of Percy adherents who occupied several castles through the winter of 1403–4.[116] At this time he had a great stroke of luck when William Serle, a former esquire of Richard II's chamber who had fled to Scotland in 1399 and busied himself with trying to stir up revolts against Henry, came to Clifford looking for support. Serle was wanted by the king for treason. Clifford held him and used him to bargain with the king. Eventually Henry agreed to pardon Clifford, and even agreed to make him guardian of Hotspur's son, and to give him 4,000 marks for this out of Hotspur's forfeited goods, on condition that Serle was delivered up to the king. Clifford duly accompanied Northumberland to his reconciliation with Henry at Pontefract in July 1404, and handed over Serle, who suffered a horrible death.[117] Clifford still had the temerity to complain that he had not received his full 4,000 marks. In the following year he rebelled again, but was once more pardoned, and was this time granted various lands in Cumberland forfeited by the earl of Northumberland. In 1408 he rebelled for a third time, perhaps on the assumption that this was the easiest way to win favours from the king. His wife was Ann, daughter and coheiress of Thomas Lord Bardolf, one of the ringleaders of the 1408 rebellion, which perhaps provides another reason for his involvement in this last revolt. Yet again he survived, was pardoned, and apparently had little difficulty in securing his wife's share of his executed father-in-law's inheritance.[118] He remained (in name) a king's knight, and under Henry V he served as constable of Bordeaux and as a diplomat of distinction before his death in 1418.[119]

The story of William Clifford indicates just how liberally some men interpreted the term 'king's knight'. Perhaps too it indicates how little control Henry IV exercised in the far north of the country, for the Cliffords were the dominant family in Westmorland, and for this reason perhaps Henry was prepared to be lenient to Sir William. But Yorkshire was much more important than Westmorland, and despite the disloyalty of a few of Henry's Yorkshire knights in 1403 and 1405, there is no doubt that the king's large and powerful following in the county ultimately paid dividends. Several of the local gentry played a vital part in the suppression of the revolts there: notably Peter Bukton, Ralph Euyr (whose lands were spread across the Yorkshire-Durham border), Alexander de Lounde, Henry FitzHugh, and Thomas Rokeby, who as sheriff was responsible for raising and leading the force which finally defeated Northumberland and ended his life at Bramham Moor on 19 February 1408.[120] All these men received rewards for their endeavours, usually in the form of confiscated rebel estates, or sometimes increased annuities.[121] And it was not just the Yorkshire gentry who proved their worth at these times of crisis: Henry's strong following in the north midlands (where many of the Duchy lands were) was also important, with king's knights such as John Everyngham from Lincolnshire, Richard Stanhope from Nottinghamshire, and Walter Blount of Derbyshire (who died with the king at Shrewsbury in 1403), all active in the fight against the Percies.[122]

It is in Yorkshire and the north midlands that we see one of the major differences between Henry's and Richard's knightly retinues: fifty (thirty-four percent) of Henry's knights came from these areas, as compared with twenty-eight (sixteen percent) of Richard's. The other really striking difference is in the west midlands and the Welsh border area, extending up into the north-west. From these areas (including Wales itself) Richard had drawn a total of fifty-five of his knights (thirty-one percent), whereas Henry drew only twenty-three (sixteen percent). This area of course includes both Hereford and Cheshire, the two counties from which Richard had retained more knights than from any others. Nevertheless, considering the immense problem posed by the Welsh revolt throughout his reign, it is surprising that Henry did not enlist the support of more of the local gentry to his cause. The result perhaps was a certain amount of backlash from Richard's reign. For Cheshire, this is a well-known fact. Having lost their status of 'most-favoured county' (as well as their annuities) in 1399, the men of Cheshire were active in support of the earls' rebellion of 1400 as well as the 1403 rebellion.[123] The men of Hereford may well have felt similarly and only two of Richard's Hereford knights became Henry IV's knights (Thomas Clanvow and John de Eylesford). Those Hereford gentry who *were* favoured by Henry were men who had not been favoured by Richard, men like John Greyndour and John Oldcastle, who stood much higher in the king's esteem than Clanvow or Eylesford[124] and it is perhaps logical to expect that there would be resentment against the man who had replaced the king under whom so many of the local gentry had found favour and fortune. Indeed, with a few notable exceptions (such as Greyndour and Oldcastle, and the king's esquires David Gam and Maredudd ap Madoc),[125] the whole Welsh problem was dealt with largely by men who were outsiders to the region. Even a man like Richard Arundel, a knight of Henry's chamber who was extremely active in the Welsh war and was sheriff of Hereford on three separate occasions, actually came from Northumberland, and held little or no land in Hereford.[126] If the attempt to suppress Glendower and his followers is seen as an 'outside job', receiving rather half-hearted support from the somewhat disaffected border gentry, this may help to explain why it took so long and caused such problems.

The links established between the king and the gentry whom he retained in a particular county, or region, were both personal and collective. Richard II undoubtedly had 'special' connections with Cheshire and Hereford, just as Henry IV had with Yorkshire and the north midlands, and these special connections have emerged clearly in local studies of these areas. The case of Richard II and Cheshire is well-known and that of Henry IV and Yorkshire has already been discussed. Another interesting example is Derbyshire. Not one of the king's knights under Richard II came from Derbyshire. There was probably nothing deliberate about this, but the situation in the county under Richard must have been very different from that under Henry. Some of Henry's closest followers came from Derbyshire, men like Richard Grey of Codnor, Walter and John Blount, Roger Leche, and John Curson.[127] In her study of the Derbyshire gentry, Dr Wright has commented on just how personal relationships between them and the king were during Henry's reign, and how the king used his duchy patronage within the county to establish good relationships with the leading families there.[128] Working together in the service of the king, these leading families were able to dominate the affairs of the county. It was, very obviously, a situation which brought benefits to the king as well as to those whom he patronised.

Apart from the geographical differences, there was another important difference between Henry's following of knights and esquires and that of his predecessor. Whereas Richard had really expanded his retinue during the second half of his reign (and particularly, as far as the esquires were concerned, after 1397), it was during the first few years of his reign that Henry built up his. By May 1400, there were already sixty-one king's knights and by the end of 1406, 133 of the 146 English knights were already attached to the king (more than twenty had meanwhile died, however, so that the total number of Henry's knights, which was at its peak at this time, stood at around 110). Thus during the second half of the reign only thirteen more knights were attached to the king. The picture is very similar for the esquires: well over a hundred of the 140 or so king's esquires were already in the king's service by 1406, and most of these had been recruited during the first two years. There are probably two explanations for this. The first is that Henry had learned from his cousin (and perhaps from his father too) the value of a sizeable following, and set out rapidly to secure the support of leading members of the gentry in a way that Richard had only really done positively *after* the setbacks of 1387–8. There being doubts about his right to the throne, he perhaps hoped to forestall any similar events (in which, as it turned out, he was of course unsuccessful, although when crises did arise some of his followers repaid him handsomely). The second explanation is that, in both reigns, the retaining policy of the king was closely linked to political events. With Richard's reign, this is clearly the case, with bursts of retaining by the king following rapidly on the heels of, firstly, the political crisis of 1387–8, and secondly the king's *coup* of 1397. The same seems to be true under Henry and it is interesting to note, for example, that it was in February 1400 that the council advised that 'in each county of the realm a certain number of more sufficient and well-respected (*de bone fame*) men should be retained by the king and associated with the said commissions, and further charged to do their utmost to save the estate of the king and his people in their localities . . .'. The 'said commissions' were set up to deal with those who had been involved with the earls' rebellion in the previous month, and there can be little doubt that it was the rebellion which prompted such advice. The council also advised the king to pay annuities to each man thus retained, using the forfeitures from the rebellion as a fund.[129] Before the end of February, a further thirteen knights had been added to the king's retinue. There was a similar burst of retaining, particularly in the north, following the Percy rebellion of 1403. From *c.* 1406, however, the real period of unrest was over (the rebellion of 1408 was a much less serious affair than those of 1400, 1403 and

1405), and Henry probably no longer felt the need to recruit new men in large numbers. Moreover, the parliament of 1406 had finally impressed upon the king the need for economies, and the granting of annuities to large numbers of men was an expensive business. It is far from surprising that retaining by both kings was linked to political events, and it was novel only in the scale on which it was done. Edward II seems to have done much the same thing when, in an attempt to build up political and military support against Thomas of Lancaster, he made indentures of retinue with 'a majority of the leading magnates' (nineteen of them have survived in full or in summary) in 1316 and 1317.[130] The difference, however, is that whereas Edward II preferred to win the support of a (relatively) small number of great lords, both Richard II and Henry IV extended the system to a much larger number of lesser men. This is significant, and will be discussed further.[131]

The general composition and *raison d'être* of Henry's knightly retinue leave little doubt that many of the same considerations were at work as in Richard's reign. Once again, personal connections were of great importance but whereas under Richard it was clans of Burleys and Walweyns who found their way into the royal service, under Henry it was clans of Watertons and Rocheforts.[132] As far as pre-1399 connections can be established, at least seventy-nine of Henry's knights as king can be shown to have been retained either by his father, or by Richard II, or by Henry himself before he became king (and this figure is undoubtedly a minimum and may well have been considerably higher). Only seventeen of these knights were attached to Henry before 1399, but the more significant point is that twelve of these seventeen became chamber knights after Henry's succession. Twenty of the seventy-nine had been in John of Gaunt's retinue (of whom three became his son's chamber knights). But the most interesting fact is that no less than forty-two of Henry's knights (including six of his chamber knights and household officers) had also been Richard's knights. Some of these men had been close to Richard, Baldwin Bereford, for example, or William Elmham, George and Simon Felbridge, and Stephen Lescrope. Moreover, many of them were attached to Henry from very early in the reign as within six months of the revolution, exactly half of the forty-two were already Henry's knights. There was obviously something of a political balancing act here: those whom Richard had considered important enough to retain were also those whom Henry considered important enough to retain. There may also have been something of a geographical balancing act. Most of Henry's (and his father's) natural followers came from the northern half of the country, the Lancastrian areas of influence. Moreover, political events during the first few years of the reign tended to draw men from the north into the king's orbit. To balance this tendency, Henry needed to cultivate support among prominent members of the county establishments in.the southern shires, and many of those who were prominent here were those whom Richard had patronised. It is worth noting that of the thirty-nine English knights who feature in both kings' retinues (three of the forty-two were foreigners), twenty-five came from the southern half of the country, and fourteen from the north. Thus there seems to be a reversal of the situation under Richard: Richard's *natural* following (Cheshire excluded) was in the south, yet after 1389 he deliberately tried to win the support of more northerners; Henry's natural following, on the other hand, was in the north, and to counter-balance it he wooed former followers of Richard in the south.

This impression is reinforced when one looks at the sort of southern knights whom Henry was retaining. On the whole they were just that sort of prominent local administrator that Richard had retained in the northern counties after 1389. The most obvious examples are William Elmham in Suffolk, Edmund Thorpe in Norfolk, John Eylesford in Hereford, William Sturmy in Hampshire-Wiltshire, and Gerard Braybrook in Bedfordshire. Not surprisingly, men of a similar type in the northern counties were also retained by both Richard and Henry; men such as John Annesley in Nottinghamshire, Richard Redman in Yorkshire, and Gerard Heron in Northumberland. Indeed it is difficult to find men of this type (locally active) who were retained by Richard but not by Henry. There could be no clearer indication of a point which it is always important to bear in mind, that is that essentially the composition of the king's affinity (and most lords' affinities) reflected, rather than created, the realities of local politics. It was, perhaps, a point which Richard II forgot to bear in mind after 1397, but that is a subject which will be discussed later.[133] For the moment, it is worth noting that as his reign progressed, Henry also retained a good number of such men who had not been in Richard's retinue, mainly it seems because they had only really risen to prominence in their localities since the revolution: men such as John Arundel in Cornwall,[134] Thomas Broke in Somerset,[135] John Copuldyk in Lincolnshire,[136] Richard Stanhope in Nottinghamshire,[137] John Greynvill in Devon and Cornwall,[138] and Edward Benstede in Hertfordshire,[139] none of whom had any apparent Lancastrian connections before 1399 but who, as M.P.s, J.P.s, or sheriffs, brought themselves to the king's notice during the early years of the reign, and were subsequently retained by him.

All medieval knights were, in theory, fighting men, even if this was not always true in practice. As suggested above, there was probably within Richard II's knightly retinue a hard core of men, numbering perhaps forty, who were retained by the king primarily for their military ability.[140] The circumstances of Henry's reign were rather different from those of his cousin's. Almost throughout his reign, Henry was faced with the need to put armies in the field and maintain substantial garrisons, often on several fronts at the same time for the situations in Wales, on the Scottish border, in France, in Ireland, and at home, were unpredictable and volatile, and made it necessary for the king to have at hand a pool of fighting men who could be called upon, often at short notice, to bear arms in his service. The general impression afforded by Henry's knights is that they were considerably more likely to see action in the field as a consequence of their attachment to the king than had been the case for Richard's knights (and the same was true of the chamber knights).[141] On several occasions, Henry issued summonses to all those who held annuities from him to come and fight for him, as for the Scottish campaign of 1400, the Welsh campaigns of 1402, 1405 and 1407, and Clarence's French expedition of 1412–13.[142] It is only possible to speculate as to whether this meant that military ability loomed larger in the king's mind as a reason for retaining men, but it does at least seem likely. Well over half of Henry's knights were regularly employed by the king in warfare of one sort or another. Naturally, many of them developed their specialities: William Farringdon, Thomas Swynburn and Ralph Rochefort were generally employed on French affairs; John Stanley, Edward Perers, Stephen Lescrope and Gilbert de Kyghley in Ireland;[143] John Oldcastle, Richard Arundel, Thomas Carreu, John Greyndour, John Penres, and Rustin de Villa Nova in Wales; and Robert Umfraville and Thomas Gray of Wark on the Scottish border. The rather scrappy nature of the warfare in Henry's reign (which consisted largely of skirmishes, raids and rebellions rather than, for example, the planned and therefore documented campaigns of Richard's reign) makes it difficult to analyse the role of the king's knights in statistical terms, but it was undoubtedly considerable. The same is true for at least some of the king's esquires, such as James Clifford, David Gam, and the indestructible Janico Dartasso.[144]

Liveries and retaining

Henry IV, then, attached knights and esquires to his person for broadly similar reasons as Richard II did, even if the emphasis may have shifted slightly. There remains the question of 'king's knights' (and esquires) and life retaining under Henry. Richard, as noted earlier, only began systematically to retain his knights and esquires for life after 1389, and I have suggested that this was in part a consequence of the controversy over livery and maintenance in the years 1388–90.[145] For Henry's knights and esquires, the facts are as follows: of the 310 or so (166 knights and 140 esquires) men described as king's knights or esquires during the reign, only seventy-nine are described as having been retained for life, thirty-six of the knights, and forty-three of the esquires. This is almost certainly not the full number, but what is clear is that, firstly, in over-all terms the life retainers were in a minority, and, secondly, being a king's knight or esquire, and being a king's knight or esquire retained for life, could be recognisably different. Certain cases demonstrate this. Roger Trumpington, for example, became a king's knight with an annuity of £40 at the exchequer some time before February 1401: in that month, 'the king now, because he has retained Roger for life, grants him in augmentation of his estate, 100 marks yearly from Michaelmas last for life at the Exchequer.' Sir John Dabrichecourt was a former life retainer of John of Gaunt. He was described as a king's knight in February 1400 and granted various lands in Kent and Rutland which had been forfeited by supporters of Richard II. A year later, in February 1401, Dabrichecourt, 'whom the king has retained for life,' had his grant of these lands confirmed, because the original grant had been technically illegal on account of the fact that it made no mention of any grants which he was already receiving from the king.[146] Even more instructive is the case of the Scottish esquire Richard Maghlyn. In July 1408 Maghlyn was given protection for himself, his men, and his lands and goods in Berwickshire (now the Borders), because he had 'become the king's liege man and done homage to the king, by which the king has retained him as one of his esquires and has given to him the livery of the collar.'[147] Maghlyn, however, who had taken the dangerous step of switching his allegiance from Scotland to England, was not prepared to settle for a livery collar and the title of king's esquire, and about a year later he submitted a petition to the council which was discussed at a meeting on 18 August 1409. The council minutes for this day record that Maghlyn 'wishes to become English, finding sufficient security'. The king therefore had offered him 20 marks annually to be taken from the issues of the county of Yorkshire, 'if he wishes to agree to this'.[148] Evidently Maghlyn did agree, and eight days later he was granted his 20 marks on account of the fact that he had 'become the king's liege man and done homage and fealty to the king, and whom the king has for that cause retained for life'.[149]

This case provides an insight into a process which no doubt was repeated many times over. Maghlyn had his allegiance to offer—as well as more tangible things, no doubt, such as military assistance on the border—but in return he wanted an agreement which gave him a more permanent sort of security, both financial and personal. Henry was prepared to buy that allegiance, but he too wanted some guarantee that his money would not be wasted. Thus Maghlyn served in effect a probationary year as a king's esquire, and once this had been completed satisfactorily, Henry was prepared to offer more in the form of a life retaining contract, and an offer of 20 marks a year. Evidently Maghlyn regarded this as a satisfactory offer, but the phrasing of the council minute suggests that bargaining over the level of the fee was not uncommon. Henry had bought his man.

But just what had Henry bought? More to the point, perhaps, what had Maghlyn sold? Was Richard Maghlyn after August 1409 in a different relationship with the king from that of the previous year, and can it be said in general that life-retainers were more closely bound to their master than mere king's knights? Before answers to these questions can be attempted, further evidence needs to be considered. The most striking point about the knights and esquires retained by the king for life is that they were nearly all retained during the first two years of the reign. Of the thirty-six knights, all but four had already been retained for life by October 1401; the remaining four were all foreign knights, and all were retained for life between January and November 1402. Of the forty-three esquires, thirty-five had already been retained for life by October 1401, and of the remaining eight, retained between 1402 and 1409 (Maghlyn was the last), four were foreigners. Thus after 1401 the king stopped retaining English knights for life, and virtually stopped retaining English esquires for life.

The next point to consider is the type of man whom the king retained for life. It is immediately apparent that a foreigner was much more likely to be retained for life than an English knight or esquire. There were twenty foreign knights in Henry's retinue, and eleven of them were life retainers: also, ten of the king's esquires who were retained for life were foreigners. This is probably quite readily explicable in terms of the security which these men desired for some of them had left their native countries for the service of the English king (such as John Hirseborn, Alfonse de Monterre, and John de Robessart), others had switched allegiance from their feudal lords (such as the Scotsmen Gawyn de Dunbarre, son of the earl of March, and Richard Maghlyn), and they wanted a more formal attachment with a guarantee of protection as well as income for life, which a life retaining contract presumably gave them. But what of the English knights and esquires retained for life? One point which stands out clearly is that they included very few men who were on close personal terms with Henry as among the knights, only John Tiptoft (the one chamber knight among them) and Henry FitzHugh were close to the king and among the esquires, only Robert Waterton and perhaps Richard del Brugge, who was Lancaster king of arms.[150] There was evidently no need for the king to retain his personal friends for life, indeed it might be that the opposite applies. Was life retaining, from the king's point of view, one way of applying pressure on a man whose loyalty was in doubt? It is interesting to note that twelve of those retained for life by Henry had formerly been retainers of Richard II's, but even so that leaves a lot of men still unaccounted for. More significant, perhaps, is that although several of the king's knights joined the rebellions against him during the first half of the reign, only two of them were life retainers but whereas the others were pardoned, both the life retainers were executed (Hugh Browe in 1403, and John Colville del Dale in 1405). This is perhaps an indication that although the reasons why the king decided to retain a man for life were varied, once that contract had been entered into, a firm expectation of loyalty ensued.

If we look further afield for reasons why the king retained for life some knights and esquires but not others, it may be that at least part of the answer lies in the livery laws enacted in the parliaments of this period. These were very much concerned with the king's retinue as well as with the retinues of lords. Parliamentary enactments and other sources in the period from 1377 to 1413 mention three types of livery: livery of hats, or hoods (*chaperons*), livery of cloth, and livery of signs, or badges (*signes, signa*). Contemporaries distinguished clearly between them, and the rules governing their distribution were significantly different. For example, when describing the statute passed in the parliament of October 1399, Adam of Usk reported that, 'it was ordained that the lords of the kingdom should not give their suit or livery of cloth [*pannorum*], or badges [*signorum*], or more especially of hoods [*capiciorum*], to anyone, except to their familiars [*familiaribus*] dwelling constantly with them, on account of several seditions in the kingdom caused by this.'[151] In fact the chronicler reported the statute incorrectly, but nevertheless the distinction which he makes is clear. They seem to have meant just what they said: liveries of hoods were, obviously, worn on the head; liveries of cloth were suits, either half-length of full-length;[152] badges were much smaller, probably not dissimilar to those delicate little badges of the white hart added to the figures of the angels in the Wilton Diptych. There are numerous references to them at this time, indicating that they could be worn either on the sleeve, the chest, or round the neck. If worn round the neck, the badges were often called collars, but for the purposes of legislation collars were equated with badges which might be very intricate, sometimes worth £20 or more, but were probably on the whole much more rough and ready than this.[153]

These liveries were used for different purposes, and were subjected to different rules. It is important to remember that at no time during this period was the practice of retaining itself the subject of complaint; the complaints related to the giving of liveries, and to maintenance, whether by liveried gangs or not. The first statute in this period to deal with the question was that of 1377, when the commons complained that men of lesser estate, by which they may have meant knights but certainly did not mean lords, were giving liveries to men from whom they then demanded money in return for a promise 'to maintain any reasonable or unreasonable quarrel'. This seems to refer to livery of hoods, for in his reply the king agreed that no livery of *chaperons*, 'or otherwise', should in future be given for the maintenance of quarrels.[154] In the parliament of September 1388 the commons requested that all liveries of signs, 'and all other lesser liveries, such as *chaperons*', should be abolished entirely, but this was not granted, and hoods were not specifically mentioned in the Ordinance of 1390.[155] Despite Adam of Usk's assertion, hoods are not mentioned either in the 1399 statute, but they are in the statutes of 1406 and 1411. The latter is virtually a verbatim repetition of the former, and on each occasion reference was made back to the statute of 1377.[156] The conclusions to be drawn from this are, firstly, that hoods were second-class ('lesser') liveries, distributed not by lords but by lesser men, and, secondly, that they were not the main subject of controversy at this time. Since a statute concerning them had been passed in 1377, there was little that successive commons could do but ask that it be enforced, to which both Richard II and Henry IV were happy to accede.

Liveries of cloth, or suits (*secta*) of livery as they were sometimes called, were first specifically mentioned in a commons petition to the parliament of January 1390. The commons then requested that their distribution should be restricted to genuine household servants, 'parentz et alliez' (which probably means relatives and kinsmen), and officers such as stewards, councillors and bailiffs. There was however no mention of liveries of cloth on the parliamentary statute roll, or in the Ordinance of May 1390. Nevertheless, when liveries of cloth were again discussed in the parliament of October 1399, much the same position was adopted: it was now enacted by statute that liveries of cloth were only to be given to the household servants (*meynalx*), officers, and councillors of a lord. The same formula was agreed in the parliaments of January 1401, 1406 and

1411, when there were complaints that the statute was not being enforced.[157] It was thus quite clear that the basic position on liveries of cloth was that they were to be used only for those who actually served the giver in a specific capacity, and not for those who were merely retained by him (kinsmen too were now excluded). As long as this was observed, no social distinctions were drawn. Guilds and fraternities were also prohibited from distributing them and, more importantly for our purposes, the king was specifically prohibited from distributing them to any but his household servants, his officers, councillors, justices, chancery clerks, and barons of the exchequer (Richard II, perhaps had been distributing them rather too widely). Finally, it is worth noting that when the 1399 statute was reiterated in the parliament of 1406, it was said that various bannerets, knights and esquires were 'jointly and severally' distributing liveries of cloth, 'sometimes to 300 yeomen, sometimes to 200, sometimes to more or less', in order to maintain their quarrels. This may have been a way of getting round the statute, for much of the efficacy of the system for enforcing it depended on being able to identify the giver of the livery, who was generally considered to be the real culprit. For groups of men simply to adopt liveries might have been (technically) a way of by-passing the law. At any rate, if a legal loophole had been discovered here, it was now closed, for the punishment for contravening the regulation was now extended to receivers as well as givers of liveries of cloth.

The real point at issue in the parliaments of this period was the giving of liveries of badges or of signs (also known sometimes as liveries of company, or marks of fellowship). In the parliament of 1384 the commons 'complained bitterly' that these were being distributed by lords in their localities in order to establish petty tyrannies over their neighbours, but were silenced by John of Gaunt's rejoinder that 'the complaint was expressed in too general terms', and by his famous remark that every lord was capable of disciplining his own retainers.[158] In the Merciless Parliament of February 1388 the attack switched to the king and the five Appellees were accused of having persuaded the king to give livery badges to a great number of people, 'as had not previously been done by any of the kings his predecessors, in order to have power to perform their false treasons.'[159] The complaints of 1384 (concerning the lords) and February 1388 (concerning the king) were merged in the Cambridge parliament of 1388, when the commons requested that 'all liveries called badges [*signes*], as well of our lord the king as of other lords . . . shall be abolished.' Those who wore such badges were emboldened to oppress the people, 'and it is certainly the boldness inspired by their badges that makes them unafraid to do these things and more besides.' Once again the lords were 'anxious to dispose of the generalised nature of the complaint', but this time the commons were not cowed and 'were firm in their demand that if the lords wanted to have peace and quiet in the kingdom they must drop the use of badges altogether'. It was at this point that the king intervened and offered to discard his own badges if the lords would follow suit. This, according to the chronicler, pleased the commons greatly, which is hardly surprising in view of Richard's attempt to use his badges to build up support during the latter half of 1387.[160] The lords, however, rejected this idea, and eventually the king said that they should be allowed to go on using their badges until the next parliament, when the whole matter would be reviewed.

In fact a more specific remedy had been suggested in the Cambridge Parliament, as is made clear in the records of the next (January 1390) parliament. In January 1390, the commons petitioned that they had complained of the problem of livery badges in September 1388, and had asked the king to provide a remedy, saying that they would abide by any judgement given in parliament, but this judgement had yet to be delivered. 'Nevertheless,' they went on, 'the king and lords of parliament have ordained such a remedy', (which the commons then detailed) 'saving always, that if the said ordinance is not a sufficient remedy, that the said commons can remain in their ancient stay of judgement until the next parliament.'[161] In other words, the king and lords had provided a provisional remedy in the Cambridge Parliament (by ordinance, not by statute), which was to be in effect for a trial period until the next parliament. This ordinance specified the general rules which were to govern the distribution of livery badges for the next decade for although later modified, the basic principles remained similar, and it is important to be clear as to what they were. Firstly, no person of whatever condition could wear a lord's livery badge unless he was retained for life by proper indenture and secondly, no person of lesser estate than an esquire could wear a lord's livery badge unless he was a genuine household servant of that lord. Having been reminded of this provisional remedy in the parliament of January 1390, the king said he would take the advice of his council and do what seemed best for the ease and quiet of his people. The result was the well-known Ordinance of 12 May 1390.[162] This essentially repeated the terms of the provisional agreement of September 1388, but with one important modification, that no person below the rank of banneret was to be allowed to distribute livery badges at all. As already noted, Richard II moved rapidly to put the ordinance into effect as far as it concerned his own affinity, either by pulling more men into his household, or by giving life-retaining contracts to knights and esquires who were not members of his household.[163]

It is evident that the statute was by no means entirely effective, however, for in the parliaments of both January 1393 and February 1397 there were petitions claiming that lesser persons (artisans, as well as lesser landholders) were wearing livery badges. The petition of 1397 formed a part of the bill drawn up by Thomas Haxey, which strongly criticised the royal household, and this may be significant for Richard had by now begun to distribute his livery of the white hart, which was apparently worn by lesser men as well as knights and esquires, and it is by no means clear that all these men were life retainers of the king.[164] It was only after 1397, however, that the king really began to abuse his power and to develop a large retinue of liveried lesser servants, notably, the Cheshire *vigilia*.[165] This was in clear contravention of the Ordinance of 1390, and is reflected in the much stricter legislation concerning livery badges enacted in the parliament of October 1399.

The statute of 1399 was the high water mark of anti-livery legislation.[166] Lords of any degree were now completely prohibited from giving livery badges, thus allowing them only liveries of cloth, which were at the same time strictly regulated.[167] In taking such a drastic step, it is likely that those concerned were probably motivated above all by the behaviour of some of Richard's closest followers among the lords, notably the earls of Rutland, Kent, Huntingdon and Somerset, and Thomas Lord Despenser, for in this same parliament they were accused of having committed numerous oppressions 'under colour of her Lordeshipes', and it was agreed 'that thei, ne none of hem, gyf no Liverees of Sygnes' ever again.[168] The only livery badge which was to be permitted from now on was the king's; he could give it to any lord, or to any knight or esquire who was a member of his household or one of his life retainers but the knights and esquires were only to wear them in the king's presence, and in particular they were not to wear them in their own localities. Moreover, even the king was now prohibited from giving his livery badge to anyone below the rank of esquire which was surely a reaction to Richard's Cheshiremen.[169]

The legislation of October 1399 thus relates very clearly to the political events of the previous few years. Moreover, it was not the end of the matter. In the angry parliament of January 1401, according to the parliament roll, the commons once again demanded that all livery badges should be prohibited excepting that of the king (the 'Coler'), which was to be subjected to the same rules as in 1399. This at least is the contemporary record of the proceedings, but a curious little episode recorded in the roll of the January 1404 parliament strongly suggests that the commons had actually asked for rather more than this in 1401. In 1404 the speaker, Sir Arnold Savage, who had also been speaker in the parliament of 1401, said in his opening address that he had heard that the king had been informed that, on a previous occasion, when he was before the king and lords in parliament, he had 'of his own authority, and without the assent of his companions', demanded that all livery badges should be abolished (including that of the king). Savage now denied that he had ever made such a request. On the contrary, he declared, he had asked that the king and Prince Henry should be allowed to distribute their liveries in the manner described in the statute. This, as will be seen, can only apply to the statute of 1401, and there is no doubt that the alleged incident referred to can only have taken place in the parliament of 1401.[170] Despite Savage's denial, it is difficult not to believe that there was an element of truth in the story (even if the idea did not come from Savage himself), and that what at least some members of the commons had hoped to achieve in 1401 was the prohibition of all livery badges, including the king's (it is worth remembering that this is also what the commons had in mind in September 1388). In fact, the legislation of 1401 represented something of a victory for the king, for he gained two concessions as compared with the 1399 statute. Firstly, the king insisted that his knights and esquires should be permitted to wear his livery badge not only in his presence, but also when they were coming to or going from his household and secondly, he insisted that Prince Henry should be permitted to use his livery of the swan in the same way that he (the king) used his livery of the collar.[171] There was one point on which the commons stood firm, however, when they reminded Henry that he had already (in 1399) agreed to abolish his valets' and yeomen's livery of the crescent with the star (the equivalent to Richard's 'lesser' livery for his Cheshire archers), and asked him now to put this into effect.

After January 1404, the controversy over livery badges seems to have subsided, at least as a subject of discussion in parliament. The statutes of 1406, 1411 and 1429 dealt only with liveries of cloth and *chaperons*. Not until 1468 does there appear to have been any further legislation on badges, and the fact that these had now once again become a point at issue is confirmed by Edward IV's denunciation of the 'giving of tokens, liveries, signs . . . ' in 1472.[172] Whether this indicates that the problem really did subside, or that the legislation of 1399 and 1401 was considered to be sufficient, or that discussion of the problem now moved away from the arena of parliament, is difficult to say. But the commons were not usually slow to complain even when there were already sufficient statutes to cope (in theory) with this sort of problem, and it does seem likely that livery *badges* were not a major issue after the early years of Henry IV's reign, even if the evils which they symbolised were.[173] Why, then, were they so important in this period? And what was the thinking behind the legislation concerning them?

The controversy over liveries in this period has usually been seen primarily in social terms, as a part of the more general problem of noble and gentry 'gangs' and the difficulties encountered in enforcing effective law and order. As far as liveries of cloth and of hoods were concerned this certainly seems to be the correct interpretation, but they were not the real point at issue at this time; badges were. When the commons raised the question of livery badges in the parliaments of 1388, they seem to have been as much concerned with the king's use of his livery badges as with the lords' use of theirs, and the same is true of the legislation of 1399 and 1401. It is indeed striking that the two periods which witnessed new legislation on livery badges (1388–90 and 1399–1401) both followed immediately after attempts by Richard II to use livery badges to extend his following at a time of political crisis. Richard's behaviour at both these times, therefore, had served to divert the argument away from its more 'social' origins and to give it a pressing political force. Would it be justified, therefore, to see this as essentially 'political' legislation?

To an extent, this seems true, but only to an extent. There were, after all, several viewpoints from which the problem could be approached. From the commons' point of view, what was objectionable was the power which the distribution of livery badges gave to lords who had a mind to establish 'local tyrannies' and when the king used the same system to bolster up a more widespread tyranny (in alliance with his chief cronies among the lords), he became the principal offender against law and justice in the kingdom. From the king's point of view, what was objectionable was the power which the system gave to lords who had a mind to rebel against the king.[174] There is no direct evidence that the Lords Appellant distributed badges to their followers in 1387, but it is very likely that they did, and Richard's attempt to do the same was probably in direct imitation of their methods. The Percies certainly saw it as a way of building up support against the king quickly. The earl of Westmorland reported to the council in 1403 that the Percy supporters were gathering in the north, 'the crescent on their sleeves', and early in the following year the constable of Bamburgh castle wrote to the king that William Clifford and other knights were still holding out in Berwick, Alnwick and Warkworth castles, and 'the said knights have procured to themselves a great multitude of your men, and given them the livery of the crescents, and have sworn to keep [the castles] by force against you and all others.' (The crescent moon was the Percy livery.)[175] It is interesting to note that it was for this offence that Northumberland was convicted in the parliament of January 1404. He begged the king's mercy for breaking various laws, 'and specially of gederyng of power, and gevyng of liverees'; the lords decided that what he had done could not be construed as treason or felony, but only as trespass. Their decision, according to the official record, was based on an examination of the treason statute of 1352 and the livery statutes of 1399 and 1401 (either of which would have served the purpose).[176]

It is not surprising, therefore, that Richard was prepared to renounce his own livery badges in 1388 so long as the lords would do the same. He had very little to lose and much to gain from such an agreement. No wonder, too, that the lords refused to countenance this, or that the commons, who saw the problem from a different angle, were delighted. Henry IV, though, did much better for himself in 1399 and 1401 than Richard had. He was, after all, in a strong position at the outset of his reign; he had just been recognised as king and was riding high on a wave of reaction to Richard's rule. His ability to secure the abolition of lords' livery badges while preserving his own must have delighted him, and the commons, mindful of the depredations of Richard's chief supporters among the *duketti*, were happy to go along with him. Nevertheless, as a precaution against any possible revival of a royal following along the lines of the Cheshire *vigilia*, he had to promise to renounce his lesser livery of the crescent and star. By 1401, the commons were apparently not so convinced of the necessity for royal livery badges, and it says something for Henry's political management that he actually managed to emerge from this parliament with further concessions on the subject (even if he was again urged to abolish his lesser livery).

The fact that the controversy surrounding livery badges was so clearly related to political disaffection (in 1387–90 and in 1397–1404) supports the view that the king saw such legislation primarily in political terms. He hoped that it would nullify, or at least restrict, the ability of his enemies to gather support against him in times of trouble. When livery badges once again became a matter for dispute during Edward IV's reign, it may well be, as Professor Lander has hinted, that the same considerations were foremost in the king's mind.[177] This does raise a further question for if this legislation was intended by the king to deal with a political problem, might it be quietly ignored at times when no danger threatened? Were the lords prepared to accept permanently

such a restriction on their power? As early as July 1404, the king issued a somewhat ambiguous directive, suggesting that the matter was not as clear-cut as the
legislation might suggest. This was on 5 July, when further rebellions were brew-
ing, and Northumberland had still not made his final peace with the king.[178] The
directive concerned livery badges ('livery with mark of fellowship'), and ordered
that no person whatsoever was to wear these, 'save only that of the king'
which was in accordance with the statute but it then went on, 'as in divers
statutes and ordinances made in divers parliaments of the king and of former
kings it is contained that no knight (or other person) shall wear such livery *save
under certain conditions therein mentioned.*' The phrase 'such livery' clearly refers
to livery badges in general, not just the king's. But the final conditional clause
certainly implies that the prohibition on lords' livery badges was not absolute,
despite the apparent finality of the statutes of 1399 and 1401. Further research
would be needed to see just how zealously the acts of 1399 and 1401 were
enforced in subsequent years. The commons would certainly have been keen to
see them enforced, and since J.P.s, who were drawn from much the same social
group as the commons, had been given the power to hear and determine cases
arising from these laws, they did in theory have the ability to do so.[179] If, however, the king was only prepared to put his weight behind the statutes when it
suited him to do so, they probably found it very difficult in practice.

If we return, then, to the question of why Richard II and Henry IV retained
some men for life and not others, it is at once apparent that the period during
which these two kings were systematically retaining men for life coincides
almost exactly with the period during which livery badges were under discussion in parliament. Richard II only indulged in widespread life retaining from
1389 onwards, while Henry IV virtually ceased to do so after 1401. Yet the
rules which linked liveries to life retaining were not altered in 1401. It is difficult, therefore, to establish a *prima facie* causal link between the legislation of
1401 and the virtual cessation of life retaining by the king. What is more significant is simply the fact that the whole question of liveries was such a controversial one during the first two years of Henry's reign. At a time when the
subject (not only of livery badges, but also of liveries of cloth) was very much
in the air, and in view of the unpopularity of his predecessor's retaining policy
during the last two years of his reign, Henry probably thought it better to be
seen to be sticking (at least partially) to the rules. A second consideration was a
financial one as a king's life retainers seem to have expected higher rewards
than those who simply became his knights or esquires without a life contract.
It was in the parliament of 1401 that the first real financial crisis of the reign
occurred, and this too may have influenced the king against life retaining. A
third consideration was political: Henry was keen to build up support early in
his reign, and the offer of life contracts may have been one way of doing this.
The execution of Hugh Browe and John Colville del Dale suggests that the
king expected a greater degree of loyalty from his life retainers than from his
other knights and esquires as the rebellion of a life retainer was evidently a

more heinous crime than the rebellion of an 'ordinary' king's knight or esquire. And this emphasis on life retaining at the beginning of the reign is symptomatic of the king's wider retaining policy, with the great majority of his knights and esquires being recruited to his retinue during the first, more violent and more politically fragile, half of the reign. Finally, there was a personal consideration in that there were certain men, or certain types of men, who either required the security of a life contract (such as foreigners), or on whom the king wished to 'lean' a little in order to encourage them to remain loyal (like some of Richard's former knights and esquires, perhaps, or like the Lancastrian retainers whom Richard retained 'to stay with the king *only*' in the spring of 1399).[180]

It is likely that the seventy-nine known life-retaining contracts which the king entered into with knights and esquires during his reign are all related to one or more of these four considerations. As with the wider retaining policy of the king, it is not always easy to fit the reason to the man, but reasons there must have been. The recruitment of the king's retinue was a question of balancing the disadvantages (basically financial) against the advantages (political and personal). Money alone, of course, could not buy men's allegiance. The first loyalty of most men was to themselves. Even with life retainers, it was sometimes recognised quite explicitly that their second loyalty was divisible. For example, when Henry retained the Scottish knight Sir John Bothwell for life in May 1402, the conditions of the contract were that Bothwell would take an oath on the gospels, in the presence of the council, that he would be 'faithful to the king and his heirs against all people except the king's adversary of Scotland and his sons, with none of whom will he go against the king and his successors, and he will never reveal the king's counsel, and if he knows anything against the king or the realm he will certify it.'[181] What Bothwell had promised, therefore, was support for the English king in all matters, except if it came to a direct clash between the king of Scotland (his feudal lord) and the king of England (his bastard feudal lord), in which case he could guarantee no more than his neutrality. (There was nothing novel in such clashes of allegiance. A classic example comes from the year 1103, when Count Robert of Flanders, the feudal vassal of the king of France, entered into a contract to provide several hundred knights for Henry I of England, 'saving his fealty to the king of France'. If, however, he was summoned by the French king to join an invasion of England, 'the Count would bring as small a contingent as he could so as not to incur the forfeiture of his fief by the King of France'.)[182] The case of John Bothwell is perhaps untypical, but, as already seen, the rebellions of 1403 and 1405 created desperate problems of double allegiance for some of the king's retainers.

Even if Richard II had tried on occasions to ensure the first loyalty of some of those whom he retained by employing an unambiguous form of words, notably in 1387–9 and 1399, there was in reality little that words could do to overcome the problem of double allegiance.[183] Henry seems never to have attached such clauses to his retaining contracts. There are only two examples from his reign of phraseology which could be construed in this way. Firstly, in December 1399, the king retained for life the esquire Robert Lamplogh and granted him an annuity of £40, 'provided that he be not retained by any other person than the king'. The second case concerns the long-serving Lancastrian Henry FitzHugh, who was retained for life by the king in November 1399. Thirteen years later the king granted FitzHugh £100 a year from the Darcy wardship, because 'at his command the said Henry has laboured at divers times ... without fee or wages except an annuity of 100 marks granted to him by the king by letters patent, of which 750 marks are due to him, and because he is retained with no other lord than the king ...'[184] Lamplogh was a man of no great significance, and it seems more likely that in both these cases the reasoning behind the phraseology was financial rather than political. According to McFarlane, Henry V at the outset of his reign 'confirmed all royal grants with the proviso "as long as he be not retained by anyone else".'[185] McFarlane assumed that this was an attempt by the king to secure the undivided loyalty of his annuitants, but the fact that Henry V adopted this policy *when confirming royal grants* might suggest that the king was telling the man concerned that he could continue to receive his grant from the king as long as he was unable to supplement his income from another source, but if he were able to find another lord to patronise him, the royal grant would cease and the exchequer be relieved accordingly. The cases of Lamplogh and FitzHugh may well fall into the same category. In FitzHugh's case, it is rather a statement of fact than a condition, and the financial overtones are clear but quite why Lamplogh should have been singled out for such treatment is not clear unless it was because of that very insignificance which makes it virtually impossible to find out anything about his career. (The fact that Henry's grant to Lamplogh was a confirmation of an earlier grant from the deceased duke of Norfolk adds further weight to the probability that it was financial rather than political considerations which prompted the addition of this clause.) The similar examples from Richard's reign do seem to be different, however: we should probably distinguish between phrases like 'retained for life, to serve [the king] above all others' (as was John Stanley in 1389), which do seem to relate to allegiance, and 'provided that he be not retained by anyone else', which may well not. Political realities had to be taken into account. Most men were probably wary of entering into contracts which were too binding (even life retaining contracts, perhaps), and which might in future restrict them both personally and financially. There was nothing to be gained from pushing men where they didn't want to go.

The affinity in politics

There remains one important question to be dealt with. Although some men were probably recruited to the king's affinity for quite specific reasons, in general the service accorded by members of it to their monarch was (in the words of Dr Morgan, describing Edward IV's affinity) 'personal and variable', rather than systematic or defined.[186] In other words, the affinity's usefulness lay in its flexibility rather than its systematic intrusion into specific spheres of political activity. This is true both of the king's knights and esquires and of the chamber knights and esquires of the household. But could kings, and did they try to, use their affinities in a more systematic way? Was it within their power or design to convert the service performed by their knights and esquires into something more permanent, more pervasive? And if it was, can they in doing so be accused of attempting to subvert the political life of the country, either in local affairs, or in national affairs, or in both? Richard II has been accused of doing so, notably during the last two years of his reign, the years of 'tyranny'. The evidence from these years needs to be seen not only in the context of the first twenty years of his reign, but also that of his successor.

Firstly, there is the evidence concerning the return of knights of the shire to parliament. Some historians, arguing either that it was the lords rather than the commons who really mattered in fourteenth-century parliaments, or that the gentry were too independently-minded to allow themselves to be manipulated by the magnates over the question of parliamentary elections, have tended to dismiss allegations that interference with elections was of any real significance. Yet there is too much evidence on the subject to be ignored. Whether or not such interference was effective, or even successful, there was clearly a widely-held belief that it *could* be. John of Gaunt, at a time when he was virtual ruler of England, was accused by Walsingham of trying to pack the parliament of January 1377.[187] In 1388 there was the well-known episode of the writs demanding that knights returned should be 'in debatis modernis magis indifferentes' (the writs had to be withdrawn and new ones omitting the offending phrase issued), and article 36 of the 1388 appeal claimed that the Appellees had persuaded the king to appoint sheriffs who would ensure that royalist M.P.s were returned.[188] In the 1399 articles of deposition, Richard was accused of interfering with the elections to the September 1397 parliament in order to secure a malleable body of knights, while both Walsingham and Adam of Usk confirm that the proceedings of that parliament were annulled in 1399 on the grounds that the knights had been chosen not 'per communitatem more solito, sed Regis violentia et voluntate.'[189] Since 1376, if not before, it had become apparent that, given the will and the leadership, knights of the shire really could make their voices heard in parliament, and could make life very uncomfortable for the government, so it is far from difficult to see why contemporaries were convinced that packing parliament might be a profitable line of action for the king.

During the first nine parliaments of the reign (October 1377 to February 1383), between four and ten (with an average of nearly seven) king's knights and esquires sat in each parliament.[190] The first sign during Richard's reign that interference with the membership of the commons might be becoming a controversial issue occurs in relation to the parliament of October 1383, to which only two king's knights (Stephen de Hales for Norfolk, and Richard Waldegrave for Suffolk) were returned. A few days before the parliament opened, however, three knights who had been returned were discharged from taking their seats: they were James Berners, Thomas Morwelle, and Thomas Camoys.[191] Berners was discharged on the grounds that he was 'of the king's retinue and household, and one of the knights of his chamber', Morwelle because he was 'of the retinue and household of Joan princess of Wales the king's mother, and is her chamberlain' and Camoys because he was 'a banneret as were most of his ancestors' and 'bannerets used not to be elected knights of the shire'. The real motives behind their discharge were probably political. Chamber knights sat quite frequently as knights of the shire, for instance, William Nevill in October 1378, John del Hay in November 1380, Peter Courtenay in 1381 and May 1382, Berners himself in 1386, Robert Witteneye and Arnold Savage in November 1391, Nicholas Dagworth and John Russell in September 1397. Bannerets may not have, but there was no law excluding them. It seems more than coincidental that these three were singled out in October 1383: Berners was a thoroughgoing courtier, executed in 1388; Camoys was expelled from court in the same year, while Morwelle, as Princess Joan's chamberlain, was closely associated with several leading figures at court.[192] Whether Richard had interfered to try to secure the return of any or all of these three is impossible to say, but it is difficult to explain why they should all three have been disallowed from taking their seats by what appear to be convenient excuses unless one is to assume some sort of move against those known to be strong supporters of the government, to which the king was forced to acquiesce. The fact that only two king's knights were eventually returned supports this view. In the event, it turned out to be a more-than-averagely troublesome parliament for the king.[193]

For the rest of the decade, the number of king's knights and esquires returned to parliament remained below ten except, ironically, for the Wonderful Parliament of 1386 when there were thirteen. In the Merciless Parliament there were nine, just about average for the period. During the 1390s, however, the number increased and in the seven parliaments between January 1390 and February 1397, king's knights and esquires numbered thirteen, twelve, twenty-two (November 1391), sixteen, twenty (January 1394), nine, and fourteen respectively. There is no reason to suspect that this increase resulted from any interference on the king's behalf. It was a natural consequence of the fact that the king was retaining more men, and indeed that he was in some cases retaining precisely those sorts of men who were already prominent in local administration. Many of those who swelled the ranks of the king's knights in these parliaments had already represented their shires in at least one, and often several, parliaments, men like James Pykeryng (Yorks.), Adam Peshale (Stafford and Salop), John Thornbury (Herts.), Edward Dalyngridge (Sussex), John Annesley (Notts.), William Sturmy (Hants.), John Trailly (Cambridge and Bedford), John Russell (Worcs.), John Bussy (Lincs.), William Bagot (Warwicks.) and Henry Green (Northants.). They owed their seats in parliament not to any royal influence but to their own standing within their counties and it was precisely this standing which the king was hoping to harness to his cause. The parliament of September 1397 has a rather different look, however. The number of king's knights and esquires returned as M.P.s now reached twenty-seven, a little over a third of all the knights of the shire, and it included a solid core of men closely attached to the king: councillors Bussy (who was speaker, and who clearly played an important part in the proceedings),[194] Bagot and Green, chamber knights John Russell, Nicholas Dagworth, and thomas Blount, chamber esquire John Worshippe, and two other men, Thomas Shelley and John Golafre, who were to remain overtly loyal to Richard in 1399–1400. Further suspicions are aroused by the fact that there were more members returned for the first time in this parliament (thirty-three) than for any other parliament since 1377, as well as by the fact that some of. the king's closest supporters appear to have been intruded as representatives of shires for which they did not normally sit.[195] Wiltshire, for instance, was represented by Henry Green and Thomas Blount, respectively landholders in Northamptonshire and Oxfordshire, which counties they had previously represented. Given the nature of the proceedings, and bearing in mind the accusation made in 1399 that Richard had tampered with these elections, it seems more than probable that there had indeed been some interference. Finally, it is worth noting that although this list of twenty-seven includes several men who had regularly represented their shires in the parliaments of Richard's reign, not a single one of them was returned to the parliament of October 1399 (although this parliament did include twelve of Richard's former knights and esquires).

The probability that Richard began to use the members of his affinity in a more systematic political role during the last two or three years of his reign is further supported by the evidence for shrieval appointments. It is most improbable that there was a direct connection between the number of king's retainers who acted as sheriffs in 1397–9 and the number of king's retainers returned to the parliament of September 1397, for nearly all the sheriffs in question were not appointed until November 1397. Yet, as with the question of interference with parliamentary elections, there is too much evidence that Richard was eager to secure complaisant sheriffs to be ignored. His reasons for wishing to do so were probably as much military as administrative. Like Henry VI, Richard II probably saw the chief value of the sheriff as lying in his ability to call out the *posse comitatus*.[196] According to the charges made, the king in 1387 had tried to persuade various sheriffs to raise forces to fight for him against the Appellants, but the response had been very lukewarm. This accusation, together with the charge that Richard had tried to secure the appointment of sheriffs who would return members of parliament favourable to the king, were both made the subjects of articles in the appeal of 1388.[197] Following his resumption of power in 1389 the king, according to the Westminster chronicler, adopted a new system for choosing sheriffs so that rather than allowing appointments to be controlled by the three chief officers of state and the barons of the exchequer, he chose them himself, in consultation with his privy councillors, and 'made them take an oath to himself that they would behave well and loyally in office'. This 'caused widespread surprise in the court', and provides further evidence of Richard's wish at least to be involved in such appointments.[198] Walsingham states that in 1398–9 the king sent orders to all the sheriffs that they must swear to obey all mandates from the king, whether under the great seal, privy seal, or signet, behind which the chronicler clearly saw some sinister motive. That he had interfered with the normal course of shrieval elections in order to secure as sheriffs men who would not resist him was also one of the charges made against Richard at his deposition.[199] Thus, as in the case of interference with parliamentary elections, there was evidently a contemporary belief that securing complaisant sheriffs could be profitable for the king.

There were twenty-eight sheriffdoms (covering thirty-seven counties) in England. Four of them may be discounted for the purposes of this study as they were held for life by members of the peerage.[200] Of the remaining twenty-four, twelve (covering sixteen counties) were held by members of the king's affinity throughout the last two years of the reign. They were Bedford and Buckingham (John Worshippe, esquire of the chamber), Oxford and Berkshire (John Golafre, esquire of the household), Cambridge and Huntingdon (Andrew Neuport, sergeant-at-arms), Cheshire (Robert de Legh, king's knight), Hampshire (William Audley, king's esquire), Hereford (Thomas Clanvow, king's knight), Lincolnshire (Henry Retford, king's knight, 1397–8, and John Littlebury, king's knight, 1398–9), Nottingham and Derby (Robert Morton, esquire of the household), Shropshire (Adam Peshale, king's knight), Stafford (William Walshale, esquire of the household, 1396–9), and Yorkshire (James Pykeryng, king's knight). In addition, the sheriff of Cornwall in 1397–8 was the household esquire John Colshull, and the sheriff of Cumberland in 1398–9 was the king's knight Richard Redman. Thus, throughout the last two years of the reign more than half the counties in England over which the king might hope to exert some influence in the matter of shrieval appointments had sheriffs who were members of the king's affinity. The view that there must have been some sort of policy behind this is reinforced by comparison with the period 1377–97. On no occasion before 1389 had the number of sheriffdoms held by members of the affinity been higher than five, and usually it was two or three. It may be that in the mid 1380s Richard had begun to follow some sort of policy of securing reliable sheriffs, but if so it never got off the ground.[201] In 1389–90 the number rose to seven, possibly as a result of the change in the method of appointment described by the Westminster chronicler, but between 1390 and 1397 it normally remained at three or four, only rising in 1393–4 (eight) and 1396–7 (six).

The situation in 1397–9 was thus quite exceptional by comparison with the rest of the reign. Taken county by county, there were only two shrievalties (Somerset and Dorset, and Devon) which never had a member of the king's affinity as sheriff, while most had royal retainers as sheriffs for between two and five years during the reign. There were three counties in which the proportion of sheriffs who were also retainers was noticably higher: Lincolnshire (eight years); Wiltshire (eleven years); and Hereford (fourteen years). There does not seem to be any especial significance in this; Richard was not trying to 'control' particular counties through pliant sheriffs. In Lincolnshire he retained a number of men who were active in local administration and continued to be so after being retained (Anketil Malorre, John Bussy and Henry Retford). In Wiltshire the proportion was swollen by two men who served long spells as sheriff (John Salisbury 1385–8, and Richard Mawardyn, 1389–90, 1393–4, and 1396–9). In Hereford, it was simply a consequence of the fact that the king retained such a high proportion of the county's gentry that by the law of averages his men were bound to provide a high proportion of the sheriffs (Thomas and John Walweyn, Thomas Barre, Kennard de la Bere, and Thomas Clanvow each served more than one term). Hereford, one might think, would be one county where Richard least needed a complaisant sheriff, for so many of the local gentry were so closely bound to his service that he could hardly have failed to find political support there.

The evidence suggests, therefore, that although Richard may have cherished hopes for a more pliant group of sheriffs for many years before 1397, only in that year was he able to realise these hopes. Just how much he gained from the realisation of his hopes is very difficult to say. No doubt his sheriffs obeyed his mandates as he ordered them to do, and some of them responded very promptly to York's call to arms in July 1399, even if it was to no avail.[202] Yet there does not seem to have been any serious suggestion that they abused their power. Indeed, eight of the fourteen royal retainers who acted as sheriffs between 1397 and 1399 either continued in office through the revolution or were re-appointed as sheriffs at some subsequent date.[203] Richard may have regarded them as his men and some of them were very much that, but they do not seem to have acted as the agents of any royal autocracy or to have performed their duties in a disreputable manner.

The evidence concerning parliamentary elections and shrieval appointments accords well with the evidence concerning judicial commissions. This was a third area in which the king could intervene in order to secure the appointment of men who would make reliable royal servants, and both Professor Storey and Dr Virgoe have again detected a distinct change of emphasis in this area dating from 1397. The purpose of the commissions of 1397 was, according to Professor Storey, 'patently political' while Dr Virgoe says that,

> 'the last years of the reign (i.e. 1397–9) seem to show a different quality in the policies pursued by the crown. . . . There appears a determination to use control of appointments to local offices and commissions, not . . . for the more effective royal supervision of local government, but for the establishment of the king's political security by direct personal involvement of the king and court with the local communities . . . '.[204]

Taken together, the evidence concerning parliamentary elections, shrieval appointments, and judicial commissions does suggest very strongly that from 1397 onwards the king was making a much more determined effort to influence local elections and to place his own supporters in the most important posts in local administration. What is perceptible here is not of course a sudden realisation by Richard that influence in parliament and local government was important (he had been well aware of this in the 1380s), but rather a change of method. His retaining policy in the years between 1389 and 1397 had been directed towards much the same end in that he retained a solid core of men from a wide group of counties who were active in the administration of those counties, in the hope that such men could be harnessed to the royal cause in a way that they had patently not been in 1387–8. This was Richard's 'softly, softly' approach. Professor Storey has suggested that Richard in effect abandoned the gentry with his volte-face over the question of liveries in 1390, but it is by no means clear that many of the gentry saw it in this light.[205] In fact he continued to woo the gentry, and with considerable success. Many of those influential shire knights who had supported the Appellants in 1387–8 were now converted to the king's cause, and several of them rose high in the royal service during the next decade. Bussy, Bagot and Green are the most famous examples, but there are many more, such as the important councillor Edward Dalyngridge, the chamber knight (and king's standard-bearer from 1395) Simon Felbridge, Gerard Braybrooke the younger, and Roger Strange of Knokyn.[206]

In 1397, quite suddenly, Richard abandoned this policy. His retaining policy narrowed drastically in geographical scope, and he began to adopt a much more high-handed approach to the question of local government. Royal attempts to control local affairs now seem to become systematic, as they had not been before. This, surely, was the moment at which Richard must have alienated large numbers of the gentry. Instead of building up a retinue which reflected, and therefore drew strength from, the realities of local politics, he was trying to establish local power-structures which reflected the image of his own court. And so unpopular had the royal court become by 1399 that, despite the loyalty of a good number of the royal retainers, there was no widespread movement among the gentry to oppose Bolingbroke's invasion.

Turning now to Henry IV's reign, the returns of members of parliament are unfortunately incomplete after 1407, but this is not a major disaster as the evidence suggesting that the king might have been interfering in elections comes from the first half of the reign. A number of chroniclers make, or report, such allegations. According to Hardyng (who was a follower of Hotspur, and thus not unbiased), one of the accusations which the Percies levelled against Henry in 1403 was that he had tried to get the sheriffs to manipulate elections so as to return men favourable to the king.[207] Which parliament they were referring to is not clear for Hardyng was writing many years later and his dates are not very reliable. Much more suspicion was attached to the Coventry Parliament of October 1404. The author of the *Eulogium Historiarum* said of the assembly that 'the king ordered that no-one who was skilled in the law should come to it, and he notified the sheriffs as to which knights and proctors of the communities he wished to have sent to it.' Walsingham also commented on Henry's desire to exclude lawyers from this parliament, and he reported that one of the articles in the manifesto proclaimed by the rebels of 1405 stated that they wished for certain matters to be reformed at a parliament in London, 'with all the estates exercising their liberties in free elections of knights of the shire'.[208] It may also be significant that the statute concerning parliamentary elections passed in 1406 declared that these elections were to be conducted not 'of affection of sheriffs', but 'freely and indifferently'.[209] Thus once again, as in Richard's reign, there is evidence that at least some contemporaries suspected interference and once again the emphasis is on the link between shrieval appointments and parliamentary elections.

The evidence of the returns can be summarised briefly. In each of the first three parliaments of the reign (1399, 1401 and 1402), thirteen members of the king's affinity sat as knights of the shire. In the next three parliaments the number rose to twenty-two in January 1404, sixteen in October 1404, and nineteen in 1406 but in the final parliament of the reign for which returns are complete, that of October 1407, the figure fell back to fourteen. Before commenting on these figures it is worth looking at Henry's sheriffs and J.P.s. On average, seven of the twenty-four shrievalties over which the king might hope to exert influence in the question of appointments were held by members of the king's affinity in any given year. This figure is higher than during the first twenty years of Richard's reign, but this does not necessarily make it sinister for it is almost certainly due to the fact that whereas Richard had only begun systematically to retain men who were locally prominent during the second half of his reign, Henry did so from the beginning of his reign. Year by year, the figure never fell below five (in 1412–13) or rose above ten (1408–9) except in 1404–5, when it stood at thirteen. This was the same proportion of 'royalist' sheriffs as in 1397–9.[210] The judicial commissions of the reign have been analysed by Dr Rogers.[211] His conclusion was that there are 'no real signs of king "packing" the local benches of justices'. Nevertheless, there are perhaps grounds for suspicion. There were three occasions in the reign when major changes were made in the personnel of the commissions: 16 May 1401 (in thirty-six counties), between December 1405 and March 1406 (in thirty-nine counties), and February 1407 (in forty-two counties). The last was the most comprehensive, and involved the removal of a large number (about thirty) of the king's servants and retainers. This, according to Rogers, 'was not an attack on household influence. . . . Nevertheless, it is clear that at some stage the influence of members of the household had been increased among the justices of the peace. This would seem to have been mostly from the end of 1404 to the middle of 1405.'

As Rogers points out, the removal of many of the king's followers in February 1407 may well have been designed to remove absentees rather than to nullify any attempt by the king to increase the number of his followers on the commissions. But the timing is important for it followed hard on the heels of Prince Henry's rise to power and his reform of the council at the end of the 1406 parliament. If we put together the evidence concerning parliamentary elections, shrieval appointments, and judicial commissions, a definite pattern emerges. It was the elections to the parliament of October 1404 that aroused most suspicion among the chroniclers; it was in November 1404 that the largest number of royal retainers became sheriffs; and it was 'from the end of 1404' that the number of royal servants on the judicial commissions began to increase. Against this must be set the fact that the number of royal retainers who sat in the October 1404 parliament actually fell (from twenty-two to sixteen) as compared with the parliament of January 1404 but if it was through the sheriffs above all that the king hoped to be able to influence elections, the shrieval appointments of November 1404 would of course have been too late for the Coventry Parliament. Yet, whether or not Henry had managed, or even tried, to influence the Coventry elections, there is no escaping the fact that it was a very much easier parliament to manage than its predecessor.

Two further comparisons are worth making between Henry's behaviour and that of his predecessor. The first is that there was only one occasion on which one of Henry's retainers remained in office as sheriff for two consecutive years. This was when Ralph Rochefort (the chamber knight) acted as sheriff of Lincolnshire from November 1404 to November 1406. Richard II, on the other hand, had kept on eleven of his followers for a second term in 1398. The second point is more significant. When one looks at the behaviour in parliament of some of these so-called 'king's friends', one is entitled to wonder whether Henry really needed any enemies. For example, the speaker of the commons in every parliament of Henry's reign except that of September 1402 was either a royal retainer or a member of the household. Yet much good it did the king. Arnold Savage, Thomas Chaucer, and John Tiptoft, all three of them men who were evidently high in the king's regard and held responsible positions at court, were all vociferous and outspoken opponents of the royal government.[212] Moreover, none of them suffered as a result of his outspokenness. The comparison is with John Bussy (whose role in 1397, there can be no doubt, was to ensure that not a murmur of dissension was heard from the ranks of the commons), and it is a comparison which tells us much both about the personalities and styles of government of the two kings, and about the reasons for Richard's downfall in 1399.[213]

To summarise this evidence, it does seem likely that, some time during the second half of 1404, Henry began to make more determined efforts to secure the appointment of some of his followers to positions of influence in local government, and to put them forward as nominees for seats in parliament. He may even have tried to do so earlier, but not on any regular basis. As a result of this he came in for a certain amount of criticism, and by early 1407 this policy (if it deserves the word) had been abandoned by the king (or perhaps he had been forced by Prince Henry to abandon it). There is no sign of a revival of it after the king's resumption of power in 1411. But as a 'policy' of interference in local government, or control of parliament, it really bears no comparison with Richard's behaviour in 1397–9. Richard had gagged and overawed the parliament of September 1397 with a massive display of military force; he had disregarded the oft-repeated request of the commons that sheriffs should be replaced each year in order to keep in office those whom he had found amenable to his wishes and he had turned the commissions of the peace into the instruments of a small handful of his greatest courtiers.[214] There was surely a great difference, not merely in degree but in kind, between his behaviour and Henry's. A certain amount of interference, of pushing one's own followers, is hardly to be wondered at, most magnates behaved in precisely the same way in their own 'countries'. But Henry did not use his affinity systematically to destroy political freedom in England. He was not a tyrant.

Conclusion

From the evidence presented in this chapter, three main conclusions can be drawn. The first is that, by about 1370, the long-favoured system by which the king retained a body of (on average) sixty to seventy 'knights of the household', had broken down. Instead, Edward III in his later years attached to his household only about five 'knights of the chamber', even though there were a number of other knights, sometimes also called knights of the chamber, or *bachelerii*, who were also closely attached to the person of the monarch. Also, when the king went to war he could still call upon knights who were of his *familia* or retinue but the number of these men was not great, and during the last fifteen or so years of Edward's reign very few of them seem to have been new recruits. The knights of the chamber were more important men than the earlier knights of the household; they were both more closely attached to the personal service of the king, and used by him in a greater variety of ways, as diplomats, special commissioners, and councillors as well as soldiers. This (in addition to their small number) was the main difference between them and the household knights of the thirteenth and early fourteenth centuries, who were essentially soldiers.

With the advent of the new reign, however, a wider body of knights and esquires came to be attached to the crown. Since the term 'knight of the household' was by now obsolete, these men came to be known as the 'king's knights' and 'king's esquires'. In other ways too they were different from the earlier knights of the household in that like the chamber knights, they were retained by the king not simply for their military usefulness (even if for some of them this may well have been the principal reason why they caught the king's eye) but were retained also for the support which they could give to the government in their localities. Here the policy of the king can be seen to reflect both the policy followed by magnates, whose retaining policy was often geared to maintaining the support of the gentry in their own 'countries', and the more long-term consolidation of 'local aristocracies' in the shires. For in the fourteenth and fifteenth centuries, local politics and administration in the shires tended to be dominated by the knights and the greater esquires, who between them had come to constitute an 'upper gentry'. The process by which this group had emerged is of course central to the whole development of bastard feudalism in late medieval England—a theme which is discussed at greater length below.[215]

The second main conclusion to be drawn concerns the recruitment and composition of the royal affinity under Richard II and Henry IV. Before 1387, Richard made no real attempt positively to recruit the gentry to his cause. Most of those men who became king's knights or esquires at this time were former followers of either his father or his grandfather, 'men in search of a master', as Morgan put it,[216] while several others were relatives of these men, whose attachment to the service of the crown was really a matter of personal connection and/or family tradition. Thus by the time of the crisis of 1387–8 the king's affinity must have had a rather old-fashioned look about it, and, more importantly, it failed to reflect the realities of local politics as they had developed over the previous quarter of a century. Realising this, the king in 1387 tried rapidly to recruit more of the 'substantial' gentry to his cause, but it was too late, his court was too unpopular, and the result was his defeat at Radcot Bridge and the rout of the court in the Merciless Parliament. After 1388, Richard set out to right this situation. Between 1389 and 1393 especially, he adopted a much more positive retaining policy, pulling in more men from the northern counties, and including a high proportion of men who had already shown themselves active in local affairs and in the parliaments of the 1380s. Dr Christine Carpenter found that in fifteenth-century Warwickshire, a magnate who wished to build up support quickly in a particular area tended, not surprisingly, to direct his retaining policy towards the top end of the market.[217] This is precisely what Richard was doing in the early 1390s and it was the knights, rather than the esquires, towards whom his principal effort was directed. From 1397, however, Richard abandoned this policy. His efforts were now very largely concentrated on the north-west, and he retained relatively few knights, but a much greater number of esquires, gentlemen and yeomen. His reasons for doing so are difficult to understand except in terms of that desperate search for physical security which both Caroline Barron and Anthony Tuck have seen as the mainspring of his actions at this time. At the same time, Richard began to use his affinity in a systematic way, to impose his will on his people, to interfere with local politics and administration, and to subvert political freedoms. The result of this was that Richard now began to forfeit much of that local support which had been carefully cultivated over the previous seven or eight years, and that his affinity now ceased to reflect local power-structures, but began instead to undermine them. This must have contributed significantly to the events of 1399. Even so, the revolution of 1399 was not quite as one-sided as it is often portrayed, and at least some of the support which Richard did receive at this time can be attributed to his retaining policy between 1389 and 1397.

Henry IV, taking his cue from both his cousin and his father, set out from the very beginning of his reign to attach to the crown a roughly similar number of the greater gentry as had Richard. During the first two years of the reign in particular, he spread his net widely. Although the geographical composition of his affinity differed in some important respects from that of Richard's (especially in that it contained a higher proportion of men from the northern half of the country, partly because this was the 'natural' area of Lancastrian influence, and partly because the political and military problems which Henry faced during the first half of his reign made it important for him to cultivate support here), in general the reasons why he recruited men were broadly similar to Richard's. For example, the fact that about forty of the knights whom he retained were men who had also been retained by Richard points to the likelihood that there were certain natural leaders of local society whom any king would have been foolish to ignore. However, the constant and unpredictable military threats which Henry faced probably meant that military ability ranked higher among his reasons for retaining men than among Richard's. After the first two years of his reign, however, Henry's recruitment of knights and esquires dropped away markedly, and during the second half of his reign only two or three dozen new names were added to the ranks of the king's knights and esquires. This is probably to be accounted for by the king's need to economise after the financial chaos of his early years, by the decline of his personal participation in government, and by the fact that the real danger to his throne was by now receding.

The third main conclusion relates to the terms in which these knights and esquires were retained by the king but it must be said that as a conclusion it is rather more equivocal than the first two. Before 1389, and after 1401 (if we are to trust the evidence of the Patent Rolls), it was most unusual for either Richard or Henry to enter into life-retaining contracts with either knights or esquires. Between these years, however, it was common for them to do so (especially for Richard between 1389 and 1399). There were probably a number of reasons why they did so. In part, it was a matter of personal security for the man involved but it was also perhaps an attempt, either in reaction to, or in anticipation of political trouble, to bind men more closely to the king's service. Perhaps too financial considerations played a part, for life retainers seem to have expected larger annuities, and Henry was facing mounting financial criticism from 1401 onwards. But probably more important than any of these considerations was the fact that the livery laws of the years 1388–1401 laid heavy emphasis on the link between the giving of liveries and the giving of life-retaining contracts. These livery laws are not easy to interpret for while the commons advocated them because they hoped that such legislation would curb the ability of lords (or the king) to establish local tyrannies, from the king's point of view their usefulness was primarily as political legislation, aimed at protecting the crown from potentially troublesome magnates. But because he supported the legislation (in principle, at least, even if not always in detail), the king probably felt obliged to be seen to be sticking (partially, anyway) to the rules, at least during the years when the controversy over livery badges was at its height. Kings were as well aware as lords or anybody else that, ultimately, no form of words could guarantee a man's loyalty; loyalties sprang from the heart or the head, not from life-indentures. It is thus probably true to say that most (though not all) of those knights and esquires retained for life by Henry or Richard were so retained because the king wished to demonstrate that he was abiding by the law of the land. Nevertheless, for a few years after 1397, there was much concern over the king's retaining policy. The statutes of 1399 and 1401, which went much further than the ordinance of 1390, reflect that concern.

Conclusion

WRITING around the middle of the fifteenth century, for the benefit of Duke Philip the Good of Burgundy, the court chronicler George Chastellain remarked that, 'after the deeds and exploits of war, which are claims to glory, the household is the first thing which strikes the eye, and that which it is, therefore, most necessary to conduct and arrange well.'[1] The rulers and the nobility of late medieval Europe would not have needed reminding of this fact. As Professor Guenée has pointed out, between the thirteenth and the fifteenth centuries a 'new style' of royal household developed as the less formalised, constantly itinerating household of the earlier Middle Ages was steadily transformed into something far grander, 'an enormous and disparate world charged with providing for (the king's) needs and glorifying his majesty'. Ceremonial occasions became ever more sumptuous but, even more importantly, there was a growing feeling that the royal household must provide a *permanent* spectacle of majesty, that splendour and luxury should be the constant accompaniments of the great. Honour must be done to all according to their estate.[2]

It is with this in mind that the size and cost of the fourteenth- and fifteenth-century English royal household need to be considered, and not only considered, but also compared with other royal households in late medieval Europe. Our first real glimpse of the French royal household comes in 1231, when a list of Louis IX's *hôtel* appears to point to a total establishment of around 260–70.[3] Early in the fourteenth century, the figure was close to 400, while the annual cost of maintaining the king's domestic establishment was estimated at 57,210 *livres parisis* (c. £15,900). By the late fourteenth century, Richard II's and Henry IV's contemporary Charles VI of France (1380–1422) was spending an annual average of about 120,000 *livres parisis* (c. £21,800) on his *hôtel*, while that of his queen, Isabel of Bavaria, cost about another £9,150 each year. Although these French royal household accounts do not allow us to work out the number of servants employed, Professor Guenée estimated that Charles VI's household numbered between 700 and 800.[4] Fifty years later, the *hôtel* of Charles VII (1422–61) often contained 'as many as 800 people'.[5] That other magnificent contemporary of Richard's and Henry's, Duke Philip the Bold of Burgundy (d. 1404), kept a household of about 250–300 persons, and spent on

average about 100,000 *livres tournois* (*c.* £14,300) on it. By the middle of the fifteenth century, however, by which time the Burgundian dukes were greater and
richer men, 400 was closer to the norm, and at times the number of servants
reached 1,000 or more. The cost of their household increased proportionately.[6]

Throughout western Europe, the same pattern is observable, for the 'necessary magnificence' of late medieval rulers meant a steady growth in the size and
cost of their households, a constant urge to proclaim and display the grandeur
of the monarch. The 150 or so household servants of Henry I's time had
become the 400–700 of the fourteenth century; the reasonably consistent
annual expenditure of £10,000 to £12,000 on the wardrobe in the period from
about 1230 to 1350 had become (on average) very close to £20,000 by the late
fourteenth century. And the size of the royal household continued to increase.
In 1450, there were over 800 servants in Henry VI's household, and by the
early seventeenth century around 1,500.[7] When we turn to the households of
the upper nobility in late medieval England, the pattern is very similar. There
is much evidence to suggest that their size too increased significantly in this
period. By the late fourteenth century, most English earls probably maintained
permanent domestic establishments of between eighty and a hundred servants.
A century earlier, it is doubtful whether fifty was often exceeded, whereas a
century later, 150 seems to have been closer to the norm. By the early fifteenth
century, even knights and esquires frequently kept households numbering
twenty or thirty servants.[8] And, as with the royal household, the tendency was
for the households of both nobility and gentry to become increasingly sedentary, and more elaborately organised.[9]

Between 1360 and 1413, the kings of England spent over one million pounds
on the wardrobe alone, at an average of almost £20,000 a year. Including the
great wardrobe, the privy wardrobe, and the chamber, the total cost to the
exchequer of the household departments was over £1,500,000, and the annual
average about £30,000 and this probably accounted, in total, for something like
a third of the total revenue brought into (or assigned by) the exchequer during
these years. While such figures are certainly impressive, they must be seen
within the contemporary European context. Richard II was very keen not to
be outshone by Charles VI, he said so, quite openly, to the parliament of
1384,[10] and when, in 1396, he had the opportunity to proclaim and demonstrate his majesty to the French king, he took full advantage of it. Equally,
Edward III's massive building programme at Windsor and elsewhere, and the
lavish expenditure on his court in the 1360s, were intended to demonstrate that
triumph of English over French monarchy which had been driven home at Poitiers and at Brétigny. The royal household was the outward and visible symbol
of royal power. But for all monarchs, necessary magnificence necessarily had its
price, and that price—criticism of royal extravagance, resentment of the constant demands made by royal servants—was as much a part of the late medieval
European household as was its splendour. For example, Edward III was sometimes advised that in the matter of purveyance he would do well to follow the
example of the king of France, who, it was alleged, did not allow his servants

to seize goods in the same indiscriminate fashion. But in fact, as M. Moisant pointed out in his introduction to the *Speculum Regis*, purveyance for the royal household gave rise to just as much criticism in France as it did in England. The *ordonnances* of the French kings record numerous complaints about purveyance, as well as purchases of exemptions.[11] Nor was it only English monarchs who were forced to expel servants from their households. In 1415 Duke John the Fearless of Burgundy (1404–19) was forced to dismiss about fifty members of his household and ten years later, Charles VII of France was made to 'cast out all the bad seed' from his entourage, and some were driven into exile.[12] It would be unfair to accuse the rulers of western Europe of being unaware of the problems created by their inability to live like other mortals. Nearly all the ordinances and regulations issued for royal households were in fact attempts at reform yet for those who were unwilling, or unable, to regulate and control both the personnel and the finances of their households, there was, inevitably, going to be pressure on them to do so.

To provide a suitable milieu for the ruler was thus one of the primary functions of the royal household and beyond this, the importance of the household lay really in its flexibility rather than its institutionalisation. The idea of 'household government', that is, of the household as an administrative haven wherein the monarch might escape the vigilance of barons or others who wished to reform his government, has little relevance to this period of English history. Nothing demonstrates this more clearly than Richard II's ineffectiveness between November 1386 and May 1389—precisely the time when, if 'household government' had ever been a feasible proposition, Richard might have tried it. The household was a centre of social life for the nobility of the kingdom; it was a point of contact, between central and local government, and for those who wished to lobby the king or his courtiers; it was the nucleus of the king's army; and it maintained at all times a substantial reserve of both cash and weaponry, which might prove extremely useful in times of crisis. In this way, it was an essential adjunct to kingship.

The fortunate survival of large numbers of exchequer and wardrobe records from the late Middle Ages puts English historians in a far stronger position than, for example, French historians, when it comes to trying to work out the size and cost of the royal household. In other respects, however, English sources are less revealing than they might be. This is especially true of court politics. French and Burgundian chroniclers give the impression of being rather better informed about the manoeuvring of factions at court, and of having a better understanding of the complexity of such matters. It is sometimes possible, therefore, to build up a picture of the different groupings at court, and of the way in which each of them was working to gain the upper hand—which meant, in practice, to achieve the greatest degree of influence with the king.[13] English chroniclers were certainly not disinterested in court politics and men like Thomas Walsingham and the author of the Westminster Chronicle undoubtedly recognised just how important a factor it was in the history of any reign. The picture which they present, however, is almost invariably a rather simplistic one, and one is left with the impression that they were not very well informed about it, except in a general sense. In other words, what they knew was common knowledge, but beyond that they knew little. The view that we are given, on the whole, is two-dimensional with, on the one hand, the king and his courtiers, and on the other hand, the 'opposition' to the court, such as the Appellants in 1387–8, or the commons of 1376. If we try to discover what groupings there were *within* the court, there is an almost unbroken wall of silence. Occasionally, it is possible to glimpse further. Walsingham, for example, recorded that before 1387 Thomas Mowbray was an intimate of the young Richard II, but in that year Robert de Vere poisoned the king's mind against Mowbray, and therefore he left the court; a few months later, Mowbray became one of the Appellants.[14] Was it as simple, or as sudden, as that? Is it possible that de Vere and Mowbray, both of whom were certainly very high in the king's favour during the early 1380s, were in fact the leaders of separate groupings at court, and thus rivals for the king's ear; that de Vere triumphed early in 1387, thus driving Mowbray and his followers into the opposition camp, and that Mowbray's temporary alliance with the more radical Gloucester and Arundel was actually an attempt to oust de Vere and thus to restore his influence with the king (in which, in the event, he succeeded, at least until 1398)? This is no more than speculation, of course, but it is surely the sort of incident about which we should hear more, and thus be in a better position to understand the obviously rather complex motivation underlying Mowbray's relationship with the king, had it occured at the court of Charles VI or VII, or Duke Philip the Good.

Alice Perrers provides another example. Walsingham devotes several pages to the task of vilifying Alice, yet at no point does he (or any of the other chroniclers of the Good Parliament) attempt to describe the undoubted currents of faction which raged around her lover at the end of his reign. Yet such currents there certainly were and when we turn to the record of Alice's trial—an official transcription, not a narrative account—we begin to see the complexity of the situation at Edward's court. Richard Lyons was obviously her friend (by 1376, anyway), while other favoured courtiers of Edward's later years, such as John Beverley and his father-in-law Alan Buxhull, were evidently her enemies.[15] The unanimity with which the courtiers deserted Alice in 1377 is instructive (even if in some cases this may well have been dictated by self-interest as much as dislike of the royal mistress). She was probably a lonely, isolated figure at court, resented for her influence and her greed, but at the same time courted by the courtiers for the favours which that same influence could elicit. It is strange that official records seem quite often to tell us more about a subject such as court politics than the chroniclers do. The events which led up to the exiling of Mowbray and Derby in September 1398, for example, are very difficult to disentangle, but what is striking—especially as this can only have been a *cause célèbre* at the time—is that those historians who have tried to disentangle it have found official records much more useful than the narrative accounts.[16] The real problem, it would seem, is that chroniclers like Walsingham and Knighton and the author of the *Vita* were not actually at court, and were not therefore in a position to understand the workings of faction there. The Westminster chronicler was, physically, closer to the court than his fellows for most of the reign, while the author of the *Traison et Mort* was probably at court for the last two or three years of the reign, but the occasional glimpses of court politics which even these two give us are not generally very revealing.[17] We are left, then, with a picture of the court as a monolithic structure, standing united against its enemies, subjected quite frequently to external pressures, but rarely to internal ones. This may well be the most important half of the story, but it is as well to remember that it is only half. Had there been real 'court chroniclers' in fourteenth-century England, we would surely be much better informed about the other half too.

Inasmuch as those who populated the court were in a good position to secure positions in the royal affinity for their friends, relatives, and clients, and without doubt frequently did so, the link between court and affinity was obviously important. Yet, although these sorts of personal considerations certainly had a major influence on the composition of the king's affinity, the evidence presented in Chapter IV of this book suggests strongly that both Richard II and Henry IV, as well as drawing political support from the personal and familiar connections of their intimates, followed something which merits description as a 'retaining policy'. Naturally, the retaining policy of each of these kings had its individual nuances, but if we discount for the moment Richard's obsession with Cheshire between 1397 and 1399, the picture for each reign is very similar. Excluding those who were described as knights of the chamber, each king retained between 250 and 300 king's knights and king's esquires, with the knights predominating both numerically and in individual importance. Although in each case about thirty or forty of these were foreigners, the remainder were native-born and drawn from all parts of the kingdom. The king's affinity was of course something which spread wider than this, at least in its broadest sense, and ultimately it is something which is quite incapable of precise definition.[18] Nevertheless, it was the king's knights and esquires, together with the other senior members of the household and those who held responsible posts in the various departments of government, who provided the real heart of the royal affinity, and the figure of 250–300 can usefully be compared with the estimated norm of sixty to eighty followers whom the greatest members of the English nobility seem to have retained at this time.[19] Clearly too, these figures invite comparison with the 220 or so knights and esquires who were apparently retained by John of Gaunt during the early years of Richard II's reign, which serves yet again to emphasise not only how untypical among English magnates Gaunt was, but also the extent to which he geared his retaining policy to his pretensions as 'King of Castile and Leon'.[20] Even for a duke and a royal uncle, Gaunt was quite untypical: his brother the duke of York, for example, seems only to have been retaining some forty knights and esquires in 1399.[21] It is probably true to say that the number of knights and esquires retained by Richard II and Henry IV was between four and eight times greater than the number retained by most dukes or earls.

This cost the king a great deal of money, especially as both Richard and Henry normally granted larger annuities to their knights and esquires than even the greatest nobles did. The normal fee for a knight retained by an earl seems to have been £20 or 20 marks, for an esquire, £10 or 10 marks. The king's sons might pay more: both Gaunt and the Black Prince, for example, often paid annuities of about £40 to their knights, and £15 or £20 to their esquires (which meant that, in total, Gaunt's knights and esquires may well have cost him about £5,000 a year).[22] The king's annuities were higher still, averaging close on £60 per knight and £25 per esquire. At this rate, the annuities payable by Richard II and Henry IV in the period *c*. 1390 to 1410 should have relieved the exchequer of about £12,000 a year. It is true of course that annuities were not always paid regularly, but equally it is the case that a great many people besides the king's knights and esquires were granted annuities by the king. Over-all figures are not easy to estimate, but it does seem that the development of a gentry retaining policy during this period led to a steady escalation of the royal annuities bill. In the mid 1360s, various exchequer estimates point to a figure of around £13,000 for the annuities payable by Edward III. This included a small number of very large annuities which Edward had granted to members of his family or to his close friends among the higher nobility, all of whom were, to the considerable relief of the exchequer, dead by 1372.[23] Richard's annuity bill by June 1378 was around £14,300, but this included £2,900 of the Black Prince's annuities confirmed by his son, and about £3,200 of new grants, so that confirmations of Edward III's annuities totalled only about £8,200—reflecting the decline of Edward's retaining activity in his later years.[24] Before 1389, the value of annuities promised by Richard probably did not increase greatly, but during the last ten years of the reign it was growing constantly, and after 1397 it soared. The Cheshiremen recruited in 1397–8 cost over £5,000 alone. All in all, the total value of the annuities promised by Richard must, by 1399, have been about £25,000.

Henry IV rapidly exceeded this figure, largely as a result of the intense recruiting drive of his first two years. Within two years, about £24,000 of annuities had been confirmed or granted either at the exchequer or on traditional exchequer revenues. In addition, the duchy of Lancaster was charged with around £8,000 of annuities throughout the reign.[25] During the next two or three years the annuities bill continued to grow, and may well have reached £35,000 by *c*. 1404–5. After 1406, however, it would certainly have decreased, albeit slowly. It might have been this high level of annuities which prompted Henry V at the outset of his reign to confirm crown grants with the proviso 'as long as he be not retained by anyone else'.[26] At any rate, the number of annuities granted by the crown does seem to have declined during the twenty-five years or so following Henry IV's death, but once Henry VI reached his majority in 1437, another steep upward trend set in.[27] In considering these figures, it is very important to remember that annuities were not paid nearly as often as they were promised. During Henry IV's reign especially, vast arrears seem to have accumulated, and on at least one occasion there were complete 'stops' on exchequer annuities.[28] Even so, the cost of royal retaining at this time was significant. At £25,000 or £35,000, it could (in theory) account for a quarter or more of all royal income, which was beginning to make the crown's budget look like a budget of noble and gentry assistance.[29] It may be true that most retainers valued the 'good lordship' of a patron more highly than the fee which accompanied it, but the annuities promised by the king were far from negligible items of income and it would be unwise to under-estimate the political and personal damage caused by 'stops' on annuities or the accumulation of serious arrears. Henry IV's annuitants were certainly worried about it, and it was one of the major elements determining the nature of the 'financial settlement' of 1406–7.[30]

The attachment to the king of this number of knights and esquires is also a development which has its place in the long-term social perspective of late medieval England. It is worth, for example, comparing Richard II's retaining policy in the 1390s with that of Edward II at a time when he too was eager to build up political support, in 1316–17. At this time, as Dr Phillips discovered, Edward drew up a series of nineteen indentures for service in peace and war with 'a majority of the leading magnates', promising a total of about £4,000 in peace-time annuities, and considerably more for service in war.[31] Thus his approach in time of need seems to have been to seek the direct support of the higher nobility of the kingdom. Edward III's retaining policy has not been analysed in detail, but to judge from the evidence of the annuities payable by the crown between 1360 and 1377, he did not retain many members of the gentry on a permanent basis, but was prepared to give very large annuities to a number of his greater nobles.[32] To suggest that Richard II ignored the greater nobles would of course be quite incorrect. The thoroughly aristocratic composition of his court clique in the 1390s, and the titles which he bestowed so lavishly on his favourites in 1385–6 and 1397, are sufficient testimony to his desire either to woo the great men of his realm or, if they refused to be wooed, to elevate around them others who could vie with them in status. Yet what is also abundantly clear is that Richard felt the need to go further than this, to appeal directly to the gentry. Even if in the end it failed to save him his throne, Richard's retaining policy did at least have the merit of originality. This sort of action is something which is frequently associated with Tudor monarchy, and as such it is seen as reflecting a 'growing shift of power at local level from the nobility towards the gentry.' Dr G. L. Harriss has remarked recently that, 'the study of both the royal and noble affinities in the Tudor age has scarcely begun, but separate studies are beginning to suggest that the crown was now more able to use the lesser nobility and gentry (often those with court connections) as instruments for direct royal influence within the shire. . . .' In his discussion of fifteenth-century affinities, Harriss saw much the same forces at work,

> the bastard feudal affinity represents an attempt by the traditional leaders of society—crown and nobility—to contain the increasingly diversifying armigerous class within the old traditions of lordship and chivalry. . . . (this) solution

disintegrated not under any attack from the crown but as cumulative wealth and access to political authority gave the broad class of landowners independence from the nobility as mediators of patronage and power.[33]

This theme of gentry 'independence' from the nobility is also taken up by Dr Carpenter, who suggests that forceful monarchical government in the shires could only be achieved once 'the gentry who administered the shires could be separated from the nobility', and this, she thought, may have taken place as a result of the Wars of the Roses.[34] Yet, as Dr Saul in particular has suggested, the 'enhanced political role' of the gentry is a trend which is clearly visible in fourteenth-century England.[35] And whether one chooses to see it as an attempt to 'contain' or to exploit the 'broad class of landowners', the retaining policy of both Richard II and Henry IV is surely evidence of the fact that both these kings were well aware of the crucial role played by the gentry, and of the consequent need for the crown to appeal directly to them.

But just how broad was this landowning class? There are further social developments which need to be taken into account. A number of local studies are now beginning to point to the existence of a reasonably clearly defined stratum of 'upper gentry' in the English shires, at least by the end of the fourteenth century, if not earlier. Thus Saul has calculated that the real 'gentry' of mid fourteenth-century Gloucestershire consisted of about fifty families, of whom about thirty were knights.[36] For Cheshire and Lancashire, Bennett has suggested an over-all figure of about 600 gentry families, but within this an upper layer of around 100 families, consisting of the knights and greater esquires. Similar studies by Dr Astill in late fourteenth-century Leicestershire, Wright in fifteenth-century Derbyshire, and Carpenter in fifteenth-century Warwickshire, have suggested 'upper gentry' figures of sixty-one, fifty-two, and about seventy, respectively. These were the families that made up the office-holding and landowning élites in their counties, who generally had the largest estates and who between them tended to share out the greater shire offices such as sheriff, M.P. and, increasingly, J.P. As several of these writers emphasise, there was a real gulf between them and the lesser gentry, consisting of the less wealthy and influential esquires together with that much broader class of quite small landowners who in the fifteenth century would commonly be described as gentlemen or even yeomen.[37] Unless those shires which have been studied are wholly unrepresentative (which seems very unlikely), then it seems possible to point to a figure of about 2,500 'upper gentry' families throughout England in the period *c.* 1350–1450. Although the proportion of knights to esquires within this group certainly dropped considerably during this period, the overall size of the group, while it may have decreased to some extent, probably did not alter significantly. Many years ago, Professor Ross suggested that in early fifteenth-century Yorkshire the normal pattern was for the 'upper gentry' to seek service with the king or local great lord, while the lesser gentry sought patronage from lesser lords.[38] The composition of the royal affinity under Richard II and Henry IV certainly supports this view as it was undoubtedly among the upper gentry that both kings sought their retainers and it was entirely logical that they should do so. It meant moreover that (when foreigners are excluded from the numbers) something close to ten percent of England's upper gentry was retained by each of these kings. This certainly did not mean that either Richard or Henry had a really committed following throughout the shires, but it did at least mean that there was a sprinkling of local bigwigs directly attached to the crown. A really committed following was not something which could be bought: it was inherited, the cumulative effect of decades or even centuries of tradition and service, stretching well beyond even the upper gentry. Richard had it in Cheshire, and Henry had it in the Yorkshire/north midlands/Lancashire heartland of his father's duchy. The retaining policy followed by these kings was rather a recognition of the crucial role played by the upper gentry, and was born of a hope that their local prominence could be harnessed, if necessary, to the cause of the crown.

The pursuit of such a retaining policy did not of course give either Richard or Henry the ability to 'manage' local politics or administration. County establishments must always have been, to a large extent, a law unto themselves, and to try to meddle with them would probably produce precisely the opposite result to that intended. For example, Professor Griffiths has argued that in the late 1450s Henry VI and his advisors at court decided to adopt the midlands (from Hereford to Lincolnshire, roughly) as their 'power-base' and a series of appointments followed, designed to place the most important posts in these shires in the hands of curialists. Yet the effect of these appointments was not in fact to rally these shires to the crown, but rather to alienate the local gentry, the natural leaders of local society who made up the county establishment, who now felt thrust aside, and to throw them into the arms of the court's opponents. This, at least, is the explanation offered by both Carpenter and Wright, for Warwickshire and Derbyshire respectively.[39] The moral of Richard II's failure in 1399 seems to be very similar: as long as the king's patronage continued to build upon and reflect, and indeed bolster, the structure of local power, that was a process from which the crown could, and probably would, draw strength; but once patronage gave way to manipulation, alienation could follow rapidly.

The real beneficiaries of the retaining policy followed not only by Richard II and Henry IV, but also by John of Gaunt and the other great lords of late medieval England, were undoubtedly the upper gentry. Astill noted that within the upper gentry of Leicestershire in the second half of the fourteenth century there was a small number of families whose influence seems to have been paramount, and that these families were generally those most closely associated with the great lord of the area, John of Gaunt.[40] Similarly, Carpenter found less than a dozen really dominant gentry families in fifteenth-century Warwickshire, nearly all of them closely associated with either the king or the earl of Warwick.[41] Cause and effect are closely intertwined here, but it is surely the case that these men drew not only money, but also enhanced prestige and authority from their associations with the great, to say nothing of 'good lordship' in all its various aspects. For the great, however, patronage of the gentry on a regular basis was by now not so much an option as a necessity, and, increasingly that meant patronage on their own (the gentry's) terms, i.e. good lordship, not political manipulation. John of Gaunt realised this, as did his son, and so too, for a while, did Richard II. The problem for Richard, however, was that after 1397 he seemed to forget it, and from this point on, he was hastening to destruction. Dr Tuck opened his study of Richard II's reign with this observation,

> In 1327 a group of nobles deposed and imprisoned King Edward II. In 1399 another group deposed his great-grandson, Richard II, and the leader of the revolution then placed himself upon the vacant throne. These two events are sufficient in themselves to suggest that the most important problem facing English kings in the fourteenth century was their relations with their nobility, the group of twenty or so men with the rank of earl and above.[42]

It is not my intention to suggest that 'counting earls' is a very profitable line of enquiry, but it is worth applying Tuck's own test to the revolution of 1399. There were in fact nineteen men who, in the summer of 1399, held an English earldom, marquisate, or dukedom. Of these, no less than eleven were thoroughly committed to Richard's cause, a further three were prevented by minority or absence from playing any part in events, while two more kept well out of harm's way. This leaves only three who actually took part against Richard in the 'revolution': Northumberland, Westmorland, and Henry himself—though technically he should not be included as he had been disbarred for life from his inheritance. Richard's deposition, in other words, was certainly not the result of any lack of support among the higher nobility. Rather, it was the failure of both the king and his great nobles to carry with them those leaders of local society who should have swelled the royal army, and who might have rallied the shires against the usurper. A few did, but not enough.[43] In the end, it was the gentry, voting, or rather, failing to vote, with their feet, who brought on Richard's downfall. The events of 1399 speak just as eloquently in testimony of the growing power of the gentry as do the retaining policies followed by the two kings whose reigns they bridged.

APPENDIX I

Accounts of the wardrobe of the household 1360–1413

| Period | (Days) | Keeper | Expenditure | | | | | Receipt | | | | Balance |
			Diet (daily ave) £	Foreign £	Total (annual average) £	Imprests £	Total £	Exchequer £	Foreign £	Debts £	Total £	£
26 May 1360–13 Nov 1361	536	William Ferriby	20,391 (38.1s)	3,250	23,641 (16,098)	1,862	25,503	13,131	10,178	1,883	25,192	311 deficit
14 Nov 1361–13 Nov 1362	365	William Manton	13,226 (36.5s)	5,514	18,740	1,473	20,213	11,332	7,493	1,321	20,146	67 deficit
14 Nov 1362–13 Nov 1363	365	William Manton	17,483 (47.18s)	4,574	22,057	1,356	23,413	15,866	7,314		23,180	233 deficit
14 Nov 1363–13 Nov 1364	365	William Manton	18,494 (50.13s)	4,930	23,424	2,492	25,916	20,465	7,612		28,077	2,161 surplus
14 Nov 1364–31 Jan 1366	443	William Manton	22,683 (51.4s)	8,116	30,799 (25,376)	3,379	34,178	20,382	11,419	359	32,160	2,018 deficit
1 Feb 1366–31 Jan 1367	365	William Gunthorpe	17,545 (48.1s)	5,391	22,936	4,134	27,070	18,472	10,689	40	29,201	2,131 surplus
1 Feb 1367–12 Feb 1368	377	William Gunthorpe	17,609 (46.14s)	5,425	23,034 (22,300)	6,300	29,334	17,353	12,329		29,682	348 surplus
13 Feb 1368–12 Feb 1369	365	Thomas Brantingham	11,262 (30.17s)	3,885	15,147	4,442	19,589	12,563	7,774		20,337	748 surplus
13 Feb 1369–27 June 1369	135	Thomas Brantingham	4,345 (32.4s)	1,400	5,745 (15,532)	3,995	9,740	3,779	5,903		9,682	58 deficit

Period	(Days)	Keeper	Diet (daily ave) £	Foreign £	Expenditure Total (annual average) £	Imprests £	Total £	Exchequer £	Receipt Foreign £	Debts £	Total £	Balance £
28 June 1369–27 June 1371	730	Thomas Brantingham	Wages of War: 74,934 Diet and Foreign: £32,608		16,304	18,801	126,343	119,832	5,289	1,175	126,296	47 deficit
28 June 1371–27 June 1373	730	Henry Wakefield	27,623 (37.17s)	7,915	35,538 (17,769)	4,518	40,056	31,003	6,490		37,493	2,563 deficit
28 June 1373–30 Sept 1374	460	Henry Wakefield	14,788 (32.3s)	3,174	17,962 (14,252)	2,585	20,547	14,256	3,962		18,218	2,329 deficit
1 Oct 1374–13 Oct 1375	378	Henry Wakefield	13,383 (35.8s)	3,456	16,839 (16,260)	3,235	20,074	21,022	5,185		26,207	6,133 surplus
14 Oct 1375–24 Nov 1376	407	William Mulsho	14,695 (36.2s)	3,810	18,505 (16,595)	3,745	22,250	17,442	4,791		22,233	17 deficit
25 Nov 1376–26 July 1377	244	Richard Beverley	9,046 (37.2s)	2,966	12,012 (17,969)	1,325	13,337	7,886	3,643	1,806	13,335	2 deficit
(Edward III's household disbanded)												
1 July 1377–30 June 1378	365	William Packington	13,368 (36.12s)	2,629	15,997	1,892	17,889	17,726	835		18,561	672 surplus
1 July 1378–30 June 1379	365	William Packington	11,380 (31.4s)	2,846	14,226	1,959	16,185	14,176	2,232		16,408	223 surplus
1 July 1379–30 Sept 1381	822	William Packington	26,570 (32.11s)	8,896	35,646 (15,828)	2,532	38,178	32,160	3,362		35,522	2,656 deficit
1 Oct 1381–30 Sept 1382	365	William Packington	15,600 (42.13s)	3,295	18,895	1,638	20,533	17,715	2,644		20,359	174 deficit
1 Oct 1382–30 Sept 1383	365	William Packington	11,033 (30.5s)	2,328	13,361	2,450	15,811	15,551	2,072		17,623	1,812 surplus

Period	(Days)	Keeper	Diet (daily ave) £	Foreign £	Expenditure Total (annual average) £	Impress £	Total £	Exchequer £	Receipt Foreign £	Debts £	Total £	Balance £
1 Oct 1383–30 Sept 1384	365	William Packington	11,442 (31.7s)	2,073	13,515	2,630	16,145	14,899	2,452		17,351	1,206 surplus
1 Oct 1384–30 Sept 1385	365	William Packington	13,904 (38.2s)	3,983	17,887	6,522	24,409	19,382	3,198		22,580	1,829 deficit
1 Oct 1385–30 Sept 1386	365	William Packington	14,017 (38.8s)	2,931	16,948	5,346	22,294	18,563	5,071		23,634	1,340 surplus
1 Oct 1386–30 Sept 1387	365	William Packington	9,550 (26.3s)	2,372	11,922	4,219	16,141	8,324	5,380		13,704	2,437 deficit
1 Oct 1387–30 Sept 1388	365	William Packington	10,412 (28.11s)	2,945	13,357	3,232	16,589	13,667	5,002		18,669	2,080 surplus
1 Oct 1388–30 Sept 1389	365	William Packington	10,745 (29.9s)	2,379	13,124	6,135	19,259	12,530	3,931		16,461	2,798 deficit
1 Oct 1389–26 July 1390	299	William Packington	10,802 (36.2s)	2,544	13,346 (16,291)	5,153	18,499	13,132	7,667		20,799	2,300 surplus
27 July 1390–30 Sept 1391	431	John Carp	16,435 (38.3s)	3,935	20,370 (17,250)	4,282	24,652	17,203	5,646		22,849	1,803 deficit
1 Oct 1391–30 Sept 1392	365	John Carp	15,460 (42.7s)	2,698	18,158	3,692	21,850	15,531	5,388		20,919	931 deficit
1 Oct 1392–30 Sept 1393	365	John Carp	15,068 (41.6s)	3,631	18,699	4,425	23,124	21,701	4,706		26,407	3,283 surplus
1 Oct 1393–30 Sept 1395	730	John Carp	30,481 (41.15s)	7,559	38,040 (19,020)	12,678	79,437	78,199	5,017		83,216	3,779 surplus

Wages of War: 28,719

Period	(Days)	Keeper	Diet (daily ave) £	Foreign £	Expenditure Total (annual average) £	Imprests £	Total £	Exchequer £	Receipt Foreign £	Debts £	Total £	Balance £
1 Oct 1395–30 Sept 1396	365	John Carp	20,999 (57.11s)	5,162	26,161	5,070	31,231	28,097	2,336		30,433	798 deficit
1 Oct 1396–30 Sept 1397	365	John Carp	32,331 (88.12s)	4,658	36,989	4,759	41,748	35,074	4,675		39,749	1,999 deficit
1 Oct 1397–30 Sept 1398	365	John Carp	29,834 (81.15s)	7,926	37,760	3,194	40,954	25,373	3,976		29,349	11,605 deficit
1 Oct 1398–30 Sept 1399	365	John Carp	26,762 (73.6s) Wages of War: 4,894	8,445	35,207	6,116	46,217	38,204	17,863		56,067	9,850 surplus
(Richard II's household disbanded)												
1 Oct 1399–8 Mar 1401	527	Thomas Tutbury	?	?	43,454 (30,096)	4,386	47,840	31,893	27,684		59,577	11,737 surplus
9 Mar 1401–30 Sept 1401	206	Thomas More	9,930 (48.4s)	2,072	12,002 (21,266)	2,289	14,291	10,677	2,940		13,617	674 deficit
1 Oct 1401–30 Sept 1402	365	Thomas More	18,144 (49.14s)	4,218	22,362	2,975	25,337	18,555	3,326		21,881	3,456 deficit
1 Oct 1402–30 Sept 1403	365	Thomas More	22,473 (61.11s)	5,034	27,507	2,831	30,338	25,611	1,936		27,547	2,791 deficit
1 Oct 1403–6 Jan 1405	463	Thomas More	25,627 (55.7s)	5,967	31,594 (24,907)	2,540	34,134	22,242	16,152		38,394	4,260 surplus
7 Jan 1405–7 Dec 1406	700	Richard Kingston	35,535 (50.15s)	13,473	49,008 (25,554)	3,801	52,809	32,969	20,956		53,925	1,116 surplus
8 Dec 1406–17 July 1408	587	John Tiptoft	26,829 (45.14s)	6,053	32,882 (20,446)	1,813	34,695	32,650	1,650		34,300	395 deficit

Period	(Days)	Keeper	Diet (daily ave) £	Foreign £	Expenditure Total (annual average) £	Imprests £	Total £	Exchequer £	Receipt Foreign £	Debts £	Total £	Balance £
18 July 1408– 30 Sept 1409	444	Thomas Brounfleet	21,044 (47.8s)	3,848	24,892 (20,463)	1,408	26,300	21,137	1,342		22,479	3,821 deficit
1 Oct 1409– 30 Sept 1410	365	Thomas Brounfleet	15,407 (42.4s)	3,918	19,325	2,409	21,734	18,684	1,176		19,860	1,874 deficit
1 Oct 1410– 30 Sept 1411	365	Thomas Brounfleet	14,114 (38.13s)	2,996	17,110	2,047	19,157	16,400	2,171		18,571	586 deficit
1 Oct 1411– 11 Apr 1413 (Henry IV's household disbanded)	558	Thomas Brounfleet	?	?	30,128 (19,707)	2,866	32,994	24,683	14,575		39,258	6,264 surplus

APPENDIX II

Recepta Scaccarii

All the sums itemised in the *recepta scaccarii* of the wardrobe account books were officially received by the keeper, from the treasurer and chamberlains of the exchequer, 'by the hands' (*per manus*) either of the keeper himself (*per manibus propriis*) or of a third party. This third party or parties might be a messenger sent by either the keeper or the exchequer officials, he might be one of the keeper's deputies in the household (e.g. the butler) receiving money with which to make purchases for his own office (*pro officio suo*), or he might be one of the wardrobe's creditors receiving payment for goods or services provided by him for the household. All sums thus delivered to the keeper were also recorded in the issue rolls of the exchequer and, if they were assignments rather than cash payments, a note of assignment would normally be made in the margin of the receipt roll under the same date. The balance between the different ways in which the wardrobe received its income is crucial to a proper understanding of household finance.

It is possible to distinguish at least seven different ways in which the wardrobe might 'receive' its income from the exchequer:

(1) In cash, directly from the exchequer. The cash would be collected by the keeper or one of his deputies, or delivered by a messenger of the exchequer. This would entail an entry on the issue roll and the keeper's *recepta scaccarii* on the same day (or almost the same day—practice is not entirely consistent), but no record on the exchequer receipt roll because no assignment has been made. Sometimes—again practice is not consistent—these cash transactions are distinguished in either the wardrobe account book, or the issue roll, or both, as being *in pecunia numerata* or *in moneta*.

(2) By assignment, directly from the exchequer. The keeper was given a tally or tallies assigned upon a specific source of revenue (a customs collector, for example). It was then up to the keeper, or one of his subordinates, to exchange his tallies for cash with that revenue collector. The entries in his own wardrobe account book and on the issue roll would be the same as for (1) above, but in this case there would also be an entry with a marginal *pro* in the receipt roll of the exchequer, recording the receipt of the sum in question from the revenue collector, and the fact of its assignment to the wardrobe. The receipt roll entry is often the only guide to the distinction between methods (1) and (2).

(3) In cash, or by assignment, from the exchequer to a wardrobe officer for his office. This involved the same procedure as (1) and (2) above, except that the cash or tallies were actually handed to the wardrobe official (e.g. the butler) and were thus recorded as having been received by the keeper *per manus* of, for example, *N. pincernae regis pro officio suo*. The official would use the money so received to make purchases for his office (e.g. the buttery).

(4) In cash, from a local official of the crown. The official might be a customs collector or a sheriff operating within the area through which the household happened to be passing, or in which one of the household purveyors was at the time making purchases. He would be ordered, usually by writ of privy seal, to hand over a certain sum to the keeper or purveyor. In return, he was given a bill of wardrobe debenture—in effect a receipt—in the name of the keeper of the wardrobe. When he next came to account at the exchequer, he would bring with him this bill as evidence that he had supplied cash to the household, and in return the exchequer officials would give him a tally of receipt which he could then use when he proceeded to the upper exchequer to have his account audited. On the day when he was issued with his tally at the exchequer, entries would be made in both the issue and receipt rolls of the exchequer recording the receipt of his sum from the local official and its issue by assignment to the keeper of the wardrobe. Under the same date in his *recepta scaccarii* (whch was invariably drawn up after the end of the accounting period and in consultation with the exchequer officials), the keeper would record the receipt of the sum from the exchequer, *per manus* of the local official. Thus the date on which the transaction is recorded is not the date on which the household received the sum in question, but the date on which the local official exchanged his bill for a tally at the exchequer and it might be weeks, months, or even years after the keeper had actually received the sum in question.

These first four methods have this in common: in each case the wardrobe, through either the keeper or one of his subordinates, should have actually received cash in hand with which to make purchases or pay for services as it went along. The acquisition of this cash sometimes depended on the ability of the keeper or his deputies to cash the tallies with which they were issued, but for the household this was not normally a major problem. Household preference at the exchequer was always high, and if tallies issued to the household were for some reason found to be uncashable, they would usually be renewed promptly.[2] Thus one can safely assume that, in the vast majority of transactions effected in any of these first four ways, the household did actually receive the cash specified. With the remaining three methods this was not the case.

(5) Under this method a household official—let us say a purveyor—took goods for which he handed over (to the 'vendor') a private tally-stock.[3] Household ordinances stated that within seven days of making the purchase, the purveyor must bring the foils of all private tallies which he had issued into the counting-house of the wardrobe. Once this had been done, the vendor could bring his tally-stock into the counting-house, and the purchase would be verified by comparing the stock with the foil. Once this had been done, the vendor might then be paid in cash in the counting-house. In this case, there would almost certainly be no record of the transaction as the money with which the vendor was paid was simply taken out of that cash which had been received in one of the methods (1)–(4) described above. But quite possibly there would not be enough cash in the counting-house to allow for payment of the debt, or else

what cash there was had been earmarked for other purposes. If this was the case, then the vendor, having surrendered his tally-stock, would be issued in the counting-house with a bill of wardrobe debenture. This bill was now his authority—his receipt, in effect—armed with which he could go to the exchequer to request payment for the goods which he had provided for the household. Once he had presented his bill at the exchequer, the same procedure as that outlined in (4) above would be followed (depending again on whether he was issued with cash or with a tally in the exchequer), the entries noting that the keeper of the wardrobe had received the money *per manus* of the vendor. Once again the official date of the transaction could be long after the date on which the goods had actually been taken by the purveyor.

Methods (6) and (7) are both variations of method (5).

(6) This entailed the provision of goods or services for the household by a local official of the crown (a sheriff, for example), that is, someone who was in his own right an exchequer accountant as opposed to the ordinary vendor considered in (5), who was not. Assuming that the sheriff received a bill of debenture rather than cash in the counting-house, then the same procedure as under (4) above would be followed. But except in cases where the exchequer issue rolls are explicit enough to distinguish between, on the one hand, cash provided by the sheriff, and on the other hand, goods or services provided by him (and usually they are not), it is impossible to distinguish these transactions from those outlined under (4) above. From the keeper's point of view, however, the difference was of importance as it meant the difference between actually receiving cash, and simply running up debts which could then be transferred to the exchequer.

(7) This last method is really a more intricate version of method (5). In this case the private tally-stock issued by the purveyor to the vendor would be replaced in the counting-house not by a bill of wardrobe debenture, but by an indenture of assignment on a local official of the crown—for instance a customs collector. This might well be preferable to the vendor, since it obviated the need for him to go to the exchequer in order to 'cash' his bill; he could instead cash it with an official who lived in his own locality. Half of this indenture would be kept in the counting-house, the other half would be presented by the vendor to the customs collector, who, in theory, would make payment to him (in practice there was often considerable delay and/or discounting involved at this stage). The customs collector was then supposed to bring the half of the indenture which he had 'bought' from the vendor into the counting-house, where it would be verified by comparison with the other half, and he would be issued with a bill of wardrobe debenture. From this point onwards, the procedure under (4) above would again be followed. Again, however, there are important differences between this method and both methods (4) and (6) above. Firstly, the household has not actually received any cash as it has under (4) above, and secondly, although both the exchequer issue roll and the *recepta scaccarii* will

have recorded the payment as having been made to the keeper *per manus* of the customs collector, he has not in fact provided anything directly to the household. He has merely acted as an intermediary for the payment of the wardrobe's debts. The real vendor has in fact disappeared completely from the official record of the transaction.

It merely remains to point out that under methods (4), (6) and (7), the issue roll entry should always be accompanied by a corresponding entry with a *pro* marginal in the receipt roll, because the local official will himself be an exchequer accountant, and any money which he hands over for household debts must therefore be technically received at the exchequer. Under method (5), however, the payment would only be recorded in the receipt roll if the vendor was paid by assignment rather than in cash.

Analysis of the different ways in which the keeper of the wardrobe received his *recepta scaccarii* at different times has the following aim: given that the major expense of the wardrobe was on food and drink (including provender for horses), and given the way in which purveyance for the household was organised, what really mattered to many of those from whom the household took its provisions was whether or not there was sufficient cash in the wardrobe to make payment for goods taken.[4] It was tacitly accepted by this time that purveyors would not normally carry large quantities of cash around with them when they went in search of victuals for the household. At the actual time of purchase, wardrobe ('private') tallies would almost invariably be handed over. It was the next stage which was the important one. If within the next few days those whose goods had been requisitioned could go into the counting-house and receive cash in return for their tallies, they probably had little to complain about. If however there was no cash in the counting-house with which to pay them, then the road leading towards ultimate payment for their requisitioned goods might be a long and difficult one, involving all the potential hazards of being an exchequer creditor which have been so carefully described by Dr Harriss.[5] The sums involved must often have been considerable. Although it was far from uncommon for household purveyors to requisition quite small quantities of victuals— a few hens, sheep, pigs, and so forth, at a time—it was naturally much easier for them to go to places such as markets in good-sized towns where they could acquire the sorts of quantities they needed without too much effort. For the officers of the household, too, a good supply of cash passing through the counting-house was obviously preferable as it saved much parchment-work, and it avoided the unpopularity and consequent obstructionism which the household so often encountered, as witness the ceaseless complaints about purveyance in parliament and in the popular literature of the time.[6] Yet this ideal, desired by both the household officials and their creditors, was almost entirely dependent on the exchequer.

Notes to Appendix II

1. See pp. 97ff. above.
2. Harriss, 'Fictitious Loans'.
3. 'Private' tallies means non-exchequer tallies. See H. Jenkinson, 'Exchequer Tallies', *Archaeologia*, lxii, part 2 (1911), and 'Medieval Tallies, Public and Private', *Archaeologia*, lxxiv (1925), where examples are shown of private tallies issued by, among others, William Manton, keeper of the wardrobe 1361–6.
4. Above, pp.83–97.
5. 'Preference at the Medieval Exchequer'.
6. See, for example, Steel, *Receipt of the Exchequer*, xxxiv–xxxv.

APPENDIX III

The staff of the household 1353–1406[1]

	1353–4	1359–60	1366–7*	1369*	1372–3	1376–7	1383–4*	1389–90*	1392–3*	1395–6	1402–3	1405–6*
Officers[2]	10	10	13	12	9	10	7	9	11	11	11	9
Chamber knights[3]	19	57	4	5	3	3	11	8	8	9	13	12
Clerks	20	24	64	21	26	22	20	23	25	35	32	32
Sergeants-at-arms	16	18		6	2	5	3	3	3	7		137
Sergeants of offices	17	33	63	74	18	21	19	19	17	23	16	
Esquires	78	63			69	68	87	128[6]	101	168	88	
Huntsmen	6	31	66	20	18	18	10	10	10	11	13	15
Falconers	7	24		13		3	4					
Valets of chamber	68	21		19	97	94	26	18	20	33	34	37
Valets of offices		65	51	60			77	81	80	106	121	163
Messengers												
Carters	15	19	19	18	21	14	13	15	14	21	16	23
Valets of stables	94	135	163	136	93	78	65	91	89	102	79	105
Cleaners	2	2	4	3	2	2	2	2	2	2	2	2
SUB-TOTAL	368[4]	579[5]	447	387	358	338	344	407	380	528	425	535
Grooms of offices	?	?	?	?	?	?	52	47	53	70	97	109
TOTAL							396	454	433	598	522	644

* = including the queen's household

Notes to Appendix III

1. Based on surviving wardrobe accounts books: PRO E101/392/12, 393/11, 396/2, 396/11, 397/5, 398/9, 401/2, 402/3, 402/5, 403/10 and 404/21; and BL *Add. Ms.* 35,115 and *Harl.* 319.
2. Includes steward, chamberlain, controller, keeper of the wardrobe, cofferer, keeper of the privy seal, secretary, almoner, physician, surgeon, and dean of the chapel.
3. Including bannerets and knights of the household in 1353–4 and 1359–60.
4. Includes 16 archers.
5. Includes 44 archers, 8 smiths, and 14 minstrels.
6. 63 esquires for the whole year; 65 for less than half the year. See above, p.40.

APPENDIX IV

Edward III's chamber knights and bachelors, 1360–77

(a)   Chamber Knights

1364 (great wardrobe account, E101/394/16, m.9)
Peter de Brewes
Richard Pembridge
John de Foxley
Alan de Buxhull
Roger de la Warde
Richard la Zouche
Bernard Brocas
Thomas Bradewell
Esmond Everard
John de Burley
John de Eynesford
William de Windsor

1366–7 (wardrobe account, E101/396/2, f.56)
Thomas Beauchamp
Peter de Brewes
Richard Pembridge
Alan de Buxhull

1369 (wardrobe account, E101/396/11, f.17)
Thomas Beauchamp
Alan de Buxhull
Richard Pembridge
Peter de Brewes
Esmond Everard

1371–2 (wardrobe account, E101/397/5, ff.43, 45)
Alan de Buxhull
Peter de Brewes
Richard Stury
Richard Pembridge (Michaelmas term only)

1372–3 (wardrobe account, E101/397/5, f.82)
Alan de Buxhull
Peter de Brewes
Richard Stury

1376–7 (wardrobe account, E101/398/9, ff. 3, 27)
Alan de Buxhull
Peter de Brewes
Richard Stury
Philip La Vache

(b) Bachelors (list of *bachelerii* provided with robes for Christmas 1366; E101/395/10)

Thomas Beauchamp
Alan de Buxhull
Richard Pembridge
Bernard Brocas
Gilbert de Spencer
Esmond Everard
William de Windsor
John de Eynesford
Thomas Murrieux
Thomas Bradewell
Richard de Arundel
Robert Salle

Peter de Brewes
Richard Stury
John de Foxley
John atte Wode
Richard la Zouche
John de Burley
Robert Ashton
Roger Elmrugge
John d'Ypres
Thomas Tirell
John de Arundel

APPENDIX V

Richard II's knights

Notes to Appendices V and VI

1. *Local interests*: most men's local interests (e.g., appointments to commissions), coincided with the areas in which they held land. On occasions, however, they did not, in which case more than one area is given. Also, some men either held land and/or were locally active in more than one area, and in these cases too both areas are given. Some men's local interests and landholding areas are difficult to determine, in which case the area is preceded by a question mark; where there are no indications of a man's local interests, there is no entry under this column.

2. *Date*: this is the first date at which the man in question is stated in those records which I have consulted as being attached to the king in the capacity under which he is listed. Thus it is the latest date by which he had become attached to the king. These first mentions are often accompanied by, for example, grants, which tend to indicate that they are close to the date of appointment or retention. So although the dates given are not fully reliable guides to recruitment dates, they are probably close in most cases.

3. *Knights of the Chamber*: the list includes all those mentioned in any source as a knight of the chamber, but asterisks are used to indicate those who received fees and robes in the wardrobe account books. The first date given is the date at which the knight in question was first described as a chamber knight or took up office in the household. The date in brackets indicates (where applicable) his first mention as a king's knight or royal retainer.

4. *Life Retainers*: (RL) indicates a knight retained for life by the king (but note that some knights were retained for life years after they first became king's knights. The date given refers to the first mention as a king's knight).

Knights of the chamber and lay officers of the household

Name (and office if applicable)	Local interests	Date
* Richard de Abberbury	Oxon	1377
* William de Arundel (RL)	Sussex/Surrey	1392
Robert Bardolf (RL)	Oxon	1386
John de Beauchamp of Holt (steward 1387–8)	Worcs	1385
William Beauchamp, Lord Bergavenny (acting chamberlain 1378–1380)	South Wales	1377
* Baldwin de Bereford	Oxon	1377
James Berners	Surrey	1383 (1382)
* Thomas Blount	Oxon/Berks	1384
Nicholas Bonde	?Cheshire	1377
Guy Brian (acting chamberlain 1377–8)	Gloucs	1377
John de Burley (RL)	Hereford	1377
* Simon de Burley (under-chamberlain 1377–88)	Hereford/Kent	1377
Roger de Clarendon	?Somerset/Gloucs	1390 (1378)
* John Clanvow	Hereford	1381 (1380)
Lewis Clifford	Devon/Norfolk	1391 (1378)
* Thomas Clifford	Westm'land/Yorks	1382

Name (and office if applicable)	Local interests	Date
* Peter Courtenay (acting chamberlain 1388–90)	Devon/Somerset	1377
Nicholas Dagworth	Norfolk	1393 (1379)
John Devereux (steward 1388–93)	Hereford	1388 (1377)
George Felbridge	Norfolk	1393 (1385)
* Simon Felbridge	Norfolk	1395 (1394)
* John Golafre	Oxon	1385
John Harleston	Essex	1384 (1380)
* John del Hay	Hants	1377
John Holand (chief chamberlain 1390–99)	Devon/diverse	1390 (1377)
Richard Lescrope (steward 1377–8)	Yorks	1377
Stephen Lescrope (under-chamberlain 1398–9) (RL)	Yorks	1398 (1396)
William Lescrope (under-chamberlain 1393–8) (RL)	Yorks/North Wales	1393 (1389)
William Lisle 'the younger' (RL)	Cambs/Oxon	1395 (1392)
John Montacute (steward 1381–7)	Hants/Herts	1381
* William Murreres	Suffolk/Yorks	1377
* Thomas Murrieux	Norfolk/Suffolk	1381 (1378)
* William de Nevill	Yorks/Durham	1377
Thomas Percy (under-chamberlain 1390–93; steward 1393–99)	Yorks/diverse	1390 (1378)
* Thomas Peytevyn	Hereford	1378
Baldwin Raddington (controller 1381–97) (RL)	Devon/Middx	1381
Robert Rous	Dorset	1381 (1378)
* John Russell (RL)	Worcs	1392 (1387)
John Salisbury	Wilts	1385
* Arnold Savage (RL)	Kent	1392 (1386)
Hugh Segrave (steward 1378–81)	Berks	1378
* Benedict Sely (RL)	Sussex	1395 (1391)
* Nicholas Sharnesfeld	Hereford	1378
John Stanley (controller 1397–9) (RL)	Lancs/Chesh	1397 (1389)
Richard Stury	Kent/South Wales	1381 (1378)
* Philip La Vache (RL)	Bucks/Oxon	1392 (1378)
Aubrey de Vere (acting chamberlain 1380–2)	Essex/diverse	1380 (1378)
* Robert Witteneye	Hereford	1392
Bernard van Zedeletz	?Netherlandish	1380 (1378)

King's knights

Name	Local interests	Date
Thomas Abberbury	Oxon/Berks	1386
John Annesley (RL)	Notts	1385
John Lord Arundel (RL)	Somerset/Dorset/Wilts	1378
John de Arundel	Somerset/Dorset/Wilts	1386
Richard de Arundel (RL)	Northumb'land	1398
John de Assheton (RL)	Lancs	1398
William Bagot (RL)	Warwicks	1398
Thomas Barre (RL)	Hereford	1386

Name	Local interests	Date
William Beauchamp of Powick (RL)	Gloucs	1392
John Beaufort (RL)	Somerset/Dorset	1392
John Lord Beaumont (RL)	Leics/Lincs	1393
Kennard de la Bere	Hereford	1386
Herman Bergo (RL)	Foreigner	1386
Edward de Berkeley	Gloucs	1378
Thomas Botiller (RL)	Gloucs	1393
John Braham (RL)	Suffolk	1392
Gerard Braybrook snr.	Bedfords	1386
Gerard Braybrook jnr.	Bedfords	1390
Thomas Brette (RL)	Gloucs/Hereford	1392
Bernard Brocas snr.	Hants	1378
Bernard Brocas jnr. (RL)	Hants	1389
William Burcester	Sussex/Kent	1396
Nicholas Burgman (RL)	Foreigner	1397
John Bussy (RL)	Lincs	1391
Alan de Buxhull	Sussex/Dorset	1377
Walter Bytterley (RL)	Salop	1395
John de Calvely (RL)	Cheshire/Leics	1394
John Camerer (RL)	Foreigner	1397
Alan Cheyne	Dorset	1381
Hugh Cheyne	Salop/Worcs	1386
John Cheyne (RL)	Gloucs	1380
Thomas Clanvow	Hereford	1395
William Clifford (RL)	Westm'land/Yorks	1397
Nicholas de Clifton (RL)	Cheshire	1396
Robert Clyfton (RL)	Lancs	1398
William Clynton (RL)	Warwicks	1381
John Lord Cobham	Kent	1378
Henry de Conwy	?North Wales	1397
Fulk Corbet	Salop	1381
John de Cornewall (RL)	Salop	1397
Philip de Courtenay	Devon	1378
David Cradok	Cheshire	1380
Richard Cradok (RL)	Cheshire	1391
John de Croft (RL)	Lancs	1398
John Daa		1384
Edward Dalyngridge (RL)	Sussex	1389
William d'Angle	Foreigner	1386
Philip Darcy	Lincs	1389
Hugh Despenser (RL)	Northants	1391
Walter Devereux	Hereford	1386
William Drayton (RL)	Oxon	1379
William de Elmham	Suffolk	1386
William Elys (RL)	Yorks	1389
John de Eylesford	Hereford	1394
William Farringdon (RL)	?Bucks	1394
Thomas de Felton	Norfolk	1381
Ralph Ferrers	Staffs/Leics	1378
William FitzRalph (RL)	?Herts	1392
Thomas Flemmyng (RL)	Ireland/Devon/Cornwall	1398
John Godarde (RL)	Yorks	1392
William Goderiche	?Lincs	1394

Name	Local interests	Date
Otho de Granson (RL)	Foreigner	1392
Henry Green (RL)	Northants	1397
Robert Greenacres		1388
Thomas Grey of Heton (RL)	Northumb'land	1389
Andrew Hake	?Gloucs/?Sussex	1397
Stephen de Hales	Norfolk	1386
Gilbert de Halsale (RL)	Cheshire	1398
Herman Hanz	Foreigner	1386
Hugh de Hastyngs	Norfolk	1381
Nicholas Hauberk (RL)	Rutland/Leics/Salop	1393
Gerard Heron (RL)	Northumb'land	1393
William de Hilton (RL)	Durham/Westm'land	1386
John de Hirseborn (RL)	Foreigner	1397
Richard Hoghton (RL)	Lancs	1398
William Hoo	Bedfords	1389
John Howard (RL)	Norfolk	1394
John de Kentwode	Berks/Cornwall	1378
Richard de Kirkeby (RL)	Lancs	1398
Dampnon Knobhill (RL)	Foreigner	1397
Thomas Latimer	Northants	1385
Walter atte Lee	Herts	1386
Robert de Legh (RL)	Cheshire	1397
William de Legh (RL)	Cheshire	1398
William Lisle 'the elder' (RL)	Bedfords	1397
John Littilbury (RL)	Lincs	1392
Nigel Loryng	Bedfords	1378
Adam de Louches	Berks	1378
John Lord Lovell (RL)	Wilts/Oxon	1386
Hugh Lutterell (RL)	Somerset	1395
Anketil Malorre	Lincs	1378
John Montacute jnr.	Hants/Herts/diverse	1383
Richard Montacute	Gloucs/Hants	1386
Thomas Mowbray	Lincs/Sussex/Norfolk	1382
Ralph Lord Nevill (RL)	Yorks/Durham/Westm'land	1395
Edmund Noon	Norfolk	1386
John Paveley	Northants	1394
Henry Percy jnr. (Hotspur) (RL)	Yorks/Northumb'land	1391
Ralph Percy (RL)	Yorks/Northumb'land	1393
Edward Perers (RL)	Herts/Ireland	1394
Adam Peshale (RL)	Staffs/Salop	1390
Thomas Peytevyn jnr.	Hereford	1386
Philip Picworth (RL)	Yorks	1394
Thomas Picworth (RL)	Yorks	1395
Ingelram de Ployche	Foreigner	1378
William de Plumpton (RL)	Yorks	1398
Michael de la Pole jnr.	Yorks/Suffolk/diverse	1386
John de Pulls (RL)	Cheshire	1398
James Pykeryng	Yorks	1390
Ralph de Radcliffe (RL)	Lancs	1397
Richard Redman (RL)	Yorks/Cumb'land	1388
Henry de Retford (RL)	Lincs/Notts	1394
John de Roches	Wilts	1378
John de Routhe (RL)	Yorks	1394

Name	Local interests	Date
Nicholas Ryvynes	Foreigner	1394
Edward St John	Sussex	1378
John St John (RL)	Devon/Hereford	1393
Digory Seys	Foreigner	1378
Peter Shaldusr	Foreigner	1386
Roger Siglem	Foreigner	1386
Ralph de Stafford	Staffs	1382
Thomas Lord Stafford (RL)	Staffs/Kent/diverse	1389
Ralph Standish	Lancs/Cheshire	1381
Walter Stiward (RL)	Scotland	1393
Roger Le Straunge	Salop	1391
William Sturmy (RL)	Hants/Wilts	1392
John de Sully	Devon	1377
Thomas Swynburn (RL)	Essex	1395
Gilbert Lord Talbot snr.	Hereford/Berks	1384
Gilbert Lord Talbot jnr.	Hereford/Berks	1392
Thomas Talbot (RL)	Lancs	1392
John Thornebury	Herts	1388
Edmund de Thorpe (RL)	Norfolk	1393
John de Thorpe	Gloucs	1377
William de Thorpe	Northants	1386
John Trailly (RL)	Bedfords/Cambs	1393
John Tryvet	Somerset	1378
Thomas Tryvet	Somerset	1378
John de Veer (RL)	Foreigner	1399
Richard Venables (RL)	Cheshire	1398
John de Vileyn	Foreigner	1379
Richard Waldegrave (RL)	Suffolk	1377
John Walsh	Lincs	1384
William de Windsor	Westm'land/Cumb'land/diverse	1379
John atte Wode	Worcs/Salop	1378
David Wogan	Ireland	1397
John Worth	?Middx/Wilts/Hants	1377
Hugh de Wrottesley	Staffs	1377
William Yssenden (RL)	Foreigner	1399

APPENDIX VI

Henry IV's knights (see Notes to Appendix V)

Knights of the chamber and lay officers of the household

Name (and office if applicable)	Local interests	Date
* Richard de Arundel	Northumb'land/Hereford	1402 (1400)
Thomas Brounfleet (controller 1401–3; keeper 1408–13)	Yorks/Beds	1401
* Robert Chalons	Devon	1402 (1399)
Robert Corbet	Salop	1401 (1399)
* Francis de Courte	Foreigner/Pembroke	1402 (1400)
* John Dalyngridge	Sussex	1402 (1400)
Thomas Erpingham (under-chamberlain 1399–1404; steward 1404)	Norfolk	1399
* Richard Goldesburgh	Yorks/Lincs	1402 (1400)
Richard Lord Grey of Codnor (under-chamberlain 1404–13)	Derbys	1404
* Nicholas Hauberk	Leics/Salop	1402 (1401)
William Heron, Lord Say (steward 1402–4)	Northumb'land/Sussex	1402
Roger Leche (controller 1403–5)	Derbys	1403 (1399)
John Littilbury	Lincs	1401 (1399)
Robert Litton (controller 1399–1401)	Essex	1399
* John Pelham	Sussex	1402 (1399)
Thomas Percy (steward 1401–2)	Yorks/diverse	1401
Thomas Rempston (steward 1399–1401)	Notts	1399
* Ralph Rochford	Lincs	1402 (1400)
* Hugh Stafford	Staffs	1406
John Stanley (steward 1404–13)	Lancs/Cheshire	1404 (1399)
* John Straunge (controller 1405–13)	Norfolk	1402 (1400)
* Thomas Swynford	Lincs	1402 (1399)
* John Tiptoft (keeper 1406–8) (RL)	Cambs	1402 (1399)
* Payn Tiptoft	Cambs	1402 (1401)

King's knights

Name	Local interests	Date
Roger Acton	Salop	1408
John Annesley (RL)	Notts	1399
John Arundel	Cornwall	1405
John Ashley (RL)	?Wilts	1401
Nicholas Athirton	Lancs	1403
William Bardolf	Norfolk	1401
Thomas Beauchamp	Somerset	1412
William Beauchamp of Powick (RL)	Gloucs	1399
Edward Benstede	Herts	1401
Baldwin de Bereford	Oxon	1400

Name	Local interests	Date
Robert Bernay	Norfolk	1401
Hugh Berwyk	Bucks	1401
John Blount	Derbys	1405
Walter Blount	Derbys	1400
John del Bolde (RL)	Lancs	1400
John Bothwell (RL)	Scotland	1402
John Braham	Suffolk	1399
Gerard Braybrook jnr. (RL)	Bedfords	1399
Thomas Brette	Gloucs/Hereford	1407
Thomas Broke	Somerset	1405
Hugh Browe (RL)	Cheshire/Rutland	1400
Peter Bukton	Yorks	1399
John Burton	Notts	1400
Andrew Butiller	Suffolk	1402
Walter Bytterley	Salop	1400
John Carbonell	Suffolk	1411
Thomas Carreu	Devon/South Wales	1403
George Chadelyche (RL)	Foreigner	1402
Edward Charlton, lord of Powys	Wales	1400
John Cheyne	Gloucs	1400
Thomas Clanvow	Hereford	1404
William Clifford	Westm'land/Yorks	1399
Walter Clopton (RL)	Suffolk	1399
John Clyfton	Notts	1400
William Clynton	Warwicks	1412
Hortonk van Clux	Foreigner	1400
John Colville del Dale (RL)	Yorks	1399
John Colvylle	Cambs	1406
John Copuldyk	Lincs	1403
John de Cornewall	Salop	1400
William Cromwell (RL)	Lincs	1400
John Dabrichecourt (RL)	Foreigner/Notts	1400
John Vaques Dalmadaam (RL)	Foreigner	1400
John Depden	Yorks	1400
Hugh Despenser (RL)	Northants	1399
John Deyncourt	Lincs/Notts/Derby	1405
Wenceslas Dorsteynour	Foreigner/Leics	1403
Gawyn de Dunbarre (RL)	Scotland	1402
John Dynham	Devon	1407
William de Elmham	Suffolk	1399
John de Etton	Yorks	1401
Ralph de Euyr	Durham/Northumb'land	1399
John Everyngham	Lincs	1405
John de Eylesford	Hereford	1401
John de Eynesford	Leics	1400
William Farringdon	?Bucks	1400
George Felbridge	Norfolk	1400
Simon Felbridge	Norfolk	1401
Henry FitzHugh (RL)	Yorks	1399
Thomas Flemmyng (RL)	Yorks	1399
Thomas Fogge	Kent	1402
Robert Fraunceys	Staffs	1399
William de Fulthorpe	Yorks	1400

Name	Local interests	Date
Luder Garescorffe (RL)	Foreigner	1401
Thomas Geney (RL)	Norfolk/Suffolk	1401
Walter Goldingham	Essex	1412
Thomas Gray of Wark snr.	Northumb'land	1400
Thomas Gray of Wark jnr.	Northumb'land	1412
John de Greily	Foreigner	1401
Thomas Grey of Heton	Northumb'land	1399
John Greyndour	Hereford/Gloucs	1399
John Greynvill	Devon	1407
Edward Hastyngs	Norfolk	1399
Richard Hastyngs	Yorks	1402
Thomas Hawley (RL)	Lincs	1401
Thomas Hemgrave	Suffolk	1408
Gerard Heron (RL)	Northumb'land	1400
Robert Hilton	Yorks	1403
John Hirseborn (RL)	Foreigner	1402
Richard Hoghton	Lancs	1406
Walter Hungerford	Wilts	1399
Walter de la Hyde (RL)	Ireland	1401
Gilbert de Kyghley	Kent	1412
Richard de Langyn (RL)	?	1401
Henry Lescrope	Yorks	1403
Stephen Lescrope	Yorks	1404
John Lisle	Hants	1400
William Lisle 'the elder' (RL)	Bedfords	1401
William Lisle 'the younger'	Cambs/Oxon	1401
Alexander de Lounde	Yorks	1402
John Luterell (RL)	Somerset	1400
William Marny	Essex	1406
Laurence de Merbury (RL)	Cheshire	1401
Alfons de Monterre (RL)	Foreigner	1400
Anthony de Montford	Foreigner	1402
Robert Mounteney	Suffolk	1402
Henry Nevylle	Leics	1401
Edmund Noon	Norfolk	1412
Robert de Ogle snr.	Northumb'land	1406
John Oldcastle	Hereford	1404
William Parr	Cheshire/Westm'land	1402
John Penres	Wales	1403
Henry Percy (Hotspur)	Yorks/Northumb'land/Cheshire	1399
Thomas Percy jnr.	?Yorks	1408
Edward Perers	Herts/Ireland	1406
Thomas Picworth (RL)	Yorks	1399
Thomas Pomeray	Devon	1400
John Prendergast	?Northumb'land	1401
Baldwin Raddington	Devon/Middx	1399
Richard Redman	Yorks/Cumb'land	1401
John Robessart (RL)	Foreigner/?Warwicks	1399
Henry Rochford	Lincs	1403
John Rochford	Lincs	1400
Thomas de Rokeby	Yorks/Northumb'land	1405
David Rouclif (RL)	Yorks	1399
Nicholas Ryvynes	Foreigner	1400

Name	Local interests	Date
John St John	Devon/Hereford	1399
Richard de Sancto Mauro (RL)	Somerset	1399
Gerard Salvayn	Yorks	1399
Arnold Savage	Kent	1403
John Sayvyll	Yorks	1403
Hans Shellendorf	Foreigner	1401
Thomas Shelton	?Hants	1405
Roger Siglem	Foreigner	1401
Humphrey de Stafford	Dorset	1399
Richard Stanhope	Notts	1405
William de Stanley	Cheshire	1405
William Sturmy	Hants/Wilts	1401
Roger Swillington	Yorks/Suffolk	1400
Thomas Swynburn	Essex	1400
Richard Tempest	Yorks	1403
Edmund de Thorpe (RL)	Norfolk	1399
Roger Trumpington (RL)	Cambs	1401
Thomas Tunstall	Lancs	1402
Robert Umfraville	Northumb'land	1402
Philip La Vache	Bucks/Oxon	1403
Rustin de Villa Nova	Foreigner/?Yorks	1408
William Walkelin	?Northants	1401
Hugh de Waterton	Yorks	1399
Thomas de Wedenesley	Derbys	1399
Thomas de Wellesley (RL)	Ireland	1400
John Wilton	Norfolk	1402

Abbreviations

All works are cited in full in the bibliography.
All references in the text to manuscript sources are to documents deposited in the Public Record Office unless otherwise stated.

Adam of Usk	Chronicon Adae de Usk
Annales	Annales Ricardi Secundi et Henrici Quarti
Anon. Chron.	Anonimalle Chronicle 1333–81
BIHR	Bulletin of the Institute of Historical Research
BL	British Library
CCR	Calendar of Close Rolls
CFR	Calendar of Fine Rolls
Chron. Angl.	Chronicon Angliae 1328–88
CIM	Calendar of Inquisitions Miscellaneous
CIPM	Calendar of Inquisitions Post Mortem
CPMR	Calendar of Plea and Memoranda Rolls of the City of London
CPR	Calendar of Patent Rolls
EHD	English Historical Documents
EHR	English Historical Review
Eulog. Hist.	Eulogium Historiarum sive Temporis
Foedera	Foedera Conventiones Literae et Cuiuscunque Generis Acta Publica
Hardyng	Chronicle of John Hardyng
Hist. Angl.	Historia Anglicana, by Thomas Walsingham, 2 vols
JMH	Journal of Medieval History
King's Works	H.M. Colvin et al, History of the King's Works, 3 vols
Knighton	Chronicon Henrici Knighton, 2 vols
Liber Quotidianus	Liber Quotidianus Contrarotulatoris Garderobiae
London Letter-Book	Letter-Books of the City of London, vols G-H
Med. Stud.	Medieval Studies
POPC	Proceedings and Ordinances of the Privy Council

PRO	Public Record Office
Rogers	A. Rogers, 'The Royal Household of Henry IV'
RP	Rotuli Parliamentorum
RS	Rolls Series
St Alban's Chronicle	The St Alban's Chronicle 1406–1420
SHF	Société de l'Histoire de France
SR	Statutes of the Realm
Traison et Mort	Chronique de la Traison et Mort de Richard II
TRHS	Transactions of the Royal Historical Society
Vita	Historia Vitae et Regni Ricardi Secundi
Westm. Chron.	The Westminster Chronicle 1381–1394

Notes

Introduction

1. L.M. Larson, *The King's Household in England Before the Norman Conquest* (1904), 76.
2. Quoted in J.O. Prestwich, 'The Military Household of the Norman Kings', *EHR*, xcvi (1981), 7.
3. Printed in C. Johnson, ed., *Dialogus de Scaccario* 1950), 129–35.
4. *Ibid.*, 1.
5. F. Barlow, *William Rufus* (1983), 134–55.
6. Prestwich, 'Military Household', 30; G.H. White, 'The Household of the Norman Kings', *TRHS*, xxx (1948), 130; Barlow, 102ff.
7. Prestwich, 'Military Household', 29.
8. S.B. Chrimes, *An Introduction to the Administrative History of Medieval England* (2nd ed., 1959), 25; White, 'Household of Norman Kings', 136. The last master of the writing-office under Henry I was Robert de Sigillo (1131–5), whose wages the king raised from 10d. to 2s. a day (*Dialogus de Scaccario*, ed. Johnson, 129). In 1141 he became bishop of London.
9. B. Wilkinson, *The Chancery under Edward III* (1929), 2.
10. White, 'Household of Norman Kings', 144.
11. William Mauduit in the later years of Henry I's reign; he ate in the *domus: assidue in domo commedet* (*Dialogus de Scaccario*, ed. Johnson, 133).
12. H.G. Richardson and G.O. Sayles, *The Governance of Medieval England from the Conquest to Magna Carta* (1963), 229–31; W.L. Warren, *Henry II* (1973), 254.
13. 'et debet habere dicas contra omnes officiales regis ut testis per omnia' (*Dialogus de Scaccario*, ed. Johnson, 134).
14. F.M. Stenton, *Anglo-Saxon England* (3rd edn., 1971), 302.
15. Larson, *King's Household*, 83–4.
16. For the *housecarles* generally see Larson, *King's Household*, 158–71, and Stenton, *Anglo-Saxon England*, 412–13, 582. For a recent and revisionist view of them, see N. Hooper, 'The Housecarles in

England in the Eleventh Century', *Anglo-Norman Studies VII*, ed. R.A. Brown (1985).
17. Larson, *King's Household*, 171.
18. Prestwich, 'Military Household', *passim*; M. Chibnall, 'Mercenaries and the *familia regis* under Henry I', *History*, 62 (1977), 15–23.
19. White, 'Household of Norman Kings', 149–50; Warren, *Henry II*, 254.
20. *Dialogus de Scaccario*, 134; White, 'Household of Norman Kings', 153.
21. Prestwich, 'Military Household', 8.
22. White, 'Household of Norman Kings', 127, 142.
23. See the Household Ordinance of 13 November 1279, printed in T.F. Tout, *Chapters in the Administrative History of Mediaeval England*, ii (1920), 158; and *ibid.*, 32.
24. *Ibid.*, 33–4.
25. *Ibid.*, 36–8.
26. Household Ordinance of 1318, printed in T.F. Tout, *The Place of the Reign of Edward II in English History* (2nd edn. by H. Johnstone, 1396), 245.
27. Tout, *Chapters*, ii, 39 nn. 1, 2; 160, n. 3.
28. B.J. Byerly and C.R. Byerly, *Records of the Wardrobe and Household 1285–6* (1977), xxviii–xxix.
29. Tout, *Chapters*, ii, 157.
30. 1318 Ordinance, ed. Tout, 276.
31. *Rotuli de Liberate ac de Misis et Praestitis regnante Johanne*, ed. T. D. Hardy (Record Commission, 1844), 110–11, 118, 122, 128, 135, 143, 159, and *passim*, shows between 10s. and 5s. shoes allowances being given to various servants, and 7s. 6d. for robes.
32. A. R. Myers, *The Household of Edward IV* (1959), 76–157.
33. For example, there were twenty carts, each with five horses, attached to the household; each esquire was supposed to keep three horses at court, and most other servants kept at least one horse at court. There were usually at least 100 sumptermen and palfreymen employed in the household to care for the horses. For a household of *c.* 500 persons, 1,000 horses is probably a conservative estimate. It is of some interest to note that when the Dalai Lama fled

Tibet in 1959, he had with him only 40 servants but 150 pack-horses.

34. See the preamble, 244.

35. J. C. Davies, *The Baronial Opposition to Edward II* (1918); Tout, *Place of Reign of Edward II*.

36. See in particular Chrimes, *Introduction to Administrative History*, 156–61; G. L. Harriss, *King, Parliament and Public Finance in England to 1369* (1975), 186–7.

37. Peter of Blois quoted in K. Mertes, 'Secular Noble Households in England 1350–1550' (Unpublished University of Edinburgh Ph.D. thesis, 1981), 325. I am very grateful to Dr Mertes for allowing me to consult her thesis. See also Warren, *Henry II*, 210; and J. C. Holt, *Magna Carta* (1965), 325; W. Stubbs, *Select Charters* (9th edn by H. W. C. Davis, 1913), 376; M. C. Prestwich, *War, Politics and Finance under Edward I* (1972), 118, for complaints about purveyance.

38. *Rotuli de Liberate*, ed. Hardy, *Misae* roll; one of the nine 'monthly' totals is missing and cannot be reconstructed since the roll is incomplete. F. M. Powicke, 'Richard I and John', *Cambridge Medieval History*, vi (1968), 222, said that the '*Misae* rolls . . . can definitely be described in John's reign as rolls of the Wardrobe', but what the 1210–11 roll clearly does *not* record are the actual daily living expenses of king and household which invariably formed the main item in later wardrobe accounts. It records the king's expenditure on such items as plate and jewels, cloth, gifts to servants and foreign dignitaries, annuities for knights who fought with the king, alms, messengers, the hiring of carts, building and maintenance of royal castles, the king's hunting expenses, and even the spending of 1*d*. 'pro uno urinali'! (164).

39. Harriss, *King, Parliament and Public Finance*, 196–7; Chrimes, *Introduction to Administrative History*, 106.

40. Harriss, *King, Parliament and Public Finance*, 201–2; M. C. Prestwich, 'Exchequer and Wardrobe in the Later Years of Edward I', *BIHR*, xlvi (1973), 8, 10.

41. Natalie Fryde, *The Tyranny and Fall of Edward II 1321–1326* (1979), 97–9, attributes such thrift to the king's 'characteristic meanness', but his subjects would hardly have been displeased.

42. E101/390/12.

43. E101/392/12. The total given is £24,760, but this includes payments to the great wardrobe of £5,690.

44. E101/393/11.

45. Harriss, *King, Parliament and Public Finance*, 214.

46. Prestwich, *War, Politics and Finance*, 220–1; Harriss, *King, Parliament and Public Finance*, 220 and n. 1.

47. Harriss, *King, Parliament and Public Finance*, 141.

48. *Ibid.*, 165–85.

49. Stubbs, *Select Charters*, 383.

50. Chrimes, *Introduction to Administrative History*,

77–8, 146; see also *The Wardrobe Book of William de Norwell*, eds. M. Lyon, B. Lyon and H. S. Lucas (1983), xxiii; Wilkinson, *Chancery under Edward III*, 95; H. Maxwell-Lyte, *Historical Notes on the use of the Great Seal of England* (HMSO, 1926), 329.

51. Wilkinson, *Chancery under Edward III*, 23.

52. Chrimes, *Introduction to Administrative History*, 77–8.

53. Tout, *Chapters*, ii, 36–8; 1318 Ordinance, in Tout, ed., 246.

54. Chrimes, *Introduction to Administrative History*, 204–5, 218; Wilkinson, *Chancery under Edward III*, 41, 47; Maxwell-Lyte, *Historical Notes*, 75ff., 84–6.

55. Chrimes, *Introduction to Administrative History*, 200.

56. See in particular Tout, *Place of Reign of Edward II*, and Davies, *Baronial Opposition*, *passim*; for a more recent exposition of the same view in relation to Richard II's use of the signet see A. Tuck, *Richard II and the English Nobility* (1973), 65–70, 130–1.

57. See refs. at n. 36 above.

58. Chrimes, *Introduction to Administrative History*, 66, 134, 136; Prestwich, *War, Politics and Finance*, 43, 57–60, 154; Byerly, *Records of Wardrobe and Household*, xvi–xxii.

59. For what follows, the principal secondary authorities are: J. E. A. Jolliffe, *Angevin Kingship* (1955), especially 226–77; Richardson and Sayles, *Governance of Medieval England*, 215–50; Richardson, 'Chamber under Henry II'; Chrimes, *Introduction to Administrative History*; Prestwich, 'Exchequer and Wardrobe', and *War, Politics and Finance*, 153–221; Harriss, *King, Parliament and Public Finance*, 186–228; and Tout, *Chapters*, vols. i–iii, which is packed with detail on all aspects of financial and other administrative matters in the thirteenth and fourteenth centuries.

60. Jolliffe, *Angevin Kingship*, 286.

61. Richardson and Sayles, *Governance of Medieval England*, 239.

62. See for instance *Rotuli de Liberate*, ed. Hardy, 110, 118, 128, 143, 159, 164.

63. Harriss, *King, Parliament and Public Finance*, 193–5.

64. Prestwich, 'Exchequer and Wardrobe', 5.

65. Fryde, *Tyranny and Fall*, 92.

66. E101/390/1, f. 36.

67. E101/391/1, *passim*.

68. See for example *CPR, 1345–8*, 79.

69. Prestwich, 'Military Household', 5–6, and sources quoted there; see also for instance John's *Misae* roll (*Rotuli de Liberate*, ed. Hardy, 125–6), where payments varying between ½ mark and 4 marks were made to twenty-six knights 'de familia regis'; some Flemish knights also received annuities from John (*ibid.*, 165).

70. The title 'banneret' indicated a superior military rank, and carried with it a certain social status; the banneret's personal retinue would be larger than

tht of a simple knight, up to 20 men, perhaps, and he received wages while on campaign of 4*s*. a day instead of the knight's 2*s*. For further discussion of household knights and bannerets see below, pp. 204–12.

71. Prestwich, *War, Politics and Finance*, 46–7, 55.

72. 1279 Ordinance, in Tout, ed., 162.

73. Prestwich, *War, Politics and Finance*, 48.

74. 1318 Ordinance, in Tout, ed., 253–4.

75. E101/398/14; E101/392/12, f. 41; E101/393/11, f. 76.

76. 1318 Ordinance, in Tout, ed., 256; 1279 Ordinance, in Tout, ed., 163.

77. Mertes, 'Secular Noble Households', 16–7.

79. G. A. Holmes, *The Good Parliament* (1975)

Chapter I: The King's Servants

1. See below, Appendix III.

2. For an inventory of vessels in the household, see *CCR*, *1377–81*, 213.

3. *King's Works*, ii, 879, 931; and see Mark Girouard, *Life in the English Country House* (1978), 53. For a fuller discussion of this, see below, pp. 204ff.

4. I refer essentially to the views concerning the social stratification of the late medieval English nobility which were first put forward by K. B. McFarlane, *The Nobility of Later Medieval England* (1973), 268–9 and *passim*.

6. R. Allen Brown, *English Castles* (2nd edn., 1976), 208.

7. *King's Works*, ii, 872–882; and iii, map 4. For Eltham and Sheen, see respectively pp. 930–7, and 994–1002.

8. *Ibid.*, 962, 967–8, 974–6.

9. Tout, *Place of Edward II*, 253, 269–71, 278–9.

10. E101/396/2; 396/11; 397/5; 398/9.

11. E101/392/12, ff. 6–33. And see Given-Wilson, 'Court and Household', pp. 111ff. and Appendix D, for this and what follows.

12. E101/394/8.

13. Given-Wilson, 'Court and Household', 115–6.

14. See below, pp. 142ff., for detailed discussion of this court clique.

15. Precision is difficult, since the number changed regularly as some were added and others abandoned or sold off: but the maps in *King's Works*, i, 85, 112, and 242–3, demonstrate this trend clearly.

16. The authors of the *King's Works*, i, 243, also suggest that the declining revenues of the late medieval English kings forced them to abandon several residences, but given the sums spent at Windsor, Sheen, Eltham, and elsewhere by these kings, this seems most unlikely; had he wanted to, Edward III could presumably have spent the £51,000 which he spent at Windsor on refurbishing several dozen of his residences, but he chose not to.

17. Mertes, 'Secular Noble Households', 16–17.

18. At Nottingham in early 1396, for example, or at Wallingford in 1390: *King's Works*, ii, 764, 851.

19. John Harvey, 'Richard II and York', in *Reign of Richard II*, 209; *Vita*, 151.

20. *Traison et Mort*, xlviii.

21. E101/402/5, ff. 7–10.

22. E101/403/10; E101/401/2; BL Add. Ms. 35, 115. Edward III also stayed at religious houses on occasions, at Bury St Edmunds abbey for 3½ weeks in January-February 1354, for example (E101/392/12).

23. *Hist. Angl.*, ii, 96–103.

24. *Winchester College Muniments*, no. 1. But it is not clear whether 'tota familia' really means the whole household. The daily expenses of the wardrobe show no real change at times when the king was being entertained elsewhere; probably he took the senior members of his household (including esquires, clerks, and perhaps valets of the chamber with him), while the 300 or so lesser servants stayed behind and were fed at the royal household's expense. Byerly noted that Edward I's household expenses sometimes fell to *nichil* when he was being entertained elsewhere. (*Records of Wardrobe and Household*, xxvii), but by the late 1330s this had ceased to be the case (*Wardrobe Book of William Norwell*, xxix), suggesting that by this time only part of the household would normally accompany the king when he went to be entertained.

25. Below, pp. 98–9, 103–5.

26. E101/402/5, f. 17.

27. *Knighton*, ii, 233, 240.

28. Tout, *Place of Edward II*, 273.

29. *Annales*, 188–94; Walsingham adds that the household lost many tents and other furnishings in a storm on the way back to England.

30. For Richard's visits to Cheshire, see R. R. Davies, 'Richard II and the Principality of Cheshire', in *Reign of Richard II*.

31. E101/404/21, and BL. Harl. Ms. 319.

32. For further discussion of this point, below, p. 182.

33. Richard II did, of course, move away from the south-east sometimes before 1394, as for example during his 'gyration' of 1387, or when he undertook the Scottish campaign of 1385, or when he removed his courts to York in 1392 out of spite for the Londoners. But it did not occur often; the surviving wardrobe account books show that in 1383–4 the household never moved further west than Corfe, or further north than Berkhamstead; in 1389–90 it never moved further west than Devizes, or further north than Oakham; in 1392-3 it never moved further north than Woodstock, or further west than Corfe; in 1393–4 it never moved further north than King's Langley or further west than Windsor, that is until August 1394 when the household and army marched to Wales to take ship for Ireland; the account book for 1395–6, however tends to confirm the king's

increased range of movement during his later years, for during the period covered by this account Richard and his household moved to Worcester in January 1396, then northwards via Coventry, Nottingham and Doncaster to York, which was reached on 23 March; returning to Windsor for the St George's Day festivities, the household spent the early summer around London before going via Canterbury and Dover to Calais, which was reached on 7 August. (E101/401/2; E101/402/5; E101/402/10; E101/402/20; E101/403/10.)

34. C. Given-Wilson, 'The Merger of Edward III's and Queen Philippa's Households, 1360–9', *BIHR*, li (1978), 183–7.

35. Below, p. 78.

36. E101/402/5, ff. 32–4. The 1389–90 account actually ends on 26 July 1390, because keeper William Packington died in office that day, but all the Easter term allowances were paid in full, as if the account had run through to 30 September.

37. *EHD*, iv, 1116.

38. Below, p. 214.

39. *Westm. Chron.*, 229; *Hist. Angl.*, ii, 172–3.

40. Below, p. 79.

41. For this and for much of what follows see C. Given-Wilson, 'Purveyance for the Royal Household 1362–1413', *BIHR*, lvi (1983), 145–63, and the Appendix, 'Consumption in the Royal Household 1362–1413'.

42. *De Speculo Regis Edwardi III*, ed. J. Moisant, 91, 105; for the dating and authorship of the treatise see L. E. Boyle, 'William of Pagula and the *Speculum Regis Edwardi III*', *Med. Stud.*, xxxii (1970), 329–36.

43. *RP* ii, 269.

44. For some examples, see *De Speculo*, ed. Moisant; Given-Wilson, 'Purveyance for the Royal Household', 149; Rogers, 'Household of Henry IV', 58–66; Steel, *Receipt of the Exchequer*, xxxiv–xxxv.

45. J. R. Maddicott, *The English Peasantry and the Demands of the Crown 1294–1341* (*Past and Present*, Supplement, i, 1975); Harriss, *King, Parliament and Public Finance*, 382–3; for examples of provisioning contracts for military needs in the period 1360–1413, see SC1/40/174, and *CPR 1385–9*, 6–7.

46. E101/405/7, 8 and 20; E101/403/29; Given-Wilson, 'Purveyance for the Royal Household', 149–50.

47. *CCR 1360–4*, 544; *ibid., 1377–81*, 287; *CPR 1374–7*, 71.

48. *CCR 1354–60*, 248.

49. Tout, *Place of Edward II*, 272–3.

50. Given-Wilson, 'Purveyance for the Royal Household', 151–2.

51. E101/624/38.

52. *De Speculo*, ed. Moisant, 99, 159.

53. *Ibid.*, 132; Given-Wilson, 'Purveyance for the Royal Household', 153–4.

54. *De Speculo*, ed. Moisant, 99, 135, 159.

55. *RP*, ii, 269; *Statutes of the Realm*, i, 266, 319.

56. *Ibid.*, 100, 132; *RP*, ii, 351; iii, 100; *Household of Edward IV*, ed. Myers, 165, where it was said that payment was to be made only if the journey exceeded 10 miles; see also P. D. A. Harvey, *A Medieval Oxfordshire Village: Cuxham 1240–1400* (1965), 110; and R. H. Britnell, '*Advantagium Mercatoris*: a custom in medieval English trade', *Nottingham Medieval Studies*, xxiv (1980), 37–50, who emphasises the rise in the cost of transport after the plague.

57. BL Harl. Ms. 642, f. 195; *RP*, ii, 269.

58. Britnell, '*Advantagium Mercatoris*' suggests that such increments were common mercantile practice in the late fourteenth century, but see Given-Wilson, 'Purveyance for the Royal Household', 155–6.

59. M. K. James, *Studies in the Medieval Wine Trade*, ed. E. M. Veale (1971), 4, n. 1.

60. E101/403/29.

61. J. J. N. McGurk, 'Royal purveyance in the shire of Kent, 1590–1614', *BIHR*, 1 (1977), 58.

62. Tout, *Place of Edward II*, 249–66, 282; *Household of Edward IV*, ed. Myers, 25, 151, 162–85; for private tallies, see Appendix II.

63. Harvey, *Cuxham 1240–1400*, 111.

64. *RP*, iii, 592.

65. Tout, *Place of Edward II*, 261; Myers, *Household of Edward IV*, 168.

66. Below, chapter 2.

67. Tout, *Place of Edward II*, 257.

68. *CPR 1364–7*, 227.

69. Given-Wilson, 'Purveyance for the Royal Household', 158–9.

70. *De Speculo*, ed., Moisant, 112.

71. *Westm. Chron.*, 225.

72. See the remarks by Caroline Barron in *Reign of Richard II*, ed. du Boulay and Barron, 197–201; also Rogers, 'Royal Household of Henry IV', 350, 357.

73. W. R. Jones, 'The Court of the Verge', *Journal of British Studies*, x (1970), 1–29. The verge extended 12 miles from the presence of the sovereign, or in his absence from the presence of the guardian of the realm (see for example *CPR 1370–74*, 199).

74. Evidence from the 1360s suggests that in practice it was frequently the steward's lieutenant who chaired the court's proceedings: from 1360 until 1371, Nicholas Carew held this post, and with the stewards often away (with the king, presumably, who was now often absent from his household), his was clearly an active lieutenancy: *CPR 1361–4*, 70; E101/256/25.

75. E101/257/2.

76. E361/1, 6, 7. After December 1406 they were no longer recorded under the wardrobe's *recepta forinseca*; they were probably now paid directly into the exchequer, or possibly into the king's chamber.

77. Three years in particular saw very high profits:

1375–6 (£350); 1379–80 (£369); and 1382–3 (£396): E101/257/2, 6.

78. *RP*, ii, 336, 349.

79. E101/256/25, mm. 2–3 is a roll of fines imposed by the clerk of the market during the years 1368–70, the majority of which were on whole towns rather than individuals. It was fitting that this petition came from the citizens of Rochester, for they had been fined more heavily (£5. 10s.) than any other town in which the clerk had held his assizes of bread and ale during this period (next highest was Ware in Hertfordshire, with £4; most towns were fined less than £2). The practice of imposing communal fines on towns had been common at least since Edward I's time (Byerly, *Records of Wardrobe and Household*, xxv, 192–3).

80. *RP*, iii, 267, 429, 596.

81. *Ibid.*, ii, 240, 297, 336. Lee had evidently acted out of malice, but genuine mistakes could also be made. In August 1375 the king advised the steward and marshal to 'behave so circumspectly' because they were about to hear a plea of debt without the king's writ, and 'although the contract and action for debt arose at the town of Broughton, Northants., which is within the verge of the king's household, the steward and marshals are purposing to take that inquisition at the venue of Broughton, Bucks, which is without the verge . . . and it is the king's will that nought be done contrary to the common law'. (*CCR 1374–7*, 154.)

82. Above, p. 33 ff.

83. *RP*, ii, 336.

84. *Ibid.*, ii, 354, 351, 368; iii, 19.

85. *Ibid.*, ii, 366.

86. *CPR 1370–74*, 265.

87. *Anon. Chron.*, 140.

88. Ruth Bird, *The Turbulent London of Richard II* (1949), 15, 25–6. C49/8/16 is a petition against the extension of the *constable* and marshal's jurisdiction, submitted to the council, which requests that the extent of the verge be limited which suggests that there may have been some confusion in the minds of contemporaries about the jurisdiction of different courts. The petition is undated, but seems to fit into the events of 1377. The most vivid, if partial, account of these events is in *Chronicon Angliae*, 119–123.

89. *Anon. Chron.*, 104–6.

90. *RP*, iii, 19, 28.

91. *Ibid.*, 267, 429, 468, 475, 539, 588, 596. And for an interesting case concerning the court in 1474–5, see *EHD*, iv, 306.

92. See, for example, a case in 1366, when the king was 'certainly informed that in a quarrel between Henry Fribern, one of the pages of the office of the saucery of the household, and William Porter of the office of the scullery, William wrathfully and maliciously took Henry's ear in his mouth and bit it, so that he tore off a large part of the upper half of his ear, whereby Henry is greatly disfigured and

might incur ill-fame and sinister suspicion.' (*CPR, 1364–7*, 348).

93. Translation in R. B. Dobson, ed., *The Peasants' Revolt of 1381* (1970), 155.

94. *Ibid.*, 119, 130, 162–3.

95. See Appendix III.

96. *RP*, iii, 223, 265–6, 318, 354.

97. *CPR, 1377–81*, 410.

98. E101/402/2.

99. *Westm. Chron.*, 187; *RP*, iii, 240; but Usk's support for Brembre against John of Northampton also seems to have been held against him at this time: *Westm. Chron.*, 315–7. He is called a king's sergeant-at-arms in September 1387: *CFR, 1383–91*, 200. It seems that he had earlier been a clerk, and he wrote the *Testament of Love.*.

100. See Tout, *Chapters*, iv, 44.

101. *CPR, 1381–5*, 216; *ibid., 1385–9*, 121; *ibid., 1388–92*, 168; *ibid., 1391–6*, 316.

102. For example, *ibid., 1388–92*, 358. (Hamond Smethwyk)

103. *CPR, 1385–9*, 395.

104. Mertes, 'Secular Noble Household', 209, 310.

105. *Winchester College Muniments*, no. 1.

106. For whom see below, pp. 175 ff.

107. Thomas More, Richard's cofferer, became keeper of the wardrobe in 1401; Thomas Percy, Richard's last steward, became steward again in 1401; Thomas Brounfleet, Richard's butler became controller in 1401, and then keeper of the wardrobe in 1408; and Richard Prentys, clerk of Richard's chapel, became dean of Henry's chapel in 1402.

108. Rogers, 'Royal Household of Henry IV', 567.

109. For Stanley, see Bennett, *Community, Class and Careerism, passim.*

110. Myers, *Household of Edward IV*, 127; *POPC*, i, 109; and below, pp. 219–20.

111. See below, pp. 217–19; and for an interesting example of the process at work in both a geographical and personal sense, see J. L. Grassi, 'Royal clerks from the archdiocese of York', *Northern History*, v, (1970), 12–33. See also G. L. Harriss's introduction to K. B. McFarlane, *England in the Fifteenth Century* (1981), xiv.

112. For a general description of the household offices see *Wardrobe Book of William Norwell*, lvi–lvii.

13. Originally the marshal was the official who had charge of the horses at court; hence the confusion of names.

114. Regulations established the number of horses which each member of the household was either allowed or supposed to keep in the household. The Ordinance of 1318, for example, said that each of the 30 sergeants-at-arms was to keep one armed horse, one hackney, and one sumpter-horse at court; the king's confessor was allowed 4 horses and one hackney, the king's physician 3 horses: Tout, *Place of Edward II*, 250–3; *CPR 1388–92*, 370.

115. There are detailed departmental lists in E101/ 396/11, E101/403/25, and E101/404/21.

116. *King's Works*, ii, 876–83, 934–5.

117. Messengers were not usually listed separately, though they were between 1360 and 1377, when their number dropped from nineteen to seven; according to M. C. Hill, *The King's Messengers 1199–1377* (1961), 136–42, after 1377 the messenger service went 'out of court', leaving only four messengers in the household to cater to its immediate needs. It is clear from the lists of *Nuncii* in the wardrobe account books, however, that all sorts of different household servants were liable to be ordered to carry the king's messages.

118. The *Constitutio* of 1136, the *Ordinances* of 1318, and the *Black Book* of 1478 all deal in detail with the regulation of liveries to different levels of servants in the household.

119. Girouard, *Life in the English Country House*, 54–5. And see the inventory of the goods of William Mulsho, keeper of the wardrobe, who died in office in November 1376: as well as eight horses, several robes, and various other goods, his personal possessions included a mattress, blankets, and a sheet (E154/6/12).

120. Tout, *Place of Edward II*, 246, 253–4.

121. *Ibid.*, 279–80; *Chapters*, ii, 160.

122. *CPR, 1370–74*, 14; BL Cotton Nero D.vi, f. 85; *Fleta*, ii, 114; BL Cotton Vesp. B.vii, 105v–107; I am grateful to Dr Michael Prestwich for these references.

123. Tout, *Place of Edward II*, 272; *CPR 1370–74*, 280.

124. J. H. Round, *The King's Serjeants and Officers of State* (1911), 97–8, 103–4.

125. Myers, *Household of Edward IV*, 129.

126. Edward III had between five and nine 'king's minstrels' in the latter part of his reign (Given-Wilson, 'Court and Household', 293–4). Richard II had between 13 and 16 at various times during his reign; in 1408–9 Henry IV had only 4 (E101/ 400/4, m. 22; 401/6, m. 17; 403/25, m. 2; 405/ 22, f. 32).

127. Given-Wilson, 'Court and Household', 295; *CPR 1391–6*, 74.

128. *Knighton*, ii, 118; *Westm. Chron.*, 343.

129. *Hist Angl.*, i, 327–8. The figures given in this paragraph are derived from surviving wardrobe account books and enrolled accounts (after 1377, however, the enrolled accounts are more summary and the figures are not given, so they are only available when wardrobe account books survive, that is, in 1383–4, 1389–90, 1392–3, 1395–6, 1402–3, 1405–6, and 1408–9; the 1408–9 document is only a tiny fragment of an account book).

130. For hunting, see in particular the splendid early fifteenth-century treatise, which may have been written by Edward, second duke of York: *Master of Game*, ed. and trans. W. A. and F. Baillie-Grohman (1909); also F. Barlow, *William Rufus* (1983), 119ff.

131. See for example E101/569/24, mm. 1–2; *CPR 1361–4*, 273; *ibid. 1367–70*, 217.

132. E101/397/20, mm. 6–7.

133. *CCR 1369–74*, 592.

134. *King's Works*, ii, 991.

135. *Original Letters Illustrative of English History*, ed. Sir Henry Ellis, i (3rd. ser., 1846), 43–4; Devon, *Issues of the Exchequer*, 189.

136. E101/397/20, mm. 8, 26, 30.

137. *POPC*, i, 100; Henry was unmarried at this time; by 'the queen', Mowbray can only have meant Isabel, the second wife of Richard II, who was still in England at this time. Mowbray was later to rebel against Henry, in 1405, and lost his life for it.

138. Devon, *Issues of the Exchequer*, 189; and see below, p. 67, and N. Orme, *From Childhood to Chivalry* (1984).

139. E101/402/15, no. 6.

140. E101/393/11, ff. 79–117; E101/397/5, ff. 54–8.

141. Rogers, 570; Armitage-Smith, *John of Gaunt*, Appendix II, 437, where the 'Order of Battle' for the 1385 campaign is printed; the word 'tynell' was occasionally used at this time to describe the royal household (see for example *RP*, ii, 336). See also N. B. Lewis, 'The Last Summons of the English Feudal Levy, 1385', *EHR*, lxxiii (1958), 5–8; these at least are the official figures for the army, and Lewis considered them to be fairly reliable.

142. Prestwich, *War, Politics and Finance*, 55.

143. Below, pp. 204ff.

144. E101/403/23, m. 2.

145. For the meaning of these terms after 1377, see below, pp. 211ff.

146. See E101/402/20, ff. 31–8 for the army of 1394–5.

147. *CCR, 1396–9*, 489; Tout, *Chapters*, iii, 489; *CPR, 1405–8*, 361–2; *POPC*, i, 121, 128; *CPR, 1401–5*, 25, 375.

148. *CCR, 1396–9*, 210.

149. E101/396/13; E101/400/27, mm. 15–20; E101/400/22, mm. 4–5.

150. As an exception one might cite John Nevill's expedition to relieve Brest in 1372; but Nevill, as well as being steward of the household, was also a peer of parliament.

151. E101/402/20, f. 31; *CPR, 1391–6*, 451, 523. On their way to Ireland, Raddington and Stanley found time to terrorise the town and abbey of Chester: see *EHD*, iv, 721.

152. *CPR, 1396–9*, 511.

153. *CFR, 1399–1405*, 310; *CCR, 1405–8*, 257, 259, 261.

154. Translation by Dobson, *The Peasants' Revolt*, 166.

155. *CPR, 1391–6*, 74.

156. See below, pp. 222–3.

157. *POPC*, i, 110.

158. See below, Chapter III.

159. Tout, *Place of Edward II*, 254–69.
160. Myers, *Household of Edward IV*, 127–8; Tout, *Place of Edward II*, 256.
161. Below, p. 182.
162. A. B. Cobban, *The King's Hall within the University of Cambridge in the later Middle Ages* (1969), 56–64.
163. Tout, *Chapters*, v, 59–61.
164. *CCR, 1381–5*, 162; *ibid.*, 1385–9, 591.
165. *CPR 1396–9*, 81.
166. *CPR, 1388–92*, 370.
167. Below, pp. 177–9; and for Henry IV's confessors, below, pp. 192–3, 197.
168. Hilda Johnstone, 'Poor-relief in the Royal Households of thirteenth-century England', *Speculum*, vi (1929), 150. And for a detailed breakdown of the royal alms dispensed in 1283–4 see Arnold Taylor, 'Royal Alms and Oblations in the later thirteenth century', in *Tribute to an Antiquary: Essays Presented to Mark Fitch*, eds. F. Emmison and R. Stephens (1976), 93–125.
169. The 1369 wardrobe account book, however, shows a higher figure of 6s. a day, but by 1371 it was back to 4s., as it had been in 1367 (E101/396/2, 11; E101/397/5).
170. This and the following information is from the surviving wardrobe account books; but see also the list of traditional king's alms in the 'Ordinance of 1323', in Tout, *Place of Edward II*, 283–4.
171. For Edward II, see Tout, *Place of Edward II*, 283. And see M. Bloch, *The Royal Touch*, trans. J. Anderson (1973), 92ff. Bloch points out that it was not until the second half of the sixteenth century that the custom of distributing royal cramp rings for epilepsy died out.
172. Myers, *Household of Edward IV*, 205. All royal residences had 'almonries', presumably situated by the gate; see Johnstone, 'Poor-relief in the Royal Household', 163.
173. Below, p. 116.
174. *RP*, ii, 325.
175. R. I. Jack, 'Entail and Descent: the Hastings Inheritance, 1370 to 1436', *BIHR*, xxxviii (1965), 6.
176. *RP, iii, 12–13*; and see below, pp. 142–7.
177. *Traison et Mort*, 194; *Vita*, 152.
178. *Annales*, 370.
179. *RP*, iii, 73, 96.
180. *Ibid.*, iii, 5, 454, 486, 647.
181. *Ibid.*, iii, 12; *Westm. Chron.*, 97, 182; Jones, 'Court of the Verge', 6.
182. See the Ordinances of 1318 for example.
183. *CPR 1377–81*, 92; compare with E101/398/9.
184. *Hist. Angl.*, ii, 96–7, 119; *Westm. Chron.*, 275, 291; *RP*, iii, 571–2.

Chapter II: Finance

1. See Appendix I, table of accounts of the wardrobe of the household (referred to here simply as 'the wardrobe', as distinct from 'the great wardrobe' and 'the privy wardrobe').
2. For alms, see above, pp. 69–70.
3. Harriss, *King, Parliament and Public Finance*, 483–4.
4. C. Given-Wilson, 'The Merger of Edward III's and Queen Philippa's Households, 1360–9', *BIHR*, li (1978), 183–7.
5. *Annales*, 188–94; *Vita*, 136; *Eulog. Hist.*, iii, 371; and see for instance *CPR, 1396–9*, 52–3, 59.
6. The author of the *Vita* (p. 156) claimed that Richard had a tunic made, bedecked with pearls and other precious stones and gold, costing 30,000 marks. No doubt this is an exaggeration, but several chroniclers remarked on the king's extravagance and his taste for luxury: *Westm. Chron.*, 163, 511, 517; *Traison et Mort*, xlii; *Eulog. Hist.*, iii, 384.
7. Tout, *Chapters*, iv, 393–407.
8. E101/397/20, m. 15.
9. For example, E101/400/4, m. 23; E101/402/12, m. 3.
10. E101/401/6, mm. 26–8.
11. E101/401/13; see also the remarks by Caroline Barron, *Reign of Richard II*, 197.
12. E101/403/5, mm. 1–2, 13.
13. *Rogers*, 347–8.
14. E101/403/8.
15. E101/398/1, m. 1.
16. During the French invasion scare of 1386, for example, when various members of the household were sent to garrison Dover, Rye, Portchester, Odiham, Sandwich, and other strongholds in the south-east, they were given substantial quantities of weaponry from the privy wardrobe: E101/400/22, mm. 4–5; E101/403/23, m. 2; E101/400/27, mm. 14–20. For the repairs effected in 1387 see E101/400/22, m. 2.
17. *Chapters*, vi, 109, has a full table of privy wardrobe receipts 1360–99, which usually matched expenses fairly closely; and see *ibid.*, iv, 463ff. for comment on fluctuations; see *Rogers*, 361–3, for expenses 1399–1407.
18. *Rogers*, 364.
19. Tout, *Chapters*, iv, 325; the last full chamber account of the fourteenth century is E101/391/1, covering the years 1345–56, which also shows considerable expenditure on the king's ships. For the chamber generally under Edward III and Richard II, see *Chapters*, iv, 227–348.
20. This is based on the supposition that between 1371 and 1376 'about half the total wool export had been diverted in this way': G. A. Holmes, *The Good Parliament* (1975), 110; the figures given by Holmes, *ibid.*, p. 81, suggest that in fact well over half was being 'diverted'.
21. These figures, which were acquired by Tout and Rogers only as a result of much patient research through the exchequer issue rolls, are taken from *Chapters*, iv, 318–24, and *Rogers*, 82, 134, 310–12, 402, 670.
22. BL Harleian Ms. 319, ff. 4–5.

23. *King, Parliament and Public Finance*, 489–502.
24. *Ibid.*, 501.
25. The relevant exchequer receipt rolls for the period November 1368 to July 1371 are E401/495, 499, 500, 501, 503 and 505; dates on which these transfers were made are: *1368*: 14 Nov., 16 Dec.; *1369*: 31 Jan., 3 Feb., 24 Feb., 5 Mar., 6 Mar., 7 May, 9 May, 12 May, 16 May, 29 May, 14 June, 4 Aug.; *1370*: 20 Feb., 25 May, 17 July, 4 Sept.; *1371*: 28 Feb., 27 June, 7 July. See also E401/510, 28 Sept. 1372; and for loans in 1367–8, *Harriss*, 580.
26. J. W. Sherborne, 'The Cost of English Warfare in France in the later fourteenth century, *BIHR*, (1977), 136ff.
27. For John Bacon, see below, p. 178. See *CPR, 1377–81*, 245–6, for the transfer of Richard's jewels and place to 'a certain place, by the advice of the council, under two keys, one to be kept by the treasurer, the other by himself (Bacon). . . . He shall not deliver up any except by mandate under the privy seal, and in case of delivery thereof in payment of any debt of the late king, he shall take acquittances whereon the sums shall be charged and discharged as in the pells of the receipt. If he sell any, and pay the proceeds by mandate aforesaid, the payments shall be entered in the said Receipt.' Bacon's accounts were to be audited annually by two or three members of the council. The exchequer seems the obvious place to transfer them to, given that the keepers of both the keys were exchequer officials. Tout discusses these transactions at *Chapters*, iv, 334–5.
28. See last note. For the sales, see Steel, *Receipt*, 38–46.
29. See *CPR, 1377–81*, 219, 340, 385, 461, 544; *ibid.*, *1381–5*, 149, 154–5; Knolles's transaction is *ibid.*, 104, occurring in March 1382.
30. *RP*, iii, 421, 439; for Richard's will, see *Testamenta Vetusta*, i, 15–16.
31. *Traison et Mort*, 263.
32. J. J. N. Palmer, *England, France and Christendom 1377–99* (1972), 173–4, 212. On 19 March 1397, 40,000 crowns (£6,666) of the dowry money was deposited in the exchequer, marked as a loan from the chamber, and arrangements made for it to be repaid to the chamber, which was promptly done. In December 1399, Henry IV paid 87,988 crowns (£14,664—almost a full year's instalment) of dowry money into the exchequer. Steel thought that this represented arrears paid to Henry in November 1399, but it is surely most unlikely that Charles VI would have made further cash available on this score to the man who had just dethroned his daughter's husband. It is much more likely that this represented money received from an earlier instalment and hoarded by Richard: Steel, *Receipt*, 75, 82, 126–7. *CPR, 1396–9*, 46.
33. *Foedera*, viii, 162; for Ikelyngton, see below, p. 180.
34. Nichols, *Collection of Wills*, 191–202.

35. BL Harl. Ms. 319, ff. 4–5.
36. E361/7/1; E101/404/10; *Rogers*, 161, 329.
37. *Rogers*, 324.
38. E101/404/21, f. 3.
39. Steel, *Receipt*, 84, 126; there was also a loan of £1,000 to the exchequer in May 1410 (*ibid.*, 100); *Rogers*, 336.
40. Given-Wilson, 'Merger of Edward III's and Philippa's Households'; also generally see Hilda Johnstone, 'The Queen's Household', in *Chapters*, v, 231–89.
41. J. Hatcher, *Rural Economy and Society in the Duchy of Cornwall 1300–1500* (1970), 7.
42. Walsingham, *Hist. Angl.*, ii, 119, remarked that Richard 'rarely if ever allowed her to leave his side'; see also *Chapters*, v, 260, n. 6; and *CPR, 1381–5, 187*.
43. *RP*, iii, 246.
44. E361/5/21–5.
45. Philip la Vache was her chamberlain; and see the interesting passage in *Traison et Mort*, 163–6, concerning the appointment of a governess for Isabel before Richard embarked for Ireland in 1399.
46. His first wife, Mary de Bohun, died in 1394.
47. *RP*, iii, 577, 588.
48. *Rogers*, 172, 373–4.
49. All figures are rounded to the nearest £100. Privy wardrobe excluded because its cost was insignificant.
50. E361/5, m. 26.
51. E361/5, m. 19.
52. E101/396/2, f. 5; E101/398/9, f. 3.
53. E361/5, m. 21.
54. G. L. Harriss, 'Fictitious Loans', *Economic History Review*, viii (1955–6); and 'Preference at the Mediaeval Exchequer', *BIHR*, xxx (1957).
55. E101/396/2, f. 1.
56. E101/401/2, ff. 2–8d.
57. See below, p. 104.
58. *Receipt of the Exchequer*, 126–8.
59. See also G. L. Harriss, ed., *Henry V: The Practice of Kingship* (1985), 161ff.
60. E361/5, m. 20.
61. Appendix I, 'Balance' column.
62. E361/5, m. 25. £3,634 of the £3,976 foreign receipt was the stock *remanencia* from the previous account.
63. E361/5, m. 26.
64. E101/394/4.
65. See Harriss, *King, Parliament and Public Finance*, 479 and n. 2. He quotes an exchequer document which suggests that between 1360 and 1362 debts amounting to £53,266 on the accounts of Farley's *predecessors* had been paid off; if this is correct, then the wardrobe's accumulated debts in 1360 must have stood at over £80,000. Yet later Harriss implies that this sum (the £53,266) was used for 'the repayment of the debts of 1356–60' (p. 495). I have not examined all these documents, but it is clear that the wardrobe's burden of debt in 1360

was very great, and naturally took a few years to be reduced. E101/393/11 gives a breakdown of Farley's £31,432 of debts: debts by bill totalled £30,387, and were mostly for wages of war; debts without bill came to £917; debts by tally totalled £128, and were mostly small sums for items of food, e.g. corn, poultry, doubtless purveyed by the household. Thus it is clear that it was very largely because of outstanding war-wages that the household's debts at this time were so vast, not because 'domestic' creditors were being ignored.

66. E101/397/5, E361/4/22d.
67. E403/454, 12 April, 12 July, 22 July.
68. E361/5/18.
69. *RP*, ii, 96.
70. E101/400/26; E101/401/9.
71. E101/400/26, ff. 3–5d.
72. The figures for the whole of Richard's reign (E361/5–6) are: 1377–8: £17,726 in 34 parcels; 1378–9: £14,175 in 24 parcels; 1379–81 (2½ years): £32,160 in 43 parcels; 1381–2: £17,714 in 105 parcels; 1382–3: £15,551 in 100 parcels; 1383–4: £14,899 in 114 parcels (making 302 separate payments in the account book); 1384–5: £19,381 in 83 parcels; 1385–6: £18,562 in 106 parcels; 1386–7: £8,324 in 51 parcels; 1387–8: £13,667 in 61 parcels; 1388–9: £12,530 in 53 parcels; 1389–90 (ten months): £8,465 in 36 parcels; 1390–91 (14 months): £17,203 in 60 parcels; 1391–2: £15,531 in 52 parcels; 1392–3: £21,701 in 41 parcels; 1393–5 (including war wages) £78,200 in 113 parcels; 1395–6: £28,097 in 58 parcels; 1396–7: £35,073 in 82 parcels; 1397–8: £25,373 in 94 parcels; 1398–9: 38,205 in 53 parcels.
73. E361/5, mm. 19–20d; in the exchequer year 1386–7, £13,349 was allocated to the wardrobe for payment of debts on previous accounts.
74. *Ibid.*, m. 21.
75. E101/402/3, f. 7.
76. *Ibid.*, f. 11.
77. Unfortunately the full *recepta scaccarii* for 1389–90 cannot be analysed, because the first folio of E101/402/3 is missing, but from the evidence of what survives it seems that about 92 percent of it was received in direct payments during the account (excluding the 7,000 marks, naturally).
78. E101/402/20. The first few folios, recording the early entries of the *recepta scaccarii*, are badly mutilated. The relevant exchequer issue rolls are E403/555, 556, 559, 561 and 562, from Easter 1397 to September 1399.
79. E361/5, mm. 22–26. It is also worth remembering that it was in January 1393 that 7,000 marks was handed over for Packington's debts, so a lot of good money found its way from exchequer to wardrobe in 1392–3.
80. Above, p. 90.
81. *Rogers*, 183, 186, 212.
82. *Ibid.*, 183–4, 186, 212.

83. E361/7, m. 5.
84. *Rogers*, 112, 184, 186; E361/7, m. 6.
85. E101/405/14, f. 2.
86. *Rogers*, 184–5, 285; E361/7, mm. 7d–8.
87. £17,110 in 1410–11; see Appendix I.
88. E361/7, mm. 9–10.
89. *Rogers*, 296; unfortunately the receipt rolls for Easter 1411 and 1412 are missing but Steel's figures confirm that receipts fell from 1409 until at least 1411 (*Receipt of the Exchequer*, 99–101).
90. *Rogers*, 185–6.
91. *Ibid.*, 229, 405–6.
92. See Harriss, *King, Parliament and Public Finance*, 466–508 for criticisms of royal extravagance at this time, but these never developed into a serious issue.
93. See above, pp. 41ff., for the organisation of household purveyance.
94. *RP*, ii, 268–70.
95. *Ibid.*, ii, 305, 312, 319, 342, 351, 352; iii, 15, 26, 47, 83, 100–1, 104, 115, 146, 158, 200, 213, 438, 473, 507–8, 510, 587, 592, 609, 624.
96. *Ibid.*, iii, 83, 158, 213.
97. *POPC*, i, 84.
98. *Ibid.*, i, 108–9; *Annales*, 337.
99. *Rogers*, 58, 62.
100. *RP*, iii, 510.
101. *Ibid.*, iii, 609. Various entries in the Calendar of Close Rolls at this time seem to be connected with the case, but they would require some unravelling (*CCR 1405–9*, 289–90, 350).
102. *RP*, iii, 6–7, 25, 100–1, 147, 213, 242.
103. *Ibid.*, iii, 339–41, 407–8.
104. *Ibid.*, iii, 523–8, 572, 577, 586–8, 624–5; *POPC*, i, 296.
105. Below, p. 130.
106. *RP*, iii, 14, 16, 73, 96, 115.
107. *Westm. Chron.*, 333.
108. *RP*, iii, 147, 213, 221–2.
109. *CPR, 1388–92*, 29ff.; and see Tuck, *Richard II and the English Nobility*, 137–8.
110. For the 1401 parliament, see A. Rogers, 'The Political Crisis of 1401', *Nottingham Medieval Studies*, xii (1968), 85–96.
111. In Richard's reign, only in 1377 and 1381 was the keeper of the wardrobe included in the list of royal officers to be appointed or sworn in parliament.
112. *RP*, iii 587–8.
113. *POPC*, i, 296.
114. Brounfleet replaced Litton as controller; Thomas Percy replaced Thomas Rempston as steward; and Thomas More replaced Thomas Tutbury as keeper.
115. Above, pp. 79–80 and 107–8.
116. *RP*, iii, 57, 73–4, 93, 100–1, 115; for Rushook, see below, p. 177–8.
117. *RP*, iii, 213, 216; and see J. J. N. Palmer, 'The Parliament of 1385 and the Constitutional Crisis of 1386', *Speculum*, xlvi (1971).

118. *RP*, iii, 221–2, 349–50.
119. E361/5, mm. 20–21.
120. *CPR, 1385–9*, 317–18, 320.
121. *CFR, 1377–83*, 182–3; *CPR, 1388–92*, 24.
122. For these clauses, see *CFR, 1383–91*, 182 to end, and *CFR, 1391–9*, 1–48, *passim*.
123. *CCR, 1385–9*, 647.
124. *CPR, 1385–9*, 371.
125. *CCR, 1385–9*, 308.
126. *Westm. Chron.*, 229.
127. See Appendix III.
128. *CPR, 1385–9*, 430, 432.
129. See K. B. McFarlane, *Lancastrian Kings and Lollard Knights* (1972), 78–101; A. Rogers, 'Henry IV, the commons, and taxation', *Medieval Studies*, xxxi (1969), 44–70; and A. L. Brown, 'The commons and the council in the reign of Henry IV', *EHR*, lxxix (1964). Rogers, 'Royal Household of Henry IV', *passim*, provides abundant evidence to support the view that for certain periods in Henry's reign the council was effectively in control of the administration.
130. *RP*, iii, 6–7, 101, 147.
131. Wardships of the heirs of: Peter Mauley, April 1383 (*CPR, 1381–5*, 364); the earl of March, November 1382 (*ibid.*, 184); Thomas Roos of Hamelake, June 1384 (*CFR, 1383–91*, 42); the earl of Pembroke, April 1384 (*CPR, 1381–5*, 388); William Bardolf of Wormegay, February 1386 (*CPR, 1385–9*, 112); the earl of Stafford, January 1387 (*ibid.*, 251); Thomas Lord Clifford, Sir Robert Hemenale, and Sir John Wingfield, November 1391 (*CPR, 1388–92*, 498); the earl of Stafford again, in July 1392 (*CPR, 1391–6*, 116); Sir John Deyncourt, November 1393 (*ibid*, 342); Temporalities of the vacant sees of: Durham, August 1381 (*CFR, 1377–83*, 266); York and Chichester, following the forfeiture incurred by Alexander Nevill and Thomas Rushook, in May 1388 (*CPR, 1385–9*, 440, 452); Bath and Wells, to be paid to the king's chamber, September 1386 (*CCR, 1385–9*, 189).
132. See last note; in addition, it is worth noting that the lands forfeited by de la Pole were reserved to the household in May 1388 (*CPR, 1385–9*, 440).
133. *CFR, 1377–83*, 61; *CPR, 1381–5*, 184; *ibid.*, *1391–6*, 50; *CFR, 1391–9*, 129: it is worth noting, however, that in October 1386 the duke of Gloucester switched his £1,000 annuity from the wool customs to the alien priories (*CPR, 1385–9*, 209, 233).
134. *RP*, iii, 366.
135. E361/4, m. 21; E403/442, 444, 446, 447.
136. BL., Add. Ms. 37, 494.
137. E403/454, 456.
138. Sherborne, 'Cost of English Warfare', 135–50.
139. *RP*, iii, 7; *CPR, 1377–81*, 99; *CFR, 1377–83*, 61.
140. *CPR, 1377–81*, 327; *RP*, iii, 66.
141. E401/534. The 'real receipt' totals used here are those estimated by Steel, *Receipt of the Exchequer*, 38ff., including cash receipts and assignments but excluding book-keeping entries.
142. *CPR, 1377–81*, 400.
143. *RP*, iii, 75; Steel, *Receipt of the Exchequer*, 42.
144. E401/537, 539.
145. *RP*, iii, 90.
146. See for example E401/537, 15 October, 23 January, 24 January (Michaelmas 1379–80); E401/541, 13 May, 20 May (Easter 1381); and E401/544, 26 October (Michaelmas 1381–2).
147. *RP*, iii, 114, 124, 134, 151–2, 167, 204, 213, 221, 244–5, 262–3, 279, 285–6.
148. E401/550, 10 August.
149. *CFR, 1377–83*, 296–7; *CPR, 1381–5*, 306, 314–15; *CCR, 1381–5*, 364; *CPR, 1381–5*, 306; this expedient also seems to have been tried for a brief while in the winter of 1382–3: *CCR, 1381–5, 191–2*.
150. *CCR, 1381–5*, 348; *CPR, 1381–5*, 279.
151. In December 1384, for example, when collectors of the half 10th and 15th were appointed, it was said that these were to be brought into the exchequer 'or other appointed place'—the implication being that it was up to the king to decide where they were to be received (*CFR, 1383–91*, 68).
152. *CFR, 1383–91*, 135.
153. E401/563, 565.
154. Steel, *Receipt of the Exchequer*, 52–6; *CPR, 1385–9*, 343.
155. *CPR, 1388–92*, 249, 362; *ibid., 1391–6*, 9; E401/572, 573, 574, 576, 579.
156. Steel, *Receipt of the Exchequer*, 61–4; war receipts overlap slightly with the Michaelmas 1388–9 and 1390–1 terms, but it would be unrealistic to include the full real receipts for these terms, especially as the system seems more or less to have ended by November 1390.
157. *CPR, 1388–92*, 362; *RP*, iii, 285–6, 301–2, 314.
158. *Ibid.*, iii, 330, 340, 368–9. Dr Alan Rogers, 'Henry IV, the commons and taxation', 50–51, gives a rather different impression of the commons' attitude to appropriation of supply in the parliaments of the 1390s, but I think that this arises from his failure to compare them with the parliaments of the period 1377–90. Moreover, whatever the commons requested, it is abundantly clear that financial reality in the 1380s and 1390s was quite different.
159. *RP*, iii, 216; J. S. Roskell, *The Impeachment of Michael de la Pole* (1984), discusses this charge but he did not consult the exchequer rolls.
160. The March inheritance was assigned to the household in November 1382, but in February 1384, after a quarrel with his chancellor, Richard le Scrope, the king was forced to grant custody to a group of lords including Arundel and Warwick (*CPR, 1381–5*, 184, 377). Tuck, *Richard II and the English Nobility*, 88–9, has the details.

161. *RP*, iii, 166.

162. *Hist. Angl.*, ii, 196.

163. Steel, *Receipt of the Exchequer*, 78.

164. *CCR, 1389–92*, 37. For other examples of household preference, see *CPR, 1396–9*, 446, 464.

165. E101/402/5, f. 30; E101/403/22, f. 33; Steel, *Receipt of the Exchequer*, 63–9.

166. The dead queen's estates provided £1,200 in 1398 (Steel, *Receipt of the Exchequer*, 74–81).

167. Rogers, 'Royal Household of Henry IV', and 'Henry IV, the commons, and taxation', with Appendix (p. 70).

168. *RP*, iii, 546.

169. 'Henry IV, the commons, and taxation', 63.

170. Above, p. 108.

171. *POPC*, i, 154; the wording is ambiguous.

172. *RP*, iii, 527–8; it seems to have been worked out in detail by the council, but formally agreed (for security, presumably) in parliament. The detailed assignments were to be: petty customs in Hull, London, and Southampton: £1,300; ancient custom in all ports except Boston: £4,000; cloth subsidy: £300; farms of shires: £2,000; hanaper: £2,000 escheatries; £500; alien priories (excepting Fécamp; see *RP*, iii, 483): £2,000. The Boston wool customs were to be assigned to the chamber and great wardrobe.

173. *RP*, iii, 586–88.

174. *CFR 1399–1405*, 251ff.

175. *POPC*, i, 286, 296; *RP*, iii, 586.

176. *RP*, iii, 568.

177. *RP*, iii, 635, 649.

178. E403/447, 449, 451.

179. Harriss, *King, Parliament and Public Finance*, 466ff.

180. *RP*, ii, 355–6; *Anon. Chron.*, 87, 91.

181. Tuck *Richard II and the English Nobility*, 72–86 and *passim*.

182. *RP*, iii, 57, 73–4; above, p. 117.

183. *RP*, iii, 115, 213.

184. *POPC*, i, 35, 85–6, 88.

185. *CPR, 1377–81*, 1–254; *CCR, 1377–81*, 1–167. Obviously I do not claim complete accuracy for these figures, but these are the grants which I counted. The new grants made during this year included £1,000 to Thomas of Woodstock and 1,000 marks to Guichard D'Angle, upon their elevation to the earldoms of Buckingham and Huntingdon respectively, £200 to the king's half-brother Thomas Holand (though it was stipulated that he was not to receive any fee for his office as keeper of the forests south of the Trent), and £100 each to John Holand (Thomas's full brother), and John d'Arundel.

186. *CPR, 1377–81*, 244, 441, 537, 561; *ibid, 1381–5*, 273.

187. C. Given-Wilson, 'Richard II and his Grandfather's Will', *EHR*, xciii (1978), 320–37; Tuck *Richard II and the English Nobility*, 88–9.

188. Below, p. 167.

189. *CPR, 1381–5*, 542; *ibid., 1385–9*, 110.

190. For the council, see below, pp. 183–8; Tuck, *Richard II and the English Nobility*, 139, also noted that conciliar supervision of grants was normal at this time.

191. *CPR, 1388–92*, 355, 358, 375, 393; also see below, pp. 137–8, and *CPR, 1399–1401*, 81–2.

192. Above, pp. 118–19.

193. *Westm. Chron.*, 483.

194. Caroline Barron, in *Reign of Richard II*, 197.

195. *CPR, 1391–6*, 450–514, *passim*; and see above, p. 128.

196. Below, p. 214.

197. Tuck, *Richard II and the English Nobility*, 180ff.

198. J. L. Leland, 'Richard II and the Counter-Appellants: Royal Patronage and Royalist Policies' (unpublished Ph.D. thesis, Yale University, 1979), 106, 114, 124. The examples quoted here are (i) Anglesey and Beaumaris to William le Scrope, February 1397 (ii) Carlisle and the West March to John Holand, February 1397 (iii) the legitimation of and subsequent grants to John Beaufort (iv) the Isle of Wight to Rutland in June 1397.

199. Below, pp. 214, 222–3.

200. *RP*, iii, 417–19.

201. Rogers, 71–2; *POPC*, i, 154.

203. Rogers, 74. Some cash sums were however made available to the household departments at times: above, pp. 91, 109.

204. Below, pp. 204ff.

205. *RP*, iii, 478–9, 508, 523–8; *POPC*, i, 283–7.

206. Rogers, 73–4, 100; *CCR, 1402–5*, 337, 382; *CPR, 1405–8*, 406. For some of Henry's larger grants, see *CPR, 1399–1401*, 34–5, 201; *ibid.*, 1401–5, 477.

207. *RP*, iii, 586–8; *CPR, 1408–13*, 35, 151.

208. B. P. Wolffe, *The Royal Demesne in English History* (1971), 86. But it was still difficult to stop the king misusing money voted to him: in February 1407, for example, out of the £6,000 from the wool subsidy granted to him in parliament to help pay household debts, Henry gave 2,000 marks to his youngest son Humphrey to help him to purchase the reversion of the lands of Sir Matthew Gournay (*CPR, 1405–8*, 297).

209. Rogers, 78; Kirby, *Henry IV of England*, 217. For examples of arrears see *CPR, 1405–8*, 330, 333; *ibid.*, 1408–13, 446.

210. *RP*, iii, 624–5.

211. Wolffe, *Royal Demesne, passim*, especially 72–4.

212. *RP*, iii, 35, 419 (Dr Wolffe's translation, *Royal Demesne*, 75).

213. *RP*, iii, 246. Note also the grant quoted earlier (above, p. 134), 'provided that the manor be not parcel of the crown'.

214. Above, p. 129.

215. *Hist. Angl.*, i, 309; E401/499, 500, 501.

216. Apart from the military expenditure, the renewal of the war also entailed the renewal (often with arrears) of the fees paid by the English king to several of the Low Countries Princes; see for example

E403/436, 27 October; E403/438, 4 May, 16 July, 25 July, 15 Sept.; F. Devon, ed., *Issue Roll of Thomas Brantingham* (1835), 333, 448.

217. Holmes, *The Good Parliament*, 72–9.

218. *Rogers*, 367–9; the severity of the problems on the Scottish border is indicated by the fact that the northern counties were frequently exempted from taxation: see for example *CPR, 1399–1401*, 444, 449; *ibid., 1405–8*, 380.

219. See for example the indentures for the garrisoning of Wales in 1405: *CPR, 1405–8*, 6; and for Ireland see *ibid.*, 431–2, where it is stated that in addition to the 7,000 marks *per annum* which he is to receive for the keeping of Ireland, the king's son Thomas is also to receive £9,000 over the next three years for the payment of his debts; this was in March 1408.

220. See for example *CFR, 1399–1405*, 317–18, for royal borrowing.

221. Below, pp. 198–9.

Chapter III: The Courtiers

1. The details of her trial are recorded in *RP*, iii, 12–14.

2. *Ibid.*, ii, 329; *Anon. Chron.*, 87; *Chron. Angl.*, 95–100.

3. See particularly M. V. Clarke, 'William of Windsor in Ireland 1369–76', in *Fourteenth Century Studies* (1937); and J. F. Lydon, ed. *England and Ireland in the later Middle Ages* (1983).

4. *Gaunt's Register 1372–6*, ii, 1343.

5. The details of the case are recorded (from a thoroughly partial viewpoint) in Thomas Walsingham's *Gesta Abbatum Monasterii Sancti Albani*, ed. H. T. Riley (3 vols. R.S. 1869), iii, 227–57.

6. *Anon. Chron.*, 90.

7. For an excellent general discussion of the political events leading up to the Good Parliament, see G. A. Holmes, *The Good Parliament* (1975). The charges made against the courtiers, and the roles of lords and commons, are also discussed in Given-Wilson, 'Court and Household', 195–254.

8. *RP*, ii, 324–8.

9. Chris Given-Wilson and Alice Curteis, *The Royal Bastards of Medieval England* (1984), 141; her bastard son John, whose father was Edward III, was probably born in 1364–5.

10. McFarlane estimated that her cash and jewels amounted in 1377 to £20,000, though no reference is given for this figure (*Nobility of Later Medieval England*, 131).

11. Quoted in Holmes, *The Good Parliament*, 103.

12. *Chapters*, iv, 162.

13. *Hist. Angl.*, ii, 322.

14. There is a detailed biography of Stury in McFarlane, *Lancastrian Kings and Lollard Knights*, 160ff.

15. *CPR, 1361–4*, 57; *CCR, 1364–8*, 150; *Chron. Angl.*, 87.

16. McFarlane, *Lancastrian Kings*.

17. *Chron. Angl.*, 87; *Anon. Chron.*, 92, 182; Sir Richard Stafford was actually one of the intercommuning committee of Lords chosen by the commons to discuss the charges with them, and thus hardly a likely target for their anger: *RP*, ii, 322.

18. *RP*, ii, 322.

19. A. R. Myers, 'The Wealth of Richard Lyons', in *Essays in Medieval History Presented to Bertie Wilkinson*, ed. T. A. Sandquist and M. R. Powicke (1969).

20. *CPMR, 1364–81*, 11.

21. *CPR, 1370–4*, 180, 323, 383, 411; *ibid., 1374–7*, 5 (*bis*), 254, 439; see also Holmes, *The Good Parliament*, 69–79, and *RP*, ii, 323–4.

22. *London Letter-Book G*, 322, 327.

23. Dobson, *The Peasants' Revolt*, 185, 249–50.

24. See for example *CPR, 1367–70*, 11, 437, 470; *ibid., 1370–4*, 50, 180, 436, 494; *ibid., 1374–7*, 5, 65, 253, 475, 477; *CCR, 1369–74*, 112, 340, 468, 532, 536; *ibid., 1374–7*, 259, 280, 424, 437–8; *CPR, 1369–77*, 307, 365; *CIPM*, xiv, 13; *ibid.*, xv, 910–20; *CIM, 1348–77*, 991; SC1/40/174.

25. *CPR, 1361–4*, 70; E101/256/25.

26. *CPR, 1367–70*, 297; S. Armitage-Smith, *John of Gaunt* (1904), 223, 441; *CPR, 1374–7*, 296.

27. *CPR, 1358–61*, 99; *CFR, 1356–68*, 321; Tout, *Chapters*, iv, 339.

28. Despite his role in uncovering Windsor's misdeeds in Ireland, Ashton enfeoffed to Alice Perrers ten manors in Dorset, Somerset and Wiltshire (*CIPM*, xv, 910–20); he played a prominent part in the politics of the last two years or so of the reign: *RP*, ii, 363; *Chron. Angl.*, 132–4.

29. *CPR, 1358–61*, 580; *ibid., 1374–7*, 341, 352.

30. E101/397/5, ff. 47, 87; *CPR, 1367–70*, 220; *ibid., 1374–7*, 381, 436. More detailed biographies of these men may be found in Given-Wilson, 'Court and Household', 118–70.

31. For discussion of the charges see Holmes, *The Good Parliament*, 108–134, and Given-Wilson, 'Court and Household', 195–238.

32. *RP* ii, 374–5.

33. Except that he was a Londoner and had loaned 13 marks to the exchequer on 20 September 1374: E403/454.

34. *CPR, 1367–70*, 74; *ibid., 1370–4*, 442; *ibid., 1374–7*, 319; *CFR., 1369–77*, 298; *Chron. Angl.*, 94.

35. E101/397/5, f. 49; *CPR, 1370–4*, 24, 398.

36. *CFR, 1356–68*, 214, 260, 292, 312, 335, 352; *ibid., 1369–77*, 133.

37. Given-Wilson, 'Court and Household', 216–21; Holmes, *The Good Parliament*, 114–18; SC8/662, 10264, 10378, and 10379, are all petitions either from Lyons and Ellis complaining of the behaviour of the men of Lowestoft (rivals to the merchants of Great Yarmouth), or from the men of Lowestoft complaining of the behaviour of Lyons and Ellis;

these are directly relevant to the charges brought against Ellis in the Good Parliament, for which see *RP*, ii, 327–8.

38. *CPR, 1367–70*, 11; *CCR, 1374–7*, 437; *RP*, ii, 328; compare the prices charged by Pecche with those in operation before he was granted the monopoly: *London Letter Book G*, 137, 149, 199, 318–19; the grant of the monopoly, in November 1373, is recorded in *CFR, 1369–77*, 225, 227, and was clearly with the consent of the king.

39. *Letter Book G*, 199; E101/509/25, 26.

40. *Letter Book G*, 205; *CPR, 1364–7*, 391.

41. *CPR, 1367–70*, 470; *ibid., 1370–4*, 494; *ibid., 1374–7*, 310; *Register of Edward the Black Prince*, iv, 284, 297, 302, 491; SCI/40/174.

42. *CPR, 1374–7*, 453.

43. *Chron. Angl.*, 94.

44. *RP*, ii, 328–9, 352; J. W. Sherborne, 'Indentured Retinues and English Expeditions to France 1369–80', *EHR*, lxxix (1964), 725–7; and Given-Wilson, 'Court and Household', 224–31.

45. *John of Gaunt's Register 1372–6*, i, 374; E101/317/2.

46. *CPR, 1374–7*, 5; *Anon. Chron.*, 89–90.

47. Holmes, *The Good Parliament*, 69–90, 108–26.

48. Above, pp. 33–5.

49. *Chron. Angl.*, 79–80, 87–8; *Anon. Chron.*, 92, 94–5.

50. What follows is taken largely from C53/145–154.

51. Holmes, *The Good Parliament*, 7–20, 46–9, 139–49, and *passim*.

52. For Wakefield's connections with the courtiers see, for example, *CCR, 1374–7*, 280; although elevated to the see of Worcester late in 1375 he remained about the court and was one of the witnesses to William Latimer's pardon by the king at Havering on 8 October 1376: SC8/180/8960. See also Holmes, *The Good Parliament*, 48.

53. *CPR, 1361–4*, 444.

43. Quoted in M. McKisack, *The Fourteenth Century* (1959), 227.

55. *Chron. Angl.*, 136–7.

56. *CCR, 1381–5*, 502, and *ibid., 1385–9*, 645.

57. *Anon. Chron.*, 93, 98–9; *Chron. Angl.*, 106–7.

58. *Anon. Chron.*, 100, 103–5; *Chron. Angl.*, 117–20.

59. E101/398/14; E101/393/11, f. 76.

60. Devon, *Issues of the Exchequer*, 166; *CPR, 1358–61*, 47; *ibid., 1361–4*, 18; *ibid., 1370–4*, 34, 61; *CCR, 1369–74*, 216–7, 226; E101/313/13; E101/317/5; *RP*, ii, 310.

61. *CCR, 1360–4*, 392; *ibid., 1364–8*, 205.

62. *RP*, ii, 316, 322.

63. *Chron. Angl.*, 121ff; and see above pp. 51–2.

64. *CPR, 1374–7*, 290. And for discussion of Beauchamp's career see Given-Wilson, 'Court and Household', 175–8.

65. Tout, *Chapters*, iv, 159.

66. *Anon. Chron.*, 89–90.

67. The *Anonimalle Chronicle* does however say that Peter de la Mare called for the dismissal of the chancellor and treasurer, but since this is not mentioned in any of the other sources, and since no action was taken on it, it may be that the chronicler is in error here: *ibid., 90*.

68. *RP*, ii, 324–8; *Chron. Angl.*, 87; *CPR, 1370–4*, 92, 166; *ibid., 1377–81*, 137.

69. *Hist. Angl.*, i, 322; also *Chron. Angl.*, 102.

70. The main sources for the council are *Anon. Chron.*, 95–6; *Chron. Angl.*, 103–8; for discussion, see Given-Wilson, 'Court and Household', 257–62, and Holmes, *The Good Parliament*, 160ff.

71. *Chron. Angl.*, 112–3; *RP*, ii, 368; *Anon Chron.*, 100.

72. *CPR., 1374–7*, 437.

73. *Hist. Angl.*, i, 327. For further discussion of the events described in this paragraph, see Given-Wilson, 'Court and Household', 255–72.

74. Holmes, *The Good Parliament*, 165–78.

75. Various other men were described in other sources as chamber knights, but for the whole question of chamber knights during Edward III's reign see below, pp. 204ff., and Appendix III.

76. *RP*, iii, 13; *CPR, 1377–81*, 104; *ibid., 1374–7*, 5; E101/398/9, f. 3.

77. E101/392/12, f. 40; *CPR, 1358–61*, 509; *ibid., 1361–4*, 458, 468; *CCR, 1369–74*, 187; *CFR, 1356–68*, 143; *CIPM*, xiv, 191.

78. He received his fee and robes for the Michaelmas 1371–2 term, but not for Easter 1372: E101/397/5, f. 45; for the circumstances of his dismissal see *CCR, 1369–74*, 420.

79. See Appendix IV.

80. E101/405/4, m. 18; *Westm. Chron.*, 43, 481.

81. E403/502, 27 June 1384.

82. *Westm. Chron.*, 273; what probably happened was that the king allowed the impeachment of de la Pole on condition that the knights were left alone. Burley had been 'prohibited from the presence of the king' on some occasion before 1388, which may well refer to this episode: *RP*, iii, 242.

83. E101/400/4, m. 21.

84. *Knighton*, ii, 296.

85. Given-Wilson, 'Richard II and his Grandfather's Will'; *Knighton*, ii, 205, actually says that Burley was made earl of Huntingdon on the 1385 campaign.

86. *Westm. Chron.*, 179.

87. *Chron. Angl.*, 375; *Hist. Angl.*, ii, 259.

88. *RP*, iii, 62.

89. *Westm. Chron.*, 72, provides the most vivid account of the affair; and *ibid.*, 115.

90. M. V. Clarke, *Fourteenth Century Studies* (1937), 119; *POPC*, i, 85.

91. *RP*, iii, 104; Walsingham, *Chron. Angl.*, 255; Tuck, *Richard II and English Nobility*, 44; *CPR, 1377–81*, 74.

92. *CPR, 1381–5*, 531.

93. C53/161.

94. *RP, 1381–5*, 531.
95. *Westm. Chron.*, 73, 213.
96. See below, pp. 175ff., for the clerks.
97. *CPR, 1396–9*, 279; he did however witness several charters in 1397–8: C53/167.
98. *Westm. Chron.*, 481.
99. *CPR, 1396–9*, 175.
100. *RP*, iii, 374.
101. *CPR, 1391–6*, 183.
102. *Traison et Mort*, 163.
103. *CFR, 1391–9*, 301.
104. *CPR, 1385–9*, 17, 18, 22, 25, 41.
105. Jack, 'Entail and Descent: the Hastings Inheritance'.
106. See below, pp. 218ff.
107. *CPR, 1391–6*, 371; *ibid., 1396–9*, 10, 284, 322, 408; McFarlane, *Nobility of Later Medieval England*, 55.
108. M. Cherry, 'The Courtenay earls of Devon: the Formation and Disintegration of a Late Medieval Aristocratic Affinity', *Southern History*, i (1979), 90–2.
109. Given-Wilson, 'Richard II and his Grandfather's Will', 328–31.
110. D. A. L. Morgan, 'The King's Affinity in the Polity of Yorkist England', *TRHS*, lvi (1973), 19.
111. M. J. Bennett, *Community, Class and Careerism: Cheshire and Lancashire Society in the Age of Sir Gawain and the Green Knight* (1983), 18 and *passim*.
112. This information is taken mainly from E101/318–320, and L. Mirot and E. Depréz, 'Les Ambassades anglaises pendant la guerre de Cent Ans', *Bibliothèque de l'école des Chartes*, 60 (1899), 177–214. Neither source is very comprehensive, and there are several examples of other embassies culled from sources such as the patent rolls, exchequer issue rolls, chronicles, and *Foedera*.
113. This information is taken mainly from the patent, close and fine rolls, and from *King's Works*, ii, 553–894, *passim*.
114. Under Edward III, the pattern is very similar. Dover castle, for example, was held successively by Ralph Spigurnell (knight of the king's retinue), Richard Pembridge, William Latimer, and Robert Ashton; the Tower of London was held by Richard la Vache (under-chamberlain of the king), then Alan Buxhull.
115. *CCR, 1369–74*, 187–8.
116. *Westm. Chron.*, 396–7 and n. 1.
117. See generally, J. A. Tuck, 'Richard II and the Border Magnates', *Northern History*, iii (1968).
118. E361/5–6, *passim*; John Beverley held this post under Edward III.
119. E101/400/4, m. 18; E101/408, mm. 16–17; E101/403/19, no. 12; E101/400/12, m. 5.
120. *CPR, 1377–81*, 27; *ibid., 1381–5*, 575.
121. E403/502, 27 June 1384; *CCR, 1381–5*, 97.
122. E403/499, 30 March 1384 (*sic*); *POPC*, i, 8.
123. *CPR, 1385–9*, 214; *ibid., 1391–6*, 433.
124. *Westm. Chron.*, 167; E101/400/22, m. 4.

125. Above, pp. 160–1.
126. For descriptions of these incidents, see Tuck, *Richard II and the English Nobility*, 87–120.
127. *Westm. Chron.*, 191; *CPR, 1388–92*, 20; for the king and de Vere see *Hist. Angl.*, ii, 148: 'tantum afficiebatur eidem, tantum coluit et amavit eundem, non sine nota, prout fertur, familiaritatis obscenae.'
128. The names are: (i) in Edward III's household: Bardolf, Beauchamp, George Felbridge, John Herlyng, John Joce, John Rose, John Salisbury (E101/397/5, f. 82, and E101/398/9, f. 47); (ii) in the Black Prince's household: John Breton, Roger Coghull, Lambert Fermer, Richard Hampton, John Peytevyn, Adam Ramsey, Philip Walweyn snr., Richard Wiltshire, and William Wyncelowe (E101/398/8).
129. E403/554, 21 July 1397; E. Perroy, ed., *The Diplomatic Correspondence of Richard II* (Camden 3rd ser. xlviii, 1933), 114. *CPR, 1396–9*, 93, 279, 498. See also C. Given-Wilson, 'The Ransom of Olivier du Guesclin', *BIHR*, liv (1981), 17–28.
130. *Traison et Mort*, 210–11; *CPR, 1399–1401*, 74, 99. J. L. Kirby, *Henry IV of England* (1970), 100.
131. *CPR, 1381–5*, 371.
132. E101/398/8, m. 3.
133. *CPR, 1385–9*, 192. During the fifteenth century the terms 'knight of the body' and 'esquire of the body' gradually replaced 'knight of the chamber' and 'esquire of the chamber'.
134. E101/397/20, m. 30.
135. He was not listed in 1377–79 (E101/400/4, m. 21), but was granted a prebend at St George's in May 1382 (*CPR, 1381–5*, 123), and was listed as a clerk of the chapel in 1383–4 (E101/401/2, f. 42). *Hist. Angl.*, ii, 112–13, 173.
136. E101/401/16, m. 17.
137. *CPR, 1381–5*, 54, 123, 219, 389.
138. E101/395/10; E101/401/16, m. 26.
139. Tout, *Chapters*, iii, 430, n. 3.
140. E101/400/4, m. 21; E101/404/21, f. 45.
141. *CPR, 1385–9*, 414; *Westm. Chron.*, 371.
142. BL Add. Ms. 35115, f. 41; *CPR, 1391–6*, 685; *Adam of Usk*, 179.
143. Rogers, 475; *CPR, 1399–1401*, 515.
144. *Westm. Chron.*, 385; C53/166–7.
145. P. Chaplais, *English Royal Documents, King John to Henry VI* (1971), 52; E101/398/8, m. 3. He was also one of the Black Prince's executors (*CPR, 1377–81*, 78); *Anon. Chron.*, 139, 141.
146. C53/166–7.
147. *Westm. Chron.*, 453.
148. E101/400/4, m. 20; Tuck, *Richard II and the English Nobility*, 56.
149. *RP*, iii, 101.
150. *Westm. Chron.*, 286, 295, 317, 382; *CPR, 1385–9*, 452; *ibid., 1388–92*, 229.
151. *Westm. Chron.*, 301–3, 345, 405; *CPR, 1381–5*, 352.
152. *Eulog. Hist.*, iii, 365; E101/401/16, m. 18.

153. *CPR, 1381–5*, 385, 516; Tout, *Chapters*, iv, 334–5, and v, 214–15; E101/398/8, m. 1.

154. *Westm. Chron.*, 145.

155. *Ibid.*, 233.

156. *CPR, 1388–92*, 178.

157. *Vita*, 134; C53/164; *POPC*, i, 1–19; E101/320/7; Tuck, *Richard II and the English Nobility*, 196.

158. *CPR, 1388–92*, 15, 325, 363.

159. *Westm. Chron.*, 435.

160. *Vita*, 151; *Adam of Usk*, 303.

161. BL Add. Ms. 35, 115, f. 41; *CPR, 1388–92*, 237; *ibid, 1391–6*, 328; *POPC*, i, 64; *Adam of Usk*, 179.

162. *Hist. Angl.*, ii, 277; *CPR, 1396–9*, 413.

163. *Adam of Usk*, 179; *CPR, 1391–6*, 320.

164. E101/403/10 (23 January 1396).

165. E101/402/10, f. 44. P. Chaplais, in *The Reign of Richard II*, 43–4.

166. *Vita*, 165.

167. *CPR, 1396–9*, 262.

168. *Traison et Mort*, 190; *CCR, 1385–9*, 319; E101/401/16, m. 25.

169. E101/403/10, f. 44; *CPR, 1396–9*, 43, 270–1, 280, 333.

170. R. R. Davies, in *The Reign of Richard II*, 270 and n. 66.

171. Nichols, *Collection of Wills*, 191–202; *Foedera*, viii, 162. The bequests included 10,000 marks to Thomas Holand, 3,000 to John Holand, and 2,000 each to Rutland and William Lescrope; also £20,000 for the debts of his household, chamber and wardrobe.

172. E101/403/13, m. 6.

173. *Traison et Mort*, 192, 258–9; *Annales*, 301.

174. *Foedera*, viii, 162; *Rogers*, 275, 692.

175. *Annales*, 390; *Adam of Usk*, 257.

176 *CPR, 1396–9*, 492; for Reade, see R. G. Davies, 'Richard II and the Church in the years of Tyranny', *JMH*, i (1975), 334.

177. *Annales*, 246.

178. *Traison et Mort*, 229, 267–9; Kirby, *Henry IV*, 141.

179. *Westm. Chron.*, 327; *Vita*, 166.

180. This is not to imply that the methods by which Richard secured sees for his household clerks were disreputable, or that they were necessarily unworthy appointees. See Davies, 'Richard II and the Church'.

181. Tuck, *Richard II and the English Nobility*, 65–70; Tout, *Chapters*, v, 200–229.

182. J. Otway-Ruthven, *The King's Secretary and the Signet Office in the Fifteenth Century* (1939), 42–3, 51.

183. *RP*, iii, 23, 44, 247, 446, 471, 528. In 1399 Richard was also accused of using the signet to impede legitimate processes in church courts: *ibid.*, 421.

184. Above, pp. 16–17.

185. Tout, *Chapters*, iii, 326ff; Tuck, *Richard II and the English Nobility*, 33–48.

186. Tuck, *Richard II and the English Nobility*, 106–7.

187. *CPR, 1381–5*, 531.

188. Tuck, *Richard II and the English Nobility*, 48–9.

189. *POPC*, i, 1–17.

190. Goodman, *The Loyal Conspiracy*, 115–16.

191. *CPR, 1388–92*, 214; *ibid., 1391–6*, 37; Tuck, *Richard II and the English Nobility*, 139–43.

192. *CPR, 1391–6*, 328, 391, 415.

193. *CPR, 1381–5*, 46; E403/554, 6 November; *POPC*, i, 76; *Traison et Mort*, 292.

194. *CPR, 1391–6*, 113; *Adam of Usk*, 179; *POPC*, i, 64. See also Tuck, *Richard II and the English Nobility*, 199.

195. J. S. Roskell, *The Commons and their Speakers in English Parliaments 1376–1532* (1965), 106, 127–30; *CPR, 1377–81*, 74.

196. *POPC*, i, 77; E403/554, 23 November; Roskell, *Commons and their Speakers*, 369.

197. *CPR, 1396–9*, 413.

198. *Ibid.*, 360, 494; *POPC*, i, 76.

199. *RP*, iii, 338; Davies, 'Richard II and the Church', 349–351.

200. Tuck, *Richard II and the English Nobility*, 199; *CPR, 1396–9*, 262.

201. *POPC*, i, 12b–d.

202. Tuck, *Richard II and the English Nobility*, 187–209; C. Barron, 'The Tyranny of Richard II', *BIHR*, xli (1968).

203. Bagot only just escaped: he was brought to trial in the parliament of October 1399 and accused of having evilly counselled Richard, and of having encompassed the death of John of Gaunt, 'which conspiracy,' remarks Walsingham, 'he could not deny'. Bagot threw the blame for evil counsel on to the earl of Rutland (with which many others seem to have agreed), while claiming that he had charters of pardon from both Richard and Gaunt concerning the conspiracy charge. (*Annales*, 303–8). This latter charge goes some of the way towards explaining the curious recognisances between Bagot and Gaunt described by Tuck, *Richard II and the English Nobility*, 208. Amazingly, Bagot's brass in Baginton church (Warwicks.) shows him and his wife wearing the Lancastrian livery! (Goodman, *Loyal Conspiracy*, 149).

204. Tuck, *Richard II and the English Nobility*, 119.

205. See above, pp. 133ff.

206. The slippery Rutland survived—but he would!; Guy Mone became treasurer for a brief while in 1402, but not in circumstances which suggest that Henry IV was enamoured of his appointment: A. Rogers, 'The Political Crisis of 1401', *Nottingham Medieval Studies*, xii (1968), 93–4. Clearly, though, he had ability, and in such men a murky past was often pardonable.

207. *RP*, iii, 577.

208. A. L. Brown, 'The Reign of Henry IV', in *Fifteenth-century England 1399–1509*, eds. S. B. Chrimes, C. D. Ross and R. A. Griffiths (1972), 1–28; and 'The Commons and the Council in the

reign of Henry IV', *EHR*, lxxix (1964), 1–29; K. B. McFarlane, *Lancastrian Kings and Lollard Knights* (1972), 61–101; A. Rogers, 'Royal Household of Henry IV', *passim*.

209. Above, pp. 113–14, 115–16; and below, n. 249.

210. *Adam of Usk*, 174; Rogers, 816.

211. *Annales*, 284–91; *Traison*, 201; *RP*, iii, 553.

212. Note also a letter patent issued on 10 September 'per consilium Thomae Rempston, militis', and the grant to Norbury on 31 August of Leeds castle, where Richard II was sent immediately after his deposition: *CPR, 1396–9*, 592, 593, 595 (*bis*); *Traison et Mort*, 215.

213. *RP*, iii, 577. For detailed biographies of all these men see Rogers, 'Royal Household of Henry IV', 697–821.

214. *Traison et Mort*, 296.

215. McFarlane, *Lancastrian Kings and Lollard Knights*, 19.

216. *CPR, 1401–5*, 108, 489; Courtenay had held Windsor castle since 1388, and died in 1405.

217. *Royal Letters of Henry IV*, ed. F. C. Hingeston, i, (1860), 149.

218. *Traison et Mort*, 296; *CPR, 1405–8*, 471ff.

219. Quoted by Brown, 'Reign of Henry IV', 17.

220. *CPR, 1401–5*, 391, 441.

221. Madeleine Barber, 'John Norbury (*c.* 1350–1414): an esquire of Henry IV', *EHR*, lxviii (1953), 66–76.

222. *St Alban's Chronicle*, 56.

223. *Rogers*, 765.

224. K. B. McFarlane, *John Wyclif and the Beginnings of English Non-Conformity* (1952), 108–15.

225 *CPR, 1399–1401*, 313; Rogers, 776.

226. *Adam of Usk*, 231–6.

227. BL Cotton Vitellius F xvii, f. 42b, quoted in *Adam of Usk*, 231–2n.

228. *CPR, 1401–5*, 412, 441.

229. *Annales*, 289.

230. One man whose support proved to be crucial was Ralph Nevill, earl of Westmorland; but it was Richard II who had elevated Nevill, and how was Henry to be sure of his loyalty, at least before 1403?.

231. *CPR, 1405–8*, 99, 260, 359; *RP*, iii, 577.

232. *Rogers*, 733; *RP*, iii, 625.

233. For his early career see M. Aston, *Thomas Arundel* (1967).

234. Brown, for example, noticed that he 'was apparently not much at Westminster' before 1406 ('Reign of Henry IV', 20), and McFarlane came to much the same conclusion (*Lancastrian Kings and Lollard Knights*, 64–5).

235. See Brown, 'Reign of Henry IV', 12–15; Roos and Furnivall both held the treasurership too.

236. See Appendix VI.

237. E101/404/21, f. 45; BL, Harl. 319, f. 46.

238. *Rogers*, 808, 815.

239. His name is in fact crossed out in the 1402–3 list

but this, as noted in the margin of the manuscript, was because he had already received his robes from the great wardrobe, not because he had been found not to be a chamber knight: E101/404/21, ff. 45–6.

24. E101/405/18, 23; E101/406/3; E361/7, mm. 8–9.

241. There are biographies of all Henry's chamber knights, as well as many other members of his household, in Rogers, 'Royal Household of Henry IV', 697–821.

242. *Traison et Mort*, 294.

243. *CPR, 1405–8*, 201; *ibid., 1408–13*, 90.

244. *Ibid., 1399–1401*, 29; E403/562, 12 July.

245. *Rogers*, 815; *RP*, ii, 374; the other three were Simon Felbridge, Baldwin Bereford, and Philip la Vache, all knights of Richard's chamber.

246. *CPR, 1405–8*, 440.

247. *Hist Angl.*, ii, 259.

248. See for example *Royal Letters*, i, 309: when Mascall was captured by Flemish pirates and held to ransom, Henry wrote in person to the duchess of Burgundy asking her to use her influence to have him freed. This incident occurred in 1404, and must have been soon after his dismissal from the household.

249. The others were Luke Feltham, a household esquire, the abbot of Dover, and 'Crosseby of the chamber'; Feltham was, in the words of the king and council 'mys a present hors des gages de mesme notre houstel noun pas en son defaute mais pur labbregement des coustages et despenses de notre houstel sous dit' (E404/18/573).

250. McFarlane, *Lancastrian Kings and Lollard Knights*, 124.

251. See for example the special pardons granted to various financial officers of the household at the end of Tutbury's term of office, relating to (often large) sums of money which had simply gone missing and could no longer be accounted for; these were said to be exceptional and under no circumstances to be regarded as setting a precedent: A. Rogers, 'Royal Household', 652–3; and see generally Rogers, 'The Political Crisis of 1401', 85–96.

252. There is perhaps a parallel in the 'Georgia mafia' of President Carter which was so heavily criticised in the months after he took up office in 1977; but to talk of a 'Lancastrian mafia' in 1399 is perhaps going too far.

253. On this subject see Brown, 'Commons and Council', *passim*.

254. Some of these men (Norbury, Bowet, Pelham and Doreward) had virtually ceased to be members of the council since *c.* May 1406, when a new council had been appointed in parliament (*ibid.*, 24–5); the effect of the changes made in December 1406 was to complete the process of replacing the king's men with the prince's men.

255. John Cheyne was the king's ambassador to

Rome in 1407; Arnold Savage went on an embassy to France in 1408–9.

256. Although retained on the council in 1407, Roos seems to have been dropped from it shortly afterwards; by 1412 he was back in regular attendance (*POPC*, ii, 31, 36; *CPR, 1408–13*, 368). For a general discussion of Roos's career see C. D. Ross, 'The Yorkshire Baronage 1399–1435' (unpublished Oxford D.Phil. thesis [1950]) 145–8.

257. G. L. Harriss, 'Preference at the Medieval Exchequer', *BIHR*, xxx (1957); 'Fictitious Loans', *Econ. Hist. Rev.*, viii (1955–6).

258. *Anon. Chron.*, 98. The figures given do not make proper sense in the chronicler's account, but the gist of the charge is perfectly clear.

259. For the charges against de la Pole in 1386, see now J. S. Roskell, *The Impeachment of Michael de la Pole* (1984).

260. On this aspect of the crisis see J. J. N. Palmer, *England, France and Christendom 1377–99* (1972), Chapters 5 and 6.

261. E101/393/15, m. 12; *CFR., 1356–8*, 214, 260, 292, 312, 335, 352; *ibid., 1369–77*, 133.

262. Above, p. 169; E. Perroy, ed., *The Diplomatic Correspondence of Richard II* (Camden Society 3rd series, xlviii, 1933), 116.

263. E101/402/20, f. 34.

264. E101/403/10, ff. 44–6.

265. Below, pp. 217–18.

266. *CPR, 1396–9*, 422, 423; Goodman, *The Loyal Conspiracy*, 102.

267. *CPR, 1399–1401*, 77, 337.

268. Ross, 'The Yorkshire Baronage', 410.

Chapter IV: The King's Affinity

1. D. A. L. Morgan's 'The King's Affinity in the Polity of Yorkist England', *RHS*, 1–25, is an excellent study of the more important personnel of the royal household, but does not really go beyond that to the wider affinity.

2. Above, pp. 53–5.

3. Tout, *Chapters*, iii, 442f; for example, estimated 120 for the chancery, certainly the largest of these departments.

4. And almost certainly before that, though the documentation is not as good: see above, pp. 5ff.

5. R. F. Walker, 'The Anglo-Welsh Wars 1217–1267' (unpublished D.Phil. thesis, Oxford University, 1954), 66–90.

6. Prestwich, *War, Politics and Finance*, 41–66. Byerly, *Records of the Wardrobe and Household*, xl–xliv.

7. This table is not intended to be comprehensive; there are other lists which could be cited; the intention is to give a broad sample of numbers over the whole period, as well as to show how rapidly fluctuations could occur, as for example in the years 1284–6, or 1312–16. The sources used are: (i) for

Edward I's reign: Prestwich, *War, Politics and Finance*, 46–7; E101/352/31; E101/352/4; *Liber Quotidianus*; and Byerly, *Records of the Wardrobe and Household*, xl–xliv; (ii) for Edward II's reign: E101/375/8; E101/376/7; E101/378/6, E101/377/1; *Society of Antiquaries* Mss. 120, 121; BL, Add. Mss. 9,951 and 17,362; and Stowe Ms 553; (iii) for Edward III's reign: E101/385/4, E101/392/12, E101/393/11, E101/398/14, E101/398/18; *The Wardrobe Book of William de Norwell*, eds. M. Lyon, B. Lyon, and H. S. Lucas (Académie Royale de Belgique, 1984), xcii, 301–3; and *A Collection of Ordinances and Regulations for the Government of the Royal Household* (Society of Antiquaries, 1790), 10–12. I am very grateful to Dr Michael Prestwich for several of the Edward I and II references.

8. The figures for 1347 are drawn from a so-called 'Ordinance' for Edward's household printed by the Society of Antiquaries in 1790 (above, n. 7); it purports to be a record of the household 'in tyme of peace', but this is surely an error; 1347 was certainly not a very peaceful year; Edward III spent most of the year encamped outside Calais.

9. Tout, *Chapters*, iv, 227–348.

10. Byerly, *Records of Wardrobe and Household*, xxviii.

11. Tout, *Chapters*, vi, 45; and ii, 157 for comment.

12. E101/13/35, n. 11. I owe this reference to Dr M. C. Prestwich who has dated it to *c.* 1301.

13. Tout, *Chapters*, vi, 45.

14. *Chronicles of Edward I and Edward II*, ed. W. Stubbs, i (R.S., 1882), 287–8; J. Conway Davies, 'The First Journal of Edward II's Chamber', *EHR*, xxx (1915), 677–8.

15. *Wardrobe Book of William de Norwell*, eds. Lyon, Lyon and Lucas, lxvi, 231–2.

16. E101/391/15, mm. 5–6; E101/395/16, m. 9. There are however no lists of chamber knights in the great wardrobe livery rolls for 1371–2 or 1374–7: E101/396/20, E101/397/20.

17. These cover parts of the following years: 1366–7, 1369, 1371–3, 1376–7: E101/396/2, 11; E101/397/5, E101/398/9.

18. E101/401/2, E101/402/5; BL, Add. Ms. 35,115; E101/403/10; E101/404/21; BL, Harl. Ms. 319.

19. *CPR, 1381–5*, 73; E101/400/4, m. 21; E101/400/24; E101/401/6, m. 16. These posts had been in existence for a long time; the Ordinance of 1318, for example, refers to the 'knight who is the earl marshal's deputy', who eats in the hall, as well as the knight chief usher of the hall and two knights marshal of the hall (one of whom is probably the same as the earl marshal's deputy), but these men are clearly rather different to the chamber knights of the late fourteenth century (Tout, *Place of Edward II*, 254–5).

20. Myers, *Household of Edward IV*, 106–8 and 240, n. 97.

21. Above, pp. 28ff.

22. E101/391/15, mm. 5–6; E101/392/12, f. 40.

Also, seven of the chamber knights listed in 1364–5 figure as knights of the household in one or both of the wardrobe account books for 1353–4 and 1359–60: E101/394/16, m. 9; E101/393/11, f. 76; and see Appendix IV.

23. E101/395/10.

24. J. M. W. Bean, '"Bachelor" and Retainer', *Medievalia et Humanistica*, 3 (1972), 121–2.

25. See Appendix V.

26. E101/404/18, 22.

27. See above, Chapter III.

28. Thus in August 1372 Thomas Bradeston and Philip Darcy, knights *de familia regis*, received wages of war at the exchequer (E403/446, 6 August, 11 August); in March 1373, the knights Gilbert Giffard and Thomas Bamfeld were each granted £50 for life at the exchequer because they were 'now of the king's retinue' (*CPR*, *1370–4*, 261–264); in February 1374 Nicholas Dagworth, knight *de retinentia regis*, received payment of an annuity at the exchequer granted to him earlier (E403/451, 27 February). In 1378 John Lord Gomeney (from Spain) had his annuity of 200 marks at the exchequer confirmed by Richard II, and was described then as being 'of the late king's retinue'; the annuity had originally been granted in 1360 (*CPR*, *1377–81*, 241).

29. *CPR*, *1385–9*, 62, 99; the men referred to were the king's half-brother John Holand, and Ralph Stafford, heir to the earldom of Stafford; the references are in connection with the brawl at Mustardthorpe in which Holand murdered Stafford. The brawl was described as 'in the king's presence', and the term 'knights of the household' was probably used loosely to indicate that the case was justiciable in the court of the verge. Both men are known to have been in the king's retinue on this campaign.

30. Myers *Household of Edward IV*, 240, nn. 95, 97.

31. Prestwich, *War, Politics and Finance*, 57–8, 273.

32. Above, pp. 169ff.

33. See Appendices V and VI.

34. In the patent rolls for *1370–4*, for example, I have discovered twenty-five men described as king's esquires, and every one of them is listed as an esquire or sergeant of the household in one or more of the wardrobe books for 1369, 1371–3 and 1376–7.

35. No doubt I have missed some, but I hope not many; I should be surprised if the actual figure passed 450. I have reserved the 'Cheshire bodyguard' recruited in 1397–8 for separate discussion: see below, pp. 222–3.

36. Above, pp. 162–4; the editor of the *Westm. Chron.* (230, n. 1) describes both Elmham and Tryvet as chamber knights but cites no reference.

37. *CFR*, *1383–91*, 310; he was described as a king's knight in both 1386 and 1390: E101/401/16, m. 26; *CPR*, *1388–92*, 338.

38. *CPR*, *1377–81*, 1–264 *passim*.

39. *Westm. Chron.*, 187.

40. *RP*, iii, 232–3; *Knighton*, ii, 291; Walsingham, *Hist. Angl.*, ii, 162.

41. Below, p. 216.

42. *Knighton*, ii, 213; see also Bennett, *Community, Class and Careerism*, 208, where it is suggested that the king may have tried to summon a force of Cheshiremen to London during the parliament of 1386; it is possible, though, that this summons was connected with the French invasion scare of that year.

43. John Lord Arundel (1378); William Drayton (1379); John Cheyne (1380); William Clynton (1381); John Annesley (1385); William Hilton (1386); John Russell (1387); *CPR*, *1377–81*, 177, 390, 490; *ibid.*, *1381–5*, 25, 571; *ibid.*, *1385–9*, 131, 372.

44. Tuck, *Richard II and the English Nobility*, 135–6; and below, pp. 238–9.

45. *EHD*, iv, 1116.

46. Above, p. 40.

47. *CPR*, *1385–9*, 112; *ibid.*, *1388–92*, 322; *ibid.*, *1391–6*, 282, 284, 552, 703, 719; E101/401/16, m. 26.

48. This includes 97 Cheshire esquires listed as retained in 1397–8, of whom 85 were 'ad terram vitae' and twelve were retained during pleasure (E101/402/10).

49. For further discussion of life retaining and the livery and maintenance legislation, see below, p 236ff.

50. *CPR*, *1385–9*, 273.

51. Goodman, *The Loyal Conspiracy*, 143, 150.

52. *CPR*, *1388–92*, 16, 101.

53. For some further examples under Henry IV, and further discussion of this question, see below, pp. 244–5.

54. *CPR*, *1396–9*, 491–593 *passim*. The knights were Henry de Hoghton, John Dabrichecourt, Maurice de Berkeley, Robert Ursewyk, Walter Blount, Hugh Huse, Ralph earl of Westmorland, John Botiller of Rouclyf, Thomas de Wennesley, William de Par, Thomas Beek, and Thomas Flemmyng (of Lancashire, not to be confused with Thomas Flemmyng, a west country and Irish landholder who was already a king's knight). I have not included any of these men (except Nevill, who was already retained by the king too) in my figures for king's knights or esquires, since they can hardly be considered as such, and certainly did not remain so for long.

55. Beltz, *Memorials of the Order of the Garter*, 257–8.

56. *CPR*, *1391–6*, 185.

57. *CPR*, *177–81*, 450; *ibid.*, *1385–9*, 16; *ibid.*, *1391–6*, 339.

58. Bennett, *Community, Class and Careerism*, 234.

59. According to his Inquisition Post Mortem he owned no land there: *EHD*, xv, 166–78; for taxable population see *EHD*, iv, 995–7.

60. McFarlane, *Lancastrian Kings and Lollard Knights*, 165

61. Holmes, *Estates of Higher Nobility*, 70; E101/394/16, m. 9.

62. *Ibid.*, 60–3; *CPR, 1396–9, 439.*

62. *Myers, Household of Edward IV*, 127.

64. *POPC*, i, 109–10.

65. Morgan, 'King's Affinity', 21–4.

66. This information is based on a variety of sources such as commission appointments, taxation lists, and inquisitions post mortem and miscellaneous; see Appendix V; and on 'regions' generally, see the sensible discussion in Bennett, *Community, Class and Careerism*, 237.

67. Devon was less well-populated than the others, but several retainers of the Black Prince came from here, where extensive Duchy of Cornwall estates were situated: the Courtenays, Lewis Clifford, John Sully, and Baldwin Raddington among others.

68. Tuck, *Richard II and the English Nobility*, 164ff.

69. Below, pp. 246ff.

70. John Godard: escheator of Yorks. 1387–8; sheriff of Yorks. 1388–9; M.P. for Yorks. 1386 and 1391; retained by the king in 1392.

71. James Pykering: escheator of Yorks. 1379–81, 1382–3, 1390–1; sheriff of Yorks. 1389–90, 1393–4, 1397–9; M.P. for Westmorland 1382, and for Yorks. 1383, 1384, 1388, 1390, 1397; retained as king's knight in 1390 (though not for life).

72. Henry Retford: sheriff of Lincs 1389, 1392–3, 1397–8; retained by the king in 1393.

73. John Bussy: sheriff of Lincs 1383–4, 1385–6, 1390–1; M.P. for Lincs. 1383, 1388, 1390 (twice), 1391, 1393, 1394, 1395, 1397 (twice); retained by the king in 1391.

74. Adam Peshale: sheriff of Staffs 1380; M.P. for Staffs 1380, 1381, 1383, sheriff of Salop 1397–9; M.P. for Salop 1394; retained by the king in 1390.

75. William Walshale: sheriff of Staffs 1381–3, 1396–9, 1406–7; escheator of Staffs and Salop 1375–7, 1378–81, 1383–4; M.P. for Staffs 1380, 1384, 1391, 1393, 1394; retained as an esquire of the household in 1389.

76. Edward Dalyngridge: M.P. for Sussex 1379, 1380 (twice), 1381, 1382, 1384 (twice), 1385, 1386, 1388. He probably supported the Appellants in 1387–8, was retained by the king for life in 1389, and was a king's councillor until his death in 1394. See above, p. 184f.

77. William Sturmy: M.P. for Hants 1384, November 1390; M.P. for Wilts January 1390, 1393, 1399; M.P. for Devon 1391; retained by the king in 1392.

78. John Thornbury: M.P. for Herts 1382 (twice), 1385, 1390, 1391; 'king's knight' in November 1388, but not recorded as a life retainer.

79. John Annesley: M.P. for Notts 1377, 1378, 1379, 1384, 1385, 1386 and 1388 (twice); retained by the king for life in 1385.

80. Below, pp. 222–3.

81. For the 1394–5 expedition those receiving war wages are listed in E101/402/20 ff. 31–40, although the last three folios of this account are badly damaged; for the 1399 expedition there is no wardrobe account, but a partial picture of the army can be gleaned from imprests made by wardrobe keeper John Carp in his enrolled account (E361/26), and from the letters of protection issued by the chancery (*CPR, 1396–9*, 22 Richard II, parts II and III).

82. See for instance the remarks made by G. L. Harriss in his introduction to McFarlane, *England in the Fifteenth Century*, x–xi: by the mid-1960s 'he [McFarlane] had, like others come to view retaining primarily as an expression of the lord's need for service in peace rather than war. The permanent nucleus of the affinity would indeed be mobilised for service in arms ... But such service was occasional and of short duration. It is in the peacetime composition and function of the retinue that its character and *raison d'être* must be sought.'

83. *CPR, 1388–92*, 101.

84. For Richard and Cheshire, see Bennett, *Community, Class and Careerism*; R. R. Davies, 'Richard II and the Principality of Chester 1397–9', in *The Reign of Richard II*, eds. Du Boulay and Barron; J. L. Gillespie, 'Richard II's Cheshire Archers', *Transactions of the Historical Society of Lancashire and Cheshire*, cxxv (1974); also the same author's 'Richard II's archers of the crown', *Journal of British Studies*, 17–18 (1977–9).

85. E101/402/10.

86. Davies, 'Richard II and the Principality of Chester', 273, quoting the Kenilworth chronicle.

87. Gillespie, 'Richard II's archers of the crown', 19.

88. Approximate numbers: household servants, 600; Cheshire retainers, 760; king's knights and esquires (excluding Cheshiremen), 250; sergeants-at-arms, 90; archers of the crown, 75; staff of government departments, 250.

89. *Adam of Usk*, 169–70; and see *RP*, iii, 418.

90. *Westm. Chron.*, 213.

91. *Knighton*, ii, 244.

92. See, for instance, *Annales*, 248–9.

93. E403/562, 20 June 1399.

94. E101/42/12.

95. See Tuck, *Richard II and the English Nobility*, 214, for the date of his arrival, which is uncertain.

96. *Vita*, 154; *Adam of Usk*, 180; *Annales*, 303–8.

97. *Annales*, 246.

98. For this see *Traison et Mort*, 192–292 *passim*; *Adam of Usk*, 152–65; *Annales*, 246ff.; Ross, 'Yorkshire Baronage', 297.

99. E403/562, 4 July, 9 July, 12 July; E101/42/12; *CPR, 1396–9*, 596.

100. Tuck, *Richard II and the English Nobility*, 216.

101. *Adam of Usk*, 174–5; *Traison et Mort*, 211.

102. See the remarks by Caroline Barron in *Reign of Richard II*, eds. Du Boulay and Barron, 201.

103. *Annales*, 245.

104. See Appendix VI.

105. *CPR, 1399–1401*, 476.

106. See for example the map in S. Armitage-Smith, *John of Gaunt* (1904), facing p. 218.

107. S. M. Wright, 'A Gentry Society of the Fifteenth Century: Derbyshire *circa* 1430–1509' (unpublished Ph.D. thesis, University of Birmingham, 1978), 199.

108. *CPR, 1401–5*, 237, 372; *ibid., 1405–8*, 50; *Hardyng*, 365–7.

109. Ross, 'Yorkshire Baronage', 426.

110. *Ibid.*, 330ff.

111. *Ibid.*, 361, 363.

112 *CPR, 1401–5*, 256; *ibid., 1405–8*, 48.

113. Ross, 'Yorkshire Baronage', 346, 361.

114. See below, p. 234.

115. *CPR, 1399–1401*, 51; Ross, 'Yorkshire Baronage', 278ff.

116. *Royal Letters*, i, 206; and see Wylie, *Henry IV*, i, 397–8, 450–1; ii, 175–7, 274, for much of what follows.

117. Above, pp. 181–2.

118. *CPR, 1399–1401*, 441; *ibid., 1405–8*, 47; *ibid., 1408–13*, 23, 95–6.

119. Ross, 'Yorkshire Baronage', 279.

120. *Hardyng*, 364; *Adam of Usk*, 284; *St Alban's Chronicle*, 28.

121. See for example *CPR, 1405–8*, 437, 444.

122. *CPR, 1405–8*, 25, 84.

123. P. McNiven, 'The Cheshire rising of 1400', *Bulletin of the John Rylands Library*, 52 (1970), 375–96.

124. See for example *RP*, iii, 577; *Royal Letters*, i, 17; *St Alban's Chronicle*, 22–3; *CPR, 1401–5*, 464.

125. For Gam, see G. Williams, *Owen Glendower* (1955) 51; for Madoc, see *CPR, 1401–5*, 212.

126. *CPR, 1405–8*, 6, 82.

127. For Grey (king's chamberlain), Leche (controller of the king's household), and Curson (the king's councillor), see above, pp. 194–6. Walter Blount was one of Gaunt's executors and died with Henry at Shrewsbury; his brother John rose rapidly in the king's service after being retained for life as a king's esquire in 1402, and received a grant 'of the king's special grace' in 1406 (*CPR, 1401–5*, 161, 499; *CFR 1405–13*, 48; *CPR, 1408–13*, 227.)

128. Wright, 'Gentry Society', 205, 221, 236.

129. *POPC*, i, 109.

130. J. R. S. Phillips, *Aymer de Valence, Earl of Pembroke 1307–1324* (1972), 148–51, 312–5.

131. Below, pp. 264–7.

132. The Watertons were Hugh (king's knight), and John and Robert (king's esquires); the chamber knight Robert Chalons was married to Hugh's daughter, Blanche; after Hugh's death in 1409, Roger Leche married his widow, Katherine. The Rocheforts were Ralph (chamber knight), Henry and John (king's knights).

133. Below, pp. 246f.

134. John Arundel: sheriff of Cornwall 1399–1400 and 1402; M.P. for Cornwall twice in 1404; retained by the king in 1405.

135. Thomas Broke: M.P. for Somerset three times between 1399 and 1404; retained by the king in 1405.

136. John Copuldyk: sheriff of Lincolnshire 1399–1400; M.P. for Lincolnshire in 1401; retained by the king in 1403.

137. Richard Stanhope: M.P. for Nottinghamshire three times in 1402 and 1404; sheriff of Notts. and Derby 1404–5, in which capacity he raised forces to help to suppress the 1405 rebellion, and for service in Wales; retained by the king in October 1405, with a £40 annuity, because he had fought for the king 'without wages, reward, or fee' (*CPR, 1405–8*, 84).

138. John Greynvill: M.P. for Devon in 1402; sheriff of Cornwall 1406; retained by the king in 1407.

139. Edward Benstede: M.P. for Hertfordshire in 1399; sheriff of Essex and Herts in 1400; retained by the king in 1401.

140. Above, pp. 221–2.

141. Above, p. 196.

142. *Rogers*, 434.

143. The first three of these had also been to Ireland under Richard II, and may have picked up a taste for Irish affairs then.

144. For Clifford, see *Adam of Usk*, 255; Gam, a Welshman but a staunch royalist, was eventually captured by Glendower in 1412, but was released and died fighting for Henry V at Agincourt (Williams, *Owen Glendower*, 51, 55); Dartasso was admiral of Ireland in 1404 (*CPR, 1401–5*, 406); his annuities from Henry totalled 200 marks, quite exceptional for an esquire, and he was retained for life by the king, as were both Gam and Clifford (*CPR, 1399–1401*, 74, 76, 191).

145. Above, pp. 214–15.

146. *CPR, 1399–1401*, 201–2, 430, 473.

147. *Ibid., 1405–8*, 545.

148. *POPC*, i, 319–20.

149. *CPR, 1408–13*, 104; it was in fact to be taken from the issues of Northumberland rather than Yorkshire.

150. For Richard del Brugge, see *Adam of Usk*, 283, 295.

151. *Adam of Usk*, 39.

152. See *Annales*, 191, where Walsingham describes the knights and esquires attending Richard II at his interview with Charles VI at Calais in 1396: 'the knights wore suits of gold cloth, the esquires cloths of say, the king's livery.'

153. For references to livery badges at this time see *Annales*, 189–90, 325; *CPR, 1399–1401*, 385; *ibid., 1405–8*, 277; *Traison et Mort*, 210–11; and other references cited below.

154. *RP*, iii, 23.

155. *Westm. Chron.*, 357.

156. *RP*, iii, 600, 662.

157. *Ibid.*, 257, 266, 428, 477–8, 600, 662.

158. *Westm. Chron.*, 82–3.

159. *RP*, iii, 233; this implies that badges, rather than hats or suits of livery, may have been something of a novelty at this time.

160. *Westm. Chron.*, 355–9; and *ibid.*, 187, for Richard's attempt to distribute *signis* of silver and gilt crowns in East Anglia in 1387, with the intention that those who accepted them 'whenever they were called upon to do so . . . should join the king, armed and ready.'

161. *RP*, iii, 265.

162. *EHD*, iv, 1116; and see R. L. Storey, 'Liveries and Commissions of the Peace 1388–1390', in *The Reign of Richard II*, eds. Du Boulay and Barron, 131–52.

163. Above, pp. 40, 214–15.

164. *RP*, iii, 307, 339.

165. That these men were given livery badges is abundantly clear even from the document which lists the king's knights, esquires, yeomen and archers receiving annuities from the issues of the Principality of Cheshire, where they are described as, for example, 'sagittarum de liberata corone', and against many of the names is the phrase 'et habet liberatum corone': E101/402/10. For the Cheshire *vigilia*, see above, pp. 222–3 and references cited there.

166. *RP*, iii, 428; *SR*, ii, 113–14.

167. Above, p. 238.

168. *RP*, iii, 452.

169. The only exception to these rules was that the constable and marshal could distribute livery badges to knights and esquires serving with them on the borders in time of war.

170. *RP*, iii, 477–78, 523–4.

171. *Ibid.*, 478, and *SR*, ii, 129–30; Henry may have regretted his generosity to his son later in the reign, but at this time it was undoubtedly on his own initiative.

172. *SR*, ii, 156, 167, 240, 426; *EHD*, iv, 1132.

173. They continually asked for the enforcement of the statute on purveyance, for example, without seriously amending it.

174. Which is not to say that the king did not care about law and order, but that other considerations were sometimes more important.

175. *Royal Letters*, i, 206; Ross, 'Yorkshire Baronage', 349; when the countess of Oxford was conspiring against Henry in 1404 she had various silver and gilt badges of the white hart made of the type that Richard used to distribute to his followers, in order to encourage men to follow her (*Hist. Angl.*, ii, 262).

176. *RP*, iii, 524.

177. J. R. Lander, *Politics and Power in England 1450–1509* (1976), 34, n. 182.

178. Kirby, *Henry IV of England*, 172; *CCR*, *1402–5*, 377.

179. *RP*, iii, 478.

180. Above, p. 216

181. *CPR*, *1401–5*, 102.

182. G. Fourquin, *Lordship and Feudalism in the Middle Ages* (1976, trans.), 104.

183. Above, pp. 215–16; Edward III sometimes did the same, as for example with Ralph Lord Stafford, who was granted a fee of 600 marks a year in 1348 'for his stay for his life with the king . . . and because he will not stay in the retinue of any other than the king.' (*CPR*, *1348–50*, 183).

184. *CPR*, *1399–1401*, 135; *ibid.*, *1408–13*, 446.

185. K. B. McFarlane, *England in the Fifteenth Century* (1981), 31.

186. Morgan, 'King's Affinity', 4.

187. J. C. Wedgwood, 'John of Gaunt and the Packing of Parliament', *EHR*, xlv (1930); and see H. G. Richardson, 'John of Gaunt and the Parliamentary Representation of Lancashire', *Bulletin of the John Rylands Library*, xxii (1938). For more general discussion of the question, see McFarlane, *England in the Fifteenth Century*, xvi–xvii, 1–21.

188. Tuck, *Richard II and the English Nobility*, 112–13; Knighton, ii, 288; *Westm. Chron.*, 267.

189. *RP*, iii, 420; the phrase is Walsingham's, in *Annales*, 302; *Adam of Usk*, 191, also claims that the cities and boroughs 'had not had free elections in the choice of the members of the commons'; see also *Annales*, 209.

190. This and the following information is drawn from *Return of Members of Parliament* (House of Commons 1878), i. Chamber knights and household esquires are included as king's knights and esquires.

191. *CCR*, *1381–5*, 398–9.

192. For Thomas Camoys' expulsion in 1388 see *Westm. Chron.*, 231, and *Knighton*, ii, 256; in June 1385 Morwelle was ordered, along with Lewis Clifford, Richard Stury, John Worth, Thomas Latymer, Philip la Vache, and several others, to 'assist continually about the person of the king's mother' while the king went to Scotland: *CCR*, *1381–5*, 553.

193. Tuck, *Richard II and the English Nobility*, 90–1.

194. *Annales*, 209ff; *Adam of Usk*, 13ff.

195. N. B. Lewis, 'Re-election to Parliament in the Reign of Richard II', *EHR*, xlviii (1933), 366.

196. R. Jeffs, 'The Later Medieval Sheriff and the Royal Household' (unpublished Oxford University D.Phil. thesis, 1960), 65 and *passim*; I am very grateful to Dr Jeffs for allowing me to consult his thesis; see also Ralph Griffiths, *The Reign of King Henry VI* (1981), 801–2.

197. *Westm. Chron.*, 266–7.

198. *Ibid.*, 405; and see Storey, 'Liveries and Commissions', 142–3.

199. *Hist. Angl.*, ii, 231; *RP*, iii, 419.

200. Lancashire, Northumberland, Westmorland and Rutland; until Earl Thomas's forfeiture in 1397, Worcestershire too was held for life by the Beauchamp earls of Warwick. This information is taken from *List of Sheriffs for England and Wales* (P.R.O. Lists and Indexes, ix, 1963 reprint).

201. Tuck, *Richard II and the English Nobility*, 99–100.
202. Above, p. 225.
203. Thomas Clanvow in Hereford; Robert de Legh in Cheshire; John Golafre in Oxford, 1404; Richard Redman in Cumberland 1401, 1411; Henry Retford in Lincolnshire, 1406; Adam Peshale in Shropshire, 1418; William Walshale in Stafford, 1406; Richard Mawardyn in Hampshire, 1403.
204. *Reign of Richard II*, eds. Du Boulay and Barron, 152, 240–1.
205. *Ibid.*, 150–1.
206. See Goodman, *The Loyal Conspiracy*, 19, 34, 37, 43 for the careers of these men and their connections with the Appellants.
207. *Hardyng*, 353.
208. *Eulog. Hist.*, iii, 402; *Annales*, 391, 403.
209. *SR*, ii, 156.
210. The two counties which most frequently had members of the king's affinity as sheriffs were Lincolnshire (ten out of the fourteen years) and Yorkshire (eight). In view of the large numbers of gentry in both these counties retained by the king, this is far from surprising.
211. *Rogers*, 596–9.
212. The speakers were: John Doreward (1399), Arnold Savage (1401 and January 1404); Henry Retford (September 1402); William Sturmy (October 1404); John Tiptoft (1406); Thomas Chaucer (1407, 1410, and 1411). Thomas Chaucer was an esquire of the household and king's butler from 1402 to 1413, apart from a brief period in 1407; Arnold Savage was steward of Prince Henry's household 1401–3, a kings knight from 1403, and a regular member of the council 1402–6; John Tiptoft was a chamber knight until 1406, then keeper of the wardrobe (1406–8), and treasurer of England 1408–9.
213. Walsingham described Bussy as cruel, ambitious, greedy, faithless, cunning, eloquent, and a geat sycophant. For once he may not have been exaggerating. (*Annales*, 209–10).
214. Storey, 'Liveries and Commissions', 152 and n. 70, points out that 'after the destruction of the old appellants, the influence of Richard's noble partisans was spread throughout the land'; Gaunt was appointed to 23 commissions, Rutland to 16, Thomas Holand to 16, John Holand to 9, and Mowbray to 8.
215. Below, pp. 264–7.
216. Morgan, 'King's Affinity', 25.
217. Christine Carpenter, 'Political Society in Warwickshire, *c.* 1401–1472' (unpublished Ph.D. thesis, University of Cambridge, 1976), 69; Dr Carpenter also noted, however, that an affinity built up in this way might not have very deep roots.

Conclusion

1. Quoted in Mertes, 'Secular Noble Households', 213.
2. B. Guenée, *L'Occident aux XIVe et XVe siecles* (1971), Chapter IV: 'Le prince et son image', especially 142–50.
3. *Comptes de l'Hôtel des rois de France aux XIVe et XVe Siècles*, ed. M. L. Douet-D'Arcq (SHF, 1865), ii. The number listed is 234, but as M. Douet-d'Arcq points out, some of the lesser servants are omitted.
4. *Ibid.*, xi, xxx–xxxiii; the accounts printed by M. Douet-D'Arcq make it clear that they cover very much the same types of expenditure as do the wardrobe accounts of the same period in England; Guenée, *L'Occident*, 148–9.
5. M. Vale, *Charles VII* (1974), 218.
6. R. Vaughan, *Valois Burgundy* (1975), 96–7, 105; Professor Vaughan states that Philip the Bold actually spent about 250,000 *livres tournois* on his court, but the 'court' here includes much that in England was covered by other departments (such as the Works), or was paid directly from the exchequer; the 'day-to-day running costs of the court' cost about 100,000 *livres tournois*. The conversion of French money into English equivalents is notoriously teacherous, and the estimates which I have provided here must only be regarded as approximate; they are obtained from the unpublished 'Interim Listing of the Exchange Rates of Medieval Europe', by Peter Spufford and Wendy Wilkinson (Keele, 1977).
7. Morgan, 'The King's Affinity', 11.
8. See especially Mertes, 'Secular Noble Households', 16–17, 213, 222; also McFarlane, *Nobility of Later Medieval England*, 109–12, and *England in the Fifteenth Century*, xiii.
9. Mertes, 'Secular Noble Households', 16, 112, 279–94, 356.
10. *RP*, iii, 166.
11. *Speculum Regis Edwardi Tertii*, ed. Moisant, introduction; *Ordonnances des Roys de France de la Troisième race*, ed. J. Laurière *et al* (1723–1846), vols. i–ix; for purchases of exemptions see for example vi, 176, and vii, 529. A good example of purveyance regulations is in vii, 784. Exemptions were normally purchased by communities who agreed instead to donate certain quantities of specified goods each year, rather like the 'composition' system which occasionally operated in England at this time and was to become much more widespread in the sixteenth century (McGurk, 'Royal purveyance in Kent').
12. Vale, *Charles VII*, 38–9; *Rogers*, 625.
13. See for example Vale, *Charles VII*, 40–41, 72, 113–4.
14. *Hist. Angl.*, ii, 156.
15. *RP*, iii, 12–14.
16. McFarlane, *Lancastrian Kings and Lollard Knights*, 43–7; Tuck, *Richard II and the English Nobility*, 207–9.

17. See for example *Westm. Chron.*, 21, 401; *Traison et Mort*, 163–6.
18. During the first year of Richard II's reign, for example, some twenty-five knights who were not, either now or later, described as king's knights, received confirmations of their annuities from the crown. These men obviously had some sort of attachment to the king, even if it might not extend far beyond the expectation of financial gain, and should be thought of as members of the royal affinity in the broadest sense of the word. Nobles' affinities are of course no more capable of close definition than the king's.
19. See Dr Harriss's introduction to McFarlane, *England in the Fifteenth Century*, xi; and Wright, 'Gentry Society', 240.
20. *Gaunt's Register 1379–83*, i, 6–13.
21. Ross, 'Yorkshire Baronage', 394.
22. McFarlane, *England in the Fifteenth Century*, xii; *Register of Edward the Black Prince, passim*; Wright, 'Gentry Society', 240.
23. For example, £2,000 to Edward Balliol, and 1,000 marks each to the Black Prince and the earls of Warwick and Stafford: Harriss, *King, Parliament and Public Finance*, 481–7.
24. *CPR, 1377–81*, 1–249.
25. Above, pp. 135–6.
26. If my interpretation of these clauses is correct: above, p. 245.
27. *Rogers*, 71–2.
28. Above, p. 136.
29. The higher figure includes the duchy of Lancaster annuities after 1399; the figure usually suggested for the nobility at this time is about ten per cent.
30. Above, pp. 135–6.
31. Phillips, *Aymer de Valence*, 148–51, 312–15; these at least are the nineteen that survive; there were very probably others.
32. See for example n. 23 above.
33. McFarlane, *England in the Fifteenth Century*, xxvi–xxvii.
34. 'Political Society in Warwickshire', 310–22.
35. N. Saul, *Knights and Esquires: The Gloucestershire Gentry in the Fourteenth Century* (1981), 260–2.
36. *Ibid.*, 34–5.
37. Bennett, *Community, Class and Careerism*, 82–4; Wright, 'Gentry Society', 9–10; Carpenter, 'Political Society in Warwickshire', 18, 22–5, 42–5, 85, 172; G. G. Astill, 'The Medieval Gentry: A study in Leicestershire Society 1350–1399' (unpublished Ph.D. thesis, University of Birmingham, 1977), 17.
38. Ross, 'Yorkshire Baronage', 424.
39. Griffiths, *Reign of Henry VI*, 800–2; Carpenter, 'Political Society in Warwickshire', 223–5; Wright, 'Gentry Society', 221.
40. Astill, 'Medieval Gentry', 161–7.
41. Carpenter, 'Political Society in Warwickshire', 46–7, 53.
42. Tuck, *Richard II and the English Nobility*, 1.
43. Above, pp. 223–5; the dukes, marquises and earls of England were (a) Richard's supporters: York, Exeter, Surrey, Oxford, Wiltshire, Worcester, Aumale (Rutland), Salisbury, Suffolk, Dorset, and Gloucester; (b) those who were not influential on either side: Norfolk (in exile), March (minor), Richmond (abroad), Devon, and Stafford; (c) Richard's opponents: Northumberland, Westmorland, and Henry himself.

Bibliography

MANUSCRIPT SOURCES

Public Record Office

C49 (Parliament and Council Proceedings)
C53 (Great Charter Rolls)
E101 (Exchequer, King's Remembrancer, Various Accounts)
E154 (Inventories of Goods and Chattels)
E361 (Exchequer, Enrolled Accounts, Wardrobe and Household)
E401 (Exchequer, Receipt Rolls)
E403 (Exchequer, Issue Rolls)
E404 (Exchequer, Warrants for Issue)
SC1 (Ancient Correspondence)
SC8 (Ancient Petitions)

British Library

Harleian, Cotton, Stowe, and Additional Manuscripts

Society of Antiquaries

Manuscripts 120, 121

Winchester College Muniments

Manuscript I

PRINTED SOURCES AND SECONDARY WORKS

A. F. O'D. Alexander, 'The War with France in 1377', *BIHR*, xii (1934–5)

Annales Ricardi Secundi et Henrici Quarti, in J. de Trokelowe et Anon., *Chronica et Annales*, ed. H. T. Riley (R. S., 1866)

Anonimalle Chronicle 1333–81, ed. V. H. Galbraith (1927)

S. Armitage-Smith, *John of Gaunt* (1904)

G. G. Astill, 'The Medieval Gentry: A Study in Leicestershire Society 1350–1399' (unpublished Ph.D. thesis, University of Birmingham, 1977)

M. Aston, *Thomas Arundel* (1967)

M. Barber, 'John Norbury (*c.* 1350–1414): an esquire of Henry IV', *EHR.*, lxviii (1953)

F. Barlow, *William Rufus* (1983)

C. Barron, 'The Tyranny of Richard II', *BIHR*, xli (1968)

J. M. W. Bean, ' "Bachelor" and Retainer', *Medievalia et Humanistica*, 3 (1972)

G. F. Beltz, *Memorials of the Order of the Garter* (1841)

M. J. Bennett, *Community, Class and Careerism: Cheshire and Lancashire Society in the Age of Sir Gawain and the Green Knight* (1983)

R. Bird, *The Turbulent London of Richard II* (1949)

M. Bloch, *The Royal Touch*, trans. J. Anderson (1973)

L. E. Boyle, 'William of Pagula and the *Speculum Regis Edwardi III*', *Med. Stud.*, xxxii (1970)

R. H. Britnell, '*Advantagium Mercatoris*: a custom in medieval English trade', *Nottingham Medieval Studies*, xxiv (1980)

A. L. Brown, 'The Commons and the Council in the reign of Henry IV', *EHR.*, lxxix (1964)

R. Allen Brown, *English Castles* (2nd edn., 1976)

B. J. and C. R. Byerly, *Records of the Wardrobe and Household 1285–6* (1977)

Calendar of Close Rolls

Calendar of Fine Rolls

Calendar of Inquisitions Miscellaneous

Calendar of Inquisitions Post Mortem

Calendar of Patent Rolls

Calendar of Plea and Memoranda Rolls of the City of London

C. Carpenter, 'Political Society in Warwickshire *c.* 1401–1472' (unpublished Ph.D. thesis, University of Cambridge, 1976)

P. Chaplais, *English Royal Documents: King John to Henry VI* (1971)

M. Cherry, 'The Courtenay earls of Devon: the Formation and Disintegration of a late medieval aristocratic affinity', *Southern History*, i (1979)

M. Chibnall, 'Mercenaries and the *Familia Regis* under Henry I', *History*, 62 (1977)

S. B. Chrimes, *An Introduction to the Administrative History of Medieval England* (2nd edn., 1959)

S. B. Chrimes, C. D. Ross and R. A. Griffiths eds, *Fifteenth-Century England 1399–1509* (1972)

Chronicon Adae de Usk, ed. E. M. Thompson (1904)

Chronicon Henrici Knighton, ed. J. R. Lumby, 2 vols. (RS, 1895)

Chronicles of Edward I and Edward II, ed. W. Stubbs, 2 vols. (RS, 1882)

Chronique de la Traison et Mort de Richard II, ed. B. Williams (1846)

M. V. Clarke, *Fourteenth-Century Studies* (1937)

A. B. Cobban, *The King's Hall within the University of Cambridge in the Later Middle Ages* (1969)

Collection of Ordinances and Regulations for the Government of the Royal Household, (Society of Antiquaries, 1790)

H. M. Colvin, R. Allen Brown and A. J. Taylor, *The History of the King's Works*, vols i–iii (1963)

Comptes de l'Hôtel des Rois de France aux XIVe et XVe Siecles, ed. M. L. Douet-D'Arcq (SHF, 1865)

J. C. Davies, *The Baronial Opposition to Edward II* (1918)

J. C. Davies, 'The First Journal of Edward II's Chamber', *EHR*, xxx (1915)

R. G. Davies, 'Richard II and the Church in the years of Tyranny', *JMH*, i (1975)

De Speculo Regis Edwardi III, ed. J. Moisant (1891)

Dialogus de Scaccario, ed. C. Johnson (1950)

Diplomatic Correspondence of Richard II, ed. E. Perroy (Camden 3rd series, xlviii, 1933)

R. B. Dobson, *The Peasants' Revolt of 1381* (1970)

F. R. H. du Boulay and C. Barron eds, *The Reign of Richard II* (1971)

English Historical Documents 1327–1485, ed. A. R. Myers (1969)

Eulogium Historiarum sive Temporis, ed. F. S. Haydon, 3 vols. (RS., 1863)

Fleta, ed. H. G. Richardson and G. O. Sayles (Selden Society, lxxii, 1955)

Foedera Conventiones Literae et Cuiuscunque Generis Acta Publica, ed. T. Rymer, 7 vols. (Record Commission 1819–1869)

G. Fourquin, *Lordship and Feudalism in the Middle Ages*, trans. I. and A. L. Lytton Sells (1976)

N. Fryde, *The Tyranny and Fall of Edward II 1321–1326* (1979)

J. L. Gillespie, 'Richard II's archers of the crown', *Journal of British Studies*, 17–8 (1977–9)

J. L. Gillespie, 'Richard II's Cheshire archers', *Transactions of the Historical Society of Lancashire and Cheshire*, cxxv (1974)

M. Girouard, *Life in the English Country House* (1978)

C. Given-Wilson, 'The Court and Household of Edward III 1360–1377' (unpublished Ph.D. thesis, University of St Andrews, 1976)

C. Given-Wilson, 'The Merger of Edward III's and Queen Philippa's Households 1360–9', *BIHR*, li (1978)

C. Given-Wilson, 'Richard II and his Grandfather's Will', *EHR.*, xciii (1978)

C. Given-Wilson, 'The Ransom of Olivier du Guesclin', *BIHR*, liv (1981)

C. Given-Wilson, 'Purveyance for the Royal Household 1362–1413', *BIHR*, lvi (1983)

C. Given-Wilson and A. Curteis, *The Royal Bastards of Medieval England* (1984)

A. Goodman, *The Loyal Conspiracy* (1971)

J. L. Grassi, 'Royal Clerks from the Archdiocese of York', *Northern History*, v (1970)

R. Griffiths, *The Reign of King Henry VI* (1981)

B. Guenée, *L'Occident aux XIVe et XVe Siècles* (1971)

G. L. Harriss, *Henry V: The Practice of Kingship* (1985)

G. L. Harriss, 'Fictitious Loans', *Economic History Review*, viii (1955–6)

G. L. Harriss, *King, Parliament and Public Finance in England to 1369* (1975)

G. L. Harriss, 'Preference at the Medieval Exchequer', *BIHR*, xxx (1957)

P. D. A. Harvey, *A Medieval Oxfordshire Village: Cuxham 1240–1400* (1963)

J. Hatcher, *Rural Economy and Society in the Duchy of Cornwall 1300–1500* (1970)

M. C. Hill, *The King's Messengers 1199–1377* (1961)

Historia Anglicana, by Thomas Walsingham, ed. H. T. Riley, 2 vols. (RS., 1863–4)

G. A. Holmes, *The Estates of the Higher Nobility in Fourteenth-Century England* (1957)

G. A. Holmes, *The Good Parliament* (1975)

J. C. Holt, *Magna Carta* (1965)

N. Hooper, 'The Housecarls in England in the Eleventh Century', *Anglo-Norman Studies VII*, ed. R. A. Brown (1985)

Issue Roll of the Exchequer Henry III to Henry VI, ed. F. Devon (1837)

Issue Roll of Thomas de Brantingham 44 Edward III, ed. F. Devon (1835)

M. K. James, *Studies in the Medieval Wine Trade*, ed. E. M. Veale (1971)

R. I. Jack, 'Entail and Descent: the Hastings Inheritance, 1370 to 1436', *BIHR*, xxxvii (1965)

R. Jeffs, 'The Later Medieval Sheriff and the Royal Household' (unpublished D.Phil. thesis, University of Oxford, 1960)

H. Jenkinson, 'Exchequer Tallies', *Archaeologia*, lxii, part 2 (1911)

H. Jenkinson, 'Medieval Tallies, Public and Private', *Archaeologia*, lxxiv (1925)

John of Gaunt's Register 1372–1376, ed. S. Armitage-Smith (Camden 3rd series, xx–xxi, 1911)

John of Gaunt's Register 1379–1383, ed. E. C. Lodge and R. Somerville (Camden 3rd series, lvi–lvii, 1937)

J. H. Johnson, 'The system of account in the wardrobe of Edward II', *TRHS.*, xii (1929)

H. Johnstone, 'Poor-relief in the Royal Households of Thirteenth-Century England', *Speculum*, vi (1929)

J. E. A. Jolliffe, *Angevin Kingship* (1955)

W. R. Jones, 'The Court of the Verge', *Journal of British Studies*, x (1970)

J. L. Kirby, *Henry IV of England* (1970)

J. R. Lander, *Politics and Power in England 1450–1509* (1976)

L. M. Larson, *The Kings' Household in England before the Norman Conquest* (1904)

J. L. Leland, 'Richard II and the Counter-Appellants: Royal Patronage and Royalist Politics (unpublished Ph.D. thesis, Yale University, 1979)

Letter-Books of the City of London, ed. R. R. Sharpe, vols. G–H (1905–7)

N. B. Lewis, 'The Last Summons of the English Feudal Levy', *EHR*, lxxiii (1958)

N. B. Lewis, 'Re-election to Parliament in the reign of Richard II', *EHR* xlviii (1933)

Liber Quotidianus Contrarotulatoris Garderobiae, ed. J. Nichols (Society of Antiquaries, 1787)

List of Sheriffs for England and Wales (Public Record Office, Lists and Indexes, ix, 1963 reprint)

J. F. Lydon, ed., *England and Ireland in the Later Middle Ages* (1983)

J. R. Maddicott, 'The English Peasantry and the Demands of the Crown', *Past and Present*, Supplement i (1975)

Master of Game, ed. and trans. W. A. and F. Baillie-Grohman (1909)

H. Maxwell-Lyte, *Historical Notes on the use of the Great Seal of England* (1926)

K. B. McFarlane, *England in the Fifteenth Century* (1981)

K. B. McFarlane, *John Wyclif and the Beginnings of English Non-Conformity* (1952)

K. B. McFarlane, *Lancastrian Kings and Lollard Knights* (1972)

K. B. McFarlane, *The Nobility of Later Medieval England* (1973)

J. J. N. McGurk, 'Royal Purveyance in the Shire of Kent, 1590–1614', *BIHR.*, l (1977)

M. McKisack, *The Fourteenth Century* (1959)

P. McNiven, 'The Cheshire Rising of 1400', *Bulletin of the John Rylands Library*, 52 (1970)

K. Mertes, 'Secular Noble Households in England 1350–1550' (unpublished Ph.D. thesis, University of Edinburgh, 1981)

L. Mirot and E. Déprez, 'Les Ambassades anglaises pendant la guerre de cent ans', *Bibliothèque de l'école des Chartes*, 60 (1899)

D. A. L. Morgan, 'The King's Affinity in the Polity of Yorkist England', *TRHS.*, lvi (1973)

A. R. Myers, *The Household of Edward IV* (1959)

A. R. Myers, 'The Wealth of Richard Lyons', in *Essays in Medieval History presented to Bertie Wilkinson*, eds. T. A. Sandquist and M. R. Powicke (1969)

J. Nichols, *A Collection of the Wills of the Kings and Queens of England* (1780)

Ordonnances des Roys de France de la troisième race, ed. J. Laurière *et al*, vols. i–ix (1723–1846)

Original Letters Illustrative of English History, ed. H. Ellis, 3rd series, i (1846)

N. Orme, *From Childhood to Chivalry* (1984)

J. Otway-Ruthven, *The King's Secretary and the Signet Office in the Fifteenth Century* (1939)

J. J. N. Palmer, *England, France and Christendom 1377–1399* (1972)

J. J. N. Palmer, 'The Parliament of 1385 and the Constitutional Crisis of 1386', *Speculum*, xlvi (1971)

J. R. S. Phillips, *Aymer de Valence, earl of Pembroke, 1307–1324* (1972)

F. M. Powicke, 'Richard I and John', *Cambridge Medieval History*, vi (1968)

J. O. Prestwich, 'The Military Household of the Norman Kings', *EHR*, xcvi (1981)

M. C. Prestwich, 'Exchequer and Wardrobe in the Later Years of Edward I', *BIHR*, xlvi (1973)

M. C. Prestwich, *The Three Edwards* (1980)

M. C. Prestwich, *War, Politics and Finance under Edward I* (1972)

Proceedings and Ordinances of the Privy Council of England, ed. H. H. Nicolas, 2 vols. (Record Commission, 1834)

Register of Edward the Black Prince, 4 vols. (1930–33)

Return of Members of Parliament (House of Commons, 1878)

H. G. Richardson, 'The Chamber under Henry II', *EHR*, lxix (1954)

H. G. Richardson, 'John of Gaunt and the Parliamentary Representation of Lancashire', *Bulletin of the John Rylands Library*, 22 (1938)

H. G. Richardson and G. O. Sayles, *The Governance of Medieval England from the Conquest to Magna Carta* (1963)

A. Rogers, 'Henry IV, the commons, and taxation', *Med. Stud.*, xxxi (1969)

A. Rogers, 'The Political Crisis of 1401', *Nottingham Medieval Studies*, xii (1968)

A. Rogers, 'The Royal Household of Henry IV' (unpublished Ph.D. thesis, University of Nottingham, 1966)

J. S. Roskell, *The Commons and their Speakers in English Parliaments 1376–1532* (1965)

J. S. Roskell, *The Impeachment of Michael de la Pole* (1984)

C. D. Ross, 'The Yorkshire Baronage, 1399–1435' (unpublished D.Phil. thesis, University of Oxford, 1950)

Rotuli de Liberate ac de Misis et Praestitis regnante Johanne, ed. T. Hardy (Record Commission, 1844)

Rotuli Parliamentorum, ed. J. Strachey *et al*, vols. ii–iii (1783)

J. H. Round, *The King's Serjeants and Officers of State* (1911)

Royal Letters of Henry IV, ed. F. D. Hingeston, 2 vols. (1860)

St Alban's Chronicle 1406–1420, ed. V. H. Galbraith (1937)

N. Saul, *Knights and Esquires: The Goucestershire Gentry in the Fourteenth Century* (1981)

J. W. Sherborne, 'The Cost of English Warfare in France in the Later Fourteenth Century', *BIHR*, 1 (1977)

J. W. Sherborne, 'Indentured Retinues and English Expeditions to France 1369–1380', *EHR*, lxxix (1964)

Statutes of the Realm (Record Commission, 1810)

A. Steel, *Receipt of the Exchequer 1377–1485* (1954)

F. M. Stenton, *Anglo-Saxon England* (3rd edn., 1971)

W. Stubbs, *Select Charters* (9th edn. by H. W. C. Davis, 1913)

A. Taylor, 'Royal Alms and Oblations in the later thirteenth century', in *Tribute to an Antiquary: Essays Presented to Mark Fitch*, eds. F. Emmison and R. Stephens (1976)

Testamenta Vetusta, ed. N. H. Nicolas, 2 vols. (1826)

T. F. Tout, *Chapters in the Administrative History of Mediaeval England*, 6 vols. (1920–33)

T. F. Tout, *The Place of the Reign of Edward II in English History* (2nd edn. by H. Johnstone, 1936)

A. Tuck, 'Richard II and the Border Magnates', *Northern History*, iii (1968)

A. Tuck, *Richard II and the English Nobility* (1973)

M. Vale, *Charles VII* (1974)

R. Vaughan, *Valois Burgundy* (1975)

R. F. Walker, 'The Anglo-Welsh Wars 1217–1267' (unpublished D.Phil. thesis, University of Oxford, 1954)

Thomas Walsingham, *Gesta Abbatum Monasterii Sancti Albani*, ed. H. T. Riley, 3 vols. (RS, 1869)

Wardrobe Book of William de Norwell, eds. M. Lyon, B. Lyon and H. S. Lucas (1983)

W. L. Warren, *Henry II* (1973)

J. C. Wedgwood, 'John of Gaunt and the Packing of Parliament', *EHR.*, xlv (1930)

Westminster Chronicle 1381–1394, ed. and trans. L. C. Hector and B. F. Harvey (1982)

G. H. White, 'The Household of the Norman Kings', *TRHS*, xxxi (1948)

B. Wilkinson, *The Chancery under Edward III* (1929)

G. Williams, *Owen Glendower* (1955)

B. P. Wolffe, *The Royal Demesne in English History* (1971)

S. M. Wright, 'A Gentry Society of the Fifteenth Century: Derbyshire *circa* 1430–1509' (unpublished Ph.D. thesis, University of Birmingham, 1978)

J. H. Wylie, *History of England under Henry IV*, 4 vols. (1884–98)

Index